The Animus

polarities
of the psyche

A series edited by Emmanuel Kennedy-Xypolitas

The Animus
The Spirit of Inner Truth in Women

Volume Two

Barbara Hannah

edited by David Eldred and Emmanuel Kennedy-Xypolitas

Chiron Publications
Wilmette, Illinois

From *MEMORIES, DREAMS, REFLECTIONS* by C. G. Jung, edited by Aniela Jaffe, translated by Richard and Clara Winston, translation copyright © 1961, 1962, 1963 and renewed 1989, 1990, 1991 by Random House, Inc. Used by permission of Pantheon Books, a division of Random House, Inc.

Jung, C. G.; *COLLECTED WORKS OF C. G. JUNG.* © 1977 Princeton University Press. Reprinted by permission of Princeton University Press.

Jung, C. G.; *DREAM ANALYSIS.* © 1984 Princeton University Press. Reprinted by permission of Princeton University Press.

Jung, C. G.; *NIETZSCHE'S ZARATHUSTRA.* © 1988 Princeton University Press. Reprinted by permission of Princeton University Press.

Jung, C. G.; *VISIONS.* © 1997 Princeton University Press. Reprinted by permission of Princeton University Press. From *Visions: Notes of the Seminar Given in 1930–1934*, C. G. Jung, copyright © 1998 Routledge. Reproduced by permission of Taylor & Francis Books UK.

Book and cover design by Peter Altenberg.
Cover art: landscape painting by Barbara Hannah.
Printed in the United States of America.

Library of Congress Cataloging-in-Publication Data

Hannah, Barbara.
   The animus : the spirit of inner truth in women / Barbara Hannah ; edited by Emmanuel Kennedy and David Eldred.
      v.   cm. — (Polarities of the psyche)
   Includes bibliographical references and index.
   ISBN 978-1-888602-46-3 (vol. 1 : alk. paper) — ISBN 978-1-888602-47-0 (vol. 2 : alk. paper)
   1. Animus (Psychoanalysis) 2. Women—Psychology. 3. Jungian psychology. I. Kennedy, Emmanuel. II. Eldred, David. III. Title. IV. Series.

BF175.5.A53H36 2010
155.3'33—dc22

                              2010003379

Contents

Foreword by David Eldred VII

Foreword by Emmanuel Kennedy-Xypolitas IX

Introduction to the Course on the Animus 1

The Animus in the Middle Ages 32

Jeanne Fery: A Case Study on the Animus, Possession,
and Exorcism 51

An Introductory Note on Plots 146

A Short Discussion on Women's Plots 149

An Introduction to Women's Plots 156

Introduction to "The Problem of Women's Plots in Marie Hay's
The Evil Vineyard" 170

The Problem of Women's Plots in Marie Hay's
The Evil Vineyard 172

Women's Plots: An Analysis of Mary Webb's
Precious Bane 237

The Religious Function of the Animus in the Book of Tobit 287

Bibliography 373

Index 383

Foreword

BARBARA HANNAH WAS A STRAIGHTFORWARD, MODEST, YET grand woman, a lover of literature, a close affiliate and friend of both Carl Gustav and Emma Jung, and of Marie-Louise von Franz. She was a first-generation Jungian psychologist, member of the Psychological Club of Zurich (1916 to the present), and among the first lecture of the Jung Institute in Zurich. She lectured both in Switzerland and England and wrote several books on C. G. Jung and Jungian psychology.

Barbara Hannah's psychological analysis of the animus is presented here in two volumes. These essays have been gleaned from Barbara Hannah's handwritten notes, typed manuscripts, previously published articles (as well as the handwritten notes of those articles), her own drafts of her lectures, and the notes taken by participants at those lectures. Barbara Hannah tackled the theme of the animus with a comprehensiveness unsurpassed in Jungian literature. Her insight and vigor stem directly from a personal grappling with her own animus while integrating the experience and reflection of many from the first and second generations of psychotherapists working directly with C. G. Jung.

The main objective of these two volumes is to present the reader with an all-inclusive synthesis of the many and complex essays and lectures Barbara Hannah presented on the theme of the animus while remaining as close as possible to the original texts. Authenticity and comprehensiveness have been set as the priorities in the editing of this work. But when lengthy passages repeat themselves identically from one presentation to the next, synthesis has been pursued. For example, Barbara Hannah discusses the animus in the case of the sixteenth-century nun Jeanne Fery in five different lectures and publications presented in these two volumes. The theme of the animus in the Book of Tobit is found in seven lectures and essays. Some of these lectures were given at the C. G. Jung Institute in Zurich, others were presented to various audiences in Switzerland and England. Naturally, a great deal of the material in her later lectures was repeated from earlier works, and much of this repetition is verbatim. If every single sentence that she ever wrote on the animus was published chronologically with no editorial adjustment, these volumes would be burdened with tedious repetition and become unmanageable in size, undermining the vitality of Barbara Hannah's style and compromising the vivaciousness of the works themselves.

Nevertheless, when the presentation of a theme would be negatively affected by such editing, repetition has been preserved from one essay to the next. Not one single idea uttered by the author has been neglected. Hand corrections, which she added to the pages of her lectures and the drafts of her publications, have been included directly in the text in order to render the straightforward manner and unfussiness of Barbara Hannah's literary style.

The editorial priority in these two volumes has been set to preserve the excellence and comprehensiveness of her work on the animus—that most complex and vexing theme—while rendering the natural and wonderful spirit of Barbara Hannah herself. It was Barbara Hannah's express wish that references and comments be included as footnotes and not relegated to endnotes, and we have respected this wish.

David Eldred
Zurich
April 2010

Foreword

The experience itself is the important thing, not its intellectual classification, which proves meaningful and helpful only when the road to original experience is blocked.
— C. G. Jung

THE TWO PRESENT BOOKS ON THE THEME OF THE ANIMUS constitute the third and fourth volumes of the series Polarities of the Psyche. The first two were *Lectures on Jung's Aion* (2004) by Barbara Hannah and Marie-Louise von Franz and *The Archetypal Symbolism of Animals* (2006) by Barbara Hannah.

Carl Gustav Jung regarded the human psyche as belonging to the most obscure and mysterious realms which we can experience. Whenever Jung writes or speaks of the nature of the human psyche, he relies above all on his personal observations of people. The anima and the animus, two of Jung's most well-known concepts, were developed through empirical observation and actual experience.

As Jung emphasizes throughout his works, intellect and theoretical knowledge alone do not suffice for the assimilation of unconscious contents and especially those unconscious contents of an archetypal, transcendent nature. Only when such contents appear subjectively out of the unconscious psyche of the individual can they become a profound experience of reality. For in the process of integration of unconscious components of our personality, we are dealing with creative processes that are steeped in mystery and can be truly grasped only by inner experience understood by Jung as "a process of assimilation without which there would be no understanding." Jung thus considered such experience as the conditio sine qua non for bringing unconscious contents into consciousness, truly understanding them, and gradually liberating oneself from their autonomous, possessive and irrational nature. Jung writes in his memoirs:

> To me there is no liberation *à tous prix*. I cannot be liberated from anything that I . . . have not experienced. Real liberation becomes possible for me only when I have done all that I was able to do, when I have completely devoted myself to a thing and participated in it to the utmost.

Complete devotion to and participation to the utmost in the "terrifying work on the animus" characterizes Barbara Hannah's lifelong struggle to come to terms with the unconscious, an *Auseinandersetzung* that began in 1929 when she began analysis with Jung and lasted nearly sixty years to her death in 1986. This charisma of her whole being was evident and even palpable to those people who were close to her. It is also manifest when one reads certain parts of her papers in this present work. Whatever Barbara Hannah said or wrote on "the vitally important archetype of the animus" was ascertained both from her own subjective experience and from the actual experience of women she knew.

Seen in this light, Barbara Hannah's truly creative writings on the complex theme of the animus are a unique and major contribution to analytical psychology. Their value lies in the fact that they stem out of direct, personal, and original experience with the darker layers of the psyche. Barbara Hannah did not gloss over, avoid, or repress but chose the path of experiencing unconscious processes to the full, which, according to Jung, is the only way to liberate oneself. She thus created an indispensable vase, a vessel to receive the contents of her unconscious with Eros, that is, her feeling relatedness.

Through an honest and conscious confrontation with the unconscious (dream analysis, active imagination, painting, creative writing) Barbara Hannah immersed herself in the inner experience of the powerful archetype of the animus. As she once stated: "It is out of my own experience—this little island and relatively firm piece of ground—that I am trying to write on the problem of the animus." Analytic practice teaches us that the individual human being to whom unconscious contents become conscious through experience is united with the impersonal center of psychic wholeness thus making the experienced center into a *spiritus rector*, a driving force of daily life.

Various dreams of and about Barbara Hannah indicate that at the end of her life she achieved as much natural wholeness as an individual human being can attain in a lifetime. In such a state of being, the animus, as it was once experienced by Barbara Hannah in an active imagination, transforms itself into the heart of the chthonic spirit of truth. In this form the animus is a mediator of the religious experience, a veritable messenger of "God." In the words of Marie-Louise von Franz, the animus becomes "the wise guide to spiritual truth . . . and the incarnation of meaning."

Emmanuel Kennedy-Xypolitas

Introduction to the Course on the Animus

Editor's Note: The following text is taken from the notes Barbara Hannah made to introduce a lecture series on the animus she gave at the C. G. Jung Institute in Zurich beginning in October 1974. In these introductory reflections, Barbara Hannah occasionally wrote comments such as "tell the story of such and such," "quote Jung from . . ." or simply "expand . . ."; she then gives no further information, apparently spontaneously reciting this information by heart during her lectures. Nevertheless, we have been able to identify and locate many of her references. In the few cases where we have not been able to pinpoint the information, we have simply left her note as is, without further comment.

WHEN I FIRST CAME TO ZURICH—NOW NEARLY FIFTY YEARS ago—we were in a more favorable position for learning to know the animus from his practical, everyday side.[1] Jung was allergic to the negative animus. So if you approached him when your animus was uppermost—even to say good morning—you were helped to realize this fact in a way you would not so quickly forget.

All of the other psychoanalysts at that time were alert to traces of the anima and animus, having learned in their own analyses with Jung to recognize them whenever they appeared. I do not know to what degree this is still the case, but we have sometimes

---

1. Barbara Hannah first sought C. G. Jung in Zurich in 1929.

been shocked when students—even on their final diploma examinations—have answered all the questions brilliantly enough, but in the voice of the animus and not in that of the woman herself. In other words, they have expressed perfectly correct opinions, but one has heard nothing of their own individual images, that is, their creative picture of it all. How easily this can happen will be demonstrated later in this course in a case of animus possession in the Middle Ages.[2]

One can learn to discern the difference between a woman's actual voice and the voice of her animus quite apart from the content of what the woman is saying. This naturally applies to oneself as well. But it is difficult to keep oneself up to the mark in this respect unless it is constantly brought to mind as it used to be when we were still in daily contact with Jung.

I am speaking here of the negative side of animus, "who" usually shows up first when he meddles in outer life. But he has a very different and most positive side when he is in his right place, and this is as the mediating function between the woman and her unconscious.

Three years ago, I gave a course on the religious function of the animus in the biblical story of Tobit. There he began as negatively as possible: he murdered seven of Sarah's husbands and was contaminated with the collective devil as well. But slowly, step by step, he was reduced to his right place and then became as positive as he had originally been negative.

In our first example this year, we will consider the case of a possessed nun from the late Middle Ages, from which it is possible to learn even more about the transformation, this time much more from the point of view of psychoanalysis, for present-day analysts can learn a great deal from the methods used by the old exorcists. I emphasize the phrase "from the exorcists" rather than "from the Inquisitors," who seem invariably to have used the worst possible methods and who had no understanding whatsoever of what they were really dealing with.

---

2. Presented in this essay is the introduction to the 1974 lecture; the actual content of these lectures is included in other essays in these two volumes.

Such medieval cases of possession are admittedly extreme, but both in principle and in their archetypal background they are similar to animus possession today. It is obviously easier to see the background of the everyday animus in such an exaggerated case. But before we start on our material, I want to make a few more general remarks about the animus himself.

By the term *animus* we mean the masculine spirit or the unconscious mind of woman. Emma Jung used to emphasize how necessary it was to differentiate carefully between the anima and the animus. The anima, as you all know, is Jung's term for the feminine soul of man, whereas the word *animus* means "spirit" or "mind." There is often still confusion here, for in his early days, when Jung was first discovering the figure of the animus in women, he sometimes spoke of the animus as the soul of woman. This was also true in his early writings. He corrected this later when he discovered, more and more, the differences between the anima and the animus. At first he became aware of the animus as the natural counterpart of the anima, and experience was necessary to teach him the nuances of the differences. And these are, in fact, considerable.

The foundation of man's search for the anima is to find his own inherited image of the inner woman and the function of Eros or relationship. These are, at first, completely in the hands of the anima. A woman's search for the animus, however, is to find her Logos, that is, her unconscious mind, and then to search for the nature of her own individual Weltanschauung. And this is, at first, entirely in the hands of the animus. To oversimplify: man is looking for clarity in what he really feels, and woman for clarity in what she really thinks.

Generally speaking, man has always projected the function of relationship onto woman, and woman has always projected her mind onto man. The goal of the work on the anima and animus is to withdraw these age-old projections.[3] The ultimate goal for woman is the development and integration of the

___
3. [Barbara Hannah has noted here: "Expand: makes one hopelessly possessive." It is uncertain what precisely she had in mind. *Ed.*]

feminine spirit, that is, the Logos in the woman. This entails its assimilation into her entire being and her outer life as a woman so that a harmonious cooperation can flourish; and not that one side or the other—for instance, the mental-intellectual or the mother-instinctual—is damned to the shadows of the woman's life.[4]

That is why creative work is so invaluable to a woman: she cannot work creatively without a direct relation to her own mind, and this particular part of her mind is, in the beginning, oftentimes unconscious.[5] This is also why so many women prefer to let their husbands do creative work for them or, as Emma Jung emphasized, prefer to have another child.

A woman's Weltanschauung consists entirely of traditional opinions gleaned during the course of her life as long as her animus has control. These opinions are those expressed by her father and the other male authorities of her youth. If she is fortunate enough to have brothers, these opinions become partially rejuvenated and revitalized anew. In these revolutionary days, the opinions gleaned from her brothers may be the exact reverse of what she assimilates from her father and other adult authority figures. But these ideas help less than one would think, for they only provide her with more one-sided opinions, in this case of a revolutionary rather than a traditional character. Missing here is the paradoxical tension that is essential in working on the animus.

Women whose animus opinions are based on tradition—and there are still surprisingly quite a few even in the younger generation—often shelter themselves behind these opinions as a strategy to attain exactly what they want; or at least what they think they want. For instance, behind a strict regard for Victorian morality, a wife secretly furthers her power motives in her wish to possess her husband. Then the woman need

---

4.   Emma Jung, "Ein Beitrag zum Problem des Animus" (1934), in C. G. Jung, ed., *Wirklichkeit der Seele* (Zurich: Rascher Verlag), p. 315.

5.   [Here, Barbara Hannah writes: "Expand." It is uncertain how she wanted to expand this theme. *Ed.*]

not see her own bad qualities, her jealousy or her passion for getting her own way. For how could she be moved by ignoble motives? She is only upholding the traditionally established and undisputedly "right" way. Jealousy of which a man or woman is not conscious is probably the most dangerous and destructive force in the world. Jung said that jealousy often comes from lack of love or the ability to love. This is undoubtedly true, but jealousy of which one is conscious—and suffers—is paid for (to some extent), because you cannot, for instance, possibly uphold a flattering image of yourself as a self-sacrificing angel if you are aware that you are torn apart by the ugly forces of jealousy and possessiveness within.

Those women whose animus opinions have a more modern nuance usually go too far in the other direction and deny tradition altogether, and they often become downright promiscuous. I remember once speaking to Jung about a woman of this nature who I was analyzing and admitting to him that I did not like finding myself in the role of a moralizing Victorian aunt, precisely the type of woman who had poisoned my own youth. He laughed and said: "Nevertheless, you will have to stop her if you possibly can, because the trouble is that too many sexual affairs destroy the woman's Eros." As Jung makes so clear in his essay "Woman in Europe," it is Eros, her relationship to the man, that is really all-important for woman; less essential is the sexual side, so all-important to man.[6]

Sexuality is, of course, natural and vital as an expression of Eros and of relationship. But if it becomes paramount, more so than the relationship itself, then, as Jung once pointed out, one may know that the animus has got hold of it and is pushing the woman out of the relationship so that he may destroy her connection with the man at his leisure. The animus, in his original untransformed shape, is just like a jealous lover himself, and he will continually try to possess the woman for himself. This "jealous lover who destroys relationships with men" will also

---

6. C. G. Jung, "Woman in Europe" (1927), in *CW*, vol. 10 (Princeton, N.J.: Princeton University Press, 1964).

be seen in the wildly possessive nature of the spirits reported by the medieval nun Jeanne Fery. The animus also loves to project himself onto the wrong man, and then when the woman is bitterly disappointed, he whispers: "Poor dear, but you know all men are the same, you will only be happy quite alone with me." And thus he gradually spins a cocoon around the woman, cutting her off entirely from her environment and the other sex.

And how he seems to rejoice in inspiring a woman to argue adamantly opinions that are all just beside the point and to make scenes that drive a man nearly crazy. This, in turn, invariably calls up his anima, and the most foolish quarrels take place in which banalities, "facts," and nasty moods are tossed back and forth with neither saying—or even knowing—what they really mean. In many marriages a great deal of time and energy is squandered in this way.

Naturally, such quarrels are not always started by the animus. The anima is also a sinner in this respect, for in her original autonomous and unconscious form she would also like to keep "her man" entirely for herself. Benoît's *L'Atlantide* is the extreme example of this constellation. His heroine was so extreme that she kept her lovers alive for only one night. Then she killed and embalmed them and set them standing upright in a grand circle of alcoves in her vast mausoleum. And she sat herself upon a throne in the center.[7]

Rather than lose ourselves in the anima, we should say a few words about the shadow, for considerable work on it is necessary before it is possible to deal with the animus at all. We must be well acquainted with our personal shadows so that we can face our own bad qualities quietly; otherwise the animus will constantly reduce us to misery by rubbing our faces in our failings which we have not yet seen or begun to accept.

It is necessary to realize that we, like everything in nature, consist of light and darkness. What could day be without night?

---

7. Pierre Benoît, *L'Atlantide* (1919; Paris: LGF, 1996). [For a detailed analysis, see "The Problem of Women's Plots in Marie Hay's *The Evil Vineyard*" in this volume. *Ed.*]

Or heat without cold? We take the light and the dark for granted in everything that exists except in our own selves. But why should this general law of nature make an exception for any of us? Yet it takes a long time, and a great deal of pain, before we realize that we also consist of an equal mixture of light and dark. There is no virtue that has not its complementary vice, and this is not even so painful when we once see that it is so, for it must inevitably be so.

There are, however, a good many pitfalls to avoid while making this realization. Anyone with a sensitive conscience is certain to be initially cast down by the realization of her bad qualities and to forget she only has them because she also has the corresponding qualities that are good. As Jung said in one of his letters to Father Victor White:

> Never have we been more in need of the Christian virtues than in the dark days we live in, when evil seems to predominate as never before, and it is just as bad to forget the good we are capable of as to be unable to see our defects and the evil we are capable of.[8]

---

8. [This statement on Christian virtues has been cited as a quotation by Barbara Hannah. It does not occur in the two published versions of Jung's letter (presumably the letter to Victor White of November 24, 1953), one edited by Gerhard Adler and the other by Ann Lammers and Adrian Cunningham, both of which omit the final two paragraphs of Jung's actual letter. In a personal communication, Ann Lammers writes that Barbara Hannah may have had access to an actual copy of Jung's letter to Father Victor White, at least briefly. She notes that Jung occasionally showed important letters to colleagues, and from evidence found in the rough draft of the November 1953 letter, we know Jung wanted several copies made (he instructed his typist to make four carbon copies of it). Therefore, he certainly could have shared it with people in his intimate circle. This letter was a major effort on Jung's part, and he knew it might be important to people other than White and himself. White got the original, of course. One carbon copy (including the final two paragraphs) went into Jung's private file. A copy of the bulk of the letter (omitting the final two paragraphs) would have gone into the secretary's file, and another was probably stored in a folder marked "Pfarrerbriefe," with all the letters to clergy that Jung was hoping eventually to publish. Lammers concludes that, by her count, one copy remains without a clear destination. It is known that, at that time, Barbara Hannah was intensively involved with questions regarding Christian theology. See Jung's letter of November 24, 1953, in *The Jung-White Letters*, edited by Ann Lammers and Adrian Cunningham (London: Routledge, 2007); also C. G. Jung, *Letters, vol. 2, 1951–1961*, selected and edited by Gerhard Adler in collaboration with Aniela Jaffé, translated by R. F. C. Hull (London: Routledge and Kegan Paul, 1976).

It is always a matter of paradox and of withstanding the opposites in ourselves. In a discussion at the Psychological Club of
Zurich, Jung was asked whether he thought that there would be
an atomic war. Jung replied that it depended on how many people
could withstand the tension of the opposites in themselves. If
enough people could, he added, then we might just avoid the
worst—as we have up until now mercifully been able to do. But
if not, then he feared the opposites would sooner or later clash
in atomic war and this would mean the end of our whole civilization. From the standpoint of the archetypal images of animals, all
that we can do is to do our best to become ever more conscious
of the extreme opposites that they represent within us and thus,
perhaps, also lay an infinitesimal grain on the scales of humanity's soul.[9]

But before we go further, we must agree that our own psyches
reach far beyond our conscious knowledge. We are not the master
in our own house. The pernicious conviction that "where there's
a will, there's a way" dies hard. We are indeed to blame if we
make no effort to know the other parts of our psyche. Like it or
not, these unconscious parts will constantly surprise us by how
they make us behave. And eventually they do make us conscious.
As Jung pointed out in his seminar on Nietzsche's Zarathustra,
our will is constantly being crossed by other unconscious wills
within us:

> It is as if you were ruler of a land which is only partially
> known to yourself, king of a country with an unknown num-
> ber of inhabitants. You don't know who they are or what their
> condition may be; time and again you make the discovery that
> you have subjects in your country of whose existence you had
> no idea. Therefore, you cannot assume the responsibility, you
> can only say: "I find myself as the ruler of a country which has
> unknown borders and unknown inhabitants, possessing quali-
> ties of which I am not entirely aware." Then you are at once

---

9. [See also C. G. Jung, "The Psychology of the Transference" (1946), in *CW*, vol. 16
(Princeton, N.J.: Princeton University Press, 1954), par. 449. *Ed.*]

out of your subjectivity, and are confronted with a situation in which you are a sort of prisoner; you are confronted with unknown possibilities because those many uncontrollable factors at any time may influence all your actions or decisions. So you are a funny kind of king in that country, a king who is not really a king, who is dependent upon so many unknown quantities and conditions that he often cannot carry through his own intentions. Therefore, it is better not to speak of being a king at all, and be only one of the inhabitants who has just a corner of that territory to rule. And the greater your experience, the more you see that your corner is infinitely small in comparison with the vast extent of the unknown against you.[10]

Once we have grasped that we are not the rulers of our psyches, not sole masters in our own homes, we are—paradoxically enough—in a much stronger position. We have escaped from our subjectivity and gained a tiny piece of objective ground from where we can see both ourselves and our fellow men and women more clearly—and more fairly. A man can ask himself whether the complaints of his wife are really genuine or if her animus is serving him up some irrelevant opinion. And still more important, he can ask himself whether or not he is really behind his own emotions, moods, and demands or if he is speaking from an anima mood. For one cannot recall too often that, if one is a man, one may just be reacting from an anima mood, and that, within but a short period of time, one may come to one's senses and feel quite differently. If one is a woman, we are likely to serve up a lot of animus opinions that we have not really thought through but that just spring ready-made from one of the other inhabitants of our so-called "kingdom," that is, usually (but not invariably) from the animus. Men are tempted to have moods that spring also from another inhabitant of that inner "kingdom," usually (but not invariably) from the anima.

10. C. G. Jung, *Nietzsche's Zarathustra: Notes of the Seminar Given in 1934–1939* (Princeton, N.J.: Princeton University Press, 1988), p. 390.

This lecture course is primarily on the animus, for I can speak of "him" from personal experience, and it is experience and not theory that counts when it comes to the animus. Particularly in places where she is emotional, a woman must continually be asking herself: "Now, do I really mean this? Or am I trying to get my own way by batting about opinions that I do not really believe?" If she is to develop and to follow the process of individuation, she must continually distinguish between her own thoughts and the opinions thrust at her by the animus who, by the way, can be eloquent and ostensibly argue most brilliantly. Yet, with certainty, he will destroy her relationships to men unless he is constantly watched and held in check.[11]

Prior to Jung, the unconscious was thought to consist only of personal material, a sort of dustbin into which we throw inconvenient things. Jung naturally recognizes this layer as well and calls it the "personal unconscious." Disagreeable as it may be for us, and though it may entail a long, weary, and at times exceedingly painful undertaking to work one's way through, the personal unconscious is not really all that difficult. The real difficulty begins when we meet the figures of the collective unconscious, for they are really unknown. The shadow is not really difficult to recognize in its personal aspect although a confrontation may be a long and often painful undertaking. The far greater difficulty comes from the contamination of the shadow with the figures of the collective unconscious. People with a sensitive conscience, for instance, will sometimes lose their sense of proportion when they first see their dark side and begin to make themselves responsible for the devil himself. The task becomes complicated and tedious when we begin to learn to discriminate between the personal sphere and the greater figures of the collective unconscious. Yet it is of utmost importance. He expressed it very plastically at a lecture at the Eidgenössische Technische Hochschule (ETH):

> As to this self-knowledge, this real penetrating knowledge
> of our own being, do not make the mistake of thinking that

---

11. [Here, Barbara Hannah notes that Jung mentioned this idea at a dinner party. *Ed.*]

it means seeing through the ego. To understand the ego is child's play, but to see through the Self is something totally different. The real difficulty lies in recognizing the unknown. No one need remain ignorant of the fact that he is striving for power, that he wants to become very rich, that he would be a tyrant if he had the chance, that he is pleasure seeking, envious of other people, and so on. Everyone can know such things of him or herself, because they are mere ego knowledge. But self-knowledge is something completely different, it is learning to know of the things that are unknown.[12]

As experience increases, one realizes more and more the extraordinary difficulty of facing the unknown. Take, for instance, the necessity of accepting and facing the tension of the opposites in oneself. And also facing the unknown realm of the *hieros gamos,* the sacred marriage, which is the only way of uniting these opposites and thus reducing the almost unbearable torture of the tension between them. We just spoke about the vital importance that Jung attached to this task.

The position seems to me to be a choice between simply acquiescing and yielding to the opposites clashing against each other in war, for they are constellated everywhere; we can no longer deny the omnipresence of evil and the number of people who have allowed themselves to be possessed by it. Or, on the other hand, withstanding the tension within and doing what one can to help the opposites unite in the *hieros gamos,* an experience that transcends the ego, our wishes, and our will. Several years after he finished his book, *Mysterium Coniunctionis,* Jung mentions this Herculean difficulty in a letter to John Trinick (which Trinick published in the preface of his book, *The Fire-Tried Stone*):

> As some alchemists had to admit that they never succeeded
> in producing the gold or the stone, I cannot claim to having

---

12. C. G. Jung, "The Process of Individuation: Alchemy I," notes on lectures given at the Eidgenössische Technische Hochschule (ETH), January 10, 1941, Zurich. Unpublished multigraph, p. 83. [This multigraph transcript was prepared by Barbara Hannah. *Ed.*]

solved the riddle of the mystery of the *coniunctio.* On the contrary. I am darkly aware of things lurking in the background of the problem, things too big for horizons.[13]

The fact that we can help by trying to reach this unknown realm in ourselves is best illustrated by Wilhelm's rainmaker story, personally of such significance to Jung that he told me to repeat it in every seminar I gave.

The renowned sinologist Richard Wilhelm tells the story of the rainmaker from the province of Schantung who was asked to come to Kiautschou where a severe drought had long oppressed the land. As soon as the man arrived he asked that a small hut be built for him at the edge of the city. When the hut was completed, he took up his abode with the request that nobody disturb him. He remained in this hut three days and three nights, and on the morning of the fourth day, a snowstorm broke over the city, a kind of storm that nobody had ever experienced at that time or season of the year. When Wilhelm heard this story, he went to visit the rainmaker and asked him how he had managed to make it snow. The man answered that it was not he who had made it snow. He was simply the person who had come from Schantung, where everything was more or less in order. Here, in Kiautschou, however, heaven and earth were separated, everything was wrong, and he needed three days and nights just to get himself in order. And in the moment when he finally was able to get himself in order, then it began to rain and snow.[14]

Both what the rainmaker called "being in Tao" and what we would call being in the Self depend a great deal on our attitude toward the opposites. If we let ourselves identify with one side or the other—that is, if we let ourselves be taken by one side or the other—we neither feel in Tao nor are we really in Tao or in our-

---

13. Jung, *Letters, vol. 2, 1951–1961,* pp. 392ff. [Commencing from a Jungian standpoint, Trinick examines the symbol of alchemical-psychological (and sexual) union, explores the power of the symbol in the work of William Blake and other less-well-known mystics, and deals with hidden undercurrents of Western and Russian mysticism. John Trinick, *The Fire-Tried Stone* (London: Stuart and Watkins, 1967), p. 7. *Ed.*]

14. See Sir Herbert Read, *Zum 85. Geburtstag von Professor Dr. Carl Gustav Jung* (Zurich. 1960), pp. 27f.

selves.[15] Yet the *hieros gamos* by which the opposites are united is such a deep mystery that one can only try constantly to keep it in mind and wait until, if ever, it reveals its own mystery.

Another example of the mystery that one should constantly keep in mind—although it often seems a hopeless task—is the mystery of life beyond death. Jung writes in *Memories, Dreams, Reflections*:

> A man should be able to say he has done his best to form a conception of life after death, or to create some image of it— even if he must confess his failure. Not to have done so is a vital loss. For the question that is posed to him is the age-old heritage of humanity: an archetype, rich in secret life, which seeks to add itself to our own individual life in order to make it whole. Reason sets the boundaries far too narrowly for us, and would have us accept only the known—and that too with limitations—and live in a known framework, just as if we were sure how far life actually extends. As a matter of fact, day after day we live far beyond the bounds of our conscious-ness; without our knowledge, the life of the unconscious is also going on within us. The more critical reason dominates, the more impoverished life becomes; but the more of the unconscious, and the more of myth we are capable of making conscious, the more of life we integrate. Overvalued rea-son has this in common with political absolutism: under its dominion the individual is pauperized.[16]

And it is just this pauperization of the individual that makes us fall victim to the animus. His opinions are the very essence of political

---

15. [Barbara Hannah's concept of freeing oneself from the opposites and finding an inner orientation in the *hieros gamos*, can be said to have certain parallels to some philosophical schools of thought. In Buddhist "mindfulness," for instance, one attempts to observe and detach oneself from the polarities of strife, physical suffering, the emotions, ambitions, and so forth. Herein, one seeks a form of union beyond the worldly realm of animus, anima, and ego convictions as well as the polarities of politics, power, jealousy, righteousness, and the like. As Jung notes, nonidentification with the opposites demands considerable moral effort. Jung, "The Psychology of the Transference," in *CW*, vol. 16, pars. 469f. *Ed.*]

16. C. G. Jung, *Memories, Dreams, Reflections* (New York: Vintage Books, 1965), p. 302.

absolutism with its state slavery and disregard of the individual. Jung used to say that the animus wanted to settle everything for the 11,000 virgins for the next 10,000 years.[17] The absolutism of the political state completely disregards the claim of the individual; it even regards it as worthless compared to the mass of the people.

To escape from the tyranny of the animus, nothing can help us more than concentrating on becoming conscious of the unknown. Even if, as Jung said, we can only confess our failure. When we concentrate on the unconscious, the animus is then in his right place as the function between consciousness and the unconscious, and thus he is prevented from interfering with our outer lives. For behind the animus is the far more powerful figure of the Self that alone can easily set the animus in his right place. I wasted a lot of time arguing directly with the animus from the ego, but he was always too clever for me and led me down the garden path until at last I realized it was really a matter of being in Tao, of being in myself, and having the right attitude. Here is where the Self comes into play and, without effort, puts the animus into his right place.

Experience has taught me, slowly and painfully, that the best way of encountering the Self is by forcing oneself to concentrate on the unknown. In his chapter on "Life after Death" in *Memories, Dreams, Reflections*, Jung says:

> The decisive question for man is: Is he related to something infinite or not? That is the telling question of his life. Only if

---

17. Jung wrote in 1940: "Optimists invariably hope that humanity learns by its mistakes, and that things will be better after a particularly foolish error. But history teaches us the opposite. It swings from white to black and black to white and, when the cycle is fulfilled, it begins all over again. Consciousness has increased, but historical evidence shows that morality has not . . . . I am sure, however, that this is a wrong way of looking at life. We should learn to think differently . . . . The individual should turn his attention to his own problems and stop worrying about the 11,000 virgins. They are really no business of ours. It is wrong to think statistically, and to worry about the state of the world in twenty years time. Other people will live then and it will be their problem; we live now and are our own concern. The modern way of thinking in terms of thousands and millions of people is really a neurosis, we simply use it as an escape from the problems of our own life. If someone really tries to answer the questions in his own life, he will have plenty to keep him employed, and he will not need to interfere with other people." C. G. Jung, "The Process of Individuation," p. 247.

we know that the thing which truly matters is the infinite can we avoid fixing our interest upon futilities, and upon all kinds of goals which are not of real importance . . . .

The feeling for the infinite, however, can be attained only if we are bounded to the utmost. The greatest limitation for man is the "self"; it is manifested in the experience: "I am only that!" Only consciousness of our narrow confinement in the self forms the link to the limitlessness of the unconscious. In such awareness we experience ourselves concurrently as limited and eternal, as both the one and the other. In knowing ourselves to be unique in our personal combination—that is, ultimately limited—we possess also the capacity for becoming conscious of the infinite. But only then![18]

One can see the difference between the effect of the ego and of the Self in the story that Jung tells in his *Memories* of their travels where, despite the heat, and with no means of transportation, they were forced to proceed on foot through a region of the Sudan. Their guides were uneasy because they had now entered the territory of a tribe that was reckoned as unpredictable. They were trekking along the southern slope of Mount Egon: the mountains higher, the jungle denser, its borders verging onto the plain, and the natives blacker, more thickly built and clumsier, lacking the grace of the Masai.

The chief, generous and friendly, had proposed a *n'goma*, a wild and stirring tribal dance around a roaring bonfire that goes well into the night. Jung could not help but recall a story told to him by one of his cousins of a similar dance in the Celebes that resulted in a European being accidentally impaled by a flying spear.[19]

I would say here that, based on Jung's own account, his "No. 1" personality (as he calls it in his *Memories*) became alarmed as the native men, encircling the women, children, and Europeans,

<hr>

18. Jung, *Memories, Dreams, Reflections*, p. 325.
19. Ibid., pp. 270f.

danced themselves into a frenzy. Jung did not know if he ought
to be pleased, honored, or anxious about the increasingly fervent
energy of the dancers, especially since all of his trekking guides
and government soldiers had somehow slipped away out of the
camp. He writes:

> It was a wild and stirring scene, bathed in the glow of the fire
> and magical moonlight. My English friends and I sprang to
> our feet and mingled with the dancers. I swung my rhinoc-
> eros whip, the only weapon I had, and danced with them.
> By their beaming faces I could see that they approved of
> our taking part. Their zeal redoubled; the whole company
> stamped, sang and shouted, sweating profusely. Gradually
> the rhythm of the dance and the drumming accelerated.
> [The natives were falling] into a state of possession. [I final-
> ly] called the people together, distributed cigarettes, and
> then made the gesture of sleeping. Then I swung my rhi-
> noceros whip threateningly, but at the same time laughing,
> and for lack of any better language I swore at them loudly
> in Swiss German [saying] that this was enough and they
> must go home to bed and sleep now. It was apparent to the
> people that I was to some extent pretending my anger, but
> that seems to have struck the right note. General laughter
> arose; capering, they scattered in all directions and vanished
> into the night.[20]

   I have experienced Jung do a similar thing in comparable situations at the Carnival Balls in Zurich, thus I was particularly interested when one of the Europeans who had been present at Mount
Egon told us that Jung seemed to grow in stature before their eyes
until he towered above the natives and easily took command of
the situation. Particularly interested, because dealing with primitives is much like dealing with the figures of the unconscious, and
the *Auseinandersetzung* with the animus can be dealt with far

---

20. Ibid., pp. 271f.

more effectively by being in oneself, as Jung was that night.[21] For if one is, then the Self can deal effectively with situations that are far too much for the ego. Or, in Jung's language, personality No. 2, not No. 1, is up to tackling all kinds of problems.

One can see a similar scene in the large group sculpture of the bride-goddess Hippodamia in Olympia in which, during the inebriated tumult of her wedding festivities, the centaurs, wildly wielding spears and daggers, try to abduct her.[22]

To return now to the practical work that is required before we can be in Tao, one cannot be in harmony within oneself unless one knows one's shadow. One can never have a proper and effective attitude to the opposites until one has thoroughly reached both the dark and the light in oneself. Until this is achieved, the animus always marries the unrecognized shadow. And this puts the ego in the hopelessly ineffective position of being one against two. In fact, you can never arrive at the animus unless you see the shadow, unless you see your own inferior sides. When you see your shadow, you can detach from the animus, but as long as you don't see it, you haven't got a ghost of a chance.[23]

Jung says, in his "Psychology of the Transference," that when you can see your shadow, then you can begin to detach from the anima or animus, a task that entails a tremendous effort and that is well portrayed in the symbolism of a crucifixion.[24] Jung writes that the encounter with the anima and animus

> means conflict and brings us up against the hard dilemma in which nature herself has placed us. Whichever course one takes, nature will be mortified and must suffer, even to the death; for the merely natural man must die in part during his own lifetime. The Christian symbol of the crucifix is, therefore, a prototype and an "eternal" truth. There are

---

21. [*Auseinandersetzung* is used here to mean coping or coming to terms with something by means of reflection, discussion, and analysis. *Ed.*]

22. [A painting, *The Abduction of Hippodamia* by Peter Paul Rubens, of the same subject can be found on the Internet. *Ed.*]

23. Jung, "The Psychology of the Transference," in *CW*, vol. 16, pars. 452ff; also pars. 501ff.

24. Ibid., par. 470.

medieval pictures showing how Christ is nailed to the Cross by his own virtues. Other people meet the same fate at the hands of their vices. Nobody who finds himself on the road to wholeness can escape that characteristic suspension which is the meaning of crucifixion. For he will infallibly run into things that thwart and "cross" him: first, the thing he has no wish to be (the shadow); second, the thing he is not (the "other," the individual reality of the "You"); and third, his psychic non-ego (the collective unconscious). This being at cross purposes with ourselves is suggested by the crossed branches held by the king and queen, who are themselves man's cross in the form of the anima and the woman's cross in the form of the animus. The meeting with the collective unconscious is a fatality of which the natural man has no inkling until it overtakes him. As Faust says: "You are conscious only of the single urge / O may you never know the other!"[25]

It is a well-known fact—quite outside psychological circles—that the soul of man is feminine. I mention only Dante's Beatrice, Petrarch's Laura, and Rider Haggard's "She." But I do not think anyone has realized clearly that the spirit of woman was masculine until Jung recognized it in his exploratory analyses of women. We can, however, find traces of it in previous times and in various places, although usually in a negative form: the demons that possess women, for instance, are usually thought to be masculine. I refer here, for example, to my discussion of the demon Asmodaeus in Tobit.[26]

The feminine mystics (Perpetua, for instance) usually found their highest spirit in the masculine figure of Christ. But as God has been thought of as masculine for at least the last two thousand years by both men and women, this fact in women has escaped special notice. Experience has certainly confirmed this, both negatively and positively: the spirit of woman almost always appears in a masculine form. Her soul, however, is con-

---

25. Ibid.
26. [See Barbara Hannah's essay on Tobit in this volume. *Ed.*]

nected with the Self, who usually, at first, appears as feminine, although the Self, as the supreme union of opposites, is actually more androgynous than either male or female. One must not forget that the great difficulty in recognizing the masculine in the spirit in woman is due to the fact that it has been projected throughout the Christian era onto our exclusively masculine Trinity, and this masculine orientation creates a real difficulty for women in re-collecting the projection and getting to know one's own animus.

In earlier and more peaceful times, the unconscious indeed fit smoothly into prevailing religions. There are a few fortunate people today whose unconscious still fits into the framework of some established religion, and we should never disturb such people if they do come to us for analysis. If they come, they are most likely being plagued by the usual modern problems; but for them answers are to be sought within their religion. Yet such people are unfortunately a minority. The analyst has to help the overwhelming majority find the psychological Self, for as Jung told me when I first began to work as an analyst, if you dig deep enough, you will find a religious problem behind almost every problem that brings people to analysis. Referring back to the quote from Jung's *Memories,* one must always keep in mind that the most telling question of one's life is whether or not a man or woman "is related to something infinite." Only if we know that the one thing that truly matters is the infinite can we then avoid fixating our interest upon futilities.[27]

I hardly need to add that it is the Self, or the "No. 2" personality in Jung's *Memories,* that is rooted in the infinite, and that the ego, or the "No. 1" personality, will inevitably waste its whole life with nonsense if it is not related to the Self. Of course, most people who come to analysis do not recognize—or are not yet ready for—their own religious problem. Then one must deal as best one can with the outer problem that brings them to analysis so that they can get on with living their lives in whatever form they feel to be theirs.

27. Jung, *Memories, Dreams, Reflections,* p. 325.

Once we have definitely realized our own shadow and are
no longer projecting our own bad qualities onto unfortunate
neighbors, and once we realize that our consciousness is only
an infinitely small standpoint in comparison to the vast extent
of the unknown, only then can we begin the task of making the
acquaintance of the animus. For we must know the figure of the
animus—and we must make it conscious—before we can afford
to have it subjugated to the Self. We must not forget that the figures of animus and anima have a personal aspect—we can speak
of my animus and your anima—yet they are also inhabitants of
the collective unconscious. Here I would like to strongly suggest
that a woman attempts to speak to her own animus when she is
having a quarrel with another woman, for this paves the way to
a real understanding of some of the more personal dynamics of
one's "own" animus.

In the spring of 1938, toward the end of his seminar on
Zarathustra, Jung went into this matter in some detail.[28] He was
speaking of the projection of the dark side and of seeing the devil
projected onto someone else:

> You see, you are a whole world of things and they are all
> mixed in you and form a terrible sauce, a chaos. So you
> should be mighty glad when the unconscious chooses certain
> figures and consolidates them outside of yourself. Of course
> that may be in the form of projections, which is not recom-
> mendable. For example, perhaps you have a sort of hostile
> element in yourself that crosses your path now and then,
> or a poisonous element that destroys all your attempts at a
> decent adaptation, and it is so mixed up with everything else
> that you never can definitely lay your hand on it. Then you
> suddenly discover somebody who you can really declare to be
> your arch-enemy, so you can say this fellow who has done this

---

28. Barbara Hannah notes: It should not be overlooked that Jung was speaking of Nietzsche's
Zarathustra and pointing out that, as Nietzsche had constructed the figure of Zarathustra,
the light aspect of the Self, he should have constructed a counter shadow figure or the latter
would—as indeed it did—fall into the "sauce" of his own psyche. Naturally, there is always a
certain danger in quoting passages out of their context.

and that against you: you succeed in constructing your arch-enemy. Now, that is already an asset which makes you sit up, because you know that there is the definite danger which can injure you. Of course it is in a way quite negative because it is not true; that fellow is not really the devil, but is only your best enemy and you should give him the credit. As a human being he is just as much in the soup as you are. But inasmuch as you succeed in creating a figure, in objectifying a certain thing in yourself which you hitherto could never contact, it is an advantage.

Now, the analyst will tell you that you cannot assume Mr. So-and-So to be the arch-devil with a hand in your own soul. That is just a projection, until the patient gradually gets to the point of saying: "Oh very well, then I am the devil"—hating it like hell, naturally, and nothing is gained. Then the devil falls back into the sauce and instantly dissolves there. So you must prevent that . . . . The analyst has to say: "Now look here, in spite of the fact that you say there is no terrible devil, there is at least a psychological fact which you might call the devil. If you should not find a devil, then you had better construct one—and quickly—before he dissolves in your own system. Make a devil, say there is one, and if you doubt it, suppress your doubts as much as you can . . . . [You] must be convinced that you have to construct him, that it is absolutely essential to construct that figure. Otherwise the thing dissolves in your unconscious right away and you are left in the same condition as before.[29]

There has been a *consensus gentium* in almost every form of human society that has believed in some kind of personification of evil per se. And it is inevitable that if we reject the reality of the figures of the collective unconscious, we shall either project collective forces onto our neighbors or introject them into ourselves. Therefore, it seems to me of vital importance that we should never forget that the animus, however personally we may take him, is also a figure of the unconscious.

---

29. Jung, *Nietzsche's Zarathustra*, pp. 1320f.

In another seminar Jung pointed out that as soon as a woman begins controlling her animus or a man his anima, then they come up against the herd instinct in mankind. Man's original state was one of complete unconsciousness, and this condition still persists in us all today.[30] When we attempt to liberate ourselves from possession by the anima or animus, we get into a different order of things, and thus we begin to be a threat to the old order. If one sheep goes ahead of the flock by itself, it will seem like a wolf to the others and thus be exposed to attack from them. Moreover, no sooner do you get rid of a devil than you have all the devils against you. If a man makes a modest attempt at controlling his anima, he will be right away in a situation where he is tested to the blood; all the devils in the world will try to get into his anima in order to bring him back into the fold of Mother Nature. The same with a woman; every devil circulating within one hundred miles will do his best to get the goat of her animus.

The truth of these words will be evident, I think, to any woman who has made a serious attempt to come to terms with her animus (or a man with his anima). On the one hand, the people in her environment are fascinated by the fact that she has gained a standpoint *au-dessus de la mêlée* [above the fray]. But on the other hand, their unconscious—particularly their animi—is irritated by the fact that something has been done *contra naturam*. Therefore, she often finds herself exposed to the most unexpected attacks, usually of a very irrational nature.

It is obvious that the animus, as a figure with both individual and collective characteristics, is particularly suitable as the intermediary between consciousness and the unconscious. But at first, in his negative form, he has little or no inclination to play this role.[31] The thing that we must never forget in dealing with the animus is that he is dual, always having a positive and negative aspect which, of course, also applies to the anima.

---

30. C. G. Jung, *Visions: Notes of the Seminar Given in 1930–1934*, 2 vols., edited by Clair Douglas (London: Routledge, 1998), p. 615.

31. [Barbara Hannah makes a note here referring to the positive and negative father complex and how the one is compensated by the other later in life. *Ed.*]

In my paper, "The Problem of Contact with the Animus," I spoke of the woman with the animus figure she called "Archibald."[32] He was most useful, a regular Admiral Creighton.[33] She told us many years ago about this animus and how much he helped her daily. And we remarked that one could not really trust a figure of the unconscious to such an extent, particularly in regards to things in the outside life, where you must make your own decisions. However, she would not listen, she was so delighted, and she gave herself more and more into his hands and eventually became completely possessed by him. What was originally very positive in the end became purely negative. But the fact that this woman personified her animus was very correct. It was the fact that she trusted him in all situations in her outer life that led to the state of possession.

Jung says in his article "The Relation Between Ego and the Unconscious" that a man must submit to a kind of prehistoric kindergarten schooling until he has won a realistic conception of the powers and factors of a world other than the visible. Thus, he would be right to treat the anima as an autonomous personality and to put direct personal questions to her. "I mean this as an actual technique," he says.[34] Naturally, the same holds true for women and the animus

He goes on with one of his clearest descriptions of active imagination. In fact, in his early writings this account—and the one in his commentary on "The Secret of the Golden Flower"—are the clearest guides possible to the technique of active imagination.[35] Altogether, active imagination is perhaps the best of all techniques for coming to terms with the animus (or anima). Although,

---

32. [See Barbara Hannah's essay "The Problem of Contact with the Animus" in volume 1 of this work. *Ed.*]

33. [Rear Admiral Sir Kenelm Creighton, ocean commodore, was called from retirement for the Battle of the Atlantic and served during the first three years of World War II as commodore of approximately twenty-five ocean convoys. He survived two sinking ships (one of which sank within two minutes after being torpedoed), and he returned to fight onward. *Ed.*]

34. C. G. Jung, "The Relations Between the Ego and the Unconscious (1928), in *CW*, vol. 7 (Princeton, N.J.: Princeton University Press, 1953), pars. 323, 370.

35. C. G. Jung, "Commentary on 'The Secret of the Golden Flower'" (1957), in *CW*, vol. 13 (Princeton, N.J.: Princeton University Press, 1967).

as mentioned before, one must guide him toward the paradoxical Self rather than argue with him directly, for he will always prove too clever for the likes of me and you.

If he tries to put over collective or one-sided arguments, it is a good plan to bring in the opposite, for example, to say: "Yes, you may be right, but the contrary is also valid." These days, he particularly likes to argue for a group or a collective solution, yet it is the individual we have to look after, for any group is only composed of the individuals of which it consists, and it can only exist on their level.

Whether we believe it or not, we shall do far more for the appalling state of the world by tending to the individual and doing our best to get ourselves and our analysands into Tao along the lines of the pattern of the rainmaker. Biologically considered, the cell's first duty is to keep its own household in order, to maintain its functioning and purpose, and to sustain its own health. Without this task set as priority, humankind, like the cell, is likely to destroy our world with a gigantic, cancer-like, malignant disease.

A woman's first task—once she has a good working knowledge of her shadow—is to try to catch the animus at work in herself. We say a lot of unconscious things in the course of a day, and it is a good idea to form the habit of carefully examining what we have said, and, at all events, we shall be surprised— certainly at first—how often we repeat opinions with which we actually do not agree. Then we ask ourselves: "Who then said that?" and we shall be on the way to making the acquaintance of the animus.

Our dreams, if properly understood, are perhaps our greatest source of information about our animus. Here, he usually appears personified as a male figure, and we can learn how much he unconsciously influences us. Jung notes that unlike the anima, who personifies herself in a single figure, the animus often does not limit his appearance to that of a singular character but may appear as a plurality of persons. The animus figure of the heroine in H. G. Wells's novel *Christine Alberta's Father* is an appropriate example.[36] Jung notes that Wells himself describes this figure as a "Court of Conscience." Christine Alberta's animus is a:

> collection of condemnatory judges, a sort of College of Preceptors, [and] corresponds to a personification of the animus. The animus is rather like an assembly of fathers or dignitaries of some kind who lay down incontestable . . . judgments. On closer examination these exacting judgments turn out to be largely sayings and opinions scraped together more or less unconsciously from childhood . . . and compressed into a canon of average truth, justice, and reasonableness, a compendium of preconceptions which, whenever a conscious and competent judgment is lacking (as not infrequently happens) instantly obliges with an opinion. Sometimes these opinions take the form of so-called sound common sense, sometimes they appear as principles which are like a travesty of education: "People have always done it like this," or "Everybody knows that it is like that."[37]

A few paragraphs further down Jung notes that the animus, contrary to the rather unified and singular personality of the anima, is distinguished by a plurality that correlates to the conscious attitude of woman.

> The conscious attitude of woman is in general far more exclusively personal than that of man. Her world is made up of fathers and mothers, brothers and sisters, husbands and children. The rest of the world consists likewise of families, who nod to each other but are, in the main, interested essentially in themselves. The man's world is the nation, the state, business concerns, etc. His family is simply a means to an end, one of the foundations of the state, and his wife is not necessarily the woman for him (at any rate not as the

---

36. H. G. Wells, *Christine Alberta's Father* (London: Jonathon Cape Ltd., 1926).

37. Jung, "The Relations Between the Ego and the Unconscious," in *CW*, vol. 7, par. 332.

woman means it when she says "my man"). The general
means more to him than the personal; his world consists of a
multitude of coordinated factors, whereas her world, outside
her husband, terminates in a sort of cosmic mist. A passionate
exclusiveness, therefore, attaches to the man's anima, and an
indefinite variety to the woman's animus . . . . [The] animus is
better expressed as a bevy of Flying Dutchmen or unknown
wanderers from over the sea, never quite clearly grasped,
protean, given to persistent and violent motion. These
expressions appear especially in dreams, though in concrete
reality they can be famous tenors, boxing champions, or great
men in far-away, unknown cities.[38]

Jung points out elsewhere that men seem to easily understand
what is meant by the anima. Many even have a definite picture of
her enabling him and are able to single out the one who comes
closest to his anima type from a group of various women.

But I have, as a rule, found it very difficult to make a woman
understand what the animus is, and I have never met any
woman who could tell me anything definite about his personality. From this I conclude that the animus does not have
a definite personality at all; in other words, he is not so much
a unity as a plurality. This fact must somehow be connected
with the specific psychology of men and women. On the biological level a woman's chief interest is to hold a man, while
a man's chief interest is to conquer a woman, and because
of his nature, he seldom stops at one conquest. Thus one
masculine personality plays a decisive role for a woman, but
a man's relation to a woman is much less definite, as he can
look on his wife as one among many women. This makes him
lay stress on the legal and social characteristic of marriage,
whereas a woman sees it as an exclusively personal relationship. Hence, as a rule, a woman's consciousness is restricted
to one man, whereas a man's consciousness has a tendency

---

38. Ibid., par. 338.

to go beyond the one personal relationship—a tendency that is sometimes opposed to any personal limitations. In the unconscious, therefore, we may expect a compensation by contraries. The man's sharply defined anima figure fulfils this expectation perfectly, as also does the indefinite polymorphism of the woman's animus.[39]

Jung's statement does apply as a general rule, yet we can see the exception in such authoritative animus figures as "Archibald," which I mentioned earlier.

In what we say and what we think—in word and thought—we can catch the animus at work. We must oblige ourselves to nail down the utterances, the unspoken statements, and the views of the animus immediately, for if we do not pin them down instantly, we naturally never catch them. Here, the fox frivolously chases its tail. To this Jung notes:

> In its primary "unconscious" form the animus is a compound of spontaneous, unpremeditated opinions which exercise a powerful influence on the woman's emotional life, while the anima is similarly compounded of feelings which thereafter influence or distort the man's understanding. Consequently the animus likes to project itself upon "intellectuals" and all kinds of "heroes," including tenors, artists, sporting celebrities, etc. The anima has a predilection for everything that is unconscious, dark, equivocal, and at a loose end in woman, and also for her vanity, frigidity, helplessness, and so forth.[40]

We can remain blissfully at one with the animus, a man with his anima, until the reality of relationships with others, as well as our functioning in the outer world, create interference and thus inevitably lead to tension, frustration, disappointment, doubt, and a generally unhappy state.

---

39. C. G. Jung, "Mind and Earth" (1931), in *CW*, vol. 10 (Princeton, N.J.: Princeton University Press, 1964), par. 81.
40. Jung, "The Psychology of the Transference," in *CW*, vol. 16, par. 521.

It is in our vital relationships to men that we usually first discover the animus in projection. As long as the projection fits, we are generally totally unaware that it exists. But sooner or later, if the relationship is important enough, it is certain to give rise to trouble. This aspect of our problem is described in an unsurpassable way by Emma Jung in her excellent article, "A Contribution to the Problem of the Animus." She writes:

> At first the spirit [that is, animus] comes toward us from outside, to the child mostly from the father or from a man who takes his place, later a teacher, an older brother, a friend, the husband, and finally then in outer objective expressions of the spirit, the church, the state, society and its institutions, and in the creations of the sciences and the arts. Most often the woman has no direct access to these objective manifestations of the spirit; rather she finds them first through a man who is her guide and her mediator. This guide, this mediator, then becomes the carrier or the representation of her animus; onto him the animus is projected. There is no conflict as long as this projection succeeds, that is, as long as the projected image is more or less covered by the man who carries it. On the contrary, this state of affairs would in a certain manner appear to be perfect, in particular when the man who is the carrier [of the animus projection] is also a man whom the woman experiences as a human being and with whom the woman has a good relationship. When such a relationship is continually maintained, then we have what could be called an ideal relationship, without conflict, whereby the woman remains unconscious. Today, however, we can no longer remain unconscious. This seems to me to be proven by the fact that many women, if not practically all, who believe themselves to be happy and content in such a presumably perfect animus relationship are plagued by nervous disorders or physical symptoms. Anxiety attacks, disturbances in sleep, and general nervousness occur, or headaches, distortions in visual perception and even problems with the lungs may arise . . . .

A total transference of the animus image may provide not only seeming satisfaction and perfection but also a type of obsessive bond to the man in question and a dependence on him that becomes increasingly unbearable.

When the disparity between the image and the man in question begins to set in, then we become aware of our confusion and dismay—and that the man who incorporated our animus image is continually behaving in a manner that does not fit our view. One may initially endeavor to fool oneself, and this often succeeds rather easily, first due to our skills to adapt, and then thanks to a rather soft and blurred focus when we discriminate. Often the woman will artfully attempt to make the man into what he should be. Not that we consciously or necessarily exercise force or pressure; rather far more often it occurs fully unconsciously and our partner is insinuated—by our own behavior—into the archetypal conduct characteristic of the animus.[41]

Emma Jung concludes with the observation that:

> The same constellation naturally occurs in a reversed manner with the man. He also wants to see the anima image that hovers before him in the woman, and through this wish, which effects her by means of suggestion, compels her to live not her own life but to become his anima figure. This situation is then coupled with the condition that the anima and animus are constellated juxtaposed to one another, that is, an anima statement on the one side conjures up the animus on the other. And vice-versa. And thus a vicious cycle is set in motion that is difficult to break and creates one of the worst complications in the relationships between man and woman.[42]

---

41. Emma Jung, *Animus and Anima: On the Nature of the Animus* (New York: The Analytical Psychology Club of New York, 1957), pp. 310–313. [Editor's translation.]

42. Ibid., p. 313.

Although there are exceptions, most women who have experienced the reality of the animus beyond all doubt feel exceedingly negative toward him. He is apparently forever thwarting our intentions, spoiling our relationships, replacing our sound instincts and feelings by a mere collection of opinions, and altogether preventing us from living our lives naturally as women. This is only too true of the animus in his negative aspect. And when we only experience this side, we are obliged sooner or later to ask ourselves: "Why do I know so little of my own mind? Why am I on such bad terms with my animus? What am I doing that he always thwarts me?" Obviously, early experiences with the projected animus—a negative father complex, for instance—play a great role here and must always be taken into account.[43] But, as Jung says in *Psychology and Alchemy*:

> no matter how much parents and grandparents may have sinned against the child, the man who is really adult will accept these sins as his own condition which has to be reckoned with. Only a fool is interested in other people's guilt since he cannot alter it. The wise man learns only from his own guilt. He will ask himself: Who am I that all this should happen to me? To find the answer to this fateful question, he will look into his own heart.[44]

If we then decide to grow up and become adult in the sense that Jung means here, and if we want to put the "fateful question" to ourselves—for which we must look into our own depths—then we shall not be in a position to answer until we have faced the *Auseinandersetzung* with our own shadow and our animus. This *Auseinandersetzung* is perhaps best done in some form of active imagination, but above all, in whatever form we face it, the sine qua non is the making of a relationship to our own unconscious

---

43. Barbara Hannah writes: I do not emphasize the father complex in this paper because its effects are comparatively well known yet, as these are exceedingly far-reaching, it would be a great mistake to underestimate them.

44. C. G. Jung, *Psychology and Alchemy* (1944), *CW*, vol. 12 (Princeton, N.J.: Princeton University Press, 1953), par. 152.

mind. Here, creative expression and creative work of some kind is of the greatest possible help.[45]

The same is true in the encounter with the animus per se. By trying to do creative work, we dedicate time and attention to our animus, which is so very necessary in order to prevent him from being hostile to us. Jung points out in *Psychology and Alchemy* that the face of the unconscious is not rigid; it reflects the face we turn to it.[46] Hostility lends it a threatening aspect, friendliness softens its features, so that, difficult as it is, it is a vital necessity to attain the right relation to the animus.[47]

Although I have already pointed out how much more important experience is than theory, I am perhaps becoming too theoretical in these general remarks, so we will now turn to the practical and everyday effect that the animus can have on a human life. And thus we will come nearer to our own experience.

---

45. [In her manuscript, Barbara Hannah writes the note: "Expand." It is uncertain what she had in mind. *Ed.*]

46. Jung, *Psychology and Alchemy*, CW, vol. 12, par. 29.

47. [In her manuscript, Barbara Hannah writes the note: "Giving credit." It is uncertain what she had in mind. *Ed.*]

The Animus in the Middle Ages

Editor's Note: The following lecture was presumably given around 1949. It serves here as a general introduction to the subsequent in-depth analysis of the animus possession of Jeanne Fery.

IT WOULD CERTAINLY BE QUITE INCORRECT TO SAY THAT THE appearance of the masculine figure in women—which Jung has called the animus—only goes back as far as the Middle Ages. In her excellent paper on St. Perpetua, Marie-Louise von Franz has shown us the existence of this figure in the dreams that Perpetua had shortly before her martyrdom circa 200 A.D.[1] And long before her, we have a wonderful description of an exceedingly negative animus in Asmodaeus, the demon lover of Sarah, who Tobit freed with the help of the angel Raphael.[2] This demon lover, as you will remember, had purportedly killed seven husbands of Sarah before Tobit took the matter in hand.

There can be little reasonable doubt that the archetype of the animus in women corresponds in certain ways closely to that of the anima in men. Presumably, it is just as old and quite as deeply ingrained in the feminine psyche as the anima is in the masculine psyche. But women are undoubtedly less conscious of this fact than men. Men have been inclined to think of their souls as

---

1. M.-L. von Franz, *The Passion of Perpetua: A Psychological Interpretation of Her Visions* (Toronto: Inner City Books. 2004).

2. The Book of Tobit is part of the Apocrypha of the Bible, most likely written down somewhere between the third and second century B.C.E.

feminine for a very long time. One recalls, for instance, Dante's
Beatrice, Poliphilo's Polia, Petrarch's Laura, and so on.[3]
Of course, ninety-nine percent of the traditional material
comes from men. As we are permeated with expressions of the
male psyche, we naturally think on those terms. Therefore, as far
as I know, it never occurred to anyone before Jung to think that
woman's spirit was probably male. In *Psychological Types* he says:

> If, therefore, we speak of the anima of a man, we must
> logically speak of the animus of a woman, if we are to give
> the soul of a woman its right name. Whereas logic and
> objectivity are usually the predominant features of a man's
> outer attitude, or are at least regarded as ideals, in the case
> of a woman it is feeling. But in the soul it is the other way
> round: inwardly it is the man who feels, and the woman who
> reflects. Hence a man's greater liability to total despair, while
> a woman can always find comfort and hope; accordingly a
> man is more likely to put an end to himself than woman.
> However much a victim of social circumstances a woman
> may be, as a prostitute for instance, a man is no less a victim
> of impulses from the unconscious, taking the form of alco-
> holism and other vices.[4]

3. [For a description of the works of Dante and Petrarch, see Barbara Hannah's "Introduction
to the Course on the Animus" in this volume. The *Hypnerotomachia Poliphili*, published in
1499, is a magnificently crafted manuscript, one of the earlier of its kind, which includes
more than 170 woodcuts. It is one of the most beautiful books of the Venetian Renaissance.
The author, Francesco Colonna, relates a dream of the protagonist Poliphilo in which he
seeks his unrequited love for the beautiful nymphlike figure of Polia. Poliphilo falls in love
with her when he first glimpses her combing her hair at a window in Treviso. Not only does
she reject his advances, but to fulfill a pledge for having survived the plague, she dedicates
herself to a life of eternal chastity. Poliphilo visits her secretly at the temple of Diana, and
when he falls into a deathlike swoon at her feet, she drags his body away and hides it. But
Cupid appears to her in a vision and compels her to return and kiss Poliphilo back to life.
Venus blesses their love, and the lovers are united at last. Barbara Hannah also adds: "Give
a few examples from primitive psychology." *Ed.*]
4. C. G. Jung, *Psychological Types* (1921), *CW*, vol. 6 (Princeton, N.J.: Princeton University
Press, 1971), par. 805. [Jung was engaged in the preparatory work for his book *Psychological
Types* between the years 1913 and 1918, a work which sprang from his need at that time to
differentiate his work from that of Freud and Adler (see Jung's Editorial Note, at the beginning of vol. 6). Jung corrected his definition of the animus to correlate not with the woman's
soul but rather with the woman's spirit and mind. *Ed.*]

But even Jung at first, if I am not mistaken, only hypothesized that the woman's soul must logically be male. In the course of his analytical work he gradually proved this hypothesis and eventually adjusted it to represent the spirit and not the soul. There were no evident proofs lying ready at hand for the animus such as Dante's Beatrice, a psychological proof of sorts for the existence of the anima. No doubt the paucity of the evidence can largely be explained by the far greater activity of men in the realms of literature, alchemy, religion, and so on. But the imbalance of evidence also lies in the characters of the anima and animus themselves. Comparatively recent literature abounds in wonderful portraits of the anima, Rider Haggard's *She* and Benoît's *L'Atlantide*, to mention only a couple, whereas portraits of the animus are exceedingly difficult to find.[5] Jung once said in a seminar that he thought the animus (naturally *l' homme inspiriteur* of the woman as the anima is the fundamental *femme inspiritrice* of the man) was loathe to give way too much of his nature and to draw portraits of himself. The anima, on the other hand, seems to regale in feminine vanity in this respect and to inspire the man to take her as his model again and again.

There are, of course, exceptions: Heathcliff in *Wuthering Heights* is a marvelous animus figure and also Latimer in *The Evil Vineyard* by Marie Hay.[6] But as a rule, the animus seems to be inclined to behave like a cunning fox that sweeps away his footprints with his tail.

Another reason, perhaps, is the more related nature of women. She studies the minutest details of the men who interest her; they form one of the major interests in her life. Therefore, when she writes, these details may be more present in her mind, and she can thus describe her male characters more from the conscious side than is usually the case with men when they write about women. If this is so, the anima would naturally have a much

---

5. Benoît, *L'Atlantide*; and Henry Rider Haggard, *She, A History of Adventure* (New York: Oxford University Press, 2008). Haggard's *She* and *Wisdom's Daughter: The Life and Love Story of She-Who-Must-Obeyed* were published in 1887 and 1923, respectively.
6. Marie Hay, *The Evil Vineyard* (London: Tauchnitz, 1923); Emily Brontë, *Wuthering Heights* (New York: Penguin Books, 1959, first published in 1847).

better chance to describe herself than the animus, even supposing the latter would like to do so, for woman's exacting individual and personal touches would disturb the archetypal picture.

A more certain reason lies in the patriarchal character of the Christian religion. All the persons of the Trinity are male and, although the Catholics endorse the worship of the Virgin Mary, she has all but disappeared in the Protestant Church. Thus the animus tends to be projected directly onto the figure of Christ, or onto God the Father, or even more rarely onto the Holy Ghost, or, in the case of witchlike psychologies, the animus tends to be projected onto their adversary, Satan.

At the end of his comments on Guillaume de Digulleville's vision of heaven in *Psychology and Alchemy,* Jung says that Guillaume had an intuition of the heretical truth when he set the queen next to the king on a throne of earth-brown crystal:

> For what is heaven without Mother Earth? And how can a man reach fulfillment if the Queen does not intercede for his black soul? She understands the darkness, for she has taken her throne—the earth itself—to heaven with her, if only as the subtlest of suggestions.[7]

Von Franz drew my attention to a Gnostic doctrine that forms an interesting parallel to this idea. According to this dogma, when a woman dies, she must undergo lengthy treatment to transform herself into a man, for only as a man can she hope to be assimilated into the Godhead.[8]

These two points of view offer us a deep insight into the whole problem of the anima and animus. They also confirm Emma Jung's idea that, at bottom, woman is often thankful to learn that

7. C. G. Jung, *Psychology and Alchemy, CW,* vol. 12 (Princeton, N.J.: Princeton University Press, 1953), par. 322.

8. [The symbolism involved in this transformation is also found in the fourth vision of Perpetua. This vision occurred shortly before her triumphant struggle and self-chosen martyrdom, a vision in which she is transformed into a man, a motif best understood within the context of deep psychological transformation. See M.-L.von Franz, *The Passion of Perpetua. Ed.*]

her spirit is male because she is thus raised into participation with what is often regarded as a "higher" spiritual order of beings. On the contrary, men tend to be, at bottom, disappointed to learn that, despite all of their exalted ideas, they are also inextricably mixed up in the "lower" feminine earth principle. Perhaps this also plays a role in the fact that so many more women than men come to psychology.

In his article "Woman in Europe," Jung points out that women who take up masculine professions have done something that it would be less possible for a man to do. Could a man, for example, take a position as a governess or be in charge of a kindergarten? In the course of my life I have met with three men—as it happens, all Englishmen and victims of a mother complex—who admitted to me that they felt more suited for a feminine profession. But these are the exceptions, and even they felt troubled facing the loss of prestige that such a decision would entail. A woman, however, gains in prestige when she adopts a masculine profession, though we are all well aware of what she loses in other respects.

Whereas the Chinese Weltanschauung is built upon the equality of the two principles ying and yang—one light and the other dark, one masculine and the other feminine—our Weltanschauung is built upon the superiority of the light, masculine principle alone. This one-sidedness has affected the psychology of Western woman in two ways: on the one side, the exclusively masculine God has tempted her to identify not only with the lost goddess but also—with far-reaching consequences—with the man's anima. On the other side, it has led to a feeling of inferiority, of belonging to an inferior species. These two problems have led in turn to an increasing tendency not to live her life as a full and ordinary woman but, if she is unable to identify with the anima, to identify with the animus instead. The evidence for the latter tendency is all too clear everywhere around us, making it unnecessary to give examples today.

As Jung has often pointed out, no matter how far our conscious ego may have moved away from the Christian religion, our whole psyche is deeply imprinted with the Christian point of view.

It seems to me, therefore, that we have to face the fact that the masculine spirit of women is in a totally different position toward the masculinity of the Christian God than the feminine soul of man. This psychological fact has probably played a considerable role in the late discovery that the woman's spirit is male. A man, confronted with a god that is exclusively male, understandably feels the need for a queen to intercede for his soul cast in shadow. But a woman in the same position will almost equally as naturally feel she will be able to get away with it, for the female sex is notably more lenient. Moreover, a great many women are actually convinced that what they want is identical with the will of God.

The woman, however, who has learned that her spirit is male through Jungian psychology and who really tries out the basic truth of this fact in her own experience, eventually realizes that the will of her ego is something very different from the will of God, and she soon is no longer so optimistic about being able to get away with it. She quickly learns of the power of the animus and that she has been possessed by him time and again throughout her life. What she thought was her own will, identical with God's, was far more often the will of the animus. As Jung makes very clear in "The Relations Between the Ego and the Unconscious," there is only one way out of this state of animus possession, and that is the way of an *Auseinandersetzung* with him.[9]

We are all trying—each in our own way—to go through this *Auseinandersetzung,* and we naturally ask ourselves the question: are we thus doing something that has never been done by women before?

When Jung was having his own *Auseinandersetzung* with the anima and the unconscious that lies behind her, he turned, as you all know, to the past and found all the marvelous parallels. But, as has often been pointed out, ninety-nine percent of these texts have been written by men. As the unconscious is fundamentally androgynous, most basic truths are undoubtedly equally true for both sexes. Moreover, Jung has often translated them into terms

---

9. C. G. Jung, "The Relations Between the Ego and the Unconscious" (1928), in *CW*, vol. 7 (Princeton, N.J.: Princeton University Press, 1953), pars. 332ff.

of the feminine psyche. But—and here I am going to say something that may arouse resistance—I have been struck by the fact that (present company naturally excepted) women are very apt to lap up all these marvelous things and yet remain animus possessed. Women flock to psychology; they are genuinely impressed by what effect it is having on the animus himself. The fact that men in our own group here are seldom very happy or impressed with these insights makes me fear the worst in this respect. I do not doubt that men have their own resistances—quite apart from anything women do or can do—but I should really like to know here what role the animus is playing: your animus, my animus, and the animus.

Once, when I was talking to my animus about the pact with the devil (which seems to be the hallmark of witchcraft in all ages and places), he made an interesting remark. He told me there were two kinds of pacts, "one with the principle of evil and one with the principle of good." The pact with the devil comes, for instance, from greed, wanting to amass worldly goods, to avoid pain, an exaggerated need for recognition, a power drive, and the wish to do as little work as possible. The pact with the good comes from fear and from leaving undone those many things that should be done and focusing then on the next world, so to speak, to avoid everything that might endanger one's reward there. Both, at bottom, are an escape from the tension of enduring the opposites, for example, the conflicting and imposing emotional forces within where one is caught between desire and morals. This battle must be fought, for this struggle is about integrating all aspects of the basic wholeness that is fundamental to the human psyche.

Before we try to answer the question of what effect psychology is having on the animus, I should like to examine briefly a few medieval cases and see if we can learn something concerning the nature of the animus. The first of these is a case of practically complete possession, a pathological case, that teaches us about the figures of the animus when they gain the upper hand entirely. The case is by no means ideal for our purpose, but the first part is described by the girl herself, which is rare in "witch material," for it is usually reported by extremely prejudiced Inquisitors and thus contaminated with men's psychology. I cannot say that I think this case is entirely free of male influence, for the girl wrote the account after she had been reclaimed by the Church and at the request of her confessors. But, as you will see, it contains some interesting points.

The girl in question was named Jeanne (or Johanna) Fery and was born in the year 1549 in the diocese of Cambrai, in what is now Belgium. Extracts from her own report are quoted by Joseph Görres in *Die Christliche Mystik*, from which I take the following.[10] Jeanne states that she was given to the devil by the curse of her father presumably around the age of four. She does not give any examples for this statement, but certainly the father played an overpowering role at that time. Her father complex was monumental and, as we shall see, she never even began to escape from it, for they could only finally get her to consent to being exorcised by promising her the exorcist as her father and the archbishop of Cambrai as her grandfather. The father figure that plays the largest role in her possession first appeared to her when she was four years old, about the time, as Jung has often pointed out, that we receive our deepest impressions. He was young and handsome and desired to become her father and, in her imagination or visions, he gave her apples and white bread. Thus she consented to regard him as her real father. The idea that he was the devil came later through the influence of the Church; at first she only thought of him as an agreeable young man who she was glad to regard as her real father. It is, as is usually the case with witch material, impossible to say whether this figure began as an actual young man or whether he was immaterial from the beginning. It is quite possible that the whole series of fantasies began with an actual incident that was

---

10. Joseph Görres, *Die Christliche Mystik*,vol. 5 (Regensburg, Germany: Verlagsanstalt G. J. Manz, 1836–1842), pp. 176ff. [Johann Joseph Görres (1776–1848) was a professor at the University of Heidelberg and later at the University of Munich. He was one of the most influential Catholic and political writers of the first half of the nineteenth century. *Die Christliche Mystik* proved a strong stimulant to the Christian faith and dealt a decisive blow to the superficial rationalism prevailing in many religious matters in Germany at that time. *Ed.*]

seized on by a nature that preferred fantasy to fact and chose to circumvent pain—and then spun on in the imagination until the image became indistinguishable from actual reality. Jeanne was certainly adept at confusing outer events with inner events but—and here she was perhaps more sensible than the average woman of today—she did not confuse her inner figures with her ego personality as we shall later see.[11]

Whether there was an outer stimulus, or whether the figure appeared as an autonomous inner figure from the beginning, Jeanne certainly fell into the well-known double-parent motif at a very early age. She says: "While I was still a child, I had yet another father who took care that I did not feel the strokes when I was beaten."

This is very confused, as we are again left uncertain as to whether the two fathers were her actual father and the handsome young man, whether one was the real father and the other a fantasy, or whether there were already two of these invisible fathers from the outset, for the punishment could also have come from the mother. At all events it is clear that some inner force was already at work protecting her from feeling the pain of the outer world.

It seems to me that here we strike an exceedingly valuable hint as to how the animus first establishes his ascendancy in the feminine psyche. He acts as a sort of anesthetic that shields us from experiencing the full impact of outer reality. Like most of his qualities, this effect is ambiguous: it can be very helpful in protecting us from intolerable or unbearable conditions and it can help buffer the shock of the contents of the collective unconscious that might otherwise overwhelm us. You will all remember the diagram in the 1925 lecture notes where Jung drew a double circle around ego and shadow.[12] The outer shield oriented toward

---

11. [For an in-depth discussion of the psychology of Jeanne Fery, see the next essay in this volume, "Jeanne Fery: A Case Study on the Animus, Possession and Exorcism." *Ed.*]

12. [The year 1925 was a turning point in Jung's professional life. He celebrated his fiftieth birthday, traveled to New Mexico and East Africa, published his first book on the principles of analytical psychology, and began his seminars in English at the Eidgenössische Technische Hochschule (ETH) in Zurich, seminars that he continued to give through the 1930s. He

the outer world was labeled the persona and the inner shield, toward the collective unconscious, was the animus.[13] But it can be very dangerous when the animus takes the place of the persona and breaks off the ego's contact with the outer world as happened in the case of Jeanne Fery.

When we consider how much of the collective unconscious is projected onto the outer world, it is in no way surprising that the animus, even in his legitimate role of mediator between conscious and unconscious, gets in between the woman and the outer world. In all fairness, we should admit that he is most often forced into this situation. According to Jeanne Fery, this was the case: he offered himself in the role of the "real father," and she accepted because, as she says, he offered her apples and white bread, a reversal of Eve and the apple.

I think, because she was so very young when this happened, we must assume that the initiative originally came from the side of the unconscious, but it is interesting that, even at that age, conscious consent was indispensable. This agrees with the definition of a sorcerer at the beginning of Bodin's *Démonomanie* where it is emphasized that conscious consent is the sine qua non of all sorcery; one finds the same criterion throughout the records of the Inquisition.[14] Kaigh also gives the same definition in speaking of magic in Africa.[15]

The motives which led Jeanne to give her consent could be seen as a desire to escape wrath or physical punishment, or maybe even greed for green apples and white bread, that is, if they were

introduced his concepts of the collective unconscious, psychological typology, the archetypes, and his theory of the anima and animus. *Ed.*]

13. C. G. Jung, *Analytical Psychology: Notes of the Seminar Given in 1925*, edited by William McGuire (Princeton, N.J.: Princeton University Press, 1991).

14. [Jeanne Bodin (1530–1596) was a jurist, statesman, and political philosopher. He was an eminent European publicist of the sixteenth century and one of the most rational and tolerant thinkers of his time despite his convictions regarding the deserved punishment of witches. Bodin recommended torture, even in cases of the disabled and children, to try to confirm guilt of witchcraft, a suspicion being enough to torment the accused because rumors concerning witches "were almost always true." See Jean Bodin, *La Démonomanie des Sorciers* [On the Demon-Mania of Witches] (Paris, 1580; English translation published by Centre for Reformation and Renaissance Studies, 1995). *Ed.*]

15. Frederick Kaigh, *Witchcraft and Magic of Africa* (London: Richard Lesley and Co., 1947).

actual, or even imaginary, gifts. But such motives are so natural to a child of that age that one really wonders why the effects should have been so disastrous. Or was she accepting the green apples and white bread in reality as a sort of compensation for an intolerable situation that generated a lot of guilt? One must remember, however, that the primitive belief of the world being full of helpful and destructive spirits was still very much alive in Europe four hundred years ago, and Jeanne was probably more or less aware that one must "question the spirits" and that one was running a risk in accepting favors under prevailing conditions.

But what of ourselves is conscious of our first childhood contact with the animus? When I look back on my own childhood, I doubt very much whether the animus has changed very much in the last four hundred years. I remember quite well that when outer reality was too disagreeable I often told myself make-believe stories in which I was not really the child of my parents but of others, either imaginary people usually belonging to another nation or the grown-ups that I happened to admire at the time. I think most children have such fantasies at times, especially introverted children who have more difficulty with the outer world. And apparently—as reflected in our material—this offers the animus an irresistible hook. Herein a powerful animus gets a start. But if we accept the evidence in our case, we can assume that, in special circumstances, the innate form of the animus can behave in a diabolical way and stake a claim, so to speak, before we are really old enough to defend ourselves.

I say "in special circumstances" because we know that children's psychology to a great extent depends on that of the parents. Jeanne says that she knows her father gave her to the devil. She writes this after the exorcists have been at work on her and she has more or less accepted their teaching that the devil is always prowling about on the lookout for human souls. This teaching is far too universal for us to dismiss it as antiquated nonsense. It is founded on empirical facts that we can experience daily if we analyze our actions and motives. I tried to show how the process works in my paper "The Problem of Women's Plots in Marie Hay's

The Evil Vineyard.[16] There, I attempted to show that Mary could not possibly have made such a devilish plot without the connivance and initiative of a peculiarly devilish animus that—as Jung pointed out in the discussion—was also the one who was leading her toward her wholeness. I refer you to Rivkah Schärf Kluger's paper on Satan, where the relativity of Yahweh and Satan is so brilliantly discussed.[17]

It is unfortunate that we do not know more of Jeanne's family life and history, as this would help us to place the figure of the handsome young man. She may be correct in attributing the blame to her father, but it would also be possible to interpret him as the animus of the mother. It is not very likely that conditions between the parents were harmonious; if it were otherwise, the girl would have been unlikely to have fallen so completely into the unconscious. Thus it is quite possible that it was the animus of the mother who appeared to her and claimed to be the real father in order to shut her off from the influence of the concrete father, and laying the blame on the father might well belong to the same picture.

We know next to nothing of the mother. Jeanne's next statement is the only reference to her:

> This condition lasted until my twelfth year when I—tired of the life in the convent where I was being educated—returned to my mother. But I was soon sent from there as apprentice to a dressmaker in the town of Berger (Belgium) where I had almost complete liberty. Then my so-called father appeared and said that as I had accepted him as my father I must now necessarily live according to his will. Until now I had lived as a child but now I must live as he directed me, as everybody lived, even though they did not admit it.

---

16. [See p. 172 in this volume. *Ed.*]
17. Rivkah Schärf Kluger, *Satan in the Old Testament* (Evanston, Ill.: Northwestern University Press, 1967). [Rivkah Schärf Kluger (1907–1987) was a Jungian analyst and teacher who recorded many of Jung's ETH lectures in the 1930s in shorthand. In Jungian circles she is known for her excellent work on the theme of Satan. *Ed.*]

He threatened to afflict her most disagreeably if she did not agree and offered her all the gold and silver and everything that she desired if she did his will. At first she resisted, but afterward she consented to everything he asked.

However much this figure was connected with the parents, he now definitely appears also as content of her own psychology, for at that time she was a considerable distance from her home. (We can hardly burden the dressmaker with this figure, as the figure is definitely the same as has been with her before.) Of course, it is possible that the father pursued her in either reality or in her fantasy—or even her actual mother—as such a figure is always deeply rooted in the family psychology. But here Jeanne is definitely faced with a personal choice. From her initial resistance we see that she was aware that something was wrong about this figure or the situation. But for the moment we must ask ourselves: if it is an inner psychological constellation, does the choice offered here ring true in the psychology of the animus? Can we find any parallel in our own experience?

These are at bottom questions that every woman must ask herself and that she will not find it easy to answer. There is, of course, the parallel in analysis that Jung often emphasizes, when the patient must cease blaming the parents and see that it is the patient himself who is standing in his or her own way. But this is a problem which we meet later in life and which we should not expect to encounter in early adolescence. If we look back on our own youth, we can—or at least I can—easily find moments when we turned a way from some adaptation to outer reality, where we knew quite well, even at a very early age, that we were ducking from something that should be faced.

I will give you an example from my own experience about the time I was ten years old. Being the youngest of the family, I was brought up alone in my nursery by an old nurse, who I adored. Although I got on quite well with other children my own age—that is, one at a time—I was actually terrified of groups of children. I was ridiculously and disproportionately afraid. My sister, who was eight years older (and thus grown up by the time

I was ten), often complained to my mother that I clung to her at parties instead of playing with the other children. This made me terribly ashamed, but the fear was stronger than the shame. My grandmother had a great Elizabethan house in the country where she always had a house party for children, a dance during the Christmas holidays. Now in that year when I was ten and my sister eighteen—and by then she had other fish to fry—I was sent alone with my nurse for the first time. We were about a dozen children staying in the house, all of them about my age or a little younger. I knew them all pretty well; two of the boys were close neighbors of ours with whom I often played alone without any difficulties whatsoever. Sensing my fear, they all locked me in a secret cupboard where Charles II had successfully hidden during a rebellion. But the next morning, presumably realizing that they had gone too far and being kinder than the girls, the boys of the party came and asked me to play with them again, promising that the housemaids would be the victims this time and that I would belong to the attacking party. I realized it was a marvelous chance to overcome my fear and was just going to accept joyfully when I heard something inside me say: "Take care, the housemaids are Nana's friends, if you join in an attack on them, you are lost." I knew I was making the wrong choice, but I obeyed the voice, refused the olive branch, and took refuge in the nursery with Nana who was with the other nurses and the babies of the party. The pattern of avoidance stuck and stayed with me for years.

The result of this decision was wholly bad as regards collective situations that then rapidly went from bad to worse. I had let them slip entirely into the hands of the animus. He had, so to speak, bribed me with my nurse. I had taken it and lost the battle. Even now it requires a disproportionate effort for me to feel at ease in a collective situation, and any carelessness will result in a regression.

I think it is in such ways that we are still faced with a decision about where Jeanne lost the battle. It is only through our cowardice, self-indulgence, and the like that the animus—in his negative form—can hook in, and it is his desire to do so that largely makes us afraid. If he had not suddenly confronted me with a fearful picture of what life would be like without Nana—a pretty unrealistic one at that—I should certainly have accepted the olive branch. So the vicious circle goes on, and one sees how humankind in general remains possessed.

When Jeanne had given her consent, she was somewhat horrified to see a crowd of these ghostlike figures before her, which was new in her experience, as she had never seen more than two or three together before. They forced her to take a pen and paper and to make the infamous pact with the devil, signed in her own blood.

The infamous pact with the devil—that is, as you know, an exceedingly common phenomenon—is a thing that has puzzled me for years. Such things do not disappear, they merely find a new form. We know from Bruschveiler that it still survives in its original form in certain places, but what I want to know is whether it has taken another form in the unconscious of women who would be horrified at the very idea of making a conscious pact with the devil.[18] Yet, if we take the commonly accepted formula, there must be conscious consent.

So far the only gleams of light I have been able to find in this very dark problem are two: one lies in the so-called devil's mark, which was characterized by complete anesthesia, in contradistinction to the stigmata of the saints, which were exceedingly painful. And the second is a turning back on the road to individuation by yielding to resistance and hate instead of accepting the given reality, with all its pain. I have seen people who funked this pain fall straight into the devil's arms.

The only way we can hope to reach an answer to this question is by examining this clear and fairly typical description and seeing what it means. The starting point is Jeanne's consent to do her so-called father's will. This immediately reminds us of Christ doing his father's will. And indeed, doing God's will instead of our own could almost be called the keystone of the Christian religion.

---

18. [See Barbara Hannah's discussion of Prue in her essay "Women's Plots: An Analysis of Mary Webb's *Precious Bane*" in this volume. *Ed.*]

Replacing the ego with the Self in psychology is founded on the same idea, with the important difference of having incorporated the alchemist's idea that we must actively redeem God and not passively wait until he redeems us. Thus the pact with the devil in Jeanne's case is saying to the devil: "Thy will, not God's, be done." God is Cusanus's *unio oppositorum*, whereas the devil demands a complete renunciation of the other side.[19] As far as the pact with the devil in Christianity is concerned, one can almost identify the devil with nature, for the first pact with the devil took place simultaneously with the crystallization of the dogma whereby nature was rejected in favor of the spirit.[20] But does this formulation hold good with the primitives where the criterion for witchcraft is also a conscious pact with the devil, or rather usually with a demon? (I remind you of the descriptions by Frederick Kaigh, who, reporting what he was told by the witch doctors, says that such pacts were usually started by jealousy or the envy of someone whose luck is better.)[21] In Jeanne's case, this father figure is, at any rate, at first more of a demon than Satan himself. (His identity as Satan, I should say, was rather pumped into her later by her exorcists.)

Jeanne also tells us repeatedly that this father demon was witty and intelligent and made her the same, and this was one of the main reasons she clung to him—not withstanding the material goods that the real father may have given, or those the demon father promised to give. The common factor is more or less always the same: the evil spirit gains possession when the person yields to ego demands.

19. [Nicholas of Cusa (Kues, Germany, 1401–1464) was a cardinal of the Catholic Church, philosopher, mathematician, reputable astronomer, and contemporary of many alchemists. He was noted for his deeply mystical writings, particularly his essay *De Docta Ignorantia* ("learned ignorance"), an approach to the possibility of knowing God with our limited human faculties. Cusa regarded antinomial thought as the highest form of reasoning. Jung writes: "What the alchemist tried to express with his . . . squaring of the circle, and what the modern man also tries to express when he draws patterns of circles and quaternities, is wholeness—a wholeness that resolves all opposition and puts an end to conflict, or at least draws its sting. The symbol of this is a *coincidentia oppositorum*, which . . . Nicholas of Cusa identified with God." C. G. Jung, "The Psychology of the Transference" (1946) in *CW*, vol. 16 (Princeton, N.J.: Princeton University Press, 1966), pars. 527n, 537. *Ed.*]
20. Barbara Hannah writes: I owe this reference to Linda Fierz.
21. Kaigh, *Witchcraft and Magic of Africa.*

We come here to the polar opposite of the *sich lassen* of Meister Eckhart.[22] If you have read *Ape and Essence* by Aldous Huxley, you were perhaps struck, as I was, by the fact that the devil established his ascendancy by what Huxley calls "detumescence," that is, subsiding from a swollen state, is the polar opposite of Meister Eckhart's view.[23] I think we come here to one of the basic roots of the whole problem. We fall into the hands of the animus because we do not let go and allow things to happen. We want to control our fate from the ego, not realizing that the ego is only a tiny piece—a weak and foolish piece—of our psyche. This gives "the devil" his chance, and the diabolical side of the animus gets the entire control.

Our ego's desires, our being unwilling or unable to let go of our willful demands, followed by issues such as jealousy and envy, all help to pave the royal road to animus possession that rapidly occurs when we fail to take responsibility for our plots. Then we end up allowing ourselves to be motivated by goals that we are conscious of in one compartment of our minds, yet ignore in the next. When we are caught up in a plot and entangled in the hands of the devil, it becomes more of a formal than an essential difference whether we delegate the responsibility externally (as with the Nazis and communists) or internally, as with Jeanne Fery. Once we have begun the way of individuation and then slip backward into contentment and leave our consciences in the hands of

---

22. [The phrase *sich lassen* can be translated here as "to allow" or "to let go." Meister Johann Eckhart (1260–1327) was a preacher, theologian, and professor, both a profound mystic and an able man of affairs. Throughout his career, he was admirably able to unite great activity with contemplation. As a preacher he employed the simple arts of oratory and gave remarkable and empathetic expression in beautiful German prose, of which he was a master. The inner position of man and the disposition of the heart were at the center of his teachings. He held little value for penances, emphasizing that man needs to turn inwardly to God and be led by him and that it is not works that justify man, but that man must first be righteous in order to do righteous works. Nor does he recommend that one flee from the world, but flee from oneself, that is, from selfishness, and self-will, otherwise one finds as little peace in the cell as outside of it. *Ed.*]

23. Aldous Huxley, *Ape and Essence* (Chicago: Ivan R. Dee, 1992). [Huxley's *Ape and Essence*, first published in 1948, is set in a dystopia similar to that of *Brave New World.* The book depicts humans as apes and baboons who, on the whole, are driven by power, greed, and will. It is a cynical and gloomy satire of the rise of dictators, tyrants, and warmongers who can be recognized in the tyrannies that dominated the first half of the twentieth century. Huxley presents a savage view of world politics set on a path of destruction and human annihilation. *Ed.*]

the animus, we do much the same as people who join the Nazis, communists, or other forms of tyranny.[24]

When Jeanne made her pact with the devil, it was enclosed in a pomegranate, and she was forced to eat it. She found it wonderfully sweet in taste until she came to the last bite, which was more bitter than she could bear. Görres compares the pact with the betrothal of the saints with Christ but points out that in this ceremony the bitterness and painful thorn come first, while the sweetness of the soul occurs at the end.[25] The German alchemist Michael Maier says something similar.[26] These two approaches to the animus seem to me very typical: there is the way of allowing oneself to be possessed which is sweet and easy at first—one gives up the struggle to take on responsibility for one's life. Or one takes up the *Auseinandersetzung* with the animus. To use the language of the alchemists: one undertakes the redemption of the god hidden in matter. If we leave the god or the animus in his natural state, he will possess us whether we know it or not. Even more so, since the natural psychic state of mankind has always been one of most easily becoming the victim of possession. Our only chance of escaping from this possession is undertaking the endless task of working on the redemption of the animus.

Jeanne was probably predestined to become a nun from the beginning. True, she ran away from her cloister school when she was twelve, but she never speaks as if there were any choice in the matter. So two paths must have been open to her from the beginning. In the Middle Ages, women with a "nun's psychology"—and Jeanne definitely had a nun's psychology from the outset—had a choice of two ways: the struggle toward the saint or the decent toward the witch. By a "nun's psychology," I mean women who were forced by their dispositions to come to terms with God or the devil, that is, women who could not avoid an *Auseinandersetzung* with something beyond everyday life.

---

24. [Barbara Hannah refers here to the behavior of Mary Carlton in Hay's *The Evil Vineyard* (1923). *Ed.*]

25. Görres, *Die Christliche Mystik.*

26. C. G. Jung, "Paracelsus as a Spiritual Phenomenon" (1942), in *CW*, vol. 13 (Princeton, N.J.: Princeton University Press), par. 183.

This is, naturally, a different situation from the one we meet in analysis today. The woman who tried to attain sainthood attempted to reach the positive pole that required effort and suffering. The witch allowed herself to be possessed; her aim was directed at power and pleasure from the beginning, but the end was generally bad. Usually, she ended up on the stake or she suffered the agonies that Jeanne did at the hands of exorcists.

Jeanne Fery

A Case Study on the Animus, Possession, and Exorcism

Editor's Note: Trance and possession are psychological phenomena found not only in the Middle Ages. The International Classification of Diseases of the World Health Organization—employed as a standard diagnostic manual worldwide—specifies these symptoms today in the category of Trance and Possession Disorders (ICD F-10 F44.3).

The American Psychiatric Association's Diagnostic and Statistical Manual of Mental Disorders (DSM) classifies these symptoms as dissociative identity disorder (DSM-IV: 300.14), a psychiatric diagnosis that describes a condition in which a single person displays multiple distinct identities or personalities, each with its own pattern of perceiving and interacting with the environment.

Possession and trance per se are characterized by a transient alteration in identity whereby one's normal identity is temporarily replaced (possessed) by a spirit, ghost, deity, or personified figure, also called an alter, alter ego, or emotional personality. The experience of being possessed by another entity (such as a person, god, demon, animal, or inanimate object) holds different meanings in different cultures; therefore, the diagnosis for this disorder today is generally culturally bound.

Contemporary psychotherapeutic theory and practice sets forth psychogenic explanations and theoretical paradigms. It documents symptoms and, on the whole, has made considerable advancement in treatment processes. Spiritual, social, psychological, and physical factors may all play an etiological role within the parameters of this disorder. The dissociative identity, trance, and possession disorders are frequently considered to have their etiology in an early history of repeated trauma and abuse, often to horrific degrees.

The diagnosis requires that at least two personalities routinely take control of the individual's behavior with an associated memory loss that goes beyond normal forgetfulness; in addition, symptoms cannot be attributable to substance abuse or a medical condition. Earlier versions of the DSM termed the condition "multiple personality disorder" (MPD), a diagnostic category that has given way to dissociative identity disorder (DID), and this is, in itself, not without controversy.

In dissociative identity disorder (DID), each identity has unique qualities as well as its own set of ideas, thoughts, ways of thinking, purposes, and so forth. One identity may be the protector or good father, as we will see in Jeanne Fery's case; another may be a child, an alter ego, a destructive figure, and so forth.

Jeanne Fery's symptoms fit the pattern of this disorder. States of dissociative amnesia, fugue, stupor, trance, and possession and dissociative motor disorders with disturbances and impediments in physical movement, convulsions, and anesthesia (for example, the lack of experiencing physical pain) constitute the basic symptoms. Additional symptoms included sleep disturbance, abysmal sadness, conversion blindness, shivering, disordered eating, contorted faces, inexplicably lost and found objects, and episodic loss of knowledge and learned skills. Compulsive suicide attempts, regression to a childlike state (particularly to the age of four with its inherent baby talk and the loss of the ability to read), along with episodes of prolonged sobbing and intense physical pain (especially headache) round off the clinical findings in Jeanne Fery's case. These symptoms are typical of the clinical picture quite familiar to contemporary clinicians working with DID. None of these symptoms—within the context of the disorder—are astounding.

There is a dramatic nature in the number and sheer intensity of the demonic figures constellated in the realm of father figures and devils in Jeanne's visionary experiences. Her demons were sometimes visualized; at times, she heard them arguing inside her head or they took over her body, causing violent pseudo-seizures. Rage attacks required restraints (from which she would escape). Regressing emotionally to the age of four would naturally raise the question of whether or not she suffered traumatic experiences at that particular age. Moreover, the second pronounced appearance of the demons occurred when she was twelve. Jeanne Fery writes:

> Then my so-called father appeared and said that as I had accepted him as my father, I must now necessarily live according to his will. Until now I had lived as a child but now I must live as he directed me, as everybody lived even though they did not admit it.

According to Jeanne Fery, he threatened to afflict her most disagreeably if she did not agree to submit to his will, and he offered her the gold and silver and everything that she desired if she did. She quotes him here saying to her convincingly: "Everyone lives like that." At first she resisted, but afterward she consented to everything he asked. Sexual abuse issues (with typical submission, consent, and extortion) can be easily read into such a statement, even if the patient has no concrete memory (psychogenic amnesia) of the event.

The clinical picture documented by Jeanne Fery, the Catholic priests, and numerous witnesses give us reason today to speculate that a possible cause of her possession lies in the suffering of repeated physical or sexual abuse. The vehement nature of the symptoms of such a possession are likely to be associated with outer transgressions of a similarly drastic nature. Due to the vehemence of guilt associated with sexuality at that time (coupled with the natural emotional issues involved with incestuous abuse), one could hypothesize that Jeanne was the victim of repeated abuse, in particular at age four and again at age twelve, and further, that she unconsciously sought refuge in, or was overwhelmed by, vehement and demonic psychic entities that served as an uncon-scious form of escape and protection from guilt, physical pain, and childhood fear.

Sexual abuse of children was certainly not unknown in France. We know from the documentation of Auguste Ambroise Tardieu (1818–1879) that sexual abuse proliferated. Tardieu was one of the most prominent figures in nineteenth-century forensic medicine, the foremost French medicolegal expert of his day, and author of an exhaustive work on forensic investigation. His court-ordered medical examinations and autopsies of children revealed anatomical sequelae of sexual abuse that, according to his investigations, could not have been simulated or contrived. Moreover, the psychic trauma of the children he interviewed showed emotional pain unmitigated even by the prospect of material advantage (which was the widely acclaimed cause of sexual abuse charges of children against their relatives). That children were manipulated by their parents to accuse relatives of sexual abuse and thus receive financial remuneration was an established tradition at the time. Tardieu's conclusion was as unshakable as it was startling: the majority of allegations of sexual abuse made by children, even very young children, could be cor-roborated and substantiated by medical evidence. Thus in the midst of the nineteenth century, sexual child abuse—even resulting in death—was, on the one hand, common enough and, on the other hand, denied, ignored, and blamed on children themselves. Further verification can be found in the works of the Marquis de Sade who describes a plethora of sexual conventions with children practiced among some of the members of the aristocratic classes in his work "One Hundred and Twenty Days of Sodom," written around 1775.[1]

1. Donatien-Alphonse-François de Sade, "One Hundred and Twenty Days of Sodom, or The Romance of the School of Libertinage," in *The Complete Marquis de Sade* (Los Angeles: Holloway House, 2007) pp. 165–301. [One can hardly describe the work of the Marquis de Sade as anything other than "depraved . . . heinous and repulsive," but one cannot ignore the fact that he was writing about sexual practices found among some of the members of the aristocratic classes in the second half of the eighteenth century. Nor can one ignore the fact that he also had a specific philosophical agenda in mind as he exposed these practices to public consciousness: "Only by contrasting Good to Evil can we fully appreciate either." De Sade was not only a "sadist" but also prolific writer, aristocrat and politician, and a reputable theorist who postulated the existence of the unconscious mind as well as the principles of

One can assume that these practices did not just suddenly appear in the mid-eighteenth century but probably evolved over a period of centuries.

That Jeanne Fery could thus have been the victim of sexual abuse at the ages of four and twelve is anything but far-fetched. Precisely this hypothesis appears in an article by Norman Simms and in the work of Onno van der Hart, Ruth Liernes, and Jean Goodwin.[2] Today, in the twenty-first century, the causes of such symptoms are readily classified within the context of dissociative identity disorders, the psychogenesis usually lying within the realm of physical and sexual abuse issues.

Moreover, in the psychogenic catharsis of the exorcism, three further elements could symbolically reflect sexual abuse motifs. The first is Mary Magdalene (the sinner and fornicator, the prostitute healed); the second is the archbishop, a positive father figure in which all features of negative fathering are purified and redeemed in a chaste and celibate father; the third is the central, male demon who served in part as a kind and protective father. These three cathartic figures would lend further support to such an hypothesis. Other traumatic causes for such psychic disturbances, however, cannot be excluded.

The features of the personality dissociation that Jeanne Fery displays also tell us something about the nature of the society in which she lived as a child. Abusers as devils and monsters are normal in the Counter-Reformation atmosphere, just as are the identities of the various male figures generated in her mind that may have helped her avoid the pain, humiliation, and desire to take revenge on her abuser(s).

In conclusion, we must note that Barbara Hannah drafted the initial essays on Jeanne Fery in the late 1940s and early 1950s.

Eros and Thantos a century before Sigmund Freud, propounded the theory of evolution a quarter of a century before Darwin, and sketched out a *republique universelle* a hundred and twenty years before the Treaty of Versailles established a League of Nations. See de Sade, *The Complete Marquis de Sade,* pp. 27ff and pp. 49f. *Ed.*]

2. Norman Simms, "Medieval Guilds, Passions and Abuse" (1998), *Journal of Psychohistory* 26(1), pp. 478–513; Onno van der Hart, Ruth Liernes, and Jean Goodwin, "Jeanne Fery: A Sixteenth-century Case of Dissociative Identity Disorder" (1996), *Journal of Psychohistory* 24(1), p. 28.

At that time, approximately forty psychiatric illnesses had been defined, and many of these would have been relatively obscure to any psychologist who was not employed for a period of years in a mental asylum.[3] This was a period riddled with the devastation of two world wars and the ongoing tyranny still cast a shadow across the American, European, and Asian continents. There was a tendency then to ascribe the causes of many psychiatric illnesses to egotism, individualism, greed, ambition, and so forth. The sexual abuse of children was popularly considered to be practically unknown.

The association of such symptoms with possible physical or sexual abuse did not become popular—or even thinkable—until several decades after Barbara Hannah composed this text. Sexual abuse themes first met general recognition long after all of her essays on animus possession were written. Moreover, dissociative identity disorder did not gain popular acknowledgment in the field of psychotherapy until after Barbara Hannah's death.

These considerations in no way detract from the content of Barbara Hannah's essay. The reader will find the analysis as valuable today as it was half a century ago. And many of Barbara Hannah's points are dead-on. For instance, she discusses the hysterical nature of the symptoms and notes their disastrous effects. She speculates that the possession was a sort of compensation for an intolerable situation that generated a lot of guilt, allies the psychogenic cause of these symptoms with childhood trauma, rejects schizophrenia, analyzes the dissociation of emotional states, and identifies the subsequent emergence of the various personifications as arising out of the dissociated elements of Jeanne Fery's personality. Thus she has identified some of the basic characteristics of dissociative identity disorder. We must keep in mind that Barbara Hannah's objective is neither diagnostics nor the psychotherapy of Jeanne Fery per se. Rather, she uses this case material as an Ariadne's thread to guide us through the

---

3. Today, a decade into the twenty-first century, nearly four hundred psychiatric disorders have been classified.

labyrinth of the multifarious and tortuous psychic phenomenon of the animus. Barbara Hannah's insights and reflections on how to comprehend, grapple with, and even guide the animus have—in the developments of modern psychiatric diagnostics—lost none of their profundity and fortitude.

Jeanne Fery
A Case Study on the Animus, Possession, and Exorcism

It has now been many years since my attention was first drawn to the striking parallels that exist between our own experience of the animus and anima and the antique and medieval reports of phenomena that were observed in the course of exorcism or, for that matter, in the whole realm of witchcraft and magic. It is extraordinarily difficult to gather objective facts that will stand up to anything like scientific investigation, for one seldom or never finds a book that was written without an ulterior purpose. The literature on possession is endless; the subject seems to exert—both then and now—all its ancient magnetic fascination, but presumably this fascination was so strong that no one dared to approach it without the safeguard of unusually strong and rigid opinions. At all events, almost without exception, the authors describing possession and extortion have an ax to grind. They write to prove this or that prejudice, and it is difficult to separate the grain from the chaff in their books.

This is, of course, particularly clear in the reports made by the Inquisitors, of which the classic example is the famous *Malleus Maleficarum*.[4] This book begins with the Papal Bull of Innocent

---

4. [The *Malleus Maleficarum* (*The Hammer of Witches*, 1486) is possibly the most blood-soaked literary work in human history. It served as a manual for judges during the Inquisition and was used to validate the prosecution, torture, and execution of outcasts, the elderly, midwives, Jews, Gypsies, artists, and nonconformists of all kinds. The death toll during the two-hundred-and-fifty-year course of the Inquisition is estimated to be from six hundred thousand to as high as nine million. Few of these victims had anything whatsoever to do with the practice of witchcraft. Its reach crossed the Atlantic to Salem, Massachusetts, for instance, where it was used as the source of reference and validation in the Salem witch trials. *Ed.*]

VIII (1484) which takes the line that all witchcraft was a fully
conscious and premeditated sin of such a heinous quality that it
was usually condemned unheard and entirely without the right
of appeal. There is no sign of ever regarding such things as misfortune, illness, or madness. The whole of this class of literature
is written with such venom and dogmatic narrowness that one
cannot avoid the impression that it is mainly written to repress
the author's own unconscious. This field is still in urgent need
of investigation, and I do not propose dealing with it at all in
this lecture.

In comparison with this class of literature comes the welcome
relief of the reports written by, or under the supervision of, the
exorcists themselves. They are indeed written from a dogmatic
standpoint and often with considerable prejudice as well, but
they are documented by men who—like ourselves—have realized
that they were up against something so real and terrifying that
all pretense and self-righteousness must necessarily come to an
end. The kind of priest who wanted to get away with a lazy attitude—who was a hypocrite, or who indeed was so frightened of
the unconscious that he was determined to repress it at all costs—
seldom or never became an exorcist. It was a highly unpopular
calling, and for the most part the exorcists seem to have been
sincere and courageous people. They do indeed naively project
their own devils onto their patients, of which a classic example
is St. Norbert, the founder of the Premonstratensian Order, who
was a highly successful and very subtle exorcist.[5] He complained
quite naively, however, when—as was often the case—a normal
man was possessed at the exact moment that Norbert arrived. He

---

5. [Norbert (1080–1134), born near Cologne, Germany, left his worldly service at the imperial court at the age of about thirty-five (after nearly being killed by lightning) and took on
the life of a penitent, a barefoot priest dressed in sheepskin. As an ordained priest, he railed
against the abuses of the clergy and was, in return, criticized and persecuted by members
of the hierarchy. In the desolate valley wilderness of Prémontré, France, Norbert laid the
foundations for his religious order, choosing the rule of St. Augustine as the guiding light
for the new community. The community was marked by its austerity, its poverty, its intense
liturgical life of prayer, and, above all, its complete fidelity to the ideal of community life.
Norbert was ordained Archbishop of Magdeburg when he was in his mid forties. A few of
the goals of the Norbertine Order are zeal for the salvation of souls, the spirit of habitual
penance, and a special devotion both to the Holy Eucharist and to the Blessed Virgin. *Ed.*]

protested that the devil was frightened of him yet always followed him around, stirring up trouble. Extreme activity of the devil in his neighborhood showed itself not only in the people who became possessed, but also in unusually violent parapsychological phenomena in the monastery that he founded at Prémontré. Yet, as far as I know, it never occurred to him that it might have to do with his own one-sided attitude, although Meister Eckhart, barely a century later, did get very near such a realization.

I only mention Norbert because his attitude is typical of that of the sincere exorcist for many centuries after his time and, as far as I know, also for the exorcists of today. It certainly pervades the most interesting *Exorcistenbuchlein* of the inner mountains of Switzerland which was written in 1729 and reprinted in Stans in 1914.[6] It then somehow disappeared under the table, so to speak. I owe my knowledge of this most interesting document to the zeal of von Franz, who chased it down through all of the Swiss libraries and eventually ran a copy to earth in Sarnen, Switzerland. The exorcists had no illusions as to the stark reality of the phenomena they were up against. They rarely blame the victims of possession in anything but a very reasonable way. They have a most genuine therapeutic aim, often show real feeling, and give credit—that is the essence of true love—to their patients. Moreover, they are well aware that the phenomena coming to light in exorcism can also attack them themselves, and that illness, injury, or even death may be the reward for their efforts. As Jung points out in the "Psychology of the Transference," they risk themselves just as the doctor is bound to do, sometimes with an astonishing courage and integrity. But they are often handicapped by their almost complete projection of evil outside themselves and their ignorance of the phenomenon of the countertransference. It is possible, however, that a few particularly intelligent exorcists were not so naive as they appear, and I should like to keep this possibility in mind as we consider the case I propose to lay before you.

But first I would like to digress here and point out that dis-

---

6. [The full title is *Das Unterwalder Exorzistenbüchlein* ("The Little Unterwalder Exorcist Book") *Ed.*].

appointment is always a shock to the feelings. It is not only the mother of bitterness but also the strongest incentive to a differentiation of feeling. The failure of a pet plan or, for instance, the disappointing behavior of someone one loves can supply the impulse either for a more or less brutal outburst of affect or for a modification and adjustment of feeling and hence for its higher development. This culminates in wisdom if feeling is supplemented by reflection and rational insight. Wisdom is never violent: where wisdom reigns there is no conflict between thinking and feeling.[7]

There are basically two different ways in which one can take a disappointment of one's feelings, either in bitterness or with wisdom. The first naturally pushes one entirely into the negative opposite, whereas the second enables the two opposites to exist side by side.

As an example of such polarity, there is the story of the two sisters who were in love with the same man. He was equally attracted to both and never could make up his mind which he preferred. The two women formed a symbiosis. (Another man in love with a girl told me he would love to marry her, but then he would have to marry her sister as well since they were really one person.) The man with whom the two sisters were in love knew nothing of psychology and after a time married a third girl, even more instinctive than either of the two sisters. The reaction of the two girls is the example I wish to give you now.

The elder sister was very angry; she gave way to fury, had terrible feelings of inferiority, and became more and more bitter. Every time she thought of the man she allowed her animus to mislead her, laying the blame on the intrigues of the third girl or the weakness of the man. In yielding more and more to her negative assumptions, she laid the foundations for becoming a bitter old maid.

The younger sister asked herself where she had been to blame in the matter and where she had her weaknesses. She refused admission to thoughts such as those harbored by her sister. She

7. C. G. Jung, *Mysterium Coniunctionis* (1955–56), *CW*, vol. 14 (Princeton, N.J.: Princeton University Press, 1963), par. 334.

gave credit both to the girl and to the man (and actually the marriage turned out well). This sister went into analysis. She discovered the weaknesses in herself that had led to the loss of the man and ultimately developed a bit of wisdom that enabled her to grow into an unusual personality in which the opposites did no violence to each other, whereas the elder sister gradually became completely possessed.

The subject of possession demonstrates that the opposites are by no means merely theoretical, but that when it comes to experiencing them in reality, they constellate an appalling conflict. Until the ego is firmly rooted in conscious reality, it is usually a mere ball tossed between the opposite powers that rule it by possessing it more or less completely. I, therefore, would like to bring an example, amplified by parallel cases, of such a tremendous fight between good and evil in a weak ego that forms just such a ball between powers much too strong for it.

Now, in order to talk about the animus we must study a case of a human being so that we have some sort of Ariadne's thread to guide us in the chaotic maze of material. Thus I propose that we take here the case of a French woman named Jeanne Fery (b. 1559). According to her own account (written in 1586), she was already demonically possessed as a child at the age of four.[8] Nevertheless, she became a nun and lived for several years in a convent before anyone noticed that anything was wrong with her. It was as an adult that she first documents her "demons." They were at times visualized, at times heard arguing inside of her head. At times they took over her body, causing violent seizures. As we will see, she also suffered from lack of sleep, impeded physical movement, conversion blindness, shivering, disordered eating, contorted faces, inexplicably lost and found objects, outbreaks of physical violence (including having herself thrown

---

8. [Here follows a short peripheral sketch of the clinical picture familiar to contemporary clinicians working with dissociative identity disorders. See the authoritative work of O. van der Hart, E. Nijenhuis, and K. Steele, *The Haunted Self: Structural Dissociation and the Treatment of Chronic Traumatization* (New York: W. W. Norton and Company, 2006). See also Simms, "Medieval Guilds, Passions and Abuse" and van der Hart, et al., "Jeanne Fery: A Sixteenth-century Case of Dissociative Identity Disorder." *Ed.*]

around the room by the demons), and then loss of knowledge and learned skills. Along with these were attacks of rage that required restraints (from which she escaped), compulsive suicide attempts, regression to a childlike state, moments of abysmal sadness, and episodes of prolonged sobbing and intense physical pain (especially headache).

In some ways it might be better to take a more modern example, but it would take far longer and would not be nearly as complete. And discretion forbids one to take a case from a woman who may in some way be known to someone here. (Although I could certainly bring in some details from modern-day cases to show how much the animus has remained unchanged since the days of Jeanne Fery.) The whole archetypal foundation of the animus has remained very much the same as it was in the Middle Ages, and indeed even the surface phenomenon remained unchanged over the centuries in its basic makeup in women until Jung exposed the whole thing. So it is to be hoped that at least a few people have changed the actual interference of the animus in their outer lives, although one must remain unceasingly watchful and conscious of him. For it is alarming how quickly he reestablishes the old order if we take our eyes off him.

This old medieval material falls into somewhat the same category as alchemy, of which Jung says: "However remote alchemy may seem to us today, we should not underestimate its cultural importance for the Middle Ages. Our own era is the child of the Middle Ages and it cannot disown its parents."[9] We would do well to keep this in mind. As I pointed out in dealing with the conversations of Hugh de St. Victor with his anima (naturally from our point of view), the dark side of the unconscious is too much repressed. Medieval man was much nearer to his instincts than we are today. Every movement becomes one-sided if persisted in too long, and the cause of wholeness now demands the inclusion of much more of the dark side of man. But we must not let this prejudice influence us. Evidently we can also get an idea from

---

9. C. G. Jung, *Psychology and Alchemy* (1944), *CW*, vol. 12 (Princeton, N.J.: Princeton University Press, 1953), par. 432.

such material as to how much we all still think in medieval terms. What was natural for Hugh de St. Victor in the twelfth century has, to a great extent, become a lazy habit with many of us today. The same is also true of our material on "possession," even if it is some centuries later. Just as mankind had to go through two thousand years of differentiation of the light in the Christian program in order to reach some consciousness of the opposites, so we have to overcome the state of possession in which we are more or less born, and for this encounter we require a fine moral sense and considerable integrity. If we become identical with our angry passions, like the elder of our two sisters, and yield to darkness and evil, the best we can hope for is an enantiodromia into the other opposite. We must accept darkness and light, for if we identify with the light side, we shall never know there is any darkness within us. One can only see and accept the darkness and evil in one's personality if the light is sufficiently differentiated for this purpose.

Years ago, I read a lot about possession, exorcism, and witchcraft as well as the lives of the saints, and when I turned to the voluminous notes I made in those years I almost despaired of ever getting any order into the chaotic material that I had collected. I am actually glad that the vote taken at the end of the last lecture forced me into condensing them. As it is, we shall cover quite a bit of extremely peculiar material. I should like to remind you of Jung's definition of the theoretical standpoint of his psychological studies:

> This standpoint is exclusively phenomenological, that is, it is concerned with occurrences, events, experiences, in a word, with facts. Its truth is a fact, and not a judgment. When psychology speaks, for instance, of the motive of the virgin birth; it is only concerned with the fact that there is such an idea, but it is not concerned with the question whether such an idea is true or false in any other sense. The idea is psychologically true in as much as it exists. Psychological existence is subjective in so far as an idea occurs in only one individual.

But it is objective in so far as it is shared by a society—by a *consensus gentium*.[10]

There is not only a *consensus gentium* concerning possession and the efficacy of exorcism in combating it, but it is an idea that we find in all ages and places with a remarkable similarity everywhere. I do not intend to discuss whether spirits really did possess their victims, nor what these spirits are. I shall try to show you a psychological fact, that is, the idea of possession and the ways in which people who had this idea used to deal with it. We also have the idea of the animus and the anima, but for those who have really tried to realize this in themselves, it is more than an idea; it is a psychological reality. We shall try to see parallels that exist in the two fields. Though our case is medieval, exorcism is by no means obsolete today. The biography of Bishop Hicks, for instance, shows that he had more than once experienced cases where only exorcism worked.[11] He once consulted an experience exorcist, a Mr. Hickson, seeking help in dealing with demons he had thrown out and was much amused to find that he banished them to the Red Sea where he visualized them hopping about. Emma Jung also related that she once met a well-known and very rational Swiss psychiatrist who was on his way to visit a Capuchin monk for exorcism with a patient he could do nothing for.

Jung once said in a seminar that mankind has always been possessed by the animus and anima, and it is incredibly difficult to change an outer fact that has existed practically forever. When I asked him if I could publish that passage, he refused his permission on the grounds that it would be badly misunderstood by the general public (much like that one sheep that I mentioned earlier that separates itself from the fold).[12] But he added that I could of

---

10. C. G. Jung, "Psychology and Religion" (1940), in *CW*, vol 11 (Princeton, N.J.: Princeton University Press, 1969), par. 4.

11. Maurice Headlam, *Bishop and Friend* (London: Macdonald and Co., 1945), pp. 78f.

12. Barbara Hannah notes: Man's original state was one of overwhelming unconsciousness, and this condition still partially persists in us all today. As soon as we attempt to liberate ourselves from possession by the anima or animus, we get into a different order of things,

course tell it to anyone who was working on the animus or anima, which I hope applies to all of you here. If so, you will not let yourself be repelled by the apparent, not necessarily antiquated point of view of the old exorcists who certainly came nearest to the animus before Jung actually discovered and identified its existence.

The girl in question was named Jeanne Fery. She was born in 1559 at Sore on the Sambre and later became a nun in the Order of the Black Sisters at a convent in Mons en Hainaut in the diocese of Cambrai in northern France, just west of the Belgian border.[13] It is a case of the possession of one individual, a possession that did not spread to other nuns as occurred in several other nunneries, the most famous example documented in *The Devils of Loudun*, which I expect many of you know through Aldous Huxley's book.[14]

The fact that the possession did not spread, as well as several other unusual, if not unique, factors in the case, was probably due to the unusual personality of the Archbishop of Cambrai at the time. This was the priest Louis de Berlaymont who was then both a secular duke as well as the Archbishop of Cambrai. The physical health of some of Jeanne's exorcists, in particular the archbishop, was severely affected at times. Another unusual factor is that there is an account of the possession starting back in her early childhood written by Jeanne Fery herself. As this account concerns the earlier stages of the possession, I propose taking it first, although it was actually written in a fairly late stage of the exorcisms. Thus at the beginning of the procedures her exorcists were still ignorant of many of the facts that her report contains (just as certain important information will only come out gradually in the course of an analysis).

Time forbids me to do more than give you the main points of Jeanne's own account and the exorcism. It is a long document and

---

and this attempt challenges the old order. If one sheep goes ahead of the flock by itself, it is a threat to the others and thus will be ostracized and exposed to attack. Moreover, no sooner do you get rid of a devil than you have all the devils against you. See "The Problem of Contact with the Animus" in volume 1 of this work.

13. [The diocese served the northeastern corner of France and western Belgium. *Ed.*]

14. Aldous Huxley, *The Devils of Loudun* (New York: Harper Perennial, 2009).

everything is given with a wealth of detail. I shall also only be able
to give a very partial interpretation.

I have already dealt with this case briefly in my essay "The
Problem of Contact with the Animus" in the pamphlet published
by the Guild of Pastoral Psychology.[15] But at that time I was only
acquainted with the account in Joseph Görres's *Die Christliche
Mystik.*[16] Since then I have obtained the original. I have also
compared Görres's work to the original *Acta Sanctorum* and other
documents. He is, on the whole, much more accurate than his
style leads one to suppose. But naturally he is also incomplete.
Moreover he occasionally gives an unintentional twist of meaning,
writing for instance: "Who are you?" as "Whose man are you?" In
all events, studying the whole document from Jeanne Fery gives
a far more complete and much more interesting account than the
one given by Görres. Jeanne Fery's account is most interesting
and, as far as I know, unique, although it was written toward the
end of her exorcism which took place over a long period of time.
She maintains that her account was written at the command or
dictation of Mary Magdalene. We could call it something related
to automatic writing. But I cannot swallow this whole. That is,
one would have had to check the veracity of the account during
the exorcism, as one does get a feeling that it might be indirectly
influenced by her exorcists. Moreover, an unconscious wish to
please the archbishop of the diocese in Cambrai may play a role
at times.

The long account of the exorcism, however, is an extremely
interesting and highly honest document, but I have been careful
to use only those parts that are confirmed by other documents.
The mistakes made by exorcists are freely admitted. Most genuine accounts of exorcism are very honest in this respect, and one

---

15. [See "The Problem of Contact with the Animus" in volume 1 of this work. The first
German edition of Jeanne Fery's work was titled: *Exorzismus—Warhafft: und gründtli-
cher Bericht, sehr wunderlich: unnd gleichsam unerhörter Geschichten, so sich unlangst
zu Bergen in Henogau, Ertzbisthumbs Cambrai, mit einer beseßnen, und hernach wider-
erledigten Closterfrawen verloffen. Auß Frantzösischer Sprach, in Hochteutsch gebracht,
Mit großem Titelholzschnitt* (Munich: Adam Berg, 1589). *Ed.*]
16. Joseph Görres, *Die Christliche Mystik,* vol. 5 (Regensburg: Verlagsanstalt GJ Manz,
1836–1842), pp. 176ff.

cannot doubt that the priests who practiced the method seriously were up against something where all pretense necessarily comes to an end. Exorcism was not practiced by the kind of priests who wanted to get away with a lazy attitude or who were hypocrites. It was highly unpopular, and only genuinely sincere people attempted to do it. We shall see some of the reasons for this later. There is, however, a class of literature about exorcism that is full of nonsense, ridiculous sentimentality, and unlikely miracles, but that is really the fault of the authors who do not know what they are talking about. The genuine exorcists—not unlike ourselves—were up against something beyond their comprehension which was highly dangerous so that they soon learned it could not be dealt with lightly. They also realized that all pretense comes to an end when facing the dark, yet invisible, reality of the inner world.

To get an idea of Jeanne Fery's life and the situation that the exorcism deals with, we shall have to follow Görres's example and briefly take a look at her own account, although hers comes at the end of the document. Chronologically, Görres's version is accurate (and for the most part exact in his rendition of Jeanne's confession), so I will just read you my original summary, adding details as we go along. For the exorcism we will follow the original text, for there Görres is inadequate.

Jeanne's own report begins with the statement that she knows she was given into the power of the devil by the curse of her father when she was four years old. We learn elsewhere that her mother had taken her to fetch him from the public house and that he evidently vented his wrath with the mother on the child. I should just like to mention here that this is a fairly common motif in literature: a child becomes possessed when the one of the parents furiously lashes out at the child. Evidently, in Jeanne's case, this had the result of driving her out of outer reality into an imaginary world, for she continues her narrative with an account of a spirit—looking like a handsome young man—who offered himself as her father and gave her white bread and apples. She accepted his offer and came to regard him as her real father. She seems to have enjoyed being with him, and also with a second father figure, who prevented her from feeling the strokes when she was beaten.

This constellation lasted until she was twelve years old, when, tired of the convent where she was being educated, she returned to her mother. Her mother, however, soon sent her away to Mons as an apprentice to a dressmaker. Here, she seems to have been left almost entirely to her own devices. The first young man then appeared to her again. He told her that, as she had accepted him as her father, she must now—being no longer a child—renounce her baptism and all the ceremonies of the Christian Church, ratify her earlier agreement, and promise to live according to his will. He told her that everybody lived this way although they did not say so. He threatened her with dire punishment if she refused and promised her gold and sliver and every delicious food she desired if she accepted. After a short resistance, she agreed to everything, and immediately a multitude of spirits appeared and forced her to sign the contract with her blood (the typical witch's pact with the devil). The multitude was a shock to her as she had never seen more than two or at most three of these figures before. They then enclosed the agreement in a pomegranate and forced her to eat it. It was marvelously sweet up until the last bite, which was more bitter than she could endure.

A great disliking for the Church ensued. At times her feet were often so heavy that she could barely reach the entrance door. Nevertheless, she did not sever her relationship with the Church. Her spirits did not insist on her doing so, but she had to give them her tongue so that they could control her confessions. Her outer confessions were naturally entirely falsified. But interestingly enough, she apparently had to confess the exact truth to one of her spirits, particularly concerning any pious action or prayer, and she was then forced to perform severe penance. She was also obliged to take the host out of her mouth at mass and hide it in her handkerchief, and then, although she tried to keep it in a clean place, it was spirited away. Her spirits taught her to despise everything to do with Christianity and to scoff at a God who could not save himself from the cross. She believed them implicitly, thought Christ worse than the thieves with whom he was crucified, and could no longer understand how people could revere such a God. They persuaded her to think herself the happiest and most privileged of mortals.

After she entered the convent, she had to sign a new contract with the spirits pledging them both her soul and body forever, and this was repeated again on the night that she took her final vows as a nun. She also had to renounce the pope and the "evil archbishop" to whom she had made her Christian vows. The spirit in possession of her tongue made her very bright and witty and, in order not to lose this gift, she gave one spirit her memory, another her reason, and a third her will. As she says, they thus entered and took up their abode in her, each in his own place. They also took possession of her body, again appearing as a legion of devils for this purpose. The so-called "spirit of blood"—sometimes called the devil or even the "god of blood"—played a great role in the ceremonies. As becomes clear in the account of the exorcism, a special devil seems to have taken possession of each part of her body, and each had to be driven out separately by the archbishop. They made her take part in mock communions held in their own honor and gave her "wonderful food" in the days of penance, while making her fast during Church festivals. One spirit, who she particularly liked, seemed always to have been with her. But some of them were very cruel.

The keynote of Jeanne's early character seems to have been, conscious or unconscious, determined to deal with suffering by repressing and detaching from it; thus she sought refuge in her inner imaginary world. This behavior could be viewed as the characteristic that delivered her over ever more intensely to her spirits, but, interestingly enough, her determination was also the impetus that eventually led to her deliverance from them.

She now realized for the first time that she had been deceived and, when she thought of the multitude and of the sign that they had been granted to her, she fell into despair. The spirits then returned and, changing their tune, reproached her for her treatment of the true God whom they now said was also their God. Her sins, they claimed, would never be forgiven, so that she had better follow the example of Judas Iscariot and hang herself with her leather girdle. At one point, she finally gave it into their hands and told them to hang her if they pleased. Although they tried to kill her in every way they could, their attempts were always thwarted. She also failed several times—despite a crowd of spirits who were rallying around her for death—to successfully commit suicide.

Then a time of great suffering began for Jeanne. Her spirits prevented her from confessing to a priest. For the first time, the authorities began to notice that she was not what she should be as a Christian and a nun. It was at this point that the people around her noticed for the first time that something was wrong. Her physical health was affected, and when the other nuns tried to help her, she only gave them insufferable rebukes. She evidently had until now existed by impressing her environment, but—in violent disunion with herself—this method no longer worked and it became only too clear that she was incapable of behaving like an ordinary sick human being. The violently rebuffed nuns reported the matter to the authorities, who soon diagnosed a state of complete possession and then took the matter in hand. This is how the matter was taken up by the archbishop Louis de Berlaymont. He took a most active part in her liberation, but, although it was her transference to him that eventually freed her, she says that the spirits initially blinded her to him. Although she had at once felt an impulse to take refuge with him, he seemed to her to be severe and terrible. She says that although the spirits tormented her with the most horrible visions of hell and so forth, Mary Magdalene appeared as her protector and never gave way. Jeanne assures us that all this really happened and was neither simply fantasy nor imagination.

I would like to give some parallel material to Jeanne's comment that she "knows it was the curse of her father that delivered her to the devil" before we consider the psychological validity of her statement.

The loss of a sense of security generally leads to feelings of inferiority. Lévy-Brühl describes such a condition as an *abaissement du niveau mental*. In an article on the transcendent function, Jung writes that the psyche is, at bottom, a self-regulating system and that when the attitude of consciousness does not move too far from nature, the regulation functions more or less automatically.[17] But the institution of the medicine man in primitive tribes shows how easily this is directly lost when there is some deviation from the archetypal pattern in the same way, for instance, as a machine can be made to run too fast thus destroying its own mechanisms. Consciousness has moved rapidly forward, splitting away from the unconscious, as is only too clearly evidenced by the First World War. And this one-sided attitude has naturally strengthened the counterpole in the unconscious to such a degree as to bring about many incredible catastrophes. When the unconscious opposite is not genuinely and fully due to one's own work on oneself, its original character becomes increasingly negative. Jung cites the cases of Nietzsche, of Nebuchadnezzar's dream in the Book of Daniel, and of a friend who dreamt he was in the mountains and became more and more elated until he walked over a ledge into space. Jung warned him to be careful, saying that he was looking for his death in the mountains and told him not to go there, or at least to take a reliable guide. But the man only laughed and refused to believe it. Six months later, the fatal accident occurred, and he dragged another man along with him to his death. Such experiences taught Jung that neither he nor his patients could afford to ignore opposition in the unconscious. Clearly a one-sided conscious attitude results in a large part of the personality falling into the unconscious where it is at the mercy of anything there, including what these old reports call demons or devils. If the conscious personality is not rooted firmly enough, it will not be able to resist the strength of the shadow, reinforced by the figures of the collective unconscious, and the result is a case of more or less complete possession.

---

17. [See C. G. Jung, *Psychological Types* (1921), *CW*, vol. 6 (Princeton, N.J.: Princeton University Press, 1971), pars. 16. 828, 924. *Ed.*]

But in the case of a child such as Jeanne Fery, who claims to have become possessed at the age of four, it is not a matter of a one-sided development of ego consciousness, for at that age there is, practically speaking, very little ego consciousness indeed. The child functions on a set of inborn patterns of behavior more or less as an animal does. Moreover, literature concerning primitive peoples is full of cases of possession of adults who are no more one-sidedly developed than a child. But in such cases it is, of course, the psyche of the parent that plays a central role.

So what about this phenomenon? Do you think that we can explain it psychologically? Naturally, the psychology of the parents plays a big role. We do not know enough of Jeanne's parents to go into this side of the problem at all deeply, but the fact that the father lost complete control of himself on his way home from an inn, presumably drunk, and cursed his four-year-old child hints at cause enough from the father's side alone. And the fact that the mother sent the child away to a dressmaker in Mons at the age of twelve, where she was under no supervision at all, does not look as if the love of the mother was strong enough to give the child any protection or firm ground from which she could develop normally.[18]

Apart from parental and environmental causes, I rather doubt if one can explain cases of the possession of children, animals, and so forth any better than one can explain why a physical illness attacks one person and leaves another untouched. One can, of course, usually find the origin of an epidemic of typhoid, for instance, in the same way there seems to be certain places where possession is more likely to occur than in others. In a chapter on lycanthropy in his *Uebersinnliche Erscheinungen bei Naturvölkern* ("Supernatural Phenomenon in Primitive Peoples"), Bozzano brings a lot of apparently well-authenticated evidence of the belief that people can only "turn into animals" by standing on earth that has been brought to the surface by black ants. In Eritrea (Italian Somaliland on the Horn of Africa), for instance,

---

18. [Barbara Hannah adds a note here saying that she should expand this part of the text. *Ed.*]

natives will not sleep on any such earth because they are afraid of becoming possessed by wild animals.

The nephew of Albert I, archduke of Austria and king of Germany, vowed to kill his uncle. He rode behind him all day, yet feared the crime of patricide. But as the king approached the junction of the Reuss and Aar rivers, the ford being an archetypal place of danger, the nephew made up his mind. "Why let that carrion lead us," he purportedly said.[19] You can act when in an archetypal situation. You are like the dragon at a ford and possessed by it. Jung talks about the dangers of the ford in his lectures at the Federal Technical University of Zurich, 1934–1935.[20] Jung also noted that the death of King Albert can also be seen as having an archetypal cause. The atmosphere of a place gets into one somehow and one is no longer one's own master. At the Eranos Conference in Ascona in 1952, Adolf Portmann spoke of the hydrophobia (rabies) virus. Jung told me afterward to bear the story in mind, for one can compare what are called "demons" in our material with a kind of psychic "minus life," much like the virus in physical diseases.[21] From the point of view of the rabies virus, everything seems to be done to enable it to achieve its objective. The person bitten wanders about, is aggressive, cannot drink water—which would reduce the harmfulness of the virus—and for the same reason cannot swallow; thus the warm-blooded animal no longer lives for itself but is

---

19. [Albrecht I of Hapsburg (1255–1308), also called Albert I, was king of Germany, duke of Austria, and the eldest son of the German king Rudolph I. Albert I was the founder of the great house of Hapsburg. His nephew was John Parricida (1290–1313). John's father was forced to waive his right to the duchies of Austria and Styria in the Treaty of Rheinfelden of 1283, thus John was deprived of his inheritance. When he came of age, he demanded a portion of the family estates from his uncle, who rejected his wishes. He swore revenge. On May 1, 1308, Albert I became separated from his attendants while crossing the river Reuss where it flows into the Aar north of Windisch, Switzerland. He was murdered by his nephew and three other conspirators. John escaped to a monastery at Pisa. Five years later he is said to have been visited by the emperor Henry VII, who had placed him under ban. His fate is unknown from this point on. The character of John is used by Schiller in his story of Wilhelm Tell. *Ed.*]

20. C. G. Jung, "Modern Psychology," notes on lectures given at the Eidgenössische Technische Hochschule, Zurich, June 2, 1934, p. 22. [The notes from these lectures were prepared by Barbara Hannah. *Ed.*]

21. [Adolf Portmann (1897–1982) was a Swiss zoologist and philosopher. See Adolf Portmann, *Die Bedeutung der Bilder in der lebendigen Energie Wandlung* (Zurich: Rhein Verlag, 1952), pp. 353f. *Ed.*]

lived through by the virus for its own purposes. In possession, the subject is also lived by a similar form of "minus life."

But we cannot explain why it is that Mr. A catches typhoid from drinking infected water and Mr. B, drinking the same water, does not. And there are many physical diseases, such as cancer, where the causes are still very much unknown. We can only say that there is a *consensus gentium* that children do become possessed. All such explanations are speculation and must be taken with a considerable grain of salt.

One could perhaps add that possession seems particularly likely to set in when one fails to live fully or when one loses opportunities for one's own development, for then libido (that is, psychic energy), which should be used to live fully or to take the opportunity to make changes in one's life, gets into the unconscious and reappears as possession. It also seems to occur if we fail to understand something. If you do not understand, you are forced to live it, to act it out.

A colleague once told me that he had failed to realize that a patient had injured herself badly in some experience. Shortly after the patient left his practice, he went out to his car and, out of pure stupidity, backed into a tree. Only afterward did he realize in the course of the case that the unconscious had forced him to act out what he had failed to understand. Analysts must watch such things after their therapy hours, for things one has not noticed tend to obtrude themselves in such ways.

Possession can also occur when one pursues a rather thoughtless and extreme way of living without limitations. Primitives are particularly afraid of being possessed when any part of their body is open, when they open their mouths to eat, in the sexual act, in emptying their bladder or bowels, and so on, activities fraught with taboos. Some primitives do not watch each other eat, which perhaps may be a remnant of this taboo. When we are too free of inhibitions, we suffer an *abaissement du niveau mental*, which we have spoken of as a source of possession.

Possession can also occur when one has suffered an injustice (such as Jeanne Fery suffering the injustice of her father).

Primitive tribes often punish the people who are the victims of thieves even more severely than the thieves themselves. Here, it is believed that the victims must have been out of themselves and offered the temptation to the thief, for such things could otherwise not happen. This may seem extreme, but if one keeps losing things or is constantly the victim of theft, then one naturally asks oneself: "What is wrong with me?" No doubt the primitives also punish the victim in part so that they may be saved from the course of evil possession. When one is inclined to resent or hate an injustice, it may well be justified, but one comes very close to the negative energy or "evil spirits" and thus endangers oneself with possession. And the tormented are particularly endangered of becoming possessed.

It is interesting, however, that Jeanne states that she accepted the first handsome young man who offered to become her father, and who also gave her white bread and apples. She also accepted a spirit as her second father—as a child she had two of these father figures—because he prevented her from feeling the strokes when she was beaten. (It may be important to note greed for food is inevitable in children who get too little love.) The building up of an intense inner world peopled by personified spirits is also the typical reaction of introverted children to outer conditions that offer them too little healthy interest, love, and options in the real world.

This spinning of such webs of fantasy has, of course, something to do with the spinning tendency in the feminine psyche and thus with plots. (Ratchford even calls her book on the Brontë children *The Brontës' Web of Childhood*.)[22] Men are by no means immune from this activity, but with them it is the anima who spins, whereas women do it themselves, although mostly subliminally. It is largely with them a matter of compartmental psychology: they know their own tendency to weave plans and plots, and even the content of their plots are known in one compartment

---

22. Fannie E. Ratchford, *The Brontës' Web of Childhood: The Miscellaneous and Unpublished Writings of Charlotte and Patrick Branwell Brontë* (New York: Columbia University Press, 1941).

and forgotten in the next. Or they know them under one aspect and fail to recognize them when they appear under another of their innumerable aspects. Men, on the other hand, have practically no direct contact with such inner plots, and they cannot find out much about them until they have made the effort to become acquainted with their anima and their shadow.

In Jeanne Fery's own account of her dealings with her spirits, we get the raw material of women's plots. It is true that until the archbishop begins to play a role in her life we know nothing of any real man whom she tried to spin into her web of fantasy. (Nevertheless, we shall find here a wonderful example of a woman plotting—highly instructive for the analyst who has to deal with the transference.) But particularly at the beginning of her own account she is mainly caught by the idea of being the femme fatale of a whole host of male spirits. She falls for their compliments, for instance, as women fall easy prey to the flattery of the other sex.

This same feminine plotting tendency, the wish to be the great *amoureuse,* or the woman who launched a thousand ships and the like, is equally apparent in the early work of Charlotte Brontë. But life corrected this tendency in her, and from the writing of the "professor" on—that is, after her experience with M. Heger in Brussels in her late twenties—she put the brakes on the plotting of her feminine psyche very sharply with her new and hard-won sense of reality. In her book to the professor she even quotes the motto: "He that is low need fear no fall," which is the leitmotif of her future work.

But in her early work, Charlotte plots as freely as Jeanne and identifies with the heroines who find themselves surrounded with demonic men who bear quite a resemblance to Jeanne Fery's spirits. Both gave free rein to fantasies of feminine plotting unduly constellated in both women by too many difficulties or too little attraction in their outer world. One great difference between the two women—even in this early stage of Charlotte's career—is how the two women reacted.

Where would the difference then be between a Jeanne Fery and the Brontë sisters? Well, for one, Charlotte Brontë attempted from the beginning to give her own inner world form by committing herself to hard work—in short, to her creativity. Jeanne, as is clear in her whole account, turned to it solely for the shelter she could get. Moreover, the Brontës risked themselves and went right into the adventures of their inner world. True, their father was not tormenting them directly, and they were siblings supporting each other. Jeanne, on the other hand, was an only child. But Jeanne turned to the inner spirits primarily to be protected and relieved from pain and to escape intolerable suffering, for instance, while she was being beaten, a form of suffering that Charlotte certainly experienced. Jeanne's attitude, however, offered her spirits no chance to enter the world creatively so that they could only do so destructively—that is, they necessarily degenerated more and more into infernal demons. And here, when dealing with the animus, one must be careful. Today we witness a similar constellation in women whose orientation is predominantly egotistical and materialistic.

Jung once mentioned a medium he knew who had an unusually rich unconscious until she began using it for money, and then she began producing the poor superficial stuff typical of professional mediums. This is what makes it so difficult to read spiritualistic literature. Moreover, using mediumistic gifts for money or personal gain is the beginning of black magic.

Contrary to the Brontës, Jeanne gave nothing consciously back to the inner world. If we can translate this into adult conditions, we see here a tendency to use the inner world for one's own egotistical purposes. This misuse results in such spirits developing in a negative way, and eventually ends in such devilishness. As Jung was looking at some pictures during the Eranos lectures in Ascona by the monk Opicinus de Canistris, he remarked that the animus, like all archetypal figures, is completely dual natured, neither good nor bad.[23] But when he becomes really infernal, it is because the human being offers

---

23. [Opicinus de Canistris (1296–before 1352) was a painter and scribe, best known for his fifty-two large drawings of the world map portraying the known continents in human form interwoven with dream and mystical motifs as well as those of creation. *Ed.*]

egotistical hooks. If solely egotistical wishes prevail that exclude the needs of the animus, then the animus turns to his negative side. Until the exorcism, Jeanne was unable to realize the needs of her animus, thus her spirits developed in a negative way and became purely devilish. Had she been able to meet them with a different attitude, they might have developed more creatively, that is, if she had been able to meet her inner spirits creatively and with a different attitude, they could have become a tremendous help instead of leading to such an evil fate. Unbridled, such inner figures can be used for practicing a kind of black magic for personal ends. One hears nothing of any destructive or malicious effect on other people—which goes much to Jeanne's credit—and this is probably the reason why she could be exorcised without destroying others. (True, we cannot overlook the negative effects on the exorcists, but such effects are almost the rule in exorcism.) Manipulating black magic for one's egotistical purposes, along with the love of destruction for destruction's sake, is a hallmark of the worst kind of witch. And such people are the hardest of all to do anything with because naturally in destroying, or even attempting to destroy, they eventually destroy themselves to such an extent that there is not enough firm ground left within. Such a case leads more or less to psychosis, or at least to a psychotic tendency.

That it was solely white bread and apples with which she was rewarded is symbolically interesting due to the connection of the apple with Eve, while white bread is a food with all the darkness thrown out (also here associated to the Eucharist, the host). How are we to take this food? Was it actual or fantasy food? Here, is a very important point, but one that is almost impossible to decide. I think that it is probably fantasy food. But there are other possibilities, such as the spirits enabling her to steal real food without being found out and then representing such food as their gift.[24] But the whole question is full of magic and difficult to decide objectively.

---

24. [This is another act which fits well into the schemata of dissociative identity disorders. *Ed.*]

In Maya Deren's book, *Divine Horsemen*, one finds an interesting yet reverse parallel.[25] Deren reports on the island of Haiti, which was populated by about two million indigenous people when discovered by Columbus. The Spaniards declared the people to be degenerate and of feeble intellect and replaced the population with slaves imported from Africa in 1512.[26] The descendants of the slaves now populate the island. They brought their gods, mainly African in character, but naturally these have undergone a change in the course of centuries and have attained a particular Haitian character. The educated classes are now largely Christian, mainly Catholic, but large numbers still keep to the old religion. The author notes, however, that each village developed a rather different aspect of the deities, and it is impossible to generalize. They have an exceedingly unrestrained demon called Ghede, a dark figure and a god of sexuality and death, who attends to the meeting of the living and the dead. If the souls of the dead enter bodies by the passage of which Ghede is guardian, the lower life forces emerge. Ghede is the lord of life as well as death, his dance is the dance of copulation, and he is also known as the beginning and the end. Obviously Ghede, not unlike our own animus, is a highly paradoxical figure, a god of sexuality and death, of good and evil. (As you know, sexuality and death are often closely connected in mythology, and there is indeed even a rational connection in the conception and birth of a child. When a child is conceived and then born, the parents have produced their successor, the one who will replace them on earth. Keats refers at one point to children as "the hungry generation" that "thread down" their parents.) The *Todeshochzeit* (dance or embrace of death) is a well-known archetypal motif. In the Haitian Ghede ritual, young men become possessed by Ghede. They enter into a form of possession, and if it is possession by a good spirit, the participants are always pleased since they go well beyond themselves when they

---

25. Maya Deren, *Divine Horsemen: The Living Gods of Haiti* (Kingston, N.Y.: McPherson & Co., 1983).

26. [The indigenous Haitian population—estimated at between two to five million—was exterminated by the usual means: massacre, genocide, illness, and the decimation of social, family, and cultural foundations. *Ed.*]

are so possessed. The participants when possessed will consume incredible quantities of real food, more than a human could manage but, when the trance is over, they are completely exhausted and ravenous as if they had eaten nothing at all. These are facts testified by numerous onlookers and show that it is possible to eat when in a trancelike state and afterward have no idea of it at all.

If so, the contrary is presumably possible, that is, Jeanne Fery would eat fantasy food and be nourished as if with real food. That such a thing is possible is testified by the Swiss Saint Nicholas of Flüe, who supposedly ate nothing at all—except occasionally the host—during the last twenty years of his life. Yet somehow he was nourished.[27] Then there is the modern case of Therese Neumann, although Jung says that he would like to know what effect she has on the people around her and whether or not they are depleted.

At all events, Jeanne Fery maintains throughout her account that her spirits completely controlled her eating and drinking, feeding her richly on days the Church fasted and starving her on feast days. One can only say here that her hunger—influenced by psychological factors—undoubtedly played a considerable role in the food her spirits are represented as giving her.

Then we come to the interesting point that, at the age of twelve, she had to ratify the arrangement with the demons because although she had given way, according to her own account, at the age of four, she was not then responsible for her actions. They held her responsible pretty young, however, since

---

27. [Nicholas of Flüe (1417–1487), also called "Brother Klaus," was a Swiss mystic whose influence was manifest in Switzerland and southern Germany. He experienced visions of such a genuine primordial nature that he was smitten with terror in every limb, so strange they were to him. Thereafter, he necessarily submitted them to the dogma of the Church which removed all taint of heresy or heathenism. His fasting was well known and even scrutinized by governmental inspection at the time. Jung writes that this is a fact "that cannot be brushed aside, however uncomfortable it may be. In the case of Therese of Konnersreuth there are also reports, whose reliability of course I can neither confirm nor contest, that for a long period of time she lived simply and solely on holy wafers. Such things naturally cannot be understood with our present knowledge of physiology. One would be well advised, however, not to dismiss them as utterly impossible on that account." C. G. Jung, "Brother Klaus" (1933), in *CW*, vol. 11 (Princeton, N.J.: Princeton University Press, 1969), par. 483; see also C. G. Jung, "The Miraculous Fast of Brother Klaus" (1951), in *CW*, vol. 18 (Princeton, N.J.: Princeton University Press, 1976), par. 1497; Marie-Louise von Franz, *Die Visionen des Niklaus von Flüe* (Zürich: Daimon Verlag, 1980). *Ed.*]

twelve years old still seems a child to us. However, it could have been a bit later, as she only says it was during the time at the dressmakers where she apparently was for some considerable time in her adolescence. Jeanne was again bribed—that is, the spirit offered her worldly advantages such as money and food (albeit probably imaginative)—but this time there were also threats of pain and punishment if she refused. One interesting point is that her so-called father asserted that everyone lived in this way. It is interesting that just at this age she is confronted with the choice.[28]

What choice do you think is meant here in terms of everyday life? The "web of childhood"—innocent enough—is torn apart and replaced by reality just about the time of adolescence. If we compare this with the fact that no one noticed that anything was wrong with her until her vision of blood from the host had thrown her into conflict, we can assume that some generally occurring condition in women is played on at this time. At adolescence the web of childhood is usually torn apart and replaced by growing reality, and things happen that cut you off from your imaginary world as a child. I remember telling something about my imaginary wolf to a sympathetic visitor who reported it to my mother, and she in turn was furious with me and put me to bed for lying. The shock cut me right off from that world. A woman once told me that as a girl she had the habit of telling her younger sister stories when they went to bed at night, and one time she introduced a real man into the story. Her sister exclaimed: "Oh, did he really do that? I didn't know," and that brought the shock.

Such shocks are necessary to get into life, and this demand to ratify the agreement was such a shock. That she got the point we can see from the fact that she resisted for a time as she knew she should not go on in the imaginary world of spirits. She had now a feeling of guilt. But she then repressed it and went on. For adults this would be maintaining an illegitimate state of childhood.

---

28. [The question also arises as to the accuracy of her memory, the possibility of selective amnesia, and whether it was the spirit-father or her actual father who approached her as a young teenager, and, finally, whether the statement "everyone lives this way" is in regards to father-daughter incestuous practices that were not unheard of at that time. *Ed.*]

We also find parallels in analysis. Mothers who eat their children without knowing it do so more or less innocently, but once they know it through analysis, they cannot do it legitimately any longer, for then there is guilt. Less and less is excused as analysis goes on. Although adolescence is the first time these kinds of choices are given to us, subsequent life is really full of these choices. And they boil down to the question: do we have the courage to accept life as it is, including our own short-comings, or are we going to allow the animus to spin us away in a cocoon of false opinions and illusions about ourselves? In contradistinction to the spirits during her childhood—where we only hear of bribes—Jeanne says now that her father figure showed her the pain she would have to suffer if she refused to satisfy her allegiance to him. This classical type of animus argument is to be found in adults where the animus says: "Don't do this or that because you will suffer if you do." This plea to avoid suffering is one of the main bribes of the animus, his primary way of attacking his opposing principle, Eros. Here, you find a feeling reaction of sorts in women that says: "If you love so and so, you will only involve yourself in suffering." And like most animus arguments it is quite true, for love does entail an extension of suffering, and not only one's own, but the loved one's pain as well. Again, like most animus arguments, it is totally beside the point because such suffering belongs to the meaning of life. If you once accept avoiding suffering as a maxim of life, you won't even own a dog for fear that its short life . . . and so on. In the end, you won't live life at all.

It is by no means only women who try to avoid suffering in this way. Men also deny a real feeling again and again lest it lead to scenes, and so on. Only women deny their own principle and fall victim to the animus when they do, whereas men are too faithful to their own principle, become one-sided, and miss the chance of an *Auseinandersetzung* with the anima and the opposite principle, Eros.

As a matter of fact, as soon as the animus is constellated, suffering becomes unavoidable. (The same holds true for the anima.) Jeanne would have suffered if she had resisted the father spirit at this age, for fighting the animus is hard work. But it is only a postponement to give in, as we shall see. Taking responsibility for what we are is painful. Jeanne was offered the very excuse we constantly find ourselves making: "Everyone lives like that." So they largely do, but evidently Jeanne was a girl who could be much more conscious. For adults, again, it comes down to refusing suffering for what and who we are.

If one looks back on one's own youth from about the time of adolescence on, one can see a lot of places where one was afraid, or too vain, to realize one's shadow. (Or at any rate I can.) And thus, like Jeanne (but to a lesser degree), one falls into the hands of the animus and replaces reality with opinions concerning reality. For that was really what Jeanne ended up doing. She escaped from her admittedly burdened reality into an imaginary world offered by her animus-demons. Now a great many children do somewhat similarly; they live in a world of make-believe. Jeanne evidently had a very inferior father who drank and cursed her and what else, and here lies the original source of her turning to an imaginary, handsome, youthful father who gave her solace and presents. Then there was another who stood between her and her real father when he beat her so that she did not feel the strokes, so real had her inner figures already become. As a child, it did not matter so much, but now it begins to matter, and she certainly knew it, for she did resist for a time.

But what do you think of the fact that after Jeanne had decided against the hard way and of saying no to the suffering, there came a multitude of spirits for the first time?

To put it in modern language, this failure to give up the outgrown fantasies of childhood and to take the hard way was answered by a dissociation, by a disintegration into the many. From the standpoint of the devils, the word goes around: "Here, is human flesh to be had . . . ," and it is then similar to a final sale where hundreds of women all crowd around to get a bargain. If one gives into one's devil, one thousand come after him. Here, this is especially true, as it is the first step that counts. Once you give way, there will be an avalanche. Such things always begin with trifles that then eat the person.

Jeanne Fery—despite numerous regressions—always cooperated in the exorcism procedures, but then mostly due to her transference to the archbishop. She says that, after signing the pact, she took a great dislike to the Church. She had, of course, opened her soul to evil, and we always hate, or are unduly fascinated, by our repressed opposite. What is interesting here in contrast to most all other reports of exorcism is that her spirits did not try to make her leave the Church but instead made her go to services for their own advantage. They made her reserve pieces of the sacrament for them, made her give them her tongue so that they controlled her confessions, and later encouraged her to become a nun.

During the exorcism it was seen that Jeanne was ambitious and much concerned with what people thought of her. (Maybe here we find a hint of why the spirits let her stay in the church. Her negative father complex undoubtedly caused her to seek a spiritual father, and at that time, the Church was certainly the only place where she could possibly find this. Now, of course, the doctor and others are possibilities.) The life of a seamstress was a very poor kind of life, probably below that of a nun in a convent. One could say that from the negative side, she stayed in the Church for power purposes, to get herself into the limelight. But from the positive side, she also did it in order to be more of a person than she would otherwise have become. Another reason is that the spirits presumably would never have got her to make a stand against an accepted general value like the Church, so they did not try since that was not her weak point. She would probably have resisted them had they tried to make her fly in the face of public opinion.

Opening your soul to evil is the inevitable result of refusing the hard way, of refusing to accept one's limitations and shadow, of refusing to undertake a creative task. If we see and know our shadow, we are in a position to deal with evil. If we do not, we inevitably open our soul to evil and become possessed by it to a lesser or greater degree corresponding to the importance of our decision. Opening your soul to evil to the extent of attempting to misuse the powers of the unconscious has a great many forms. They really include all destructive wishes and the injuring of other people. If you make people angry, you are endangering them, bringing them to a place where they may get possessed. Another way, more common today than one would think, is using active imagination on other people. And yet another is seeing that a projection is doing another person harm, and then not doing everything one can do to take it back. Such things can happen in the transference.

In point 5 of *Das Unterwalder Exorzistenbüchlein*, we find that a very strong projection is quite a difficult thing to live with. If someone has a very negative father or mother complex and expects you to behave like a parent, you have to make a great effort not to do so. If you do not try to take back the projection, then in this way you can open your soul to the influences of evil. In this book of instruction for exorcists, the question is asked how one can know whether the exorcism is being useful or harmful to the soul's salvation.

The healing powers of the unconscious are powers which are always helpful and open to salvation. But when the possessed person obstinately holds to his sins, or refuses the effort to change his previous immoral or malevolent way of life, and if there is no sustained moral improvement before the actual exorcism occurs, then neither the priest nor the person will be able to do anything with the devil, and he will always return to his old lodging.

If a person's soul is persistently open to evil, remaining manipulative, malicious, and destructive, there is nothing to be done. In other words, no exorcism can succeed without the cooperation of the one who is possessed. This is, by the way, equally true for patients in analysis.

The diabolical cleverness of the way in which the devil always attacks the weaker points reminds one of the Nazis, who kept note of such traits so as to be able to use them as a hook. They also were clever enough not to have allied themselves with similar forces, just as we have here in this case. As for getting her spirits to control her confessions, there are several modern parallels for this. For instance, there is a tendency to use analysis for destructive gossip, especially in borderline cases. Or a woman pretends that she must confess this or that but actually is always conniving to discuss something negative about someone else. Furthermore, when Jung and a few priests compared notes, they noticed that both in confession and analysis there is a considerable tendency to confess the lesser sins or make a fuss about trifles and thus avoid seeing the really painful things within.

The animus is an archdemon in this way. He artfully pulls the wool over women's eyes to prevent being discovered himself. It is interesting that in this old and naïve document from Jeanne Fery, the strategies of the animus so clearly parallel analytical experience.

More unusual in the literature, although by no means unique, is the fact that, while the spirits falsified her Church confessions, they insisted on a real confession with no subterfuge being made to themselves. We see something of the same situation in *Christina Alberta's Father* by H. G. Wells.[29] Christina Alberta does all sorts of nonsensical things during the day, but in the evening she holds a sort of court of conscience that tells her exactly what she has really been up to. This is a kind of inexorable thinking from which she cannot get away, and it is a good illustration of the autonomous working of the unconscious mind of women. But in Jeanne Fery's case it was a reversed confession, as she had especially to confess any pious actions or prayer for which she had to do severe penance; everything good had to be confessed, and to the utmost, but nothing evil. The spirits are, therefore, seen as archaic and hold her by being completely one-sided. As Jung so often emphasizes, all nature spirits, as well as the animus and anima, are really dual natured, neither good nor bad per se. As mentioned before, it is only the attitude of consciousness that can make them infernal. When they are one-sidedly dark, they are abnormally fascinated by the light and want to know everything about it. They are fascinated, but do not know whether they could love it or whether they want to destroy it, and thus they are much like ourselves in a reversed way: we are similarly fascinated in

---

29. H. G. Wells, *Christina Alberta's Father* (London: Jonathon Cape Ltd., 1926).

knowing them. We can observe the same phenomenon in our own animus in the passionate way he interests himself in analysis and in the transference to the analyst, and so on. Evidently, Jeanne's egotism is unbroken. She is defenseless against one-sided devils as is still the rule with ourselves today.

As our material is dynamic and comes close to most of us, I would like to add a few words about its dangers and its practical use. One of the chief dangers is that this material may lure us into the unconscious and provide a great temptation to the animus or anima to slip into our weak spot. Therefore, it is more than usually necessary for us to remain alert and watch the effect of the material upon ourselves. Another danger is that the material is so medieval in language and point of view that it is fatally easy for us to think it has nothing to do with ourselves. Therefore, I try to link it up with practical experience, for stripped of its medieval trappings, it is simply a case of animus possession and of a weak ego caught between the polarities of the psyche and tossed from one side to the other. In more or less modern language, it is the case of a child who became possessed, that is, taken out of its normal playful development with children of its own age by psychological factors and who, not linking up to its outer surroundings, succumbed more and more to a fantasy life whose features conformed to its wishful thinking.

It is interesting that Jeanne Fery's spirits are, for the most part, so one-sided. It is only a completely one-sided attitude that can make them infernal. Evidently, Jeanne is defenseless against such devils. She could not understand how people could worship such a feeble God as Christ who allowed himself to be crucified, showing he could not even save himself from the cross. Yet feeling as she undoubtedly did about the Christian religion, and with the demons making her worship them, she yet took the veil. Although she had to sign another document renouncing her vows, the pope, and the "evil archbishop" to whom she made her vows, the demons made no effort to stop her from becoming a nun. This is by no means usual. As a rule in cases of possession, the demons are violently opposed to their victims taking the veil.

I would like to give you a short account of a case of possession related by Hieronymus Radochio, prior of the Abbey of Vallombrosa.[30] The monastery had extremely good effects in cases of exorcism, but I have not succeeded at all in tracing the manuscript itself as the monastery has in the meantime been replaced by a forestry school. The story is told by the girl's father, who held a respected position in a small town between Florence and Pisa. About five months before he took his daughter to be exorcised at Vallombrosa, there were several young girls from good families sitting and spinning just outside a window of his house. Then "the devil" threw a small stone out the window at the girls. Now since the father and daughter were standing together near the window, the girls and their families got very upset and threatened them both. The father was only able to calm them down with difficulty. The girl denied even having thought of throwing a stone and was forbidden to look out of the windows afterward when the girls were there. Nevertheless, another stone was thrown the next day, and a girl was hurt. The father prayed for help, as did the daughter who had a vision of an old woman lying on the bed with her right hand between cheek and pillow. She approached to see who it was and the figure raised its head and looked at her with wild eyes and said: "Take care what thou art doing." The girl called on the Virgin Mary and rushed to her father, who tried to persuade her that it was all nonsense. The father could not see the old woman, but a younger sister could.

A priest then tried to exorcise the spirit with water and prayers and compelled it to leave the room. Then they all heard a voice crying that it could not stand such suffering much longer. On being questioned, the "old woman" said that she could be helped by a Gregorian mass for the dead, and the priest promised to help but told her that she must then go where she belonged. She claimed to be the great-grandmother of the girl. Then at night, when most everyone was fast asleep, the demon woke the girl and told her: "You act in your own way and not in my way. Do

---

30. [The monastery of Vallombrosa, a Benedictine abbey in Tuscany founded in 1038, is still located today about thirty kilometers from Florence. *Ed.*]

you hope to do so for long? You will never do so again with my permission." The girl called on the Virgin Mary.

The father, hearing the voices, came into the room. The demon then moved to the bottom of another bed and began to trouble the boy sleeping there. The father rushed to the boy, the demon called to the girl, and in the end the neighbors had to come in and help. Among them came the priest, who was terrified by the bad effects of his former exorcism. If an exorcism does not succeed, and one does not get down to the bottom, it makes things much worse. As the doors had been locked and the father had been unable to leave the child, the neighbors had to break in through the window. When they asked what was the trouble, the father said: "God help me, it's my own sins, help me!" They were unable to drive out the demon, and the father was then in despair. Yet the daughter encouraged him not to give up. He then let the priest enter the room and waited to see what would happen. The daughter received three hard slaps on her cheeks from the devil and then rushed to an image of the Virgin hanging on the wall and begged for help, promising to devote her whole life to her service. The demon abused the girl again.

Soon thereafter, it repeatedly acted as a poltergeist, becoming more and more violent. Once, when unable to free herself, it caught the girl around the waist and carried her away in spite of her resistance. Everyone witnessing was terrified. The girl even tried to comfort the mother and assure her that she was not hurt. The demon continued its attacks until the father asked what it wanted and why it picked only on them out of all the families in town. He promised to do what was asked as long as it was not wrong. After the demon asked for the daughter herself and was refused, it said it would suffice if she would promise not to become a nun. She insisted that she would become a nun just the same, and the demon was infuriated. Then the father prayed for release by his own death, but he was persuaded by the family to let the girl go to the local convent at once. Once there, the demon stole money from the convent and plagued the nuns, who lost all faith in themselves and sent the girl back home again. The demon then entered the girl, who went about doing all the things it had previously done. It also reproached the neighbors with all of their sins, so they too were terrified. Then they thought of the monastery at Vallombrosa and undertook the journey despite the fact that it was now in the dead of winter.

What is the difference between Jeanne Fery and this other girl? Well, first of all, in this latter case, the demon bitterly opposed the girl becoming a nun and succeeded in having her driven out of the convent that she had recently joined. Jeanne's devils, on the other hand, made no opposition whatsoever. Then we mustn't overlook the role that the fathers played, for they both had their own personal plots. Although the second girl's father openly took the blame, he may have secretly wanted to keep her from the nunnery. Jeanne Fery's father was most likely glad to be rid of her. (Most of the cases I have read on possession emphasize that the demons are opposed to the woman becoming a nun. There are also several cases of entire convents becoming possessed. In such cases, it may be brought back to the one nun who, presumably like Jeanne Fery, was possessed before she entered the convent.

The father and the neighbors are on the girl's side from the beginning, and the father takes the blame, saying that the whole thing is a punishment for his sins. This confession is the exact opposite from the approach of Jeanne Fery's father. Also, the story came out at once, not as in the case of Jeanne where everything was "hush-hushed" away, a tendency that opens the sluices to witches and demons and that one should always be careful not to give in to. As a rule, it is almost impossible to be too discreet in analysis, but when it is a matter of "hush-hush," one must sometimes tell the analysand that the story must come right out into the open. One of the reasons why the Vallombrosa exorcism came to a good end in a few months, and not twenty years, was because there was no hushing up over the matter, although the situation must have been exceedingly embarrassing for a respected family. Moreover, in the second case, the incident itself comes out into the open at once.

The second girl was also surrounded by relationships, for not only is the girl related to her father from the start, but the mother is much attached to her daughter as well and calls in other mothers to help. Furthermore, the original possession took place when the girl was with a group of girls who were evidently shocked beyond measure at a stone being thrown, presumably since it was so unlike the girl's usual behavior. This firm rooting in her social environment lends a background that makes it possible to assail the issues. An imminent danger is when you are alone with such things and have a lot of fantasies. In the majority of borderline cases that go over the edge, it is due to lack of relationships—or due to something inherently wrong in the relationships. But this is not only the case with borderline personalities. Jung once related how a woman who had committed a successful murder came to him and confessed. She had been living in isolation but had a horse (or was it a dog?) with whom she was constantly in contact. But when the animal died, she could not stand having no relationships at all anymore. After telling Jung, she felt that she could bear it again, but he never heard of what became of her, and he actually did not even know her name.

The animus attacks every woman no matter how well or badly adapted she is. It all depends on how the attack is met. It is difficult to know what we could assume from the story of the throwing of the stone, but as there seems to be very little bridge between this girl and the demon, possibly he sought to draw her attention to his existence. We might also assume that the girl was well related herself. Even when the manifestations are as demonical as here or in the case of Jeanne Fery, there is always a purpose behind the one-sided manifestation.

In a discussion after a lecture on women's plots, Jung said that plot was one of the famous devices of the wise old man, a figure who could also play the role of the devil. In a lecture in Ascona, he told the fairy tale of a poor orphan boy who, ill treated by a peasant and his wife, slacked off in his duties as cowherd and was dreaming of a princess or whatever and inadvertently became the victim of an evil old man who made his cow run away. And thus he had to run away himself.[31] Soon thereafter, starving, exhausted and in despair, he meets an old man. The old man says: "If you wander on for seven days you will come to the great mountain" (the great mountain here indicating an ascent to his inner Self).[32] So the old man sets the poor boy on the quest for himself, giving the lad good advice and showing him the way to his destiny. It turns out that this is the same old man who had made the cow run away. When you look at him from the dark side only, he appears to be an evil old man. But at the end of the story you see that it all turns out for the best. If the boy had carefully looked at the old man's plot, he would have possibly discovered that he ran away because he was fed up with that peasant and his wife, and his dream came true. Now on the personal level this is all nonsense, personal daydreams and the like, but if one follows them, then they may lead to one's true calling, which was the collective, superpersonal aspect of the plot. In one's own analysis it is much the same thing. At first you get the most unfavorable picture of yourself, but it has another side if you are courageous enough to go it through to the end. Most people get shocked in the beginning about themselves: "This is the devil's scheme." That is, it seems fully to be the wrong thing. But if you have the courage to go on with it and follow the lead, the ego will be stolen. If you are missing the courage, then all that matters really is adaptation and living out this life.

Jung once said that though we cannot quite accept the Indian doctrine of reincarnation due to the lack of scientific evidence, it is actually a psychological fact that people seem to have souls of different ages. It is as though one person was sent into this world to find out the most elementary things: what is a mountain, what is a table? Whereas other people, who seem to have gone through a great many reincarnations and experience déjà vu–like memo-

---

31. C. G. Jung, "The Phenomenology of the Spirit in Fairytales" (1948), in *CW*, vol. 9i (Princeton, N.J.: Princeton University Press, 1968), par 401.

32. C. G. Jung, "The Process of Individuation," notes on lectures given at the Eidgenössische Technische Hochschule, Zurich, Nov. 15, 1940, p. 18ff. [This multigraph transcript was prepared by Barbara Hannah. *Ed.*]

ries, seem to be compelled by superpersonal destinies. (It does seem generally true in analysis that one should try to find out the age of the soul that you are dealing with.)

I want to mention one more extract, namely, the Siberian fairy tale of the one-sided old man. He is a powerful spirit who gives good advice to the hero of the story who, by his own stupidity, exposes himself to the effects of evil powers. He must be killed several times by devils and is always revived by the wise old man. The remarkable thing is that the wise old man is one-sided, that is, he has one leg, one hand, one eye, and in the ultimate fight when he helps the hero kill the bad spirit, the hero kills him as well. One sees here that the bad spirit is really the other half of the one-sided old man, both actually being one and the same. He is an incomprehensible power of life, a wholly paradoxical figure, that presents itself first in a negative and then in a positive way. One cannot think the two things together, that one and the same thing could be both good and evil, but it is so.

This gives us an idea of the positive possibilities behind the story of Jeanne Fery and her spirits. Jung has often said that quarrels between married people and people living too close to each other frequently have the purpose of creating more distance. Then there is the story from Konrad Lorenz of the male stickle-back fish, which is so quarrelsome that if a couple are isolated in an aquarium, a mirror has to be put in between them so that the male can fight his own reflection and thus be nice to his wife instead of fighting her.[33]

Now, the girl who was possessed was evidently almost too related, whereas Jeanne was highly unrelated. Therefore, from the deeper layer of the animus, even from within the infernal one-sided form of Jeanne Fery's animi, there is an effort to reach the greater totality. And from this point of view, the convent would be

---

33. [The sticklebacks belong to the *gasterosteidae* family of fish, and they can be found in northern temperate climates including Britain, Europe, Alaska, and Japan. Konrad Lorenz (1903–1989), an Austrian zoologist, often considered one of the founders of ethology, shared the 1973 Nobel Prize in physiology and medicine with Karl von Frisch and Nikolaas Tinbergen for their discoveries concerning organization and elicitation of individual, social, and fixed behavioral patterns in sticklebacks, gulls, and butterflies. *Ed.*]

poison for the related girl and the collective crowd to which she would belong like a drop in the sea. Whereas to a woman as unrelated as Jeanne in those days, it would have been the only hope of ever reaching a related life at all. From one point of view, Jeanne Fery's spirits played the best card they could, and by letting her become a nun they were in a position to possess her more completely and obtain things, such as pieces of the host and the like.

On the superficial level, the animus goes all out to possess the human being completely, but this is not really a satisfactory solution even for him, so that if one digs deeply enough, one finds the contrary motion behind the apparently devilish possession. The animus, or perhaps the Self using the animus as a tool, is trying to put the human being on the path to wholeness. It was only by the help of the whole convent that Jeanne Fery escaped from the possession.[34] As a highly unrelated girl, she could only have become more and more possessed outside the convent. Thus, on the deeper level, the demons acted against their own interests in the service of the greater whole.

We do not know enough of the Florentine girl, not even whether she entered a convent in the end, but I do regard it as quite possible that her real destiny was marriage and that the apparent wholly devilish demon may have been also pressuring her against the wrong decision. However one-sided and infernal the animus becomes—and he just about reached the limit with Jeanne Fery—it would still be a mistake to forget his intrinsically dual nature or to forget that extremes meet and that the more one

---

34. [The exorcism began on April 10, 1584. Canon Mainsent was the priest both for the Dominican convent and the laywomen of the Beguinage. The Beguines constituted a women's communal organization, one of the few pro-feminist forces in that era. They evolved in northeastern France, Belgium, the Netherlands, and northern Germany around the time of the Crusades. The Beguinage consisted of housing communities associated with and built onto convents, in particular the Dominican convents, where women gathered and lived, in essence serving God without retiring from the world. These communities arose in part out of the surplus of women resulting from war, which took the lives of so many men. Great numbers of women had no option but to unite and collectively secure the aid of benefactors while serving social and religious purposes. Their communities, with their silent chapels, walled gardens, and proximity to flowing water, were sanctuaries for women. Not only were the Beguines familiar with the realities of violence against women, but they also cultivated the idea that women could take control of their lives and function in areas usually restricted to men. *Ed.*]

goes into one's opposite, the more likely an eventual enantiodromia becomes.

Sometimes in analysis it is necessary to support a one-sided attitude until "the bubble bursts." Any effort on the part of the archbishop or anyone else would have been worse than useless at the earlier stages of Jeanne Fery's development. If she had come to analysis, one could probably have found oneself under the disagreeable necessity of tolerating the demons for a time. But it is most unlikely—in fact almost impossible—that anyone at this stage of possession could come to analysis at all.

The next question is why the pact was repeated when she entered the convent and then again when she took her vows. Presumably these pacts served to annul the vows. Otherwise she would have been exposed to the opposites that, at this stage, would have united neither the superficial level of her complete possession nor the deeper level of totality. But in annulling the vows, the spirits really had gained a lot by having her in a convent, for all the time set apart for meditation could be used for the purpose of worshipping them. And indeed that went to far greater lengths in the convent than ever before.

For some time, the spirit in possession of her tongue had made her very bright and witty, but now, in order not to lose this gift, she had to give one spirit her memory, another her reason, and a third her will. Now how are we to understand this in practical psychological experience? Well, one example would be when one begins to let the animus speak instead of asking oneself if one really agrees with what flows from one's tongue. Then it soon goes further: one's memory is falsified, one's reason does not work any longer (one is in fact quite unreasonable), and one's will has practically faded altogether. It is a process one can watch in every case of increasing animus possession. First, it is just allowing the desire to be witty and to shine gain the upper hand, but the person is still aware she is not being very truthful. Before long, she is no longer so clear about what is truth and what is falsehood. She lies to herself, and that is then much the worst kind of lying. A spirit possesses her memory and twists it at will, and she takes no responsibility. Second, perhaps it is just a sort of wish to charm others or to gain some advantage by being a little unreasonable. Women by nature tend to be more unreasonable than men. Or maybe it is an egotistical wish to have more than is reasonable, and so the limitations are swept away and a demon has her reason. Then try as she may, she cannot be reasonable any longer and soon even forgets what it is. We all suffer from the idea that we can stop evil habits whenever we like. For instance: "I'll do it just today, tomorrow I will change." And before we know it, there is a demon in possession of our will, and we are living his way instead of our own.

This sequence in Jeanne Fery mirrors what we meet in psychology. The ego becomes so weak that it is practically only the ball of the unconscious. So-called animus-possessed women are terrifically sure of themselves, but when they do become uncertain, they are suddenly frightened little girls longing for someone to tell them what to do. When one's energy falls into the hands of the animus, we are possessed. Cecil Woodham Smith, in her biography of Florence Nightingale, reports that Florence was neurotic and often ill between bursts of energy during which she pushed through with her will like a man.[35] At the outset of the Crimean War, there was a time when she became neurotic about her mother and sister.[36] Afterward she became active in the hospital work, and at the end of her life she fell a victim to infatuations for young nurses. This marvelous woman had bursts of animus energy, but in between she really regressed into being a young girl.

---

35. Cecil Woodham-Smith, *Florence Nightingale* (New York: Grosset and Dunlap, 1951).

36. [The Crimean War (1853–1856) entailed a conflict over the Holy Land and was fought between Imperial Russia and an alliance including France (who originally aggravated the war), the United Kingdom, and the Ottoman Empire. Most of the conflict took place on the Crimean Peninsula, a vast landmass in the Black Sea. Due to the introduction of the electric telegraph, infamously incompetent military strategies and disastrous logistical planning on the part of the generals were exposed by journalists for the first time. Informed newspaper readership actually led to the resignation of the prevailing British government due to the reporting of the dreary shape of the British forces deployed to the Crimea. Approximately seven times as many French and British soldiers died of disease and wounds as died in battle. The scandalous treatment of wounded soldiers reported by war correspondents prompted the work of Florence Nightingale, Mary Seacole, and many other women who served as army nurses and introduced modern nursing methods. *Ed.*]

Later, Jeanne Fery had to give various devils different parts of her body. During the exorcism, these spirits made her seriously ill. At one point, her doctor gave her up, convinced she could not recover, and she herself wanted to die. Psychological problems that are not met psychologically do seem to have a tendency to get into the body, and it strikes me as valuable and reasonable to say that the animus can have a physical effect on the body. I should not like to go further because we have no valid information, but we could amplify the subject by remembering that the archetypes have often been projected onto parts of the body. We know in astrology, for instance, that Capricorn has to do with the knees and Leo with the heart, and astrologers are anxious even today to warn people born in these signs to be careful with these parts of their bodies. The primitive medicine man can get an indication as to what demon is causing the trouble and possessing the patient, and Navajo medicine men touch the body and diagnose accordingly: the bear demon, for instance, requires the bear dance to cure the patient, and so forth. Furthermore, we betray our complexes by our movements. The signs are even more obvious in cases of schizophrenia, where people can fall apart into archetypal factors, and the dread of anything of this kind is deeply implanted in us all.

In *Psychology and Alchemy* Jung writes:

> The dread and resistance which every natural human being experiences when it comes to delving too deeply into himself is, at bottom, the fear of the journey to Hades. If it were only resistance that he felt, it would not be so bad. In actual fact, however, the psychic substratum, that dark realm of the unknown, exercises a fascinating attraction that threatens to become the more overpowering the further he penetrates into it. The psychological danger that arises here is the disintegration of personality into its functional components, i.e., the separate functions of consciousness, the complexes, hereditary factors, etc. Disintegration—which may be functional or occasionally a real schizophrenia—is the fate which

overtakes Gabricuas (in the Rosarium version): he is dissolved into atoms in the body of Beya, this being equivalent to a form of mortificatio.[37]

It is these functional components that get projected onto the body, especially in "imaginary" illnesses, that is, psychological disorders. A nervous tick might possibly be said to be a complex that has settled down in that part of the body. Some of the old alchemists declare that all physical diseases have two natures, a "coarse" physical nature and a "subtle" psychic nature. They prefer to deal with the subtle end. Paracelsus, for instance, is full of such ideas, finding equivalents to diseases in the inner firmament. Most certainly it is extremely unwise to regard any illness as only psychological. And if there was anything the matter with us while working with Jung, we were always sent to see a general practitioner. Many people go much too far in regarding any illness as psychological. But all the same, it is my experience that if I funk a psychological problem, it may revert to my body. But I should not like to assert that every time I have been ill there was a psychological cause. Jeanne Fery was originally in possession of her body, and it is interesting that her spirits had to get her permission to possess it. Some people, particularly intuitives, never know their bodies, and then the animus can take over the body without permission.

Alongside all these physical factors, the spirits continued their blasphemous parodies of church services and constantly made Jeanne recant whenever she had taken part in communion. Particularly, they continued making her steal pieces of the host, which they spirited away. It is rather interesting that they required pieces belonging to other parts, a motif that reminds me of a modern dream where the matter was indeed reversed. Here, a young man dreamed of a struggle between two supernatural beings who he associated with Ohrmazd and Ahriman in Zoroastrianism.[38] He was afraid that the dark side was going to

---

37. Jung, *Psychology and Alchemy, CW*, vol. 12, par. 439.
38. Zoroastrian philosophy personifies the warring kingdoms of good and evil, light and darkness, right and wrong in the divine figures of Ohrmazd (Ahura Mazda) and Ahriman

overcome the light when a little bit of the dark changed sides and joined the light. In a similar way these demons seemed capable of holding onto their one-sided sway over Jeanne only by the possession of little pieces of that light side. Here, we recall how they punished her severely for any allegiance to the other side yet longed for pieces of it which they could only get through her.

What would be the psychological equivalent of this motif in modern women and her animus? There are in fact cases where people seem to come to modern analysis in order to steal information for their demons greedy for gnosis. In one case, anything told to the patient was promptly used to make trouble with somebody else. Then such people try to set the analyst by the ears or have some other destructive trick. A less-obvious abuse is when people get ahold of psychological or religious truths and do not keep them in consciousness. That is, something impresses a woman very much and she thinks "that is for me," but she allows herself to forget it. But if she lets it fall into the unconscious again, and if she has a strong twisting animus, it will appear on the outside and will be much worse than if she had never known it.

For instance, a woman in analysis had learned about the shadow but because she lacked a certain moral integrity, she did not really suffer (as normal people do) when she discovered bits of her shadow. She thus failed to keep them in mind but got over the whole problem with clichés, such as Jeanne Fery's spirits gave her: "Oh, everybody is like that . . ." or "Of course I am not pure white, no woman is." Therefore, things which would have hurt her if she had realized them were promptly forgotten and not allowed to inconveniently remain in her mind. The animus

---

(Angra Mainyu). Ohrmazd is the supreme deity, the principle of good, creator of the world, and guardian of mankind. As the omniscient lord of light, he is also the lord of life and truth, of prayer and hope and all of the sublime and delightful creations of nature: roses, ruby-plumaged birds, and the like. Ahriman is the omniscient demon of darkness, of death and lies, of agonized thought, and the creator of all negative forces on earth: doubt, debauchery, winter, noxious insects and plants, and so forth. These two archetypal antagonistic powers perpetually clash over the mastery and possession of the soul of man. The real world was thought to be the result of their personal struggle. Ohrmazd, the good and light, will triumph in the end; Ahriman will be annihilated forever. Man is considered to be instrumental in this struggle and in bringing about victory. *Ed.*]

got fat on such excellent nourishment and persuaded her into all sorts of things under the cliché of "I am living my shadow." She even went so far as to rewrite her analysis, noting not what the analyst said but what "she knew he meant." In the end, she was fifty times worse than before she had become acquainted with Jungian psychology. Just as Jeanne Fery was worse off every time she went to mass, so we are the worse off for any truth we learn that remains un-integrated. Integration demands applying the truth to ourselves and suffering the pain.

Jeanne Fery, who was becoming discontent in her state of possession, began now for the first time to doubt if she really was the happiest of mortals. The spirits persuaded her that she was the most intelligent person they had ever met and that they had never before known anybody to whom they could teach so much. But in time this conviction began to wear a bit thin. (This is apt to be the case in animus possession. At first there is identification with being more than oneself, but this will eventually have to be paid for.) As time went on, the spirits became extremely critical and began to punish her severely. Jeanne then began to wonder whether Christians had a better God and thought she might worship him, too, in addition to her own, if he would give her a sign. Here, the spirits became angry and made her take a piece of the host and pierce it with a knife. But no sooner had she done so than blood flowed from it and a great radiance poured out of it. We cannot get away from theological consideration that this practically amounts to killing Christ. This is substantiated by the benevolent sign that is vouchsafed: blood pours from the host. Here, she is actually treated like doubting Thomas who disbelieved the stories of Christ's resurrection until Christ told him to put his hand in the wound in his side in order to prove to him that his body was real. On the one side, Jeanne had committed a terrible blasphemy, but on the other, she had made a great effort to obtain certainty. The knife represents Logos, that is, discrimination. The libido, seen here as the blood, was now in the despised, neglected, and repressed opposite that also had the light, the illumination. One could say that for a girl brought up in a convent as Jeanne Fery was (the same holds true for parsons' daughters and other children who have too much of a good thing), there is no libido, no energy, no meaning left; one is too used to it all. It all becomes empty form. For a girl like Jeanne Fery in those days, accustomed to it all in a convent school, there was really only one escape: to go right over into the opposite. Evil, evidently already well constellated in the father, held the manna, and she got possessed by it. And it had to go on until it reached its zenith, until she had had enough of it (and that was, at any rate, for quite a long time). When she committed the supreme blasphemy and imitated the soldier who pierces Christ's side with the lance, it was revealed that the libido had moved into all that she had previously reviled and hated.

It depends indeed on the temperament of the individual. My sister, for instance, never wavered in her faith in the Church, but then she was grown up by the time we went to Chichester; she did not get such a bad dose of it as I did.[39] And she was, by her nature, not rebellious.

All the demons now left Jeanne for the moment, and she was alone and terrified, realizing for the first time that the spirits had seduced her. Now she was really in despair and no longer able to escape suffering as she had done up until now. Her efforts to do so had landed her in far worse suffering than she had expected. After a time, the demons returned and behaved in a way most characteristic of the animus when he is in the stage of a possessing demon. They admitted that they had deceived her but, taking no responsibility for what they had done, they turned right around and told her that the Christian God was the only true God—they also worshipped Him.

If what we do turns out badly, we can rely on the animus to behave negatively. He is a past master in saying "I told you so," even though, as in the case of Jeanne's demons, they had told her nothing of the kind. The voices that schizophrenics hear may be

---

39. [Chichester is a small city in West Sussex on the south coast of England. Barbara Hannah's father was the dean of the Chichester Cathedral from 1902 to 1909. The family lived at the deanery. *Ed.*]

extremely helpful and full of common sense, and then suddenly they turn around and are destructive and may even go as far as murder. The voice that has hitherto been helpful may say: "Take a knife and kill that child."

Although a patient I had is now far away from the Jung Institute, I must ask for your discretion if I tell you this instance in her case. She had had a very bad time. She had been in an asylum and had been given insulin, which had done her no good at all. She had been taught that the voice was a sign of madness, but nevertheless, she often obeyed it blindly without discrimination. Her analyst taught her to treat the voice with greatest respect and caution. Often it gave her good advice and was wise, so that one could only say: "Do what it says, but be careful." Fortunately, she had an intelligent husband who was cooperative and clever at managing her. We had warned him to be careful about the voice which might at any time turn negative, and after they moved away, such an event occurred. While in Zurich she had dreamed of a cave at the top of a mountain, a place of extraordinary value, where she might receive a great treasure. And she actually found such a cave in another country. Then she had two dreams that ought to have made her suspicious (mercifully, the husband smelled a rat). The extremely positive figure that had so far helped her now appeared curiously attired in a checkered suit and top hat, looking altogether suspicious; the husband became anxious. Then she dreamed that she was to be made a living sacrifice, and the husband thought that that might be the end of her. When they arrived at the actual cave, the guide became hysterical with fear and would not let them enter. She was madly keen to do so, but the husband was nervous and pulled her away, saying that they would not go without ropes and reliable guides. Eventually, her love for her husband prevailed, so she came away. Afterward, when they inquired, they discovered that nobody had ever gone to the back of the caves, though a Frenchman had tried but never came out again. It was believed that there were asphyxiating gases within. However, she was in a frightful state and could hardly be got to the airplane to fly home. She wrote me asking whether or not she should go back, and I replied that she should not. That voice had been so helpful to her and yet would have led her to her death with no thought of remorse.

Trying to look at what a person has done while in the possession of the animus is admittedly difficult, if not impossible, for the animus. And here is where the negative animus still today advises suicide. The negative spirits apparently suggested suicide at this particular time because this was the first occasion on which Jeanne had threatened to move over to the other side. From the negative point of view, the animus would prefer to destroy her. The Catholic Church teaches that despair is one of the mortal sins, one of the very worst, and it is one of the most dangerous. These spirits have come to the end of their tether and could only act as they did. There was the risk from the negative side that Jeanne might become an active agent for the good just as she had been for the evil. There is no better Christian than a repentant sinner. Think, for instance, of St. Paul. Such a person, and this includes Jeanne Fery, is much better equipped to act for the other side than someone who has never strayed from the fold because he has knowledge of the ways of evil spirits. He is like the top secret man who knows the plans of the other camp. In psychology, it is the man who knows his own abyss who can really understand. Jung often quotes Carpocrates: "Thou canst not be redeemed from a sin thou hast not committed," a great truth for the man who knows what he is talking about.[40] Therefore, it was important for the demons to prevent

---

40. [Jung writes: "'No man can be redeemed from a sin he has not committed,' . . . a deep saying for all who wish to understand, and a golden opportunity for all those who prefer do draw false conclusions. What is down below is not just an excuse for more pleasure, but something we fear because it demands to play its part in the life of the more conscious and more complete man." C. G. Jung, "Woman in Europe" (1927), in *CW*, vol. 10 (Princeton, N.J.: Princeton University Press, 1964), par. 271. Carpocrates (c.130–150) was an Alexandrian philosopher, founder, with his son Epiphanes, of a Hellenistic Gnostic sect whose beliefs had an antimonial bent. Jesus, they held, was but one of several wise men who had achieved deliverance. The Carpocratians believed that men had formerly been united with the Absolute and that one's imprisoned eternal soul must pass through every possible condition of earthly life. The material realm could be transcended, thus they were bound to no religious law or other morality, all of which were held to be human opinion. Moreover, transcendence could be achieved within one lifetime. According to Irenaeus, the Carpocratians did notoriously licentious things so that, when they died, they would not be compelled to incarnate but

Jeanne from changing sides. On this level they would have enormously preferred her death.

The demons from now on complained that they suffered. Demons cannot stand their opposite and will never voluntarily accept it. If we try to live on the dark side alone, we inevitably meet destruction. That is why we have needed two thousand years of the differentiation of the light. One can only hope that the light is sufficiently differentiated to stand against the destructive forces—similar to Jeanne Fery's demons—that are threatening our whole civilization today. If you think of the things that happened in the concentration camps, for instance, you will not be tempted to dismiss Jeanne's demons as medieval nonsense. She had opened her soul in such a way that she was then open to evil. It is only logical and to be expected that evil then tries to destroy her utterly. The demons failed to get her to commit suicide, and although they put her through hell, they could not kill her either.

We can ask ourselves what then happened here? Once she had seen the miracle of the host—the blood and the blinding light— the libido then began to move to the other side and thus offered the demons less of a hook. She was no longer completely possessed. If the storm from the demons had come to her before the visions of blood and light, she just might have committed suicide. But once she knew that they had deceived her, this knowledge was apparently enough to preserve her life.

Once you accept something absolutely, then it no longer really wishes to go against you. Jeanne Fery was wise enough not to kill herself, but she offered her spirits the possibility. In her case, this meant fully accepting her fate, but then she had also seen the miracle of the Host. Perhaps if it had come to this earlier, she might been successful in one of her actual suicide attempts, but she knew now that she had been deceived, and this particular knowledge was enough to preserve her. This is a place where one should be careful not to lay down the law. Sometimes the danger of suicide is acute when the other side comes up, and sometimes

would return transcended to God. Differences in class and the ownership of property were proclaimed as unnatural; property and women were to be held in common. *Ed.*]

it is worse before. One can only say that, by the grace of God, Jeanne Fery did not go through with it, although the temptation was evidently acute. It is a "just so" story and depends entirely on the individual. This is why the analyst has to exercise the greatest care in such cases and never let himself be lulled into security. Things are usually more dangerous when one is not alarmed. Jeanne knew now that she was practically certain to be found out and that she faced great disgrace, and, therefore, it was an enormous temptation not to go on.

Remember the many attempts that Doris (in our active imagination series) had made since her adolescence?[41] But once she really understood that she was possessed, it stopped at once. The great difficulty is to get borderline cases, such as Jeanne Fery and Doris presumably are, to realize that they are possessed. There is no safety until they do become conscious of this, and then a big battle has been won. It was not yet been entirely won in Jeanne's case, as we shall see in the exorcism, but it is greatly to her credit that she went through this preliminary stage by herself and did not commit suicide at this point.

Interestingly enough, it was not until now, after the blood and light had issued from the pierced host, that the authorities noticed that there was something wrong with her. While she was at one with her spirits, it was not observed that she was practicing a religion contrary to that which she outwardly professed. No one seems to have had any idea. Both animus and anima are great liars and deceivers and can get away with something as no simple human can. Animus-possessed women and anima-possessed men lie very cleverly.

People who are highly one-sided, in no conflict with the opposite, can often function well. People who are possessed are usually particularly gifted at lying and deception. It is amazing how they can deceive other people and themselves. It is striking in wars, for instance, how borderline personalities function normally while they have a job that requires only a one-sided effort.

---

41. [Barbara Hannah refers here to a case she discussed in her lecture series on active imagination. See Barbara Hannah, *Active Imagination* (Boston: Sigo Press, 1981). *Ed.*]

They are quite all right until some conflict occurs. Unfortunately, nowadays many jobs are so specialized that it is extremely easy to carry on without developing other sides of the personality. Evidently, Jeanne thought herself quite justified in deceiving her whole environment; she assumed they were wrong, and it worked smoothly in a sort of compartmentalized psychology. We see something similar in people who live a double life . . . until the two sides collide.

The Archdeacon of Wakefield, for instance, had a tiresome wife, who was also an invalid, and he was a virile man and a good preacher. Convinced that he was in the right, it was easy for him to argue within himself that, without an affair, he could not carry on functioning. However, he saw to it that a man in a similar situation was defrocked, and this man set detectives on his trail. The archdeacon also made the mistake of taking his lady love, the secretary of a prisoner's society, to Cathedral Close at Salisbury. It was not until the two opposite sides came together in the second Court that he realized his guilt and collapsed. Jung also had a patient who went up in the air at the mention of polygamy and who, on being shown that he was polygamous, became impotent for a time thereafter. Such instances prove how the animus and anima can lie so well that one does not even know it oneself. This collision of the two worlds also applies to Jeanne Fery and Doris; once the collision occurred, then of course she could no longer function smoothly.

But evidently something had been happening to Jeanne of which she was totally unaware, and it is to a great extent the point around which the whole case then began to revolve. The clue here is the central worldly figure Louis de Berlaymont, whose personality eventually contributed largely to her cure. She knew of him only in that she had made her vows as a nun to him and then again when the spirits had forced her to renounce both the pope and that "evil archbishop." Now we hear that at the height of her conflict she felt an impulse to take refuge with him, but the spirits blinded her eyes, and he seemed so "severe and terrible" that she did not dare approach him.

This was the first touch of human relationship. She may have had an unconscious transference to him even before the beginning of the exorcism. This was the first movement against her relatedness to her imaginary world, and it was probably this transference that made her wonder whether it would not be as well to have Christ along with the other gods, for Christ was the archbishop's God. Prior to this moment, she had only despised other people for believing in a God who could not save himself from the Cross. I am inclined to think that it was the initially strong unconscious transference to him that brought about the sudden positive feelings toward Christ. At all events, it will become clear that the archbishop was the deciding factor just as the transference to the analyst makes it possible to confront a great and necessary change.

Our information now comes from the long and detailed account of the exorcism that is a carefully compiled document vouched for by an unusual number of prominent people. When published in 1586 together with her own account, it not only went into more than one edition in France but was translated into German and published in Germany within two years. Görres used this German edition in his *Die Christliche Mystik,* but the only copy I have run to earth is the original French in the Bibliotheque Nationale in Paris.[42]

When the doctor could do nothing for her, he said—as medical doctors often do—that it was a psychic problem. The nuns, moved by Jeanne's suffering—both physical and mental—now took compassion on her and were kind and sympathetic. Jeanne was unable to respond, and this and her unsupportable replies made them first suspect that there must be something wrong with her. Thus they went to the authorities. Evidently she had not been intimate with the other nuns and had got away with being witty and clever. She impressed people but was hardly related to them, and when her illness and misery pulled her down from this superior attitude and she was obliged to suffer outright, she then

---

42. Joseph Görres, *Die Christliche Mystik,* vol. 5 (Regensburg: Verlagsanstalt GJ Manz, 1836–1842).

seemed more human and aroused sympathy and kindness from other people.

One sees such people in modern life. Where there is no human response to other humans, something quite inhuman may function for years. But when human demands are made, there is no longer any power of disguise. I was at school with such a girl. She was a shining light at games, held the tennis cup, and so on. Of course, she was enormously admired in sport-loving England and kept going well for years on the adulation she received. But she had next to no friends, and she always suspected that no one really trusted her. She had a peculiar, rather rigid look that I have since learned to associate with animus possession. But back then it only made me feel uncomfortable. She was three or four years younger than I, and sometime after I left she became head of the school. The headmistress told me afterward that she went right to pieces in this responsible post, for she simply had not developed the human qualities that are indispensable in close contact with girls. The headmistress said: "She somehow isn't human." An "animus hound," we might say today, that is, a woman who fails to respond humanly in relationships. There is no "human being" present to reply to normal human reactions with related human reactions, and then something rather inhuman reacts. The woman can cover it quite well when she is on top of a situation, as Jeanne Fery was for years, but she has no power to disguise the problem once human demands are made on her.

At this time, Jeanne was completely possessed. Almost immediately afterward she declares that she still prefers her spirits to everything else, so presumably the blessing, like the pieces of the host, would only have benefited the demons if her ego had received it and the figure of Mary Magdalene had not intervened. Jeanne would thus have been worse off, as can happen in analysis, if the animus—and not the human being—gets hold of the matter. If the positive feminine figure gets it, the effect will be quite different. For example, several things that Jung said in my earlier analysis I did not understand at the time. But something in me knew they were important and should be remembered.

Such things I never did forget, and the animus never got hold of them and twisted them. After many years, I understood them. One could say that a more mature personality had intervened and preserved them from the animus.

Jung says that, in cases of psychosis, one should pour in a lot of psychological knowledge, as it is very much needed, and even if it is not understood, something in the person retains it. In a lecture at the Eidgenössische Technische Hochschule of Zurich, Jung said that a person who has read a thousand books and forgotten them is still in a totally different position from the person who has never read any at all. That Mary Magdalene took the blessing for Jeanne meant something along these lines.

We hear that the demons, feeling themselves threatened and enfeebled by this one blessing of the archbishop (that they were able to twist because it was safe for them), made another violent onslaught on Jeanne herself. They made her promise never to abandon them, to which she gladly agreed, for the visions that they gave her still pleased her much better than the resplendent vision of light. Such an attack on the part of the negative animus may always be expected to appear when an important relationship is likely to be established, or even at the beginning of an analysis. And then the attacks by the animus get much worse after a relationship or analysis begins, for the demonic side feels itself threatened. It is clear from her preference for the demons that Jeanne is still quite caught in her plots to look good and shine, and she is by no means willing to allow another woman, even Mary Magdalene, to outshine her. Since her demons were all men, it may be that she is now ready to admit Christ as another admirer, but not another woman. It may seem strange to speak of Christ as an "admirer," but Jung tells the story of how, at the time he was an assistant at Burghölzli (the psychiatric clinic of the University of Zurich), he was attending church one morning when one of the patients leapt up and said: "He is my Christ, and you are all whores." That is how people are awfully inclined to feel in a transference. We do not realize how much we let the animus deceive us in this way. Interestingly enough, in the first attempt at exorcism, the demons spoke the truth. When asked by the merits of which saints they would depart, Ninon, one of the central spirits, spoke in the name of them all, and said: "By the merits of Mary Magdalene." Apparently they acted entirely against their own interests here. They had just made Jeanne promise never to abandon them, and later they fought every inch of the way.

I remind you of Jung's remarks after the lecture on women's plots, where he said that if you have the courage to go on, the animus leads you to something meaningful in the end. Here, these misleading demons yet bow to Mary Magdalene as a symbol of the Self. In the surprise attack on them in the first place, they had acted positively. We often see the same thing in analysis when there is perhaps an extraordinary success at the beginning and everything may seem to be going well in the case of the animus-possessed woman, or an anima-possessed man. Later the old negative animus (or anima) recovers and learns the new methods and begins to twist them for his or her own ends. Ninon announces that they will only disappear in the name of Mary Magdalene, thus the archbishop asks if there is a picture of her in the convent. This he had taken to Jeanne's room, where it was especially blessed by him, and proved to be of great use afterward when the demons complained of this manna. One should observe here that the wise exorcist is willing to learn from his enemies, the demons. This is the first mention to be made of Mary Magdalene, and it has come from the demons. The archbishop knew there had been a figure, but Jeanne had not mentioned her. This is very much the wisdom of the serpent recommend by Christ: "Be ye, therefore, wise as serpents and harmless as doves" (Matt. 10:16). Usually it is only the people— evil or not—with such wisdom who then are open to learn from their enemies. Hitler purportedly said that he learned more from his chief enemies, the Catholics and Jews, than from anyone else. Many good men are unfortunately too proud or too narrow to do this.

The first exorcism had no effect at all on Jeanne herself. In fact, it was observed more and more how far she had moved from the faith to which she had made her vows as a nun. For this reason, the archbishop now formed a committee of about five or six men, all priests in high positions and including Canon Mainsent, priest for both the Dominican convent and the lay-women of the Beguinage as well as the priest who served as the archbishop's chief assistant in the case. In fact, until he was obliged to intervene by one of Jeanne's later visions of Mary Magdalene, the archbishop left the practical work to Mainsent, who also had assistants to relieve him. But the archbishop remained the deciding authority, all difficulties being reported to him wherever he was.

The chief therapy applied at this time could be compared to the case of the little elephant at the Circus Knie (Swiss National Circus). The little elephant had been born in captivity, and when it was about a year old it suffered from serious diarrhea. The best vets were brought to see it, yet nothing successful could be done. When the little thing was on the verge of death, the district medical officer suggested that the owner call in a Capuchin monk. This monk was said to be very good at effecting cures where other doctors could do nothing. The monk was a wizened little man, and all that he did was to stroke the elephant and whisper in its ear, and then every now and then he turned to other people watching and said: "No, he won't." But at last he turned around beaming and said: "It is all right, he will!" The diarrhea was cured. Jung said that this type of therapy at bottom is the most important type there is. The monk's explanation was that the little elephant had a dreadful grudge against life. It had been born in captivity, without trees, forests, or natural surroundings, and the old monk, by accepting the little elephant and its grudge while giving the little animal wholeheartedly his own personal energy, made up a bit of what the elephant had never received. He gave his own psychic energy to the case. Jung thought that this was more important than the psychological methods one uses and the psychology one gives. I have seen cases where I was convinced that a man who really accepts the patient and gives himself to him or her with his full energy will succeed more—

even with all the wrong ideas—than the man who just properly applies that which "is right."

At this point Jeanne was wholly resistant, and it is doubtful whether one exorcist could have swung it alone. The Church has means that we do not possess, but this shows the importance of the cooperation of colleagues with difficult cases and of not trying to carry them entirely alone. Jeanne had fallen back into her demons, who were recovering from their first shock, and the committee then could only report complete failure. The archbishop could not realize at first how much depended on Jeanne's transference to him. He, therefore, instructed them to follow all the usual methods and recommended her to the Church with which she was to be reunited. Therefore, they made more or less rational attempts to make her conscious of her state. They took her around to all of the sacred places in her environment and exposed her to the relics with reputations of working miracles. In short, they tried an easy way of hoping for a miracle, like at Lourdes or at Einsiedeln. In my experience, miracles only occur if you never rely upon them. If there is one, it will most likely be after you have done everything you possibly can. In this case, the effect was close to nil, although some minor devils are said to have fled. They soon, however, were back. This corresponds to the efforts one makes in analysis to avoid opening up the collective unconscious. We also try to avoid going the hard way by opening up to the collective unconscious, which should be opened up to only if this proves absolutely necessary. The exorcists tried to show Jeanne something of her personal shadow, that is, to show her how completely she had fallen away from the Church. And they made efforts to employ the means of grace (which we have not got) in order to get her back into the Church without a "deeper analysis" so to speak, without what they would presumably call a complete exorcism.

The priests also put her in a dark and narrow prison cell in order to subdue the malicious spirits of whom, it is admitted, the priests themselves were afraid. This method is the well-known attempt to repress the whole matter, a method that might well be indicated in certain cases. Interestingly enough, we are told here that in other cases it had been "good and necessary," that is, successful. But in this case, it proved worse than useless, so after keeping her imprisoned for three days and nights they wisely desisted and returned her to her accustomed place, which, at that time, was the convent infirmary, for she was also physically very unwell.

Then the archbishop tried the effect of baths in Gregorian waters, as a result of which certain things were expelled—bad odors and so forth—but the main possession remained untouched. After these more or less rational attempts, the exorcists realized that they were in for a long and thorough battle and that all cheaper efforts were doomed to failure. And that is when, in our language, only the process of individuation itself can help. For at this point, Jeanne Fery is confronted with a highly individual fate. We should be sure that it is indicated before encouraging the patient to go this difficult way.

After six weeks of this kind of treatment, the archbishop went away to his residence in the Ardennes, leaving Jeanne in the hands of Canon Mainsent and an assistant priest. But in his absence, the demons got a much better hold on her so that the nun who was nursing her, Barbara Deruillers, had great trouble in preventing her from being smothered. The demons also prevented her from eating and drinking for three days and nights so that there were the beginnings of a danger that she would die. They also persuaded her to throw herself from the convent into the river below. The suicidal attempt came nearer to success this time, but the spirits could not quite extinguish her wish to live, for once in the water she shrieked for help and her fellow nuns were able to rescue her and bring her back to bed. Three attempts to convince her to throw herself off the roof were also foiled. But they did slowly succeed in making her life so miserable that she went on a hunger strike and attempted to starve herself to death. Moreover, her devils had made her so stupid that she could only communicate in writing. This amounts to somewhat of a catatonic state.

Although possession did not spread to the other nuns as it did in Loudun,[43] the nuns were all very unhappy with the whole affair, particularly Jeanne's personal nurse. But they felt more sorry for her afflictions than angry with her. Presumably, this sympathetic human attitude, along with the fact that they gave her credit and avoided negative assumptions, preserved them from succumbing to the infection, for such things are terribly infectious, as we only know too well in psychotherapy today. Cases are known where the doctor or nurse has taken over the psychosis while the patient would be particularly well at times. The archbishop must have been an unusual man, for the attitude of both priests and nuns is characterized by moderation and common sense.

The archbishop remained away for several months, but with the archbishop's constant advice, Canon Mainsent was beginning to understand the case better. He did a lot of the preliminary work (such as recovering the stolen pieces of the host and undermining the position of the demons), although the conviction that he had successfully exorcised them always proves to be too optimistic.

At this point, the official report of the exorcism becomes the clearer account, but before going on to this subject, I should like to discuss briefly a few facts in Jeanne's own account which gives us the main information we have as to the conditions that led to her possession.

Now if you had to give a modern label to this case, how could we diagnose it? The dramatic and exaggerated psychological states that occurred seem to point toward hysteria rather than to schizophrenia. There is indeed a tremendous dissociation of her emotions and a personification of these and other parts of her

---

43. [Jean-Joseph Surin (1600–1665) was a French Jesuit priest famous for delivering the nuns at the convent of Loudun from demonic possession. The extraordinary events were popularized by Aldous Huxley in *The Devils of Loudun* and by Ken Russell in the film *The Devils* (1973), both of which focus on the shocking and spectacular aspects of the story. France was rife with beliefs in demonic activity at that time, so when the relationship between the priest, Urbain Grandier, and the nuns at Loudun acquired erotic overtones, he was accused of bringing the devil into the convent and was tortured and burned at the stake on charges of witchcraft. In the meantime, chaos reigned among the nuns, who behaved erratically, acting out symptoms such as rage, exaggerated sexual activity, and so forth. See Aldous Huxley, *The Devils of Loudun* (New York: Harper Perennial, 2009). *Ed.*]

personality. Yet her ego—weak as it was—was never obliterated. There was always someone there to whom these things happened; she never thought she was one of the spirits, for instance, and during the exorcism she proved herself capable of reeducation. She eventually became a more or less ordinary nun. But as the archetypal foundation remains the same in the sick or "normal" psyche, I would prefer to use the ordinary psychological language with which I am more familiar and leave the diagnosis to the medical doctors.

And what do you think of her family situation? We do not have enough facts about Jeanne's home life to speak with any certainty, but I think we may safely assume that it was far from happy. The father presumably drank—a sober man would hardly have cursed a child of four when returning from the public house—and Jeanne's account does not sound as if the mother had bothered about her at all. The fact that Jeanne's figures were all men points, of course, to a father complex although maybe to an animus-possessed mother as well. There is a complete and striking absence of any feminine figures until the beginning of the exorcism.

The first father figure, the handsome young man, wins her allegiance with white bread and apples, presumably delicacies that were rare in her outer life and symbolic enough in themselves. The second father figure prevented her from feeling the strokes when she was beaten, so presumably she was a sensitive child who was quite unable to bear her hard lot and whose emotions thus split off and became autonomous. It is, of course, a very common reaction for sensitive, lonely children to live in a world of imagination. A classic example can be found in Fannie Ratchford's book *The Brontës' Web of Childhood*.[44] It seems to me, therefore, that in some ways Jeanne's life as a child with these imaginary father figures was by no means extraordinarily abnormal, and similarities can be seen in the reactions of many other children in comparable surroundings.

---

44. Fannie E. Ratchford, *The Brontës' Web of Childhood: The Miscellaneous and Unpublished Writings of Charlotte and Patrick Branwell Brontë* (New York: Columbia University Press, 1941).

The ratification of the pact during her adolescence, how-ever, becomes more ominous. To live in a "web of childhood" is innocent and common enough, but most children, in the con-vent school where Jeanne was educated or as an apprentice to a dressmaker, would begin to accept the outer world—with its pleasures and knocks—and no longer live entirely in the inner world. Charlotte Brontë, for instance, although she always loved her inner world beyond everything, took her education—when sent to school at the age of sixteen—very seriously and also made two lifelong friends. Put in everyday language, one might say that Jeanne's pact with her figures represented a more or less conscious refusal to grow up, to face the disappointments and imperfections of life and, above all, the shortcomings in her own character. Her spirits flattered her, and she chose to believe these illusions and eventually wove—or was compelled to weave—a drama with herself as the one woman in a host of men relatively oblivious to the outer facts. I say it was a more or less conscious decision because we hear she resisted for a time; that is, she was aware that she was doing something wrong. Moreover, she had had a warning in the sudden multiplication of her figures that we hear terrified her. Evil had received overwhelming reinforce-ments in such a simple form that one could surmise even Jeanne might have understood.

And this appearance of a crowd (that could be, for example, collective opinions) in its turn leads to the famous pact with the devil that we find everywhere in witchcraft literature. (The sim-plest definition of a witch is a person who attempts to use the powers of the unconscious for personal ends. Although it may seem that witches have disappeared and passed away, they have just taken on a more modern form.) Jeanne has to sign this pact with her blood—the invariable formula—and then put it in a pomegranate and eat them both, a symbol that is more unusual. The pomegranate is marvelously sweet until the last bite, which is then unbearably bitter.

We really find the whole trouble depicted in the symbol of the pomegranate. Marie-Louise von Franz tells me that this fruit belongs to Dionysus as well as to Persephone in her underworld aspect. It has the special attribute of making you forget this life: the dead eat it in order to do so, and the living should never eat a pomegranate while in the underworld or they will be unable to return to the upper world again. So it is symbolically very interesting that it is a pomegranate in which the adolescent Jeanne eats her pact with the spirits. It was very sweet to the taste until its intolerably bitter end, just as it seems sweet to avoid the suffering of the outer world and to go off with the animus into a hysterical imaginary drama. This is also a way to live—more common perhaps than we think—but a terrific bill will always be presented in the end. The whole future development of Jeanne's case was already present in this symbol in a simple form.

The animus uses a symbolic language, and if we cannot or do not understand it—as Jeanne cannot or does not understand the intolerable bitterness that will follow the sweet fruit here—then we open the door to his twists and distortions in the concrete world. One cannot even blame him, for it is not his world. A woman who was talking to her animus in active imagination one day was astonished to hear him remark: "We are in a very awkward position linked together like Siamese twins in totally different realities." He then explained that her reality was as nebulous and invisible to him as his was to hers. She asked him indignantly why he was so fond of interfering in a reality that he could so little see. He replied that if she left things undone, it formed a vacuum, and he was then obliged to fill it as best he could.

From this point of view, when one fails to stand up against the manipulations of the animus—as Jeanne failed—or when one cannot face or understand the bitter end of the pomegranate, a vacuum is made in this world that is then filled with "demons." One then allows one's consciousness to be wrapped away in a cocoon of illusions and animus opinions as to what life is, a thing that most women have experienced to some degree in one area or another where they have failed to live.

One of the first things that happened after Jeanne had sealed her pact by eating the pomegranate was that she had to give her tongue, then her memory, reason, and will, and subsequently all the parts of her body each to a separate demon. In return they promised her various advantages of which the most striking was to make her clever and witty so that she could impress her environment. We are all familiar with the animus using a woman's tongue and how maddeningly eloquent and beside the point that can be. Yet it can be impressive to naïve people—to mention but one example: what Hitler achieved in a similar manner—so it is not surprising that Jeanne Fery seems to have made quite an impression on her environment. We are also only too familiar with the way the animus can twist a woman's memory and reason, and of course there is little question of free will in such conditions. The fact that she had given them—or that they took over—her body leads into very complicated material, with which I have no time to deal in the context of this lecture, although we shall see that her body had to be freed—piece by piece—during the exorcism.

We will now turn to the exorcism using the original Paris document that was carefully put together based on a great many witnesses who apparently attempted to give an objective account of what happened. That is, the reality of the exorcism was witnessed by a great many people who verified that the account of the events was accurate. Thus we can certainly say that a *consensus gentium* testified to its validity.

Now, returning to Jeanne's initial lack of response to the nuns, and at the time when the archbishop was already considering the case with his assistant exorcists, there was the critical moment when Jeanne overcame her fear of him (which had so far enabled the spirits to hold her back). The archbishop, who was evidently highly interested in such things, went to the convent himself at the first hint of trouble, and we hear that Jeanne threw herself at his feet. This was a significant event right at the beginning (it is omitted by Görres). She had indeed felt a similar impulse before, but according to her account, the spirits had prevented her from such action. Now they advised her to do so. Yet it had a crucial result, for as she lay at the feet of the archbishop, she had her first vision of an impressive feminine figure who radiated a great light and who took the archbishop's blessing in Jeanne's name. We see the Luciferian principle of individuation at work here, for it was the spirits who advised Jeanne to throw herself at the archbishop's feet. It was her subsequent transference to him that won the battle against them.

Moreover, this first gesture of submission toward a human being was apparently sufficient to constellate the first appearance of a feminine figure, a representative of the principle of Eros, that had so far been lacking and that would become the demons' great opponent. And yet it was one of the spirits that soon afterward was the first to name this figure and said they would only depart by the merits of Mary Magdalene. Nonetheless, on the very evening that Jeanne had her vision at the feet of the archbishop, they tormented her into promising never to leave or abandon them, which we hear she did willingly, for she still greatly preferred them to the unaccustomed light of the divine feminine figure.

Now Mary Magdalene will later prove to be the great inner opponent of the evil spirits. But her initial obeisance, which is particularly emphasized by Görres, was said to have been insincere when it became clear that Jeanne had not entirely given them up. However, I do not quite agree with this. I believe that—as far as she existed separate from the possession—she was sincerely impressed by the archbishop. But naturally much of her was still possessed and not under her control so it would appear insincere to the outsider. Throughout the document no allowance is made for the duality of Jeanne's motives.

It is apt that the demons hit just on Mary Magdalene, the great sinner, who overcame through love, for she represents Jeanne's situation and her only hope. They have already made Jeanne reproduce Mary's action when she threw herself at the feet of Christ (in Jeanne's case at the feet of the archbishop). Mary Magdalene plays a considerable role in the dogma of the Church, thus the vision more or less corresponds to dogmatic expectation and could thus be readily accepted by her exorcists.

The figure of Mary Magdalene intervenes and takes the archbishop's blessing in Jeanne's name. Now why is this step neces-

sary? Presumably if Jeanne had received it directly, it would have
been taken over by her demons much like the pieces of the host.
Jeanne would then have been worse off instead of better. This is
similar to our modern-day animus when he gets hold of a psychological truth and, for example, twists it. Moreover, as previously
mentioned, certain truths that we are not yet able to understand
and integrate seem to be preserved by someone or something in
our unconscious that is wiser than our conscious and are given to
us intact at the right moment. One feels that it is with some such
wise purpose that this great feminine figure intervenes and takes
the blessing in Jeanne's name.

It is interesting that the archbishop was quite willing to learn
from his enemies, the demons. As soon as he hears them say they
would depart only by the merits of Mary Magdalene, he gives the
orders for a picture of her to be found, blesses the picture himself,
and has it placed in Jeanne's cell. The archbishop then appointed
a whole committee of priests, including Canon Mainsent, who
afterward became his chief assistant in dealing with the case.

There is a vast arrogance in people who are animus possessed,
and here Jeanne separates herself to a certain extent. The transference to the archbishop, demonstrated in this obeisance, turns
out to entail a relatedness strong enough to become a human
relationship in which she commits herself to him. Presumably it
is the first time that a human being really impressed her, and she
has, even though she is still very much afraid of him, an unconscious relation to the archbishop. This makes it possible for the
unconscious to manifest positively, and it is the reason why it
is initially dangerous to do active imagination without a strong
human relationship, that is, until one has learned the method.
The aim eventually is to help the patient become independent,
but from the analyst's point of view, he or she should be careful
to be sure that the rapport between analyst and patient is good
and will hold in emergencies before the method is recommended.

Hitherto, there has been no positive animus figure in Jeanne's
life, and all of the demons were male figures strongly contaminated with the collective unconscious. Mary Magdalene was a sym-

bol of the Self that is inclined to occur in feminine symbols in the case of women. The Self in women is almost always a feminine figure, particularly at the beginning. Later it may take on a more hermaphroditic character, but it is always inclined toward the feminine side in women and to the male in men. If the vision had been of a masculine figure—one of the saints or even Christ himself—it would have meant the usual conflict between light and dark. Mary Magdalene is a far more meaningful symbol. Jeanne's feminine side has been constellated by the transference and the transformation. Before, while weaving plots with her demons, she saw only herself as great feminine figure. Now, for the first time, she sees that figure objectively as well as connected with herself. But this figure is complex. On the one side, Mary Magdalene plays a role in the dogma of the Church. On the other, she has a strongly individual nuance and fits Jeanne's position very aptly, for Mary Magdalene is the great sinner who overcame through love and, from the point of view of her time and environment, Jeanne Fery was certainly a great sinner. Moreover, Mary Magdalene threw herself at Christ's feet just as Jeanne Fery threw herself at the feet of the archbishop. Certainly in those days Jeanne could only proceed by acknowledging herself a sinner, though we could be a bit more lenient and point out that a lonely child with such a father and very little help from the mother had had a life in which the human elements of love, Eros, and relationship had had no place.

There is a legend of the Three Marys who, after Christ's death, purportedly traveled to Marseilles, where they settled and later died. They are Mary Salome, Mary the Mother of Christ, and Mary Magdalene. The cult of these three women apparently mixed in well with the old Celtic Tres Matronae, the three mothers or three earth goddesses, and this legend played a major and widely known role in French tradition. The legend would reinforce the idea that Mary Magdalene presumably stood in Jeanne's psychology for the Self in her Earth Mother aspect. Throughout the official Church literature connected with the Inquisition, possession and witchcraft are regarded as a deliberate sin. When

I began reading the *Malleus Maleficarum,* Jung told me to keep an eye out for any possible signs of madness that were treated as illness or misfortune, but I have never come across such an attitude in official medieval Church literature. In the old stories we find a more lenient attitude. For instance, in the Book of Tobit no blame is placed on Sarah. Her possession is attributed to the wickedness of Asmodaeus, a demonic figure who possessed her, and she is considered to be his victim. But in the Middle Ages, when the witch cult was at its height and the Inquisition on its trail, witchcraft was a most heinous crime. This is particularly clear in the official documents that, naturally, were written mainly by the Inquisitors themselves.

An extract from a papal bull of Innocent VIII in 1484 states: "It has lately come to our ears that in some parts of Germany many persons of both sexes, unmindful of their own salvation and straying from the Catholic Church, have abandoned themselves to devils and to incubi and succubi . . . ." No mention is made of the possibility of these persons being victims. Possession was regarded as a deliberate sin; it was believed that people voluntarily and by conscious decision abandoned themselves to the devil. It is assumed in the papal bull—as throughout the *Malleus Maleficarum* to which it appears as a preface—that this was the case. Such people were delivered over to the full power of the Inquisition, and the Inquisitors were given absolute authority to inflict any punishment that might seem good, rejecting any right of appeal. The Inquisitor could—with papal authority—aggravate the incident and then renew the penalty as often as he wished, calling in, when desired, the help of the secular arm.

The archbishop, knowing how difficult it was to deal with these devils, was a great deal more human in his approach to Jeanne Fery than this bull of Innocent VIII written about one hundred years earlier. The bull would have permitted him to deal with her in a different way, but the exorcists, no doubt knowing from bitter personal experience something of the difficulties, were far more human and regarded possession to a great extent to be an affliction. The Inquisitors were evidently men who had never tried to come to terms with any devils in their lives. The psychological point of view is more or less that guilt only consists of consciously agreeing to the possession and then continuing to go along with it after it is realized. We find exactly the same idea in the Swiss *Büchlein* in which it is said that possession is only harmful to the soul's salvation if the person persists in his evil attitude. The decision has to be made: "Am I going to fight my negative animus, or am I going to give in to him?"

The exorcists themselves almost always showed considerable compassion and treated possessed people more as patients, particularly before witch persecution grew to greater dimensions. St. Norbert, who lived about the same time as Hugh de St. Victor, himself a great exorcist, put most of the blame on the demons. He once went to Vivars (Soissons) in northern France to appoint a new abbot. When he was approaching the town, a villager, drinking from a stream, saw an extraordinary dark black shadow in the water and became possessed and raving mad and had to be put in chains. In the evening, after Norbert had appointed the abbot, this man was brought to him, and he immediately exorcised him, after which the man became reasonable and seemed to be quite all right. The people were pleased that the thing could be finished so quickly, but Norbert said that he could not rest because there was a horrible smell coming out of the man's nostrils, that is, the devil was still in him. Norbert then said that it was not without reason that the man was possessed with a devil and that the man must pay his debt, so he told the people to leave the man in the clutches of the devil until morning so that he may suffer, yet the people might pray for him (that is, the man was a victim yet had presented a hook for the devil). Norbert always asserted that the devil followed him and gave him personal attention. He was rather naively sure that the devil honored him as such, but he never connected this "attention" with his own psychology. Such convictions belonged to the age, and Norbert had a very fine sense of smell as to whether or not a devil had left the person and thus did not allow himself to be deceived. The point in this story is mainly in the remark that the man, who was victimized, was not delivered over to this hostile power without reason. And thus Norbert left him in the clutches of the devil overnight so that "he can pay his debt by suffering." Here, Norbert really goes to the root of the matter and judges much as he should. The man was the victim, yet such a fate belonged to him as well. Moreover, paying "the debt" with suffering is exactly what Jeanne now needed to do, for holding out through suffering is the only way in which such debts can be paid.

Under these circumstances it is not astonishing that Jeanne took a dislike to the Church. But one is distinctly surprised that she became a nun. In those days, however, there were no real careers open to women, and her dressmaking may not have offered enough scope to an ambitious girl like Jeanne. The only alternatives for such a girl were marriage, becoming the mistress of someone above her rank, or entering a convent, and we have already seen that the two former possibilities were probably closed to Jeanne. Therefore, becoming a nun was really the only life in those days that offered her intelligence and her intellectual ambition some scope, particularly as her great-aunt was the mother superior of the convent that she entered. Moreover, despite how infernal the animus becomes, he is yet connected with the Luciferian *principium individuationis,* and it was the best chance that her spirits had of leading her into a situation where she could become more conscious, for although the demons hate the light, they are also fascinated by it.[45] I hope to be able to give you convincing proof of this assertion when we come to the details of the exorcism.

In the meantime Jeanne was completely possessed by evil, and her spirits did not hesitate to inspire her to "murder," for piercing the host with a knife amounts to killing Christ. The evil principle has reached its summit, so to speak, and tries to rid itself forever of its opposing principle. But as the Chinese say, when yin is at its

---

45. [Barbara Hannah, in a handwritten note on the manuscript, points out that Gil, in James Hogg's *Confessions of a Justified Sinner,* pressed Robert toward consciousness. In this story, Gil Martin—the Luciferian principle—incites the protagonist, Robert, to commit murder. See James Hogg, *Confessions of a Justified Sinner* (London: David Campbell Publishers, 1992). *Ed.*]

darkest, yang is born. So here, that which is despised and rejected flames up like the rising sun.

Jeanne's attitude up until now has been primarily egotistical and materialistic. She believed in her spirits because she could seek refuge in them, and she had experienced advantages such as "good food" and a witty tongue that they produced. Therefore, she has not hesitated to renounce vows that meant nothing to her on the very evening they were made. But blood is the symbol of the living par excellence and was undeniable proof that all she had denied was alive and valid. Her world went down, so to speak, her familiar spirits fled, and there was nothing left for Jeanne but fear and despair. The bitter end of the pomegranate had begun.

The demons were soon back to assure her that Christ indeed was the only God, whom they also worshipped. Now what is to be made psychologically of this turn of events? They apparently simply ignored the fact that it was they who had taught her to despise a God who was too feeble to save Himself from the cross. This manner of capriciousness we often meet in our dealings with the animus and anima. Like nature herself, they are unhampered by any logic or moral considerations, and if it suits their purpose to ignore it, then what they maintained yesterday no longer exists today.

It is indeed quite possible that the blood and light convinced the demons—as well as Jeanne—and that they now realized for certain that the other side was alive and must be reckoned with. They placed a high value on blood in their previous dealings with Jeanne, and one of the worst demons was called Sanguainaire. According to their destructive nature, they proceeded to convince Jeanne that she was worse than Judas Iscariot and persuaded her to make more than one attempt to commit suicide. These attempts recurred during the first part of the exorcism rituals, but seeing that they also were a hysterical dramatization of the situation, they never succeeded. She would throw herself into the river, for instance, but just where some nuns who were working in the garden would hear her cries and rescue her.

Jeanne's hysteria was in one way highly successful. The archbishop along with several important priests, to say nothing of the whole convent, were now concentrated upon her and her affairs.[46] Really not a bad effort for a small dressmaker's assistant. She screamed the place down indeed, all being impressed by her sufferings, but possibly somewhere she at first secretly enjoyed being the center of this wonderful drama now occurring in the outer world as well.

We may be pretty sure that this was not without influence on the fact that the first efforts of her exorcists were a failure. As previously mentioned, the usual forms of exorcism were used: the exorcists talked to the demons, they commanded them to depart by the crucifix, they took her around for six weeks to every miracle-working relic within reach, they bathed her in Gregorian water, and so forth. But the demons remained unimpressed, and Jeanne still could not detach herself from them. The exorcists then realized that it was going to be a long fight. They made one more attempt at a quick cure by imprisoning her in a dark and narrow cell in order to subdue the malicious spirits, of which, it was later admitted, the priests were afraid. We are assured that this method had been successful in other cases, but it was worse than useless with Jeanne, so after three days and nights it was also given up.

The archbishop then went away to his summer palace in the Ardennes, leaving Jeanne in the care of Canon Mainsent. This made things much worse, and Jeanne's attempts at suicide were renewed. She even attempted a hunger strike and, affirming that her spirits had made her dumb, she only communicated in writing with her nurse, Sister Barbara, and her exorcists.

Presumably these were hysterical attempts in part to bring back the archbishop, but he remained away for several months. Probably this check in the success of her drama had a salutary effect. At all events, Mainsent began to have more success in his treatment and there as was a second appearance of Mary Magdalene who, with the light that always emanated from her,

---

46. [People inclined to histrionics tend to talk about and draw attention to themselves. Yet attention-seeking is also considered to be important for patients with dissociative identity disorders who have been severely neglected and/or abused in childhood. *Ed.*]

formed a rampart between Jeanne and her demons. We are told that Jeanne was thus able to tell her secret, that is, to give Mainsent his first information about her earlier childhood life and how she became possessed. There is, however, considerable doubt as to whether she spoke herself, as her spirits afterward maintained that they always spoke through her and that she herself had not as yet uttered a word. Do we ever meet such a thing today?

Mary Magdalene was the symbol to which the demons had declared their willingness to submit. Jeanne is still quite unable to understand their language and just wants to keep her spirits in their old familiar form. So it is really by no means out of character for the demons to give the information first, to show Mary respect themselves (for they purportedly vacated that part of the room), and then to torture Jeanne for failing to do so.

Mainsent was able to use the information he had received, and during this period several pieces of the stolen host were recovered. When they were assembled on a table where Jeanne was, the demons approached Mainsent and inquired, scoffing at him, if he thought he could deal with this secret by himself and then advised him to send for the archbishop. They then enforced their point by making Jeanne particularly violent so that her nurse could no longer manage her, thus more exorcists and the whole convent had to be mobilized to deal with her.

Mainsent sent an SOS to the archbishop, who responded only by sending them advice. Their subsequent measures led to a third appearance of Mary Magdalene, who then spoke to Jeanne for the first time, exhorting her to abandon her demons and promising to obtain a real father for her in their place. This time Jeanne seemed more able and willing to attend. Her exorcists were pleased by their subsequent progress, but their success seems to have been more apparent than real, for Jeanne was just as possessed as ever, and her demons soon informed Mainsent that she would die immediately if they were forced to abandon her, a threat that the exorcists took quite seriously.

After the recovery of all the pieces of the host, Mainsent appealed to the archbishop, and it is thanks to the latter that they were able to prevent the demons from recapturing the pieces of the host. This led to a paradoxical advance on the part of the unconscious: on one side, the demons threaten Jeanne with a forced regression to the mentality of a child of four, obtaining once again her promise never to abandon them; and on the other side, Mary Magdalene appears for the third time, and this time she finally speaks. She goes right to the root of the father problem, exhorts the girl to abandon her spirits entirely, and promises to obtain for her another father who will teach and indoctrinate her seriously so that all of her difficulties will vanish. She also advices her to endure her present sufferings and promises to be with her throughout. I must omit the theme of the pieces of Jeanne's own flesh cut out by the demons, which were the alleged cause of her physical illness. The return of these pieces, interestingly enough, took a great deal more effort than the return of the pieces of the host, but with the exception of this obstinate malady, the exorcism suddenly became remarkably successful. Just while they were rejoicing over these improvements, the archbishop (who had returned to his palace in Mons next door to the convent) was stricken with a grievous illness. The exorcists apparently concluded that his illness was connected with Jeanne, but in a consultation with the archbishop in his sickroom they decided that such dangers—as well as the possibility of the girl's death—must be risked and that the battle must be continued to the end. I mention this to show how far the sincere exorcist was willing to risk himself and how much he felt himself involved. Those who have read the essay "Psychology of the Transference" will remember what Jung says about the doctor being as much concerned with the successful outcome as the patient.

The psychological parallel here today would be everyday analytical work. At the beginning, one analyzes the dreams more to understand them oneself than with any other hope of the patient's understanding them. Usually it is at the dramatic turning points that the battle is won or lost, but the routine work must be done most conscientiously. The analyst must find out the facts of the case and get a line on the individual psychology, seeing where and how the animus is twisting the whole thing. Recovering the host would amount, with us, to finding those psychological truths that the animus is storing up for his own purpose should the patient become cooperative later. The patient may sometimes eventually understand the things twisted by the animus much better than those that have never touched her at all.

An interesting point is that the spirit-demons themselves give Mainsent the advice that saves the case. Although recovering from the shock of the first attack—they were fighting every inch of the way—it was they, as mentioned above, who asked Mainsent if he thought he could swing the case alone, and then they told him that he had better send for the archbishop. Undoubtedly, they hope to make him jealous, confused, and uncertain. Yet it is they who point out the importance of the archbishop, thus showing their dual nature. They fight according to their nature, which is purely destructively, yet they also seem to want redemption. And every now and then they take an active step (although generally wrapped up in a negative form) so that Mainsent would be undermined.

Several weeks later the archbishop returned, afflicted himself with a "grievous malady" that was reported to be connected with Jeanne's demons. Just as he was right to refuse to give in to Jeanne's hysterical dramatizations in the first place, one yet suspects that he may have been unwise to delay his return when the demons themselves told Mainsent to get him, for several weeks elapsed before he came. At all events, they were all now in an extremely serious situation: Jeanne seriously ill in her convent, the archbishop at his house in the immediate neighborhood. Perhaps the archbishop's dilemma could be compared here to that of a modern analyst who would almost certainly be right not to give into a hysterical plot of the patient's (for instance, the drama staged when the archbishop first left). He would rather be wise to regard statements in a dream or active imagination more seriously, for example, the demons' advice that he should return. We have seen before that the archbishop was quite willing to learn from them when they brought in Mary Magdalene, an openness that is frequently found in the cases of exorcists in the literature, but apparently not if their advice interfered with his own plans too much.

Mainsent reported to the bedridden archbishop. They were seriously worried about the possibility of the girl's death. But they decided that death—as well as any possible injury to themselves—must be risked, for it was impossible to keep the girl in her present state. Thus, a time was set for Mainsent and another exorcist to enter Jeanne's room in the convent and the room of the archbishop in his home simultaneously, where exorcisms then took place. The demons were asked to smash a pane of glass as a sign of their departure. (Such arrangements are frequently made between exorcists and demons, and they usually—although not always—are a sign that the exorcism has been successfully completed.) After a struggle that lasted most of the night, and during which we hear that Jeanne endured "such excessive sufferings as would move marble hearts to pity," the agreed-upon sign was given at the arranged hour and the pane of glass was smashed to pieces.

When we consider the breaking of glass, we must not forget that this substance was much more valuable in the sixteenth century than it is today. Now, why is the breaking of glass used as a signal of completion? Presumably it was given as a sacrifice to obtain a full—or in Jeanne's case—partial expulsion of the devils. A glass from which a toast has been drunk is still broken in some ceremonies (for instance, the salamander ritual among Swiss students today). Moreover, it is by no means rare for a glass to be broken by invisible means when someone is about to die. Jeanne's life had been threatened by the demons, there was an evident tension that had to explode, and presumably the idea was that the glass should be broken in her stead.

The sacrifice of the glass is followed by Jeanne's own sacrifice of Cornau, of the sweetness that he gave her and the sacrifice of her wit and intelligence. (Does a parallel with our own egotism here strike us as familiar?) We must not forget that Mary Magdalene had exhorted her to give up her demons and promised her a father in their place. Presumably Jeanne recognized the fulfillment of this promise when she heard that Mainsent had the masculine version of her own Christian name. Then, for the first time, she acted in obedience to the feminine principle and against her own egotism, for it was the archbishop who fascinated her, there never being a sign of a transference to Mainsent. Moreover, the sacrifice of her wit and intelligence, which Cornau represented, must have been especially humiliating and bitter.

One is reminded of the twenty-third hexagram of the *I Ching*: bō, "Splitting Apart." Just as in the first four lines of that hexagram, Jeanne has split into a thousand pieces. But, as in the sixth line, a large fruit remains that has not been eaten, so Mary Magdalene, the positive figure that replaces the demons and perhaps even represents her feminine Self, has remained intact in all the splitting up on both the emotional and the masculine side.

At all events, Jeanne had to submit to being looked after as if she were a child of four. For some time she just lay in bed murmuring "pretty Mary." Suddenly one day she added "Grandfather." Mainsent was afraid that Cornau had reappeared under this guise but then learned that the "good lady" had appointed the archbishop as Jeanne's grandfather and had made him, not Mainsent, personally responsible for her. Jeanne now had to go to the archbishop's sickroom daily—it took her half an hour to walk fifty paces—where he gradually, by blessing her tongue and each separate part of her body, gave her back the use of her limbs and her intelligence. She had to relearn everything, including her ABCs.

The archbishop and Mainsent then made a concerted attack on the demons, fixing an hour when they should all use the same form of exorcism simultaneously. This resulted in the first concrete sign of an effect, for during this combined attack the demons actually broke a piece of glass in order to show that they were leaving. This was the sign previously arranged. Such things still happen, but being more rational than the old exorcists, we do not welcome them so warmly. In fact one might say that, when such things occur, we are only then first convinced that something tangible can manifest and be capable of producing psychic as well as physical effects. Here, we approach an unknown realm between spirit and matter that I only mention in passing.

We are told that now all of the extraneous devils had left Jeanne and only the two father figures of her childhood remained. In modern analysis, this would correspond to having more or less succeeded in separating the personal from the collective unconscious so that one is left with the more individual factors. The second of these two father figures, called George, left fairly easily, but the first father figure, known as Cornau, was tenacious. He did not really give way until the final scene when the arch-bishop was in command and the whole nunnery assisted. Cornau asserted that he had more power than all of the others because he was the first and represented the whole of her intelligence. They then obtained the girl's admission that his first appearance occurred when she was four years old, this being the first time they had heard this confession. Cornau addressed them directly via Jeanne's mouth claiming that so far she had not spoken a single word herself; the animus alone had spoken, Jeanne still being completely possessed.

Although this was by no means the end of Jeanne's possession, it yet marked a tremendously important step in the exorcism. Just as her consent to signing the pact brought about a great reinforce-ment of her devils, so this concerted effort of the sick archbishop and the exorcists in Jeanne's room correspondingly weakened her devils, for the multitude evidently did leave her when the pane of glass was smashed. At all events, but a few days later Mainsent discovered that only the two original father figures remained. The second of these—the one who originally prevented her from feeling the strokes when beaten—left easily enough, but the first, the "handsome young man," who called himself Cornau, flatly refused. He assured Mainsent that if he did leave, he would take all of Jeanne's intelligence with him and reduce her to the condition of a child of four years old. Mainsent greatly preferred this prospect to the possession, but Jeanne clung desperately to Cornau saying that he had given her much sweetness for over twenty years whereas she had only known Mainsent for nine months. "I will not do it," she declared. Mainsent stuck to his point and offered to take Cornau's place as her father. This idea had little attraction for Jeanne until she heard that Mainsent's Christian name was Jean. This struck her so much that she agreed to the "terrible departing" with Cornau, who was then obliged to leave her. He fulfilled his threat, however, and Jeanne was actually reduced to the level of a little girl of four and could only lisp the words "father" and "pretty Mary."

In the meantime, the devils had by no means given up the struggle, but we are told that it was now an obsession and no longer a possession. She had frequent regressions, and the struggle was so fierce that Mary Magdalene now commanded the archbishop to take Jeanne out of the convent and, along with her nurse Sister Barbara, to give her room and board in his own house. He also was commanded to feed her at his own table after which she would be completely freed. This was obviously awkward from the point of view of the archbishop, and though he reluctantly obeyed, he soon yielded to adverse criticism and sent her back to her convent trying to buy his way out by paying himself for her food there. But Jeanne was immediately tortured worse than before. Mary Magdalene then appeared and told Jeanne that she must tell her grandfather that he had incurred the wrath of God for his disobedience. Mainsent reported this to the archbishop who listened patiently, but although he had done all that was humanly possible, he felt it was too much to risk his honor by taking a girl of twenty-five again out of the convent and into his house. He was not, however, happy about his decision, and he reflected deeply about his quandary, telling Mainsent that he longed for more experience and a feeling of certainty. He tried yet another compromise and decided to send her food from his own table and to send an extra priest to guard her at night from the demons.

Do such subterfuges actually help? As many modern analysts know from experience, when something beyond reason is demanded of them in special cases, such subterfuges are worse than useless, and Jeanne then was tormented more fiercely than ever before. And a further effort to escape on the part of the archbishop—who then put his vestments to bed with her—was such a failure that he thought the nun would soon die.

This last event convinced the archbishop of the genuineness of the command. He faced the raging scandal, submitted, and took Jeanne back into his house where at last she was at peace and could sleep. But then she became severely ill. The archbishop called in doctors, perhaps hoping once more for relief in his own dilemma, but Jeanne declared that these were useless and that only he himself could help her. Her pain ceased when the archbishop himself put his finger in her mouth to make her vomit into a silver bowl.

From then on Jeanne's more orthodox visions increased, and she frequently fell into the same kind of ecstasy as one reads of in the lives of the saints. Another important point—that I have so far omitted and that time only allows me to mention briefly—is that, from her third appearance onward, Mary Magdalene encouraged Jeanne to write, and indeed Jeanne's texts are often the dictation of Mary Magdalene. This writing culminated in her own account of her possession of which we have previously spoken. Therapeutic value of creative work in dealing with an overwhelming animus seems to have come spontaneously to the surface in this sixteenth-century case.

As to the troubles of the archbishop, I think they speak for themselves and require little comment. They remind one of the prophet Hosea who, at God's command, was obliged to marry a prostitute. We do not know enough of the archbishop to analyze this matter from his point of view, but I feel convinced that it must all fit into his psychology as well. Anyone who has had any such experience will know what he went through in order to meet the demands of such a special case. This report also shows clearly that such therapy must be guided by the Self, for it was only by obedience to Mary Magdalene that the archbishop made any progress, his own conscious suggestions and evasions falling hopelessly wide of the mark.

The next months passed in the archbishop's house, where Jeanne, still tortured by her demons, was ill-behaved and difficult. But her studies (mainly conducted by the archbishop) progressed steadily. (I need hardly point out how important these studies were to develop her mind, which was originally quite autonomous in her demonic possession.) But some five months after his last attempt to return her to the convent, the archbishop again yielded to gossip and scandal. He himself blessed and prepared a cell in the convent, and she was then transferred out of his house.

The immediate result was possession worse than ever. The demons made use of the nun's limbs and attacked the archbishop so violently that his life was apparently in danger. Mainsent and two dignitaries of the Church, to whom the archbishop applied for aid, were equally violently attacked. Mainsent barely escaped the brutal onslaught. The archbishop realized that once again he had made a serious mistake in disobeying the command and took her back into his house "in spite of the scandal against his person," upon which she returned to her senses and to her accustomed ways.

Presumably it was Mainsent this time who persuaded the archbishop to discontinue laying himself open to all this juicy gossip. At all events, Mary Magdalene again appeared to Jeanne and told her to spend most of her time praying for Mainsent, who would have a grievous illness for his share in the archbishop's disobedience. A few days later he was taken ill with palpitations of the heart and violent vomiting so that he thought his final hour had come. He took refuge, however, with Mary Magdalene and gradually recovered, as he realized the magnitude of his error.

The archbishop then kept Jeanne in his house and continued her education himself. There were, nevertheless, frequent relapses, but on the whole she was able to sustain considerable progress in her studies. Then, four months after the archbishop's last attempt to escape his fate, and about nine months after Jeanne first became an inmate in his house, Mary Magdalene gave permission through Jeanne to her "grandfather" to return the nun to her convent. Thus the archbishop was relieved of three of the originally stipulated twelve months. But there were conditions attached. Jeanne must have a retired cell, be kept as quiet as she was in the archbishop's house, and so forth. These were not carried out, and the devils tormented her unbearably all night. Mary Magdalene then appeared again to Jeanne and told her to rebuke her grandfather and to tell him that the things he might think trivial were yet of great importance in the sight of God.

The commands were obeyed in every detail the next morning, but this incident again was followed by a severe physical illness in which Jeanne's life was actually given up by the doctor. But by invocation of Mary Magdalene, she gradually recovered.

After some time, Jeanne began to take a real, active part herself, but she was not much interested in Mainsent and kept on murmuring "Gran'-père." Mainsent tried to find out who she was speaking of, and she eventually murmured "Louis" (the archbishop). Mainsent was then satisfied that Mary Magdalene had given Jeanne the archbishop as a grandfather. Jeanne then began having frequent visions of Mary Magdalene, in the course of which she reported that Mary Magdalene had placed her under the special care of the archbishop, who must now undertake her instruction himself. The latter immediately accepted the charge. She had to be taught the ABCs before he could begin, and then she could at first only manage single words. Jeanne was taken to his bedside for these lessons and for his blessings. He had to bless her tongue and all the different parts of her body separately. After this she recovered the normal use of her legs—before it had taken her half an hour to walk fifty paces to the archbishop—and she also could talk intelligently like an adult. Her transference was evidently the motivating force.

Soon Jeanne announced that Mary Magdalene had said that the archbishop must keep her in his house for a year together with her nurse. The archbishop obeyed for about six weeks but did not like the gossip that evidently started up, so he returned her to the convent. This was a failure, although he sent her food from his table so that she was still in essence his guest. But neither the devils nor Mary Magdalene fell for such simple wiles; the former tormented her while the latter said she should tell her grandfather that he was incurring the wrath of God by his disobedience. But he did not want to risk his honor by keeping a young woman of twenty-six in his house, nun or not. He tried putting her to bed with his "accoutrements" (presumably his vestments), but this was such a failure that he feared she would die on the spot. Reluctantly he gave in and kept her in his house and under his instruction for the stipulated time. He was obliged to take over the exorcism himself, for the devils continued their torments, although now more in the neighborhood of the girl than within her. They were objectified and no longer subjectively identical with her.

The poor archbishop was not let off easily. He had to hold the bowl himself when she vomited and was often attacked by the spirits as well. And they all held on. Although relapses were common, a gradual development of her mind was attained. However, things deteriorated before they finally improved. At one point things regressed so badly that her mental torment by the devils drastically worsened, and the doctors despaired of her life.

The day was now approaching when complete deliverance had been promised. The archbishop had obeyed the commands given him, and Jeanne herself had done everything in her power to resist the demons, to learn from the archbishop, and turn toward Mary Magdalene. Mary Magdalene now appeared again to Jeanne while she was in ecstasy and gave her full instructions as to how the final ceremony was to be conducted. The archbishop, following these instructions, assembled all the exorcists, the whole convent, the doctor, and a number of important clerical and laypeople from the diocese in a large room on the appointed day at three in the afternoon. Mary Magdalene also warned Jeanne that the fight would be severe, and indeed the demons got steadily worse as the time approached, presumably following the natural law of the darkest hour being before the dawn.

Then Jeanne, speaking for the first time herself, declared she must retain Cornau, as she was terrified of regressing to the state of a child of four. But Mainsent obtained her consent at last when she discovered that his name was Jean and that he would be her father from now on. Mary Magdalene now appeared again and took up the fight with Cornau, thus demonstrating that there is a possibility of development other than that of animus intelligence alone.

The final scene is dramatically described. The nun lay on a couch while Mary Magdalene, immobile and silent, stood at the foot of the bed on the right. The air was filled with a multitude of demons presumably having received reinforcements for the final struggle, as this is the first time we hear of a multitude since the breaking of the glass. It is important, however, that Mary Magdalene had sent instructions to the archbishop and Mainsent that they must on no account regard the demons as being still in Jeanne's body, that is, as possessing her, but as pressing in on her and tormenting her from the air around.

Although it was announced earlier that Jeanne was no longer possessed but only obsessed, the report is, nevertheless, somewhat vague in this respect, sometimes speaking of torture and sometimes of possession (presumably re-possession) when things went wrong. This is the first clear statement as to what is actually meant: the demons are no longer in Jeanne, that is, identical with her, but around her, tempting or torturing her. A certain objective distance has been gained and on no account could be lost.

There is a striking change in this final scene: although the archbishop stood before Jeanne holding the crucifix, neither he nor the other exorcists addressed the demons directly as they had done earlier and as would be usual in exorcism. Instead, Jeanne was left to fight her own battle. The archbishop indeed gave her advice and support, but only when she actually asked for it. It is also interesting that when she directly confronted and fought the demons, telling them, for instance, that they were lying when they asserted that their power over her was unbroken, their strength over her increased. She told them that if God gave them power over her, she would endure it voluntarily. But the torture increased to such a degree that at last she cried: "What will become of me, I can endure no more," and then she appealed to the archbishop who pointed out that God had not spared his own son a similar fate. Jeanne then told her demons that this would be her satisfaction. Thus she lay quietly, enduring her agony as best she could. Finally the demons left her and her tortured body, and Jeanne slowly returned to normal.

When she had recovered sufficiently, she told the archbishop that Mary Magdalene now released him forever of all material obligations toward her; he would, however, remain in charge of her conscience all the days of his life. The same evening she was able to go to the refectory with the other nuns and to resume the normal life of the convent.

Many years ago, in a seminar, Jung said that while men overcame their unconsciousness by killing the dragon, women could only do so by accepting their suffering.[47] Certainly this was the case with Jeanne Fery. She became possessed originally because she could not endure the suffering of life and thus escaped into a hysterical drama. As is usually the case, the inability to endure suffering catches up with one in a far worse form. Here, she gained sufficient consciousness to accept her suffering voluntarily, even to the point of having no idea what would become of her and letting herself go fully into it. And only then did the demons retire, presumably in submission and some form of consciousness of what their torture had produced in Jeanne.

She proved the sincerity of her submission by her subsequent sacrifice of all material advantages in her relation to the archbishop, by separating herself from her hysterical drama and becoming just one of a number of nuns.

One could not, of course, speak of Jeanne's case as anything like a fully conscious realization of the process of individuation, although this pattern is clearly visible in the material world. It is true that she took an unusual amount of responsibility herself in the last scene. But she was very much enabled to do so by the enormous amount of support and help she had received throughout, particularly from the archbishop. It was indeed no mean achievement for Jeanne to admit her complete dependence on

---

47. [Elsewhere, Barbara Hannah writes: "I have often quoted Jung's statement that men overcome by killing the dragon and women by accepting their suffering, but in a full process of individuation—for either a man or a woman—both have to be done." Barbara Hannah, *The Archetypal Symbolism of Animals* (Wilmette, Ill.: Chiron Publications, 2006), p. 318. *Ed.*]

the whole group and to ask their help—as Mary Magdalene commanded her to do—when she sketched the final scene.

Perhaps indeed the most striking factor in the whole case is the gradual emergence of the figure of Mary Magdalene. She comes after Jeanne makes her first gesture toward accepting her transference onto the archbishop by falling at his feet. That is, Jeanne moves toward replacing an imaginary drama by respect for a human man where power would have to be sacrificed and replaced by the principle of love. This was not only an individual matter for Jeanne, for her possession caused a profound disturbance in the life of the community, to which balance could only be restored by concerted communal effort. One might liken Mary Magdalene to the framework of the crystal in the solution as Jeanne, the archbishop, Mainsent, and the whole community of nuns are gradually drawn into her originally invisible pattern, a pattern that the demons were the first to foresee. It is also striking that the exorcists dealt directly with the demons—except in the final scene—whereas all of Mary Magdalene's commands came thorough Jeanne. Here, we have a vivid picture of the way the negative animus can be replaced by a positive source of influence and control and an image of the way the ego can be replaced by the Self, which is, however, only possible in relationship. As Jung also once said in a seminar: "One cannot individuate on Mount Everest," a statement that applies as well to a case such as Jeanne's.[48]

If the demand to live in the house of the archbishop had come from the ego, it would have represented a gigantic plot. But as

---

48. ["One cannot individuate on top of Mount Everest or in a cave somewhere where one doesn't see people for seventy years: one only can individuate with or against something or somebody. Being an individual is always a link in a chain, it is not an absolutely detached situation, in itself only, with no connection outside . . . . If you think with concentration, you realize how much you are connected with other human beings, how little you can exist without being related, without responsibilities and duties and the relation of other people to yourself . . . . Individuation is only possible with people, through people." C. G. Jung, *Nietzsche's Zarathustra: Notes of the Seminar Given in 1934–1939* (Princeton, N.J.: Princeton University Press, 1988), p. 102f. Jung defines individuation as: "a process of differentiation . . . having for its goal the development of the individual human personality . . . as distinct from the general, collective psychology." C. G. Jung, *Psychological Types* (1921), *CW*, vol. 6 (Princeton, N.J.: Princeton University Press, 1971), par. 757. *Ed.*]

it came from the figure of Mary Magdalene, one needs to ask oneself from Jeanne's point of view (as we do not know that of the archbishop) why such a plotlike set up was encouraged, or even instigated, by this superhuman figure. I cannot answer this question, for the figure of Mary Magdalene goes beyond what I can understand. But it fits in with what I have seen of deep, fatal plots. (I am not speaking of the superficial plots that we see every-day.) While a woman, for instance, is unable to get even a whiff of what is meant by an unreasonably strong transference, the unconscious will rub her nose in its concrete side so that she does understand; it almost obliges her to make the most unreasonable demands (such as forcing the archbishop to face a raging scandal in his own diocese). Then it will compel her—very likely for reasons she herself is not yet conscious of—to sacrifice all demands of every kind on the material side as Jeanne does here. Only after such a sacrifice can the meaning of a powerful transference come to light, symbolized here by a spiritual relationship between nun and confessor.

Returning now to Mary Magdalene, we must note that she is not an easy figure to label, as is always the case with religious and mythological personalities. While speaking of the terms *ego, shadow,* and *Self* in his *Mysterium Coniunctionis,* Jung says in a footnote:

> Since I have no wish to construct a world of speculative concepts which leads merely to the barren hair-splitting of philosophical discussions, I set no particular store by [reflections on these three terms]. If such concepts provisionally serve to put the empirical material in order, they will have fulfilled their purpose.[49]

Now, we do require some such terms to clarify this material, but undoubtedly it would be quite inadequate should we just label the Mary Magdalene figure as the Self. Since she first appeared to Jeanne when kneeling at the feet of the archbishop,

---

49. Jung, *Mysterium Coniunctionis, CW,* vol. 14, par. 129, n66.

she may also have something to do with the archbishop's anima. In fact, as we shall later see, he undoubtedly got somewhat caught in the countertransference, so we shall probably not be too far off if we assume that there was actually some connection between the anima of the archbishop and the divine feminine figure in Jeanne's unconscious.

A detail we should not overlook is that it was Mary Magdalene who received the blessing from the archbishop in Jeanne's name. We are expressly told that Jeanne only saw a great light and a divine feminine figure and that initially she did not recognize the figure as Mary Magdalene. We are not told whether or not the archbishop saw her, but it is pretty clear from what comes afterward that he did not. So we should first consider why the figure is so interesting. We could take Mary Magdalene as the more mature personality in Jeanne, or at any rate as a part of her psychology, and obviously it would be that part that would receive the blessing. God is, so to speak, on the side of this part and grants it his grace. Actually, man (that is, the unredeemed ego) cannot take God's grace directly; it can only be assimilated in so far as man has an immortal soul, a similar nature as God, and only this part of man can receive the positive effect of God's grace. Jeanne did receive it directly two years afterward, but then at the demand of Mary Magdalene.

In *Psychology and Alchemy* Jung says:

> It would be blasphemy to assert that God can manifest Himself everywhere save only in the human soul. Indeed the very intimacy of the relationship between God and the soul automatically precludes any devaluation of the latter.[50]
>
> The fact that the devil too can take possession of the soul does not diminish [the] significance [of the soul] in the least.[51]
>
> It would be going perhaps too far to speak of an affinity; but at all events the soul must contain in itself the faculty of relation to God, that is, a correspondence, otherwise a con-

---

50. Jung, Psychology and Alchemy, CW, vol. 12, par. 11.
51. Ibid., n5.

nection could never come about. This correspondence is, in psychological terms, the archetype of the God-image.[52]

It is, therefore, psychologically quite unthinkable for God to be simply the "wholly other," for a "wholly other" could never be one of the soul's deepest and closest intimacies—which is precisely what God is. The only statements that have psychological validity concerning the God-image are either paradoxes or antinomies.[53]

The exorcism, the vision of Mary Magdalene, and the agreement that Mainsent should be her father, resulted in Cornau retiring to the extent that Mainsent concluded that he had been driven out. But Cornau carried out his threat to reduce the girl to the state of a four-year-old child, an arrangement that was accepted by the exorcists. Although preferable to the devil's intelligence, Jeanne was, nevertheless, reduced to the simplicity of childhood and only able to say "Father Jean" and "pretty Mary," showing preference for the latter. The more Mainsent persisted in the exorcism, the nearer and more real Mary Magdalene became.

There are parallels to patients being reduced to a state of childhood. One example is of a patient in a clinic who was unable to eat and was being fed artificially when another patient suggested that the food should be given in a bottle. When the bottle was brought, the patient behaved as though feeding from the breast and soon thereafter could be fed by mouth.

The main psychological significance of the final scene is that, like the little elephant, she was finally convinced that they all meant well by her, that she could risk living as an ordinary nun in that convent, and that she did not have to hang on to that brilliance that the devils provided. She admitted that the archbishop had discharged his obligations with regards to her outer nourishment but told him he must remain in charge of her conscience for the rest of her life. Apparently he accepted this charge, and she became quiet and normal and went off to the refectory with the

---

52. Ibid.
53. Ibid., n6.

other nuns. This condition was maintained and apparently there was no relapse, that is, not in the few years prior to the publication of the documents.

In a way, the solution of finally throwing out the devils and leaving good in possession of the field seems rather unsatisfactory from our point of view. But after all, the prototype in the story, Mary Magdalene, did the same, for she had lived as a prostitute until she met Christ, whom she evidently loved, and she changed into her own opposite.

I should like to turn to *Mysterium Coniunctionis* and read Jung's reflection on the nature of such transformations:

> It is obviously a moment of supreme possibilities both for good and for evil. Usually, however, it is first one and then the other: the good man succumbs to evil, the sinner is converted to good, and that, to an uncritical eye, is the end of the matter. But those endowed with a finer moral sense or deeper insight cannot deny that this seeming one-after-another is in reality a happening of events side-by-side, and perhaps no one has realized this more clearly than St. Paul who knew that he bore a thorn in the flesh and that the messenger of Satan smote him in the face lest he be "exalted above measure" (2 Cor. 12:7). The one-after-another is a bearable prelude to the deeper knowledge of the side-by-side, for this is an incomparably more difficult problem. Again, the view that good and evil are spiritual forces outside us, and that man is caught in the conflict between them, is more bearable by far than the insight that the opposites are the ineradicable and indispensable preconditions of all psychic life, so much so that life itself is guilt. Even a life dedicated to God is still lived by an ego, which speaks of an ego and asserts an ego in God's despite, which does not instantly merge itself with God but reserves for itself a freedom and a will which it sets up outside God and against him. How can it do this against the overwhelming might of God? Only through self-assertion, which is as sure of its free will as Lucifer. All distinction from

God is separation, estrangement, a falling away. The Fall was inevitable even in paradise. Therefore, Christ is "without the stain of sin" because he stands for the whole of the Godhead and is not distinct from it by reason of his manhood. Man, however, is branded by the stain of separation from God. This state of things would be insupportable if there were nothing to set against evil but the law and the Decalogue, as in pre-Christian Judaism—until the reformer and rabbi Jesus tried to introduce the more advanced and psychologically more correct view that not fidelity to the law but love and kindness are the antithesis of evil.[54]

I think this passage may answer several of our questions and shows clearly that Jeanne Fery, like her prototype Mary Magdalene, was long in the stage of one after the other. The solution which we have to strive for today is admittedly much more difficult. Although it is still one after the other, I, at all events, have learned quite a lot from this medieval example.

---

54. Jung, *Mysterium Coniunctionis, CW*, vol. 14, par. 206.

An Introductory Note on Plots

IN ORDER TO GIVE YOU, AT THE VERY BEGINNING, A SUPERFI-cial idea of what I mean by the term *plots,* one could perhaps say that they are the phenomena that can be observed wherever the irresistible force of nature meets a relatively immovable obstacle made by the human mind, such as civilization, religion, tradition, and so on. Perhaps the most marvelous examples are to be found among the Anglo-Saxons where the ideals of the "gentleman" are woven with their counterpart, the "lady," in a tradition that is most formally rooted. But lest this be seen as a direct invitation for projection, let me hasten to add that they are by no means confined to the Anglo-Saxon race. The underly-ing causes are the same everywhere. Plots manifest differently according to the tradition in which they are constellated. And more over, plots are by no means the monopoly of women, but also manifest in men.

It is difficult to stay put on such an island of discourse, for it is surrounded with enticing speculations. And even if one suc-ceeded in doing so, it is very difficult to know what to say about them. For on the one hand, things that one experiences on that island seem new to oneself, and one naively supposes that they are new to other people as well. And on the other hand, certain thing become familiar, and then one assumes that everyone knows them. Both presumptions may be wide of the mark. Thus, at best, this lecture will have the value of subjective testimony. At worst—and the worst is not shy—I do not want to help plots to appear.

A woman of forty, who, owing to her upbringing, was particularly far removed from her instincts and who describes her first encounter with plots as a painful reality, told me the following story. She had been in analysis for some years when she then began an analysis with a male analyst to whom she developed a strong transference that was also in part erotic. She had no difficulty accepting this, even its worst implications, but she was unfortunately a past master at the art of "nothing but." Thus her analyst had a hard time bringing about anything like an actual feeling realization. One day, as she was leaving an analytical hour in which she had been rather more successful than usual, she caught sight of an advertisement for automobiles. She gladly took refuge in less painful issues and began to think about how soon she could afford to buy a car as she actually needed one. The thought struck her, as she put it, "Why couldn't my analyst [who was well off] solve this problem and just give me a car?" Now this thought was so far from reality that she pleasantly played with this childish idea for few minutes when, like lightning, a second thought struck her: "You must tell him all this next time," which was followed by such a feeling of shame like she had rarely felt before. For her, it was somewhat like having a nerve exposed "along a six-inch surface." As such things happen, she chanced to hear from an outside source that evening that he was in fact actually buying a new car. This rubbed salt on that exposed nerve, because now there was an actual car to be had and he just might think that she really wanted him to give it to her. There were four days until her next hour, and they seemed to pass like four months. She knew that she had to tell him the experience, and the pain never let up for a moment. When, at last, she was actually in his consulting room, she began her hour by making an awful fuss about something quite extraneous. She was always straightforward and upright with him, so she was struck and quite troubled by the realization that something in her was wildly sidetracking the real issue in an exaggerated and dishonest manner. The tension mounted within her to the point that she simply burst into tears. Now, he had recently told her that women seldom cry solely from grief but often have some other purpose, which was even more painful because she had to admit to herself that those tears were actually a concrete plot to get that car. With no more room for subterfuge, she managed to confess the whole thing and was most grateful to her analyst for having the cool, common sense and understanding to meet the situation openly. As the pain lessened, she saw for the first time the driving force of a plot autonomously working within.

So the plot then disappears—one is hopelessly optimistic about having "outgrown them." It took many years, and many equally painful situations, to teach me that plots are always with us. But I learned one thing from my first experience: as soon as one is exposed to a new source of pain, a plot begins to stir under the surface and will soon be trying to work its way into reality. In themselves, they are pleasant, so pleasant that I think many women spend most of their lives bathing in them. But when they break unconsciously into reality, they are one of the greatest sources of pain one can suffer.

A Short Discussion on Women's Plots

I SHOULD LIKE TO MAKE CLEAR FROM THE VERY BEGINNING that I in no way regard the phenomenon of so-called "plots" as the monopoly of women. They belong rather to nature, to the dark unconscious side of human nature, and thus manifest in both men and women. Now in this dark and bewildering realm one finds that all the cats are gray, and the animus and the witch eternally battle for their very existence as autonomous beings. Their fight is to the last ditch, with every weapon in their armory employed. In this incomprehensible melee in the twilight of consciousness I have only found one relatively firm piece of ground on which I can discuss plots. And that is my own experience.[1]

The outer variations in the manifestations of plots are endless, and it would not be possible—and certainly anything but desirable—for any woman to experience more than the smallest fraction. But under these outer manifestations there seems to be a pattern—a sort of fundamental framework—on which all plots are based. This framework is apparently quite simple, but being largely outside our perception of space and time, it cannot be comprehended. It can only be experienced much as we experience other phenomena of nature, above all spiritual phenomena. This framework touches the surface in a characteristic manner, and here apparently there is a considerable difference between its manifestation in men and in women. The aim of women's plots

---

1. [Barbara Hannah writes in a footnote: "It is from this little island that I am trying to write this lecture." *Ed.*]

agrees with the nature and the main aim of woman as woman; the hooks with which she is presented in her everyday life are manifold. But the aim of women's plots does not agree with the nature and main aim of man as man, and, therefore, the hooks with which he is presented are much better concealed, at any rate to me. For this reason I am confining myself to speaking of plots as they manifest in women.

What then is the aim of these plots? It seems to be intimately connected, or even identical with, the aim of nature to continue herself by means of reproduction. It is a sort of blind urge of *extraordinary* strength and of absolute disregard for any rational facts. It is like the hen that will sit patiently on a china egg, or like a kind of tick that, as scientists have discovered, will wait for as long as fourteen years on a bush or branch in the hope of a warm-blooded animal passing underneath, onto which it can drop and hatch out its eggs.[2]

In the purely natural state, for instance in the animal realm, there is of course no question of plots. This force only becomes dangerous when it is opposed. The nature of plots has much in common with water which seeks the lowest place. If this urge is dammed up, it behaves much as water does under similar circumstances. It will wash for years (as against a stone cliff in nature, or a building, or even a human being), slowly discovering the weak spots and working on the weak spots where everything originally appears strong and secure. Then suddenly it finds its way through a crack that has opened, and slowly, or even quickly, the whole thing collapses . . . and no one understands how the catastrophe came about. People often speak of the inscrutable ways of fate much as a foolish miller might after neglecting to examine the walls of his mill beneath the water line. Though indeed they have more excuses than a miller, when the reproductive urge or the urge for control or dominion is dammed up, then it flows back out of our space and time into the unconscious where it discovers things that have been lying dormant, perhaps even for centuries. Or it finds things that

---

2. [This hypothesis has since been refuted. *Ed.*]

actually belong to the future, things which seem to act upon it like an invisible magnet.

When I first began my work on plots—now about thirty years ago—I had a fixed idea that their driving urge was due to personal repression. Experience slowly taught me that it was more a matter of a "cosmic urge" so to speak, and that personal repressions were only its opportunity for finding weak spots, as it were, in my walls. Moreover, I soon found that personal repression was by no means the greatest danger. I learned this from the fact that women who apparently had full lives as women, including marriage, children, lovers, and so on, were by no means immune to plots. In one sense they seemed to be even more exposed, because the woman who has not lived fully as a woman is usually at least aware that she bitterly regrets this fact, and she is thus more on her guard.

It is very dangerous not to realize that the driving force of plots is something cosmic and far beyond our personal control. There is a natural instinct, if we listen to it, which warns us in this respect. I began to notice, for instance, that I always spoke of *the* plot, and that if I said *my* plot, or if someone spoke to me of *your* plot, I felt an uncomfortable sense of hubris and fascination, much as we all do when reading about some great political or personal plot. We are more in a position of people living on the banks of a great river which has risen far beyond the limit recorded in history. If we do not want to imitate the foolish miller and go on talking about the inscrutable ways of fate and pitying ourselves as its helpless victims, we are bound to ask ourselves the question: "What's Hecuba to me or I to Hecuba?"[3] Though a comparison between a swollen river and Hecuba may seem far-fetched, this river is actually very nearly related to Hecuba, and indeed to all the mythological figures, particularly in their feminine aspect.

---

3. [In Greek mythology, Hecuba was the queen and wife of King Priam of Troy. Her mother was said to be a daughter of the god of the river Sangarius, the principal river of ancient Phrygia. According to one tradition, when fortune overturned the pride of the Trojans, King Priam was killed, his kingdom fell, and Hecuba was captured and imprisoned. After finding her son Polyxena dead and then discovering the corpse of her son Polydorus on the beach, she was driven mad by sorrow and began howling like a dog. *Ed.*]

One can draw an analogy between Hecuba and Scylla on account of the similarity in the legends of their deaths and transformations. Therefore, to define our river as the river of Hecuba gives us a hint as to its strange paradoxical nature. It is the dreadful sea monster Scylla before she was changed into a rock. It is she once again in a transformed state. It is the water flowing past and, in certain circumstances, it is also its own opposite: Charybdis, the sea monster sucking water in. It is very closely connected with the female principle and yet, when one least expects it, it appears as the male. It is as though the Ouroboros was just beneath the surface, forcing the unconscious human being to swirl round continually chasing his or her own tail.[4] When one is involved in such a plot, it feels to be—and actually is—a tragic fate. But probably it is all a comedy in the eyes of the gods.

What then is this Hecuba river to us, and what are we to it? We are, so to speak, its actors. We represent it on earth. But as it is nature, it will certainly not protect us from its own catastrophes unless we do everything in our power to protect ourselves. If personal repressions are not the greatest danger, it is evident that just living our biological lives more fully will do very little—or nothing at all—to protect us. But as far as my experience reaches, there are two main ways of protecting ourselves from plots: one is to increase our consciousness, and the other is to reduce our ego. For undoubtedly the two most dangerous building materials for plots are unconsciousness and the hubris of the ego. A complete unconsciousness indeed is a certain protection—as mentioned earlier, there are no plots in the animal realm—but an animal cannot protect itself from the greater, or even many of the lesser, misfortunes and catastrophes of nature.

In the animal world the male is the active partner in almost all relationships between the sexes, though there are of course exceptions such as the flight of the queen bee. It is the male bird,

---

4. [Ouroboros (or Uroborus) is an ancient symbol depicting a serpent or dragon swallowing its own tail and thus forming a circle. It generally symbolizes cyclicality and primordial unity in religion and mythology, as well as the *prima materia*, primordial unity, and the *opus* and *lapis* in alchemy. See C. G. Jung, *Psychology and Alchemy* (1944), *CW*, vol. 12 (Princeton, N.J.: Princeton University Press, 1953), par. 404 and fig. 147. *Ed.*]

for instance, that wears the bright plumage to attract the passive female, and with very primitive peoples the same principle tends to prevail. Perhaps, therefore, we could say that when the art of attraction goes over to the female, she begins to take up, at first quite unconsciously, her bisexual nature, and the Ouroboros thus rises nearer to the surface. It then becomes her imperative need to come to terms with her bisexual nature, but, as she does not recognize the male within, she finds it projected onto men. Her passive role is thus disturbed, and she begins to chase men herself. She chases them and runs away from them at one and the same time.

Man has had some notion that his own soul is feminine since ancient days. I think this plays more of a role in his relationships and attitudes toward women than is generally acknowledged. But the knowledge that her spirit is masculine—or rather, strictly speaking, appears to her subjectively in its masculine aspect—seems somehow to be rather lacking in women. The fact which has so often been mentioned here, that about ninety percent of the symbols that we possess come to us from man, may perhaps have formed many layers over the original image in her unconscious. Moreover, the Judeo-Christian religions have provided her with an external, masculine image in which, presumably, her spirit is better contained than the feminine soul of man. At any rate, in England the congregations at church services consist of about seventy-five percent women. She is thus even more accustomed than man to seek the spirit or soul outside herself. We cannot be surprised then that woman is so absolute in her relation to man: he not only represents himself but also to a great extent her hope of immortality.

The projection of the soul onto the other sex is of course common to both men and women, and as we all know, men also sometimes project it entirely onto one woman when they are completely contained by her. We also know that a great deal of the more absolute quality in the attitude of women to men can be explained by biological reasons: it is her duty as a mother, for instance, to keep the man's interest centered on herself and to fight off other women, so that his time and libido (or to put it more bluntly while leaving all higher considerations out of the question—his money) may all be spent on her and her children. Whether or not there are any children, the nature of her outer relationship to the man (if there is any relationship at all) plays little role whatsoever in this blind urge. It is, as we have seen, like the hen, and even if there are no real eggs, there is never any lack of substitutes.

There is, however, a tendency to panic, which I have frequently observed both in myself and in other women, when a projection identified with one particular man begins to move away from him or even onto another man. As far as my observation goes, which admittedly is not very far, man does not suffer from this kind of panic, at any rate not so often or as severely.

I do not think that the biological urge explains it sufficiently; the hen does not mind which cock fertilizes her eggs—or as a matter of fact whether they are fertilized at all—and we know that women can be quite as promiscuous as men, if not more so. It therefore seems to me that women are less aware that their spirit is masculine than men that their soul is feminine. Thus when there is any sign that the projection is moving, she is inclined to become absolutely disoriented and prey to blind panic. Or, to express it differently, is it not more difficult for women to take back the projection of the spirit onto men than vice versa? Perhaps because she has forgotten, or never knew? That is, until Jung discovered the animus and that her spirit is masculine.

In any case it seems to me that it is exceedingly important for us to keep in mind that it is a matter of the projection of the spirit, or else we shall certainly be in danger of interpreting the plots from too negative an angle.

Before we turn to the empirical material on which I propose to test out the speculations I have been unable to resist, I would like to say a few words about the moral aspect of the matter. There is no question of good and evil in the blind underlying urge in a plot. It apparently does not consider its own results any more than the wave considers whether there is a human being on a rock when it breaks over it. It merely follows its own nature and is itself. The very consideration of good and evil belongs to the obstacles with which this force has to contend. It does not consider whether the path to its own purpose will agree with the moral conscience of the human being that it is using as its tool. And here, as the walls of civilization and increased consciousness have driven the blind force of plots further and further back, it seems as if the animus, that is, the woman's spirit, has made a plot itself with the devil to keep women unconscious at any price in order that she will continue to take the apple blindly and give it to Adam. Perhaps Adam has to some small extent realized the consequences of eating the apple, but has Eve? The very existence of the plot seems to prove that she has not, but I must make it very clear here that by Adam I mean the male side of the total human being, and by Eve the female side.

An Introduction to Women's Plots

IT HAS NOT BEEN SO VERY LONG SINCE WE STUDIED THE ANI-
mus of creative women as rendered by women authors in English
literature.[1] This time we will look at the animus from a very different standpoint, that of animus possession in women, a standpoint that we unfortunately often meet in practical analysis. In a
seminar, Jung once went as far as to say that mankind has always
been possessed by the anima or the animus.

To publish such a statement and to talk about it in a seminar
are two very different things. So here today you can ask questions,
you can bring your own experiences, you can object and so on, so
that there should be no fear of a misunderstanding.

If I understand Jung correctly, he meant the following: as far
as we are comfortable being collective entities, herd animals as it
were, living by traditional values, opinions, codes of morals, senti-
ments, and so on—without having it out individually with any or
all of the above—then, whether we know it or not, we shall be
possessed in the sense of living for a foreign will, be it that of the
animus or the anima or whatever. The less we know it, the more
we are possessed.

Now in this century it is possible more than ever to ask ourselves directly: "Why did I do that?" And even to answer: "I
don't know." Even answering in the negative is a step toward
breaking the possession, for at that moment we are already no

---

1. [See Barbara Hannah's essay "Animus Figures in Literature and in Modern Life" in
volume 1 of this work. *Ed.*]

longer identical with the animus (or anima) in their original state. Nevertheless, it is indeed easy to go along the familiar given paths during an entire lifetime without even asking this simple question.

Last summer, I joined several cousins for lunch whom I had not seen since I was a child. Two of three brothers and a sister were all still living in a house inherited from their parents; everything exactly in the pattern I remember so well from my childhood. Instead of new horses they spoke of new cars, which was one of the few differences I could detect. They are good-natured, easygoing people, so we all got along quite pleasantly. Yet as far as I could see, also quite meaninglessly. I remember Jung once said to me of such a life: well, if the Tibetans are right and there is a Bardo where we go between existence, Mr. So-and-So will very soon not be able to remember this existence at all.

In the case of my cousins, it is not only meaningless, but three of the four remained unmarried; the old pattern has so encompassed them that they presumably have each been cheated of his or her individual life.

When that good-heartedness is somehow missing, then things can go terribly wrong. In fact, Germany in the time of the Nazis taught us that this good-heartedness is only a protection when the outer world has some stability, for the Germans as a whole are very good-natured. And even under such conditions that good-naturedness can hold, as it did with some cases in Germany.[2] However, it can also give way most disastrously. For many "good-hearted" people were unable to stand their ground and found themselves "possessed" by crimes that apparently were otherwise foreign to their nature. I found out from my experience with one case—this person was not in analysis with me—something similar can happen even without the collective background. There are also quite nice people who are apparently living as their ancestors had done. They are very rich, so they manage somehow or other to maintain a household much as we all did in my youth, but which in my case, and in ninety-five percent of the other cases, had collapsed long ago for want of money.

---

2. [Barbara Hannah mentions here an aunt named Herda. *Ed.*]

Now my cousins' father died young, so the three sons and a daughter lived on with their mother. The sons did go to work, so they got away by day at least, and sometimes they were away longer for business trips. The daughter however remained in the set up, slept in her mother's bedroom, and played the role of the indispensable daughter, sacrificing herself for the beloved mother, although there actually were several servants and a resident hospital nurse. The mother died before I knew the family, but she was undoubtedly the prototype of the self-sacrificing and secretly devouring mother of the very worst kind. Although the mother was originally to blame, there was then also her mother before her, and a long ancestral line of women all caught in a similar self-sacrificing pattern.

One interesting thing was the effect of the mother's death on the daughter. She was nearly forty when the mother died and had remained more or less anonymous, unnoticed in the background up till then. True, she spoke about a profession she longed to follow, but she nevertheless stayed at home playing the self-sacrificing martyr, naturally without coming out into the open about it. She was indeed a pleasant girl, but when the mother died she proved herself to be equally possessed by what may well be called the "family animus" or "family spirit." One brother had married a woman who was very much suited to his mother, that is, a girl she could well manage. And after the mother's death, one of the other sons was at least able to realize how much he loved a woman he knew. Now, his sister had applied for a position in the profession she had always longed for, and almost by miracle—due to her age—she was accepted. However, the very day she learned that her brother intended to marry, she secretly gave up the appointment, said it was her sacred duty to make a home for her brothers who "could not live without her," and proceeded to settle down to destroying their lives much as her mother had done before. In fact, she went a good bit further, attacked the marriage that her mother had tolerated in order to have that brother also in her power. Though all three of these cousins are endangered by a hereditary tendency toward alcoholism, the sister determined to convert their large house into a hotel and to have the most endangered brother always at home managing, of all things, the bar.

This is naturally a rather dramatic case of negative animus possession, but it serves to show how innocuous these patterns are and how they can function unconsciously in the background unnoticed by all. Of course similar patterns are at work in us all. It takes a lot of courage and is often for many long years a daunting task, because a long-established state of affairs is not changed in a day. But if we want to know who we are and live our own genuine individual pattern, it is absolutely unavoidable. Analysis is the greatest possible help, but one can achieve a lot by hard work, as we see in the case of Jane Austen, who produced an extraordinary change in her animus and carried an amazing objectivity by sheer realism and by taking apart and refusing illusions on principle.

People often complain that we talk too much here of the negative animus, and that they want to hear about the positive animus. However, if we are in a patch of bad weather, it is not much use saying we would prefer the sun. Furthermore, it is an empirical fact that the animus appears first in his negative aspect, and only if this negative aspect is completely accepted and grappled with does he show his positive side in anything but sporadic flashes. This is the pattern we are all faced with. Are we going to take the risk? Every attempt to come to terms with the animus hinges on this. In a way, it is like the story of Moses of the Qur'an.[3]

However, it won't be explained to us or become evident until we have lived its bitterness through to the end. To take the example of the girl and her brothers: now if she could face the fact that she is literally cultivating a situation that will lead to her brothers' death, if she could accept her plot consciously, then immediately it would begin to change. But while she deceives herself—playing the role of the self-sacrificing sister, fostering illusions and delusions—her plot may well succeed with one or more of her brothers, and she may easily discourage one or the

---

3. [Barbara Hannah refers here to the story of the angel Chidr. See her discussion of the Book of Tobit in this volume. *Ed.*]

other to death . . . or at least into becoming hopeless drunkards. In women's plots, which are always rooted in animus possession, one can see the truth of Christ's logion: "If thou knowest what thou doest, thou art blest, but if thou knowest not, thou art curst and a breaker of the law."[4]

Naturally, I could not tell you how the sister's plot would work out if the girl was up to becoming conscious of her plot, because consciousness is never able to guess the infinite days of the unconscious. I can say, however, that I never yet saw a plot come out destructively when the woman was able to see it and go forward "through the dark cloud." Then, as far as my experience goes, it always had a positive conclusion. The trouble is that just seeing it intellectually is not nearly enough; you have to see it totally, you must have the courage not to retreat. This takes valor and substance.

Many of you may remember the marvelous passage from Richard de St. Victor when he speaks of self-knowledge as a great and high mountain, the greatest value of all.[5] Plato, Aristotle, and many philosophers failed in their search because they did not realize that the greatest truth of all is "know thyself." The prototype of the problem can be found in the fairy tale (which Jung related) where an old man first steals the cow, that is, shows himself first in a purely negative role, and only then helps the boy.[6]

This story also shows the prototype of the animus problem per se. At first, the animus apparently has to be negative. How could he have got the boy on the path that led to the mountain

---

4. C. G. Jung, *Visions: Notes of the Seminar Given in 1930–1934* (London: Routledge, 1998), p. 1226.

5. [Richard of St. Victor, a Scot, was one of the most important mystical theologians of the twelfth century in Paris, the intellectual center of Europe at that time. He was a student of the great German mystic Hugo of St. Victor, whose principles and methods he adopted and elaborated. Greater interest belongs today to his mystical and devotional theology which is mainly contained in two books on mystical contemplation entitled respectively *Benjamin Minor* and *Benjamin Major* along with an allegorical treatise on the Tabernacle. His career was strictly monastic, and his relations with the outer world were few and slight. Richard was the prior of the famous Augustinian Abbey of Saint-Victor in Paris from 1162 until his death in 1173. *Ed.*]

6. [Barbara Hannah discusses this fairy tale in "Jeanne Fery: A Case Study on the Animus, Possession, and Exorcism" in this volume. *Ed.*]

of self-knowledge unless he had hooked him out of his traditional pattern of servitude with peasants? Once the boy had lost the cow, he dared not return, for the peasants would have beaten him to death. It is as if the animus forces us to act, yanking us out of our traditional background by preventing our return to those patterns.

My cousin, who relatively unconsciously works toward destroying her brothers, is a woman embedded in her family psychology. She was raised by old-fashioned parents who thought they had children for their own convenience. And the mothers, sacrificing the development of their own animus potential and remaining in the protective confines of motherhood, pass the pattern on to their daughters who then fool themselves as well by pledging their lives to similar convictions: "It is a girl's true and honored duty to sacrifice herself and look solely after her brothers" (or parents or whatever). And so doing they avoid struggling to develop their own mental and spiritual needs. Now really the only thing the animus can do when caught in such a dilemma is react negatively, that is, make this woman destroy something, in this case her brothers. Because only the shock of realizing what she is doing, namely, that she is actually setting up a situation in which they cling to her and drink themselves to death, could possibly convince her that she was anything but their guardian angel. Now the sooner such a family pattern is broken up the better. It also gives the brothers a chance; because they have fallen into the age-old woman's plot in this family, they are themselves beyond taking anything in hand and would rather be comfortable, mollycoddled, nurtured, and directed—neatly avoiding their own mental and emotional development—than face their weaknesses in a man's world and with women. Such a plot is so obvious that even a mother-bound man should have little difficulty seeing it for himself.

Now, if she could see her plot and take on the intense depression and fear, which includes that black cloud through which she would have to pass, then she would be well on the way toward a positive end. For it takes a lot of courage and integrity to see that all of your wonderful and altruistic plans are just a camouflaged plot of Queen Antinea with her mausoleum of dead men, and that you are more of a destructive witch than a guardian angel.[7] Although perhaps you are not quite so bad, for fortunately we do not all aspire to be such angels, it is pretty much the same pattern for us all. Only if we can see and accept the negative plots in which our animus has entangled us is there any hope of our reaching his positive side and winning through to a worthwhile end.

There is a Siberian fairy tale in which the animus appears as a one-legged, one-handed, and one-eyed graybeard who awakens a dead man with an iron staff. In the course of the story, the protagonist is killed by a murderer several times, and each time he is brought back to life by this one-sided figure. Finally, after being brought back to life several times, he succeeds in killing the murderer, but in that struggle he also kills the one-sided old man, the identity of the two victims being affiliated, the old man possibly being essentially his own opposite, a life-bringer as well as a death-dealer, as is said of Hermes.[8] In a Balkan fairy tale, an old man in the guise of an evildoer is caught up in all the twists and turns of an individuation process that ends suggestively with the *hieros gamos*.[9]

Here, again, in the fairy tales of this one-sided old graybeard and the evil murderer, we see why it is so difficult to see our animus plots, and we see how the animus can be negatively constellated in the beginning with no hope in sight. We all originally think one-sidedly. People like Tertullian, who can think paradoxically, are very rare.[10] One can learn to do so to some extent, but it

---

7. [Barbara Hannah is referring to the startling beauty, Queen Antinea, the granddaughter of the great kings of the mythological Atlantis. She keeps an underground mausoleum with the numbered and labeled bodies of her former lovers, who spend one glorious single night with her before she has them murdered. See footnote 28 in "The Problem of Women's Plots in Marie Hay's *The Evil Vineyard*" in this volume. *Ed.*]

8. C. G. Jung, "The Phenomenology of the Spirit in Fairytales" (1948), in *CW*, vol. 9i (Princeton, N.J.: Princeton University Press, 1968), par. 413.

9. Ibid., par. 418.

10. [Barbara Hannah refers here to the Catholic patriarch Quintus Septimus Florens Tertullianus (Tertullian), circa 160–225 A.D., born in Carthage. Tertullian is known for his sublime confession: *Credo quia absurdum est* (I believe, because it is absurd), which is a great simplification—or misquote—of what he actually wrote: "The Son of God was crucified: I am not ashamed—because it is shameful. The Son of God died: it is immediately

is a much later stage in the process than first seeing our own plots and the animus behind them. Therefore, when we turn and face ourselves and our animus negativity, we are bound to go through the black cloud as if it were the only reality. If this woman with the three brothers ever went into analysis, no analyst could or should spare her the devastating realization that she truly wanted somewhere within her unconscious to destroy her brothers. And if you have enough conscience and ethos to see and face down such a thing at all, then you are going to suffer hellishly. The other side will only become visible after you have suffered sufficiently.

There is one aspect which I have left out and which must certainly be mentioned, otherwise we may fall into the error of thinking that plotting is only a matter of women and their animuses. In reality, some of the most ingenious and unconscious plots I have ever seen were the plots of men. Here is one of the great differences between the two sexes in respect to plots. Jung notes that women's plots are more personal, while men's are more distant in a sense and more likely to be coming from the collective and superpersonal layer of the unconscious. Our discussion started with a comment from Jung in response to mine: that men's and women's plots were very different, as men's were anima plots. Jung commented also then that men's plots were more mythological in nature.

One can see this essential difference quite well if we compare two great political leaders such as Churchill and Hitler. In one way, one could say that they were both striving for a similar spiritual ideal: a new Europe, or even a new world. But Hitler was hopelessly idealistic and mythological about his vision despite the intense personal nature of his dream. The Third Reich was to center primarily around Hitler as a mythological hero of all time and also around the German people only in so far as they were supermen and superwomen destined to subjugate and rule the inferior races of the rest of the world. Hitler was practically

credible—because it is absurd. He was buried, and rose again: it is certain—because it is impossible." Also see Jung's discussion of Tertullian in *Psychological Types* (1921), *CW*, vol. 6 (Princeton, N.J.: Princeton University Press, 1971), par. 17. *Ed.*]

unrelated to the personal, everyday side of people, particularly so with women. Whereas he had practically no relationships of a personal nature with men, he had for all intents and purposes no down-to-earth relationships whatsoever with women. He never consummated sexual relations with Eva Braun, his so-called partner and secretary, who calculated and secured her relationship to Hitler by means of this savior complex, cleverly staging several suicide attempts at appropriate times on his premises, thus effectively sealing their fates. Here one sees the personal nature of the woman's plot, cunningly and shrewdly positioning herself to become the one and only woman in Germany to possess the glorified Hitler (even though she had little other than the glory and the illusion). Her plot is far different in nature to Hitler's ideological ambitions for Germany and an Aryan world. Their relationship took place in a rather imaginary realm, the down-to-earth relationship being filled with quarrels and fights. For Hitler, relationships with women hovered in the mythological realms of the gods, of which he was one. He did attempt to make relationships with some men as a buffer between himself and his anima's appalling personal travesty of the idea of a new world.[11] Yet it all ended in complete destruction: the Thousand Year Reich deteriorated into total self-annihilation within twenty years after its conception with Hitler taking millions upon millions with him to their—unfortunately—very personal and down-to-earth deaths. Sheer destruction of unimaginable dimensions was all that was accomplished by Hitler's anima-possessed ideology, his grand mythology, and his wildly ambitious plot to rule the world.

Winston Churchill was by no means without personal ambition. In his boyhood and youth he was unpopular on this account. But he was able to learn from personal experience (a thing which the dictators seem to forget) and, at least in his own way, tried to do what he could with the so-called "nearest compartment,"

---

11. [Hitler's asexuality with women, his megalomaniac and inhumanly ice-cold manner in dealing with his own soldiers and the German people at large, as well as certain pedophilic and homosexual interests, are documented in a scholarly psychobiography by Manfred Koch-Hillebrecht. See Manfred Koch-Hillebrecht, *Homo Hitler: Psychogramm eines deutschen Diktators* (Munich: Wilhelm Goldmann Verlag, 1999). *Ed.*]

that is, his anima. He did manage to stay married for over fifty years and had several children, and they gave him a lot of trouble, which he seems to have done what he could do to resolve. No doubt he was a difficult father, but at least he did not funk this vital side of life. One of his daughters once said that her father had always wanted to relate to exceptional women—such as great actresses—but he just didn't know how.[12] She said that he was like a schoolboy in this respect, never really growing up but never discouraged by his invariable failures. He just went on admiring them from a distance.

Before he was called upon by the Second World War to play a leading role in world politics, Churchill had done what he could to learn something of the compartment nearest to men and to do something about the nuances of his feeling life and a certain kind of relatedness in a down-to-earth fashion in the real world. In other words, he had not starved and ignored the finer nuances and worldly needs of his anima as had Hitler. Churchill was able to offer a very different level to the spiritual idea of a united Europe or world and to be satisfied with what he personally had without being driven blindly by his anima to strive at absolutely all costs—to everyone—as had Hitler. Out of this differentiation it was possible for England to play its leading political role worldwide during Churchill's career. He was even able to give up the idea of the British Empire (terribly dear to nearly every Briton) and substitute the idea of the Commonwealth. In other words, Churchill was able to live out his mythological plot also in a positive, down-to-earth manner and to work toward a constructive goal for all—and not just his own anima. God knows to what extent he has actually succeeded, but at all events one feels he had done all he could, and much of that was very much personally related to the everyday man and woman. So much for a very short look at men's plots in comparison to those of women.

Now, the animus is the real originator and plotter of every

---

12. [His marriage proposal to Ethel Barrymore was turned down, yet his interest apparently did not recede and was again fostered by his daughter, Sarah, an actress and dancer who, for instance, costarred with Fred Astaire in the film *Royal Wedding. Ed.*]

far-reaching plot in women, that is, he thinks them out almost entirely "behind the woman's back" so to speak . This I hope to show in a couple of our examples. Yet in that compartment which is next to our consciousness, we have all sorts of semiconscious wishes and goals that we don't make conscious, even though we could. If we knew these, the animus's plots could be far less destructive and less personal.

In "Woman in Europe" Jung says:

> The indirect method of woman is dangerous, for it can hope-lessly compromise her aim. That is why she longs for greater consciousness which would enable her to name her goal and give it meaning, and thus escape the blind dynamism of nature.[13]

It is this inability to name our goal that makes us reluctant to enter the compartment nearest to our consciousness, namely the animus. It is as difficult for us as it is for a man to take up and differentiate his feelings and develop his relatedness in his near-est compartment. Not doing so will have the same result in both cases. If women do not know what they really want, the plot will turn out destructively, just as Hitler's did, largely because he had done little about his nearest compartment—that is, feeling and relatedness. Jung says further in "Woman in Europe":

> Masculinity means knowing what one wants and doing what is necessary to achieve it. Once this lesson has been learned, it is so obvious that it can never again be forgotten without tremendous psychic loss.[14]

Therefore, to enter that nearest compartment for women means entering masculinity. Even unconscious men usually do know what they want and do their best to achieve it. But unconscious

---

13. C. G. Jung, "Woman in Europe" (1927), in *CW*, vol. 10 (Princeton, N.J.: Princeton University Press, 1964), par. 275.

14. Ibid., par. 260.

women never do. They all too often—like the woman with three brothers, though this is admittedly an extreme example—are convinced that they really want their brothers' best good or that they are sacrificing what they want, their "chosen profession," for this illustrious end. But then why give up that profession the very day the brother gets engaged and veers toward independence? What was the need to give it up at all?

I am convinced that my cousin has no idea what she really wants, and from my experience of such women it is also the last thing she wants to know. Unconscious women take refuge behind such clichés as: "It doesn't matter what I want, it is what other people want" or "I live for other people" and such tripe. In all fairness to them, this is the way they were educated and drilled from the time they could talk, as was their own mother and the mothers before them. But they are really avoiding the effort of moving into the masculine realm of "knowing their goal."

In the same way, unconscious men (with certain exceptions) often do know what they want to do in life and have outer goals, but they get terribly upset when they have to discover and face what they feel, how infantile, moody, or whatever else they are, or who they really want, to relate to, and who not, and so on. They are all too inclined to leave all that feeling stuff blindly to the anima who will kindly produce sentimental moods and ideals or project herself onto who knows what kind of a woman. Thus the anima fascination—which probably has little to do with the actual woman herself—can settle the problem on her own, and he can comfortably allow himself to be seduced and pampered in order to go along. And in a similar manner, animus opinions settle the problem for women. In both cases, however, it has really been settled by anima or animus possession, but we don't notice it, for as Jung said, mankind has always been possessed.[15]

It is, of course, an almost superhuman effort to question things that have always been taken for granted. The easiest and most

---

15. See C. G. Jung, "The Meaning of Psychology for Modern Man" (1934), in *CW*, vol. 10 (Princeton, N.J.: Princeton University Press, 1964), pars. 287, 309; "After the Catastrophe" (1945), in *CW*, vol. 10 (Princeton, N.J.: Princeton University Press, 1964), par. 431.

tempting thing is to go on in the old rut with woman blindly letting her animus look after her goals and man making himself the
fool in pursuit of his feelings and his love life through the fascina-
tions of his anima. But once it has been realized that women can
know their goal, that is, what they—and not what their animus—
want, and men learning to follow themselves—and not what their
anima dictates and others want them to feel—then, the freedom
and the consciousness gained "is so obvious that it is never again
forgotten without tremendous psychic loss."[16]

Anyone who has really tried to apply Jungian psychology to
herself or himself, that is, not just using it as an intellectual pursuit, will have realized this, and then we can only go forward, for
to go back to unconsciousness means too great a loss.

Jung says that the thinking out of the plot is not so much the
actual business of the anima. Right behind the plot, on a large
scale at all events, there is always the archetype or the archetypal
idea. As ideas are in the direct hands of the animus, so here the
animus has a more direct connection to the plots than the anima
does. For while she stands unseen between the man and his
plots, she will twist them to her feminine and personal purposes
rather than think them out herself. Where the animus convinces,
the anima tantalizes. So it is essential for the man to begin by
becoming conscious of his anima and her world of feelings and
relatedness, for he really cannot see his plots or hers until he has.
Whereas plots lie much closer to a woman's personal calculations,
it is also her own personal (though too unconscious) wishes that
are nurturing them along.

But we will now leave the plots until we come to the example
that concerns them and try to get a more direct idea of the
animus in the first place—as these lectures primarily concern
him—but also of the anima, for our examples can be analyzed
from both sides.

Before we start on our material, I should just like to present
to those who were there, as well as those who were not, a very
brief resume of "putting the animus in the resin" which we used

16. Jung, "Woman in Europe," in *CW*, vol. 10, par. 260.

as a sort of leitmotif in our last lecture on the animus.[17] The idea comes from a patient's visions which Jung used for over a period of eleven terms in his seminars, and in this particular vision, the woman found a piece of amber in which there was the suffering face of a man. This man she eventually freed from the amber.[18]

Amber, as you know, is made of resin that has been under the sea for a long period of time. Quoting Jung, and turning to our own material that we were then discussing, we spoke about the over-activity of the animus that occurs when we are in a state of animus possession. This over-activity is reduced by pinning him down—mostly by becoming conscious of him and struggling with him—a process which, in the text of the legendary alchemist Maria Prophetissa, is portrayed as sticking the man in gum arabic or resin, in which the anima is stopped. It is Maria Prophetissa who emphasizes the importance of the sticky substance in her maxim, "Marry gum with gum in true marriage," which was repeatedly quoted by the later alchemists. In *Psychology and Alchemy* Jung comments that "originally it was gum arabic, and it was used here as a secret name for the transforming substance."[19]

I do not want to go into this aspect in any detail again but just wanted to explain briefly what I mean when I use the term "put the animus in the resin," for we used it so much last time that I am sure it will slip out from time to time again here.

17. [See Barbara Hannah's essay "Animus Figures in Literature and in Modern Life" in volume 1 of this work. *Ed.*]

18. Jung, *Visions: Notes of the Seminar Given in 1930–1934*, p. 611.

19. C. G. Jung, *Psychology and Alchemy* (1944), *CW*, vol. 12 (Princeton, N.J.: Princeton University Press, 1953), par. 209.

Introduction to "The Problem of Women's Plots in Marie Hay's The Evil Vineyard"

WE WILL TRY NOW TO OBSERVE OUR *SPIRITUS RECTOR*—THAT IS, our animus—in an extreme example. Jung speaks about Marie Hay's *The Evil Vineyard* already in 1925.[1] And when I said I would like to write a lecture on "women's plots" he recommended it to me as the best example he knew. We took the liberty to regard it then, and I shall take it again now, as an actual plot in real human life, just the type of plot that real women spin unbeknownst to themselves when they have no idea of their animus or what he is up to. It is far more favorable, of course, when the *spiritus rector* spins his plot in a novel and not in the woman's actual life, and this is one of the reasons why creative work has such a favorable effect: it gives one an opportunity to see the kind of cocoon that one's particular animus is likely to spin.

When I use the word *plot* in the sense of women's "plots" (not as in novels but in real life), I mean that their animus is spinning a plot with a purpose or goal of which the woman herself is relatively unconscious. As we shall see in this book, it is not wholly unconscious, but it is more a matter of compartmental psychology.[2]

Now, men also occasionally get caught up in plots, but with men, plots tend to be wholly in the realm of the anima. It is not

---

1. Marie Hay, *The Evil Vineyard* (London: Tauchnitz, 1923).
2. See below the example of Jung's patient who was having five affairs and managed to keep his own consciousness of them compartmentalized.

so much compartmental psychology; they are actually unaware of them and cannot even know them until they become conscious—to quite a high degree—of their anima. Moreover, when anima plots play a role, her work is best considered in men who are outright anima possessed. (And here they can amaze one by being even worse than a woman's.) But with most men, they play less of an overt and blatant daily role and are best seen in extramarital affairs, political convictions, and high-level crime where men seem to be rather in a fog about what they are doing. These plots then have the characteristic of a "mist-ifying" and highly feminine psychology. As we shall see, women tend to have a certain consciousness of their plots. Thoughts concerning them shoot through their mind but are immediately forgotten again because it would disturb their *spiritus rector* (in his nefarious role). For these plots aim at the goal he is attempting to bring into reality. We find this same process described in Goethe's *Faust* in the incident of Philemon and Baucis.[3] Faust just petulantly wishes they would give him over their ground, as it is a sort of Naboth's vineyard in his enormous estate.[4] Mephistopheles brings his wish into fulfillment by killing Philemon and Baucis, and then Faust is full of injured innocence and reproaches. Goethe, however, makes it very clear that when Faust wishes for something at all passionately, Mephistopheles will go to any lengths to fulfill his desire, and we see exactly the same process at work in women's plots. They want something passionately, and their animus will spin the web by which they attain it. Unconscious women keep an aim tightly locked up in one compartment and—although they know of it somewhere all the time and sometimes enter the compartment themselves—they are careful always to keep it locked up so that there shall be no fusion among compartments.

3. [The elderly Philemon and his wife Baucis live in poverty in a hut on the edge of the city, yet are extraordinarily generous in hosting two unknown guests. These then turn out to be two gods who reward the couple with a golden temple and priesthood. Goethe adds the formidable twist that Faust, desiring their abode, sets Mephistopheles to the task of forcing them to move, which leads to them being murdered when they refuse. *Ed.*]

4. [Naboth's vineyard (1 Kings 21) is a reference to the story of Jezebel who perfidiously plots Naboth's death so that her husband, King Ahab, can append Naboth's vineyard onto his palace gardens. All ends in disaster, Ahab and Jezebel both condemned to be eaten by dogs. *Ed.*]

The Problem of Women's Plots in *Marie Hay's* The Evil Vineyard

WHEN I USE THE WORD *PLOT*, I MEAN A PURPOSE OR GOAL that we ignore. In masculine psychology the plots belong in the realm of the anima, and men really do not know their plots until they know their anima.[1] But with women it is more a matter of compartmental psychology. We know them quite well in one compartment, yet forget them entirely in the next. Or we know them under one aspect, yet do not recognize them when they appear under one of their many other aspects. In either case, we tend to attach too little importance to them. Thus they lead a more or less autonomous life and motivate us without our knowledge. There is a passage in "Woman in Europe" that goes right to the heart of the matter:

> The indirect method of woman is dangerous, for it can hope-lessly compromise her aim. That is why she longs for greater consciousness which would enable her to name her goal and give it meaning, and thus escape the blind dynamism of nature.[2]

---

1. [The following essay is based on the notes for Barbara Hannah's lecture delivered at the Psychology Club, Zurich, on June 15 and 19, 1948. The lecture, in a revised form, was subsequently published. See Barbara Hannah, "The Problem of Women's Plots in *The Evil Vineyard*," The Guild of Pastoral Psychology, lecture no. 51 (East Dulwich: H. H. Greaves Ltd., 1948). *Ed.*]

2. C. G. Jung, "Woman in Europe" (1927), in *CW*, vol. 10 (Princeton, N.J.: Princeton University Press, 1964), par. 275.

As long as a woman is being motivated by hidden goals that secretly support "the blind dynamism of nature," she will be misled—and will be misleading herself—when she talks about aspiring to loftier goals.[3] As Morienus says: "Take that which is trodden underfoot on the dunghill; for if thou dost not, thou wilt fall on thine head when thou wouldst climb without steps."[4] Women's plots are literally on the "dunghill"; they have been thrown away by women for generations, perhaps always. For up until the last decades, how often has woman ever been in the position to openly and honestly reflect upon and realize her goals? Let alone actually "name her goal"? To quote again from "Woman in Europe":

> Masculinity means knowing what one wants and doing what is necessary to achieve it. Once this lesson has been learned, it is so obvious that it can never again be forgotten without tremendous psychic loss."[5]

Now, when attempting to integrate her masculine side, the woman of today is put in an awkward position. If you will excuse a lame analogy, it is rather like suddenly having to ride a bicycle consciously, a thing that can really only be done instinctively. If one thinks where one should put one's weight, one falls off at once. Therefore, the temptation not to think about our plots is almost irresistible. But, once we have learned the value of "naming our goal," we must face the inevitable consequences, painful and laming as they are.

The Evil Vineyard can be a great help to us in this respect, for it is the story of a very unconscious woman who was involved in,

---

3. [Barbara Hannah notes: This means that if one refuses to accept what one has spurned, it will recoil upon oneself the moment one wants to go higher. See C. G. Jung, *Psychology and Alchemy* (1944), *CW*, vol. 12 (Princeton, N.J.: Princeton University Press, 1953), par. 514. *Ed.*]

4. [Romanus Morienus was an obscure hermit and Byzantine monk who purportedly taught the art of alchemy to the royal figure Khalid (ca. 668–704), the first in the Islamic world to order the translation of alchemical texts into Arabic. Morienus authored numerous alchemical epistles. Legends abound in Arabic literature about Khalid's relationship with this alchemist-monk whose works were translated from Arabic into Latin as early as 1182 a.d. *Ed.*]

5. Jung, "Woman in Europe," in *CW*, vol. 10, par. 260.

or rather brought about, a terrible tragedy through her inability to "name her goal." In a discussion on the anima and animus, Jung noted that:

> whenever the anima is projected, she immediately surrounds herself with a peculiar historical feeling which Goethe expressed in the words: "In times gone by you were my wife or sister." Rider Haggard and [Pierre] Benoît had to go back to Greece and Egypt to give expression to this insistent historical feeling . . . .[6]

> This historical feeling always has the quality of momentousness and fatefulness, and therefore leads to the problems of immortality and divinity. Even the rationalistic, skeptical Benoît describes those who have died of love . . . . Not to mention the full-blown mysticism of Rider Haggard in *Ayesha: The Return of She*—altogether a psychological document of the first rank . . . . The animus, not having these emotional qualities, seems to lack entirely [this] aspect . . . yet in his deepest essence he is just as historically minded as the anima . . . . I know of only one unprejudiced document of this sort, a novel by Marie Hay, *The Evil Vineyard*. In this very unpretentious story the historical element in the animus comes out in a clever disguise that was surely not intended by the author.[7]

From the literary point of view it is certainly no masterpiece, but as it is the most genuine feminine material that I have ever come across. It is—even as fiction—very much worth analyzing. Jungian psychology provides a key with which we can try to approach the underlying psychological implications of this work,

---

6. [Pierre Benoît, *L'Atlantide* (Paris: LGF, 1996); see discussion in footnote 28 below. Henry Rider Haggard, *She: A History of Adventure* (New York: Oxford University Press, 2008). *Ed.*]
7. C. G. Jung, "Mind and Earth" (1931), in *CW*, vol. 10 (Princeton, N.J.: Princeton University Press, 1964), pars. 85ff.

particularly as Jung mentioned this book in a seminar in 1925.[8] I am attempting to analyze the book from the standpoint of the modern woman who is "longing for greater consciousness . . . and the power of naming her goal." In my efforts to find my way through this dark material and to analyze how such a tragedy can be averted, or at least understood, it is probable that I will sometimes judge the leading figures too harshly, for they had no psychological knowledge and show remarkably little common sense.

The material is so genuinely feminine that it permits me to examine the book as if its heroine were a real woman.[9] But it may interest you to know a few facts about the author. Unfortunately I know very little, and I also do not know the origin of the legend. Marie Hay is the daughter of Viscount Dupplin and Lady Agnes Duff, whose father was the Earl of Fife.[10] This means that she is connected with many of the old Scottish families, for these form one great web through intermarriage. Therefore, there would undoubtedly be haunted houses in her family. It is suggestive that she uses her own Christian name for her heroine, and it would be very interesting, were it ever possible to collect enough facts, to establish a possible connection with her own psychology. She was born in London in 1873 and married Herbert von Hindenburg in 1903. He was a diplomat and was attached to the German Embassy in Berne, Switzerland, at the end of the First World War. She died in Berlin in 1938.

I will start here with a concise synopsis of Hay's story and delve into more detail at various points during the lecture. Our story begins in Bern in the spring of 1918. The heroine, Mary Latimer, born Mary Carlton, looks out of her hotel window

---

8. C. G. Jung, *Analytical Psychology: Notes of the Seminar Given in 1925* (Princeton, N.J.: Princeton University Press, 1991).

9. [Barbara Hannah presents a highly detailed and in-depth psychoanalysis of the two fictional protagonists of this story. The psychological details of these personalities are ubiquitous, occurring everywhere and at all times throughout history. The material is profoundly feminine—and thus also profoundly archetypal. *Ed.*]

10. [Agnes Blanche Marie Hay was born on December 6, 1873. She was the daughter of George Robert Hay (Viscount Dupplin) and Lady Agnes Cecil Emmeline Duff. She married Herbert Baron von Hindenburg in February 1903 and died on December 13, 1938, at the age of 65. *Ed.*]

onto the great bridge over the Aare, the main river that flows
through the center of the city, and lets her thoughts wander
back to her childhood and youth. She was brought up in a big
English country house and eight years previously—when still
a young girl of nineteen—had married a famous archaeologist,
nearly thirty years older than herself. The Latimers had been
living these eight years in Rome with an interval of two or three
years for war work in London, and Mary Latimer is now waiting
for her husband to take her to an old castle that he has bought
near Locarno, Switzerland. He has restored La Vignaccia (here,
the evil vineyard), also called the Casa di Ferro, exactly as it was
three hundred years ago.[11]

While she is in Bern she learns that the house is haunted
and that there is a legend connected with it. She also makes the
acquaintance of a Mme de Villeneuve who, as Mary remarks
afterward, was "destined by fate" to help her in the final tragedy.
The next day she goes to the Casa di Ferro with her husband.
Mary says: "It was like a stage setting, so perfect in every detail,
that the illusion was complete and one felt instinctively that
thus the Vignaccia looked in the far-off days when Signor Enrico
lived there."[12]

Signor Enrico (or, as he is usually called, Heinrich von
Brunnen) was the main actor in the tragedy that took place in
the house in 1640. He was apparently the owner of the castle and
the captain of a troop of mercenaries, for the Casa di Ferro had
been a training school for *Landsknechte* in the Middle Ages.[13]
He was a turbulent man who terrorized the whole countryside.
He brought back a girl in a curtained litter from one of his military expeditions. Apparently he was very much in love with her
but suspected her of loving a younger member of the troop. He
murdered them both, and since that time, the Casa di Ferro has

---

11. [Locarno is in the Canton Ticino, the southern most canton in Switzerland. The town
borders on the northern end of the romantic Lake Maggiore, which extends southward into
Italy. *Ed.*]

12. Marie Hay, *The Evil Vineyard* (Leipzig: Bernhard Tauchnitz, 1924), p. 115.

13. [*Landsknechte* were mercenary soldiers (*knecht* being uneducated, unskilled farm labor-
ers) coming from impoverished backgrounds. *Ed.*]

been empty, for everyone who tried to live there was frightened away by the ghosts.

George Latimer, a famous archaeologist and scholar, became completely possessed by this medieval figure, and Mary found herself, apparently innocently, in the role of the past "Lady of the Casa di Ferro." At first she was terrified, especially as George Latimer spoke as if he had lived there before when he took her around the castle for the first time. "He might have been showing her the home of his youth." But then she is reassured by a supernatural experience in which a tangible presence assures her: "Have no fear, have no fear. I watch over you, I guard you until you pass from my keeping to his, until he comes for whom you wait."[14]

A few weeks later, a Maurice Drummond appears. He is a young cousin of George Latimer and has come to visit his relatives. He soon finds himself cast in the role of the young medieval lover. George Latimer makes a feeble attempt to end the story as it ended in the Middle Ages, that is, with the murder of the young pair. But Mary is warned by the supernatural presence and flies to the bedroom of Mme de Villeneuve, who is also staying at the castle. Latimer dies unaccountably while he is stabbing Mary's empty bed and is found lying "humped and limp like a discarded cloak flung down by angry hands." When they look at the dead man's face, there is "no cruelty and no madness" in it, but "only a great weariness as of one who rests at last—having accomplished a task of a magnitude almost beyond his strength, a task imposed by a cruel task-master."[15]

The next day, Mary says to Maurice Drummond: "It has sometimes seemed to me that we have been caught in a trap—George and I—and you too. Or that we have lost our way in a labyrinth—that there was no way out save death."[16]

Maurice then insists on declaring his love for Mary, saying that there is only one thing clear to him in it all: they "belong together

14. Hay, *The Evil Vineyard*, p. 134.
15. Ibid., p. 231.
16. Ibid., pp. 240f.

and have belonged together always."¹⁷ This blunt statement horrifies Mary, but Maurice persuades her that he is surely the man for whom she has been waiting. She then consents to marry him when the time of mourning she "owes" is past. She once again feels the touch of the "gentle fingers" of the unseen presence on her brow, and it then seems to pass out "over the tranquil water of the lake."

Once more the evil vineyard is deserted, but the peasants are more afraid of it than ever. Their priest tries to reassure them and to tell them that its lad is "living safe and happy in a far-off country." But they shake their heads doubtfully, for they believe that one more troubled spirit now wanders through those desolate rooms behind the barred windows of the Casa di Ferro.

THE HEROINE'S BACKGROUND

I have described here the end of the book in more detail because I think it is important that we should not lose sight of what actually happened, of what everything led to. It is always easier to distinguish a plot when you can look at it from both ends. But we must now return to the beginning of the action and see what we can learn from the material and about the trap in which they were all caught.

In order to understand the plot concealed beneath the surface of this book, we must first consider the heroine's background (which is not unlike the author's). The Carlton family had lived for many generations on its country estate. You can find an excellent picture of the life on such estates and their decay in a book called *English Saga*, published in 1940, that contains an interesting investigation of the hundred years that preceded the beaches of Dunkirk. Bryant says: "The life of a great county house afforded a microcosm of the State . . . and was a masterpiece of smooth and intricate organization."¹⁸ He especially emphasizes the old libraries "lined with golden volumes and all

17. Ibid., p. 241.
18. Arthur Bryant, *English Saga: 1840–1940* (London: Collins, 1940), p. 40.

the more curious and costly books" and says that the children of such houses took scholarly tastes from their fathers' libraries into a wider world.

While agriculture was the chief industry of England, these houses were its natural center. But Bryant says that the bad harvest of 1879 and the following years "marked the end of an era."[19] The foreigner began to feed Britain, ushering in the beginning of the demise of the country estate.

From a psychological point of view, we were much nearer the opposites in England a century or so ago. Bryant speaks of

> a strong native paganism that the Church, even in the age of faith, had never wholly eradicated. A heathen folklore and tradition that died hard took the place of a half-hearted theology. More than one eighteenth-century church was clandestinely dedicated to the Devil by the local Morris dancers. If many . . . had ceased to believe in Christ, they had not ceased to believe in his great adversary: "Old Scraper" could almost be heard by the imaginative on moon-light nights pattering through the undergrowth. Every village had its tales of ghosts and witches, of bygone murders and haunted crossroads and gibbets.[20]

The great Lord Melbourne also recognized the power of evil, for "it was his creed that it was best to try to do not good and then one could do no harm."[21]

The British had peculiar "notions of propriety" even in those days. For instance, in 1852, in Roget's thesaurus of English words

---

19. Ibid., p. 232.

20. Ibid., p. 34. [Morris dances include many forms of folk dances from the British Isles as well as dances involving agricultural motifs, jigs, sword dances, and much more. *Ed.*]

21. Ibid., p. 24. [William Lamb, the second viscount Melbourne (1779–1848), was a British Whig statesman who served as Prime Minister (1834 and 1835–1841). He was a mentor and close friend of Queen Victoria as she came to power. He first met general recognition under disreputable conditions: his wife had a public affair with Lord Byron. Melbourne is credited with a considerable list of reform legislation including a reduction in the number of capital offences, reform of the Poor Laws, and reforms of local government. Melbourne's most lasting memorial is the city of Melbourne, Australia, which was named after him in 1837. *Ed.*]

and phrases, everything was classified except the human body, which was discreetly scattered about the book.[22] Stomach is to be found under "receptacle" and the genital under "production." Bryant explains this by saying that the English were only half-civilized; they could not keep pace with their fortunes. Therefore, the moment they relaxed their "puritanical decorum," then out popped "the rude native Adam, so full of nature and vitality." According to the prime minister Benjamin Disraeli, this Adam evidently still had a considerable say in the fortunes of the nation even in the 1860s.[23] His opponent, Lord Palmerston, was then seventy-eight, and it was rumored on the eve of an election that he was having an affair with a clergyman's wife. Disraeli groaned and said: "For God's sake don't let the people of England know, or he'll sweep the country." Yet by the turn of the century the slightest breath of such a scandal would have ruined the chances of any candidate for Parliament.

I hope this is sufficient to give us some idea of the things that were slumbering below the surface on the estates of Great Britain during the time that our leading figure, Mary Carlton, was growing up in Darnfield. She would have been born in the late eighties of the nineteenth century, when the Victorian veneer was at its thickest and when the country houses still seemed secure, although they were dangerously hollowed out from beneath. Mary's family had really staked its all on the security and strength of conventions.[24] Looking back at Darnfield from the Casa di Ferro she says: "What safety there had been in that trivial conventional life."

---

22. Ibid., p. 141.

23. Ibid., p. 149. [Benjamin Disraeli, first earl of Beaconsfield (1804–1881), was an English statesman and literary figure. Disraeli served in government for three decades, twice as prime minister. He was the first and thus far the only person of Jewish parentage to do so, although Disraeli was baptized in the Anglican Church at an early age. Disraeli's most lasting achievement was the creation of the modern Conservative Party. Before and during his political career, Disraeli was well known as a literary and social figure, although his novels are not generally regarded as belonging to the first rank of Victorian literature. He is unusual among British prime ministers for having gained equal social and political renown. *Ed.*]

24. [In the course of her essay, Barbara Hannah discusses Mary Carlton's parents, Sir Arthur Carlton and Lady Carlton, and James, one of a number of otherwise unnamed brothers. *Ed.*]

Though the conventions had won out in the house, nature still had her sanctuaries out of doors in the gardens, stables, and farms. The children of such houses were, therefore, daily in outward contact with nature. But this had led to an overvaluing of sport in the case of Marie Hay's fictional Carlton family. We read:

> The Carltons considered learning to be a kind of reprehensible affectation. They expected a learned man to be a crank . . . who must necessarily be a middle-class person. It was in this milieu that Mary had grown up, but her mentality had wandered from the Carlton's paths. Her parents had seen no harm in allowing her to spend many hours in the old library, and here she had found treasures which had enthralled her; apparently other generations of Carltons had not despised the written word.[25]

Sir Arthur, indeed, enquired whether there was any "French trash" that the child could get hold of, but Lady Carlton assured him that there was no danger because they were all "well-bound books" ! Mary was the only girl in a large family of boys, who all chaffed her unmercifully: "Where's Mary?" her brothers would ask, and the usual reply was: "Oh, doing the literary in the library." We hear that the "thoughtless teasing crashed like a handful of stones flung into the enchanted garden of her mind."[26]

The excitement when she had her "coming out," that is, her debut, had at first swept Mary's thoughts away from books. Her family was reassured about her, for she had danced vigorously at hunt balls, gone to shooting parties and local races—in fact "behaved like a rational being," as her family said. Then she spent two seasons in London where the Carltons took a house with the avowed purpose of exhibiting their only daughter in the London marriage market. In her own circles (the dull, conventional, aristocratic life that centered round the court) she was a tremendous success. But she turned impatiently from her suitors; they were

---

25. Hay, *The Evil Vineyard*, pp. 14f.
26. Ibid., p. 15.

"commonplace youths," they wanted her "to share their dullness" or "to tread the prosaic path" of their life.[27]

On the other hand, she was evidently longing to play a role in the literary and artistic circles. But there she found that the Carltons were not in the swim; in fact, they were despised as being provincial. The opera and concerts were part of "the social campaign" and were, therefore, duly patronized by Lady Carlton, although they bored her to death. Mary was full of enthusiasm that earned her many snubs from her mother. Very soon Lady Carlton announced that the opera was too expensive, and Mary begged to be allowed to go to the cheap seats in the gallery. Lady Carlton rose in her wrath, demanding to know: "What new nonsense this?" Mary explained that she had been reading du Maurier's book and had been impressed by Peter Ibbetson hearing all "the beautiful things . . . better than the people in the boxes." Lady Carlton threatened to stop her subscription to Day's Library if she took what she read seriously, and we hear that Mary then had been vanquished.[28]

This defeat was more serious than it seems at first glance, for it amounted to a betrayal of Mary's feelings as an individual woman. The "enchanted garden of her mind," that had first appeared in the old library, evidently reappeared in the gallery at the opera. The result of her choice was that she exchanged the "golden volumes" of her ancestral library for the toxins of modern novels, and she also listened to the cackle of her girlfriends and tried to fall in love. Naturally, she failed in this endeavor for, at this period of her life, young men simply did not contain the mystery for her. This often seems to happen to girls with many brothers, and Mary appears to have been weak in relationship from the beginning. It is remarkable, for instance, that there is never any mention of a friendship with one of her brothers. Therefore, it seems to me that the "enchanted garden of her mind" had appeared, as it were, autonomously, and that she could only accept this fact and stand to her feeling wherever it appeared. "God can appear in a blade

27. Ibid., pp. 21f.
28. Ibid., pp. 17f.

of grass," as a Somali tribesman once told Jung.[29] But it would be undoubtedly awkward for Mary if God actually made some form of appearance in the gallery at the opera, for it would bring her up against the whole collective force of British society, and she had nothing to guide her except the instinctive urge of every living creature toward its wholeness.

Lady Carlton followed up her victory with a destructive and fatal blow. She was, of course, annoyed that Mary had refused so many advantageous proposals. We must remember that in the London marriage market prior to the war, a girl was expected to marry in her first season and was almost dubbed a failure if she did not marry in her second. But all the same it was incredibly inhuman of Lady Carlton to assert frequently and ruefully that her daughter had not "got it in her to fall in love" when she was only nineteen.

We hear that Mary concluded that Lady Carlton was right and that this conclusion had hastily sent her once again in search of the treasures of the mind. To Lady Carlton's dismay, she had taken to stealing away, accompanied by her highly bored maid, to the British Museum. This renewed her brothers' teasing which stung her sensitive young pride and, at the same time, encouraged her to feel herself as one apart from the rest of the family, apart and a bit superior as well. Mary's inability to respond to the endless taunting of her brothers gives us a good example of the extent to which Mary was cut off from an instinctive ability to defend and assert herself and how it came to be that she passively and submissively secedes where she should take action, choosing an indirect and unconscious way of circumventing adverse circumstances.

There was undoubtedly an effort to find her way back to the enchanted garden of her mind. But unfortunately the harm had already been done. She had believed that falling in love was the only right thing, and this had, as we shall see, become a vital goal. Lady Carlton's poisoned dart then did its deadly work. Such

---

29. C. G. Jung, *Visions: Notes of the Seminar Given in 1930–1934*, vol. 1 (London: Routledge, 1998), p. 111.

women are just barely bearable on their husbands' estates, for they use their energy in ruling their miniature kingdoms, including its king. But their worst side is apt to come out in London when they find themselves of no particular account. They have usually married the estate, not the man, and are, therefore, filled with repressed feelings and unconscious plots that can be exceedingly destructive to their daughters, who are indoctrinated with maternal ambivalence and dishonesty while still in their cradles. Such women are determined to get their daughters married, and equally determined that they—like themselves—shall not marry for love. But if Mary had been able to stand by her original feeling and had not believed that she should fall in love, she would have been protected, at any rate to some extent, from the poisoned dart. But now it is only too clear that her mother has made her feel hopelessly inferior as a woman, and that she is seeking a compensatory superiority in the "treasures of the mind," thus using them as a refuge from an unsolved problem. So naturally the teasing now gets further under her skin, for her love of the things of the mind is no longer unadulterated but infected by other motives.

MARY'S GOAL

The next passage is one of the more important in the book. For we see, first of all, the compensation for her feelings of inferiority and then her misery reflected in a childlike, grandiose fantasy. We read:

> At the end of the second season, when the Carltons returned to Darnfield, Mary spent more time than ever in the library. She had decided that she would never marry, and though she was wise enough to recognize that she had no literary gift, she dreamed of being a leader of an intellectual circle. She would have a salon in London, a brilliant house where all the poets, authors, actors, and musicians would find a second home.[30]

---

30. Hay, *The Evil Vineyard*, p. 23.

If we glance at this fantasy for a moment from the final point of view as well, jumping briefly to the end of the story, we see that it contains the germ of the whole development. It is a reflection of the future, a condensation such as one often sees in dreams. The salon motif belongs to George and Mary Latimer's life in Rome. We are told that all sides of Roman society were open to Mary, not only the fascinating Roman intellectual life that all foreigners effect, but also Italian society and the high-spirited, carefree world of the hotels and embassies. The London element belongs to the early years of the war which, as we have heard, were spent in London. Looking back after the event, one can understand Mary's feelings of a trap, of a fatal destiny from which there was no escape. And Maurice Drummond did feel drawn to the Casa di Ferro as a sort of "second home" during his stay in Switzerland. He gives two reasons for having proposed himself without an invitation: he wanted to see someone with whom he could talk about his people at home, and he had heard that the house was a wonderful old place.

What was Mary's goal as shown in this fantasy? There is not much left of the old, naïve and natural Mary who wanted her cheap seat at the opera. She has evidently vacated the field and taken over her animus's version of the enchanted garden of the mind. Such a salon would have made sense to Mary's ancestors in the days when the children of the country houses carried scholarly tastes from their father's library into a wider world. But it laid Mary open to a plot on a grand scale. The circumstances precluding her conviction that she would never marry and the subsequent development show us that the goal of this "brilliant house" was principally to give Mary the best possible opportunity to meet a man with whom she could fall in love. Naturally, had she been a girl who doubted her own attraction for men, the goal would have been to have all these men at her feet. But Mary did not doubt herself in this respect. The weak point where she could be misled by animus opinions—be they her mother's or her own—lay in her uncertainty with regard to her own feeling life. Had she been able to recognize and stand by her feelings, the animus would not have been able to interfere in this realm which is not his own. And had she been a girl who was in touch with her instincts, she would never have believed her mother's dictum. But instinct had been subordinated to convention at Darnfield, and nature had been banished to the stables and farms where it was in the realm of "Old Scraper" who "pattered through the undergrowth." If Mary cannot stand by her individual feelings, her animus will be able to cut her off from her instincts or deliver her over to the "blind dynamism of nature" just as he pleases.

I shall bring evidence later to show that the goal of falling in love was never far from Mary's consciousness. In other words, in one compartment she was aware of this longing. She did not know how to achieve it, however, so evidently she ignored that compartment and just hoped that it might happen of itself. That is, she chose a passive role. But at the same time she was spinning a web of wishful fantasies and thus providing Old Scraper with every hook he could desire.

When any woman is so passive, she naturally forces someone in her neighborhood to take over the active role, and when she uses all her libido in daydreams, we may be pretty sure that someone will be moved, via the unconscious, to do something about them. And in the very next paragraph her father does do something that gives her fantasy the opportunity to materialize in outer reality.

Going back now to the beginning for a more detailed rendition of the story, we read:

> Then one day Sir Arthur announced that George Latimer, the archaeologist, had been invited by a local antiquarian society to come down and give his opinion on some fragments of Roman pavement which had been discovered in the neighborhood.
>
> "It is rather a bore, but I suppose we must invite him to stay for a couple of nights. I believe he's quite a decent fellow, though, if he hadn't got a bee in his bonnet about digging up things," Sir Author said. "By the way, he'll be something

for Mary. Eh! Miss Girton-Girl." Mary blushed and turned away . . . .

"Oh, look at Mary blushing" one of her brothers cried. "Dear old blue stocking, was she going to have a learned old buster all to herself to flirt with?"

For once in a way Lady Carlton came to Mary's rescue. "Leave your sister alone, Jim. I believe Mr. Latimer is a charming man," she said. Perhaps she remembered that George Latimer's family was fully as old as the Carltons themselves, and until his advent had been just as devoid of interest. Possibly too the maternal instinct recollected that, as the Latimer property lay in and around a large manufacturing town, George Latimer must be rich.

"What sort of aged man is he?" she had asked casually.

"Oh! Well over forty, I should think," Sir Arthur answered. Hereupon Lady Carlton's interest in the famous archaeologist promptly evaporated and Jim's chaff was suffered to continue unchecked.[31]

The Carltons evidently did not know Latimer, and they certainly had nothing to do with archaeological societies. Moreover, Sir Arthur himself connects his invitation with Mary. The brothers tell her pretty clearly what she is likely to be up to, and even her mother gives her the opportunity to realize that George Latimer is rich. That salon and brilliant house will obviously need a great deal of money, and Mary herself will have next to none. The Carlton estates were impoverished, and the lion's share always goes to the eldest son in such families in order to preserve the estate. Had Mary taken her fantasy seriously, she would have been on her guard where rich men were concerned. On the other hand, if she had realized the force of her goal to fall in love, she would not have laid such a trap for herself nor set the bait for an elderly scholar whom she had never seen. But, as it is, it seems

---

31. Ibid., pp. 23f. ["Girton girl" is a reference to Girton College, an all-girls school established in 1869 as one of the constituent colleges of the University of Cambridge in England, first admitting undergraduate males in 1979. *Ed.*]

to me that the trap was laid well before George Latimer arrived on the scene.

On the afternoon that Latimer was expected, Mary developed a "charitable" wish to visit an old tenant of Sir Arthur's who lived three miles away and thus she could avoid the family's sarcasm. Therefore, she first inspected George Latimer through the drawing-room window from the safe distance of the rose garden. She was surprised to see someone far removed from her idea of a celebrated scholar and archaeologist. He was a tall, broad-shouldered man and looked like a soldier or an explorer. To her astonishment the Carlton family seemed to be listening spellbound to what he was saying. He had vanquished the Carlton prejudice against learned men before he ever set eyes on Mary.

Latimer was evidently socially well adapted before his marriage. He lingered on for several days at Darnfield, leading the ordinary life of an English county house, shooting, going round the home farm, and working in Sir Arthur's study. The text reads:

> At first Mary alone of all the family remained unbending and formal in manner towards him . . . but she frequently felt his gaze upon her and a tremor as of fear had come to her at those moments. Yet his conversation was as prosaic as the Carltons' own . . . and Mary went back to her reading and dreaming in the library with only a tinge of disappointment in her mind that the first scholar she had met should prove so commonplace in everyday life. Then, one evening after tea . . . Latimer followed her into the library . . . and asked her to show him her books . . . . Latimer's whole being seemed changed as he talked; it was as though he had removed a mask and Mary saw him for the first time.[32]

We see here that, as a nineteen-year-old, Mary's instincts were not entirely silent but sent her a friendly warning in these "tremors of fear." If she had stood by her fear, the animus

---

32. Ibid., pp. 29f.

could not have cut her off from this contact with the instincts which could have prevented her marriage with Latimer. But she represses the instincts with conventional opinions: Latimer's conversation is "prosaic" and he is "commonplace." So she returns to the library and her daydreams of that salon and brilliant house.

Again, these fantasies have an immediate effect on her surroundings, this time on Latimer himself. He is exceedingly rich and famous, the ideal fulfillment of every dream except love. One is reminded of Mephistopheles and Faust, for really only the devil could have produced such an overwhelming temptation.[33] But we must not forget that the animus was only bringing Mary's own fantasy into reality, and that she had, as it were, asked the devilish side of her animus to help her. He could never have interfered in this realm had she stood by her feeling or even her fear. But as is usual for women in such circumstance, it has now become a sort of vicious circle: she cannot stand by her own simple instinctual reactions because of her plot, and she cannot see her plot because she has lost these simple reactions.

Mary's vanity reacted at once to this attention from the "famous scholar" and within a few weeks she "found herself engaged to him." We hear that she was as proud as though she had won a scholarship at the university and was reassured about

---

33. [The legend of Faust, first set into print in Frankfurt in 1587, is seemingly woven around several actual men who eventually comprised the character Faust. There were probably several Fausts. One was Dr. Johannes Faustus, a German scholar living approximately between 1480 and 1540. What is fact and fiction concerning this man is unclear. It was thought that he traveled throughout Europe as one of many magicians, astrologists and necromancers during the Renaissance, entertaining at fairs and at royal courts. Stories have it that he sold his soul to the devil for magical powers with the hopes of enjoying immunity when delving in those pleasures and acts that medieval ethics had branded as stemming from cardinal sins. The "Faust-book," or *Faustbuch*, was hastily translated throughout Europe, gaining rapid appeal. An English translation inspired Christopher Marlowe's (1564–1593) play *The Tragicall History of D. Faustus*. In this adaptation, Faust turns to magic with high expectations of gaining the services of Mephistopheles in order to attain a life of "all voluptuousness." He thereby loses his soul and is swept off by devils into the mouth of hell. In Goethe's version of the story, Mephistopheles is the infernal spirit who arduously attempts to fulfill Faust's wish to reach contentment and thereby to gain possession over his soul. The otherwise obscure character Faust has come to be preserved in legend as the representative magician of the age—an age of schism, unorthodoxy, witchcraft, and inquisitions—flourishing with occultists, seers, necromancers, and more serious "doctors" and philosophers of that time. *Ed.*]

herself, for if she were the absurd, affected Mary doing the literary, as her family ridiculed, why should this learned man be so interested in her mind?

We are particularly told that Mary did not think of Latimer as a lover at all but as the wise and kindly guide to the "hoarded beauty of the ages." Evidently the animus has sprung into Latimer, and Mary no doubt really thought she was walking into the enchanted garden of her mind. But clearly she was not attaching enough importance to her goal—which was to fall in love—for she certainly knew from the beginning that she was not in love with this man. She simply did not enter this compartment, possibly because she hedged a largely unconscious conviction that the brilliant house would also provide a lover in time. Of course she did not allow this conclusion to be drawn all too consciously—or all that long—for she would have seen from the beginning that Latimer was the "cloak" for her purpose and that he would have to be "discarded" when the lover arrived. Therefore, she obviously could not have married him had she allowed herself to think of him as that actual one-and-only lover. This gives us an idea of how we play hide-and-seek with our plots so as not to impede their fulfillment.

It must be emphasized that her family did not push Mary into the marriage; it was her own wish. We hear that the Carltons were aghast at first, for Latimer was nearly fifty and Mary not yet twenty. And Latimer himself asked: "Am I too old for you, Mary?" and she answered—deceiving herself as well—that she could dream of nothing better than to be with him.

And what about Latimer? Why has he fallen headlong into her trap? We must not forget that the book is written by a woman and that we can, therefore, see well into Mary's mind but hardly at all into Latimer's. We can only get an approximate idea of him, for we always see him through Mary's eyes; moreover, we know very little of his life before his marriage except that he had spent a long time in Egypt. The very fact that Latimer is an archaeologist suggests a powerful anima, for we know that she is in her element in antiquity and in the sepulchers of the dead. I remind you, for instance, of the enchanting and commanding anima figure of Antinea in Benoît's *L'Atlantide*.[34] It is also evident that Latimer had lived almost exclusively in his brilliant mind and had never had any serious relation to a woman. Therefore, we may assume that his anima had become exceedingly possessive. If Latimer is to be allowed a real woman at all, it is best if she is a young and inexperienced woman who is partially weakened by her own unconscious plot, because such a woman will never get her own feelings clear enough to function as a serious rival to the anima. Latimer's anima most certainly projected herself onto Mary, and thus drew him into Mary's plot. And apparently his anima made a counterplot of her own. (We will speak more about this later.) His anima was certainly in possession of Latimer's instincts, and she seems to have prompted him to pretend a great interest in Mary's mind. It is interesting how the anima kept him convinced of potential love and a sexual embrace from his attractive, young wife and did not let him see that Mary was not thinking of him as a lover at all. Mary says later that she had always held the knowledge but never discerned the fact that she was waiting for another man, whereas Latimer was evidently always in the dark concerning his anima and her plot.

It seems to me that this is a typical situation. The woman, even when she is as young as Mary, really has to carry the responsibility for the plots simply because she does know something about them, whereas the average man is simply in the dark. Not that I wish to clear Latimer of blame in marrying Mary. He had cer-

---

34. Pierre Benoît,, *L'Atlantide* (Paris: LGF, 1996). [First published 1919, Benoît's story takes place in the French Sahara where an officer and a monk have been asked to investigate the mysterious disappearances of other officers and explorers in the vast reaches of that desert. Eventually they are drugged and taken prisoner, and when they awaken, they find themselves in a royal palace hidden within an unbreachable mountain range and overlooking a beautiful palm oasis. Queen Antinea (a startling beauty of Atlantis and Egyptian royal lineage) keeps an underground mausoleum with one hundred and twenty alcoves filled with the numbered and labeled bodies of those former lovers who were blessed with one glorious night with her at the subsequent cost of their lives. In the center of the mausoleum stands the throne where Antinea will sit and rest for eternity once all the niches have been filled. The book has been made into a movie approximately six times in the grandiose tradition of *cinema fantastique. Ed.*]

tainly used his work illegitimately as a refuge from life, and his mind alone could have told him that he was taking no ordinary risk in marrying such a young girl.

In 1925 Jung said that such a marriage always begins with a violent outburst of sexuality on the side of the man.[35] Hay writes:

> Mary was miserable for a time. Yet she was so full of the enjoyment of being able to buy all the books she wished for, of haunting picture galleries, of meeting men and women of intellect, that she was frequently able to forget the discomforts of married life.[36]

Latimer's anima evidently knew what she was doing. Mary is simply absent. She does not even stay with her misery but forgets it by escaping into her fantasy, which is beginning to come into reality with the men and women of intellect. When Latimer tries to reach her, she is not there. Disappointed and rejected, he falls straight into the outstretched arms of his own anima and her plots.

Her mother's conventional marriage no doubt made it difficult for Mary. We are given a vivid picture of this side of Lady Carlton in the following words: "The worthy lady, though a large and healthy progeny proved her to have been a competent wife of Sir Arthur, always spoke and behaved as if life had left her in blissful ignorance of some of its undoubted if unpleasant facts."[37] It is then no surprise that Mary herself identified with this point of view: she gave up a friendship that she valued with a German lady in Rome when she found that it involved the discussion of marital experiences. She then drew back with the reflection that she preferred her own insular methods of reserve.

---

35. Jung, *Analytical Psychology: Notes of the Seminar Given in 1925.*
36. Hay, *The Evil Vineyard*, p. 37.
37. Ibid., p. 38.

FAILURE OF A PROJECTION

The situation had forced Latimer into a primitive and inferior role that, as Jung pointed out, he could not maintain as a civilized man. Such circumstance naturally cooled his passion exceedingly quickly, and he began to leave Mary a good deal alone. The book says: "There was certainly an advantage in this for her, but being young and inexperienced, she wondered if she had failed in her duty to her husband."[38] If Mary had stood by this doubt, the whole tragedy might have been averted, for we shall see that her determination to play the role of a completely innocent victim forced Latimer to take over the opposite role. Of course his own unconsciousness was largely to blame, but we must not overlook the fact that Mary never again considers the possibility that she may have failed in her duty to her husband in any way until after his death. This one doubt is attributed to "youth and inexperience," and thenceforth all blame is projected onto Latimer.

But Latimer also makes a mistake at this point. We have seen that Mary regarded him, as she says, the "wise and kindly guide to the hoarded beauty of the ages." At first Latimer carried this projection, answered all of her questions, talked to her about art and literature, and even of his beloved archaeology. But as his passion cooled, his patience and interest in her mind waned. In a comment on this story in 1925, Jung emphasized that it was a tragic misunderstanding; he thought she wanted him as a lover, and she thought he cared for her mind. Both were bitterly disappointed. Just as Mary refused to carry the projection of his anima (of course without realizing what she was doing), so now Latimer, equally unconsciously, refuses to carry the projection of the wise old man, and he thus escapes back into his beloved archaeology where his anima reigns supreme. Mary's animus draws her more and more into her goal "to fall in love," and Latimer's jealous anima refuses to allow Mary to enter the only realm where she might have formed a real relationship to him as the wise old man.

No doubt Latimer was too childish on this side to be able to carry such a projection when not helped by the force of passion.

38. Ibid., p. 38.

Moreover, Mary's animus probably withdrew the projection when it suited his own means. One understands Latimer being terribly disappointed that Mary did not love him and downright irritated when he found that her interests were limited to the treasures of his mind. But it seems to me that this brilliant mind, or just simple common sense, might have informed him that, when marrying a girl young enough to be his daughter, he would have to—like it or not—take over something of the responsibility of a father. Had he been able to see this and give her time to grow up, if he had helped her with the development of her mind, it seems to me quite possible that they might have found a real relationship to each other. At any rate, he would probably have avoided her hostility, for when she found herself excluded from his real life, that is, "the life of his brain," and up against the inhuman coldness of his anima, she evidently secretly declared war on the very thing she had originally admired: his brilliant mind.

Back to the outer setting of our story. We see that Mary's fantasy is now a reality. The salon is established in an apartment of the Palazzo Barberini, and, as the wife of a famous scholar, Mary's dream of being a leader of an intellectual circle is fulfilled.[39] She is "la belle Madame Latimer" and a figure in Roman society. She enjoyed all of this for a time, and especially Rome itself; but as for her daily life with Latimer, we read that he was vaguely kind and accepted her as pleasantly existing. She, on the other hand, realized that she was now only a portion of the unimportant "machinery of everyday life," not unlike his house and his servants. She then admitted to herself that her marriage was an irreparable mistake, but she did not say so to him. She should

---

39. [The Palazzo Barberini, towering high above the piazza of the same name in the center of Rome, was contracted by Pope Urban VIII (Maffeo Barberini, who reigned from 1623 to 1644). Barberini was a builder and art patron who was fortunate in having two great architects of the Baroque period, Borromini and Bernini, to work for him on this palace. They created a complex layout of rectangular and oval staircase halls, with suites of rooms and state apartments. In the rear part of the building, one finds a subterranean Mithraic chamber dating from around the second or third century A.D. In the Palazzo Barberini, the High Baroque found its fullest expression. In past centuries the palazzo has housed state and private apartments, and today it is the home of the Galleria Nazionale d'Art Antica, curators of one of the most important collections of paintings in Italy. It was the perfect place for Mary to entertain the intellectual circles of Europe. *Ed.*]

certainly have asserted herself in some way or other, told him he was failing her just where she needed him most, made some sort of dramatic scenes, or flirted with another man. She should have done something to show that she was not just "part of the machinery." But unfortunately it fitted exactly into her plot to be part of the machinery, to keep absolutely quiet and play the role of the neglected wife of an "old and satiated man."

POWER OF THE FANTASY

The outward life of the Latimers seemed smooth enough for the first four or five years of their marriage. The first sign that Mary's fantasies were again affecting Latimer came at the outbreak of the First World War. We hear that Mary's soul awoke to an ardent, childlike patriotism and that she thrilled to the martial glory of England. Latimer was irritated by the disturbance that the war brought into his studious, self-centered life and smiled coldly at Mary's enthusiasm. The two returned to England, however, and he was valuable to the Foreign Office where he worked with unenthusiastic conscientiousness. Thus far, we can accept the book's explanation that it was a concession to the collective opinion of the moment. But then a peculiar thing occurred; Latimer resigned the Foreign Office and volunteered for the front. Latimer must have been over fifty then, and there has been no mention of any previous military experience. Therefore, it would have required a most unusual effort and a great deal of influence on his part to reach the front at all. We hear that Mary "rejoiced," believing that under his impassive manner there lurked after all some warmer, more generous feeling. She told him tremulously that she was proud of his decision to do his bit, which, however, had an exceedingly irritating effect.

Latimer's military adventure was of short duration. After a few months he was sent home as an invalid, suffering from shell shock. So they returned to Rome, and he became more than ever absorbed in study and steadily refused to mention the war. "I take absolutely no interest in it," he would answer coldly if anyone ventured to ask his opinion or to mention the news in the papers. It was said that he had had terrible experiences at the front and that this, together with the shell shock from which he had suffered, had made him a little "odd." But Mary knew now that no shell and no terrible experience could shatter the man's relentless egoism, that he had simply returned to the aloof, impersonal realm where he lived the only life that meant anything to him.

I do not think that it is possible to doubt that it was Mary's fantasies that moved Latimer to this adventure. One begins to wonder whether there was not something unusually evil at work. For this is really not a nice story. The net result is an alibi for Mary: everything can henceforward be put down to Latimer's being "odd." Yet we are told that Mary does not believe in the shell shock but attributes everything to his "relentless egoism," which is certainly a case of the pot calling the kettle black. When we remember how well adapted Latimer was socially before his marriage, we can only explain his downright rudeness when the war is mentioned by something that must have happened to him since his marriage and during his experience on the front. Presumably he does not understand why he volunteered and, therefore, gets angry when anything reminds him of the war.

Latimer's behavior evidently needs a deeper explanation than the reasons he had given to Mary: convention and a mild curiosity. Perhaps he was unconsciously trying to play the role of Mary's young hero animus and to reach her as a lover after all? And perhaps his unconscious was trying to warn him, saying, as it were, "Look what your wife is doing to you. You know that her soul 'thrilled to the martial glory of England,' and you know that yours did not. Can you not see what you are doing, just acting out her fantasies? You have escaped with your life this time; wake up before it is too late." And Mary herself gave him a chance at this point, for we hear that she "sometimes had actually hated him" and "was often irritable and even hostile in her manner to him, but he seemed not to notice her." In fact, he buried himself in his work and behaved as if there was no war and as if he had no wife.

Had either Latimer or Mary faced the situation, the tragedy might still have been averted. Latimer could have asked himself, for instance, what he was doing in the role of a young man at the front. And Mary could have stood by her hatred and drawn the logical conclusion. Latimer could not have avoided noticing her if she had asked for a divorce or announced her intention of leaving. Moreover, it was no more than her duty to realize that she desired Latimer's death. But not at all; she is "bound to this strange being for all the days of her life" and "marriage is a life sentence." In other words, Latimer has escaped with his anima to his beloved archaeology, and instead of standing by her hatred, Mary once again escapes with her animus into her plot. Latimer at least used his energy in work, whereas Mary did nothing at all.

The salon has proven to be a disappointment; it has not produced the man with whom Mary could "fall in love." There were men who made love to her, it is true, but these are only interesting in that they prove that Mary was to some extent conscious of her goal to "fall in love." She tells us quite naively that "they had no charms for her" or that they "failed to attract her." Therefore, she now discards the salon, and her unused energy goes into a new series of fantasies. She again calls on her animus to help her, and he responds by producing the medieval figure of Heinrich von Brunnen (the tragic proprietor of the Casa di Ferro in seventeenth century).

The leitmotif in Mary's new fantasies is that of the cruel jailer and the little bird in the gilded cage. Jung said in 1925 that he had often met with similar fantasy material, which centers on the figure of a young hero who will free the girl from the incarceration of the old tyrant. The salon has been exchanged for a prison, and the many men of her earlier fantasy for one man.

It is not long before these fantasies have their effect on Latimer. Mary's extreme passivity obliges him again to take over the active role. With the same suddenness that he showed when he resigned from the Foreign Office, he abandons his studious life in Rome and announces one day that he has business in Switzerland. He intimates that Mary can accompany him, but she prefers to remain in Rome.

We must not forget that she "prefers to remain in Rome," for this choice establishes her own pretense that Latimer was entirely responsible for the Casa di Ferro. Had she gone with him, she would have been obliged to abandon her passive role and either to oppose the purchase of the castle or to accept half the responsibility. But by staying in Rome she provides herself with a watertight alibi in the eyes of the world.

It is certain that in Rome Mary decided to remain in a compartment of her psychology where she had no idea what she was doing. But one does not quite understand how she reconciled this fact with her image of Latimer as her jailer. We hear that "she spent the summer pleasantly enough at Abetone and then returned to Rome," the two then living separately.[40] Latimer was busy in Switzerland for almost a year, and when he came back he was already identical with Heinrich von Brunnen.

How has such an extraordinary thing been brought about? We see that Mary fails to stand by her hatred just as she fails to stand by any of her feelings. She again vacates the realm of relationship, and again she calls on her animus to help her with wishful fantasies in which, of course, the hatred reappears. Evidently she has touched a deeper layer of the collective unconscious; at any rate, the animus has gone right back to the Middle Ages. Since Latimer failed to please as a modern hero, he shall now appear in a more romantic guise as a sixteenth-century condottiere who terrorized the whole neighborhood and who excelled in skilled killing and murder.[41] What a dramatic figure; surely Mary will "fall in love" with him this time! One is reminded of the arduous efforts made by Mephistopheles to fulfill Faust's wishes and thus take his soul to hell. Probably, if asked, Mary's animus would complain, like Mephistopheles, that she had no idea what hard work it was to fulfill her desires!

---

40. [Abetone is a village in the mountains north of Florence; today it is a ski resort. *Ed.*]

41. [A condottiere is a leader of mercenary soldiers in Italy during the incessant wars of the fourteenth and fifteenth centuries. The condottieri organized and led troops of mercenaries and dealt directly with the cities, states, or lords which requested their services. They and their troops were strictly for hire, and they fought for the highest bidder, switching with no qualms from one contractor to his opponent if opportunity arose. *Ed.*]

When Mary's animus projected itself onto Latimer in the form of the wise old man, he was unable—or refused—to carry the projection. It belongs to the nature of a positive projection that it will not force us to carry it. But force does belong to the nature of negative things, and when Mary's animus projected himself onto Latimer as the evil condottiere, he apparently found himself obliged to carry the projection. There was no possibility of bringing this figure into reality in Rome. Latimer is always represented as calmly and even happily absorbed in his work, and Mary, though bored and miserable, as completely free. Just as the projection of the young hero seems to have hounded him to the front, so now the projection of this hateful, incarcerating tyrant seems to drive him on a journey where he must wander about until he can find a form into which the projection will fit.

One wonders why his anima allowed him to leave this studious life among the antiquities of Rome. Apparently Mary and her animus have undermined his life. It only looked secure, and, therefore, the supremacy of the anima was again threatened. It is evident from Latimer's behavior when he got to the Casa di Ferro that his goal was to find the love that Mary had denied him. One, therefore, presumes that his anima was repeating her tactics at Darnfield: throwing him into Mary's plot with a deadly counterplot of her own in the background. It will certainly be no more and no less than the age-old plot of a man's anima to entice him forward into her hopeful, promising outstretched arms while stealthily, mercilessly driving him—from behind—into a fatal and eternal embrace. How many men have followed their anima, beckoning like a Joan of Arc, into heroic—and unnecessary—self-sacrifice? She must have encouraged him to believe that he would find Mary's love at the Casa, yet knowing full well that Mary would again be absent, this time given to fantasies of her younger lover. In such a building and such a role, this deadly anima could be more certain of her prey.

There is a consideration that should perhaps be indulged in, or at least mentioned, although I am unable to estimate its importance. About this time, Mary tells us that both of her parents have died and that her eldest brother James, obliged to let Darnfield to a whiskey distiller, has since been killed himself on the front. Some ghosts are said to remain in old houses through every change of ownership, and others to follow the family. We never hear that Darnfield was haunted, but I have stayed in a good many such old houses, and my experience has led me to suspect that there is always a kind of ancestral deposit. One could imagine, for instance, that it might have been a remnant of Mary's book-loving ancestors that led her footsteps to the old library when she was a child. At all events, Mary developed at this time a passionate long-ing for a home, a place on the earth where she belonged. Rome had satisfied her in this respect before, and she even says that she had learned to love it with the clinging personal love that we give to the home of our youth. Apparently the Roman apartment was not given up, for Latimer only says that he intends to live a good deal of the time at La Vignaccia in the future. Therefore, it is conceivable that there were ghosts, ancient and modern—or if you will, autonomous psychological complexes connected perhaps with unfulfilled longings and deficiencies in her ancestral past— who were pressing Mary to find them a more suitable dwelling.

Latimer at last returned to Rome. At the first mention that he had bought La Vignaccia, Mary noticed a curious quality in his voice unlike his characteristic deliberate utterance. "Why are you so reticent," she asks. "My dear Mary," he answers, "you used not to be inquisitive."[42] Here he may be reacting much as he had reacted to all mention of the war after his military adventure. Or maybe his anima possession has sealed the next step of his fate. For he then felt that he must explain himself to a certain extent and owned that the strange old place interested him so much that he got almost nervous when he spoke of it. He also admitted his interest in Heinrich von Brunnen whose personality is dominant in the few records of the villa. So his anima has moved from youthful wartime heroism on the front to a higher form of martial fascination, that of the merciless condottiere. Mary asked him why this "not unusual type" should interest him so much? "It is a

---

42. Hay, *The Evil Vineyard,* p. 46.

question of destiny beyond our control, like so much else after all"
is Latimer's fateful answer.

Latimer was half like a possessed thing and half more friendly
and human than he had ever been since his marriage. Sometimes
he was nervous and irritable, sometimes, she admits, natural and
friendly. Mary also came more into the open. There would have
been again a chance here of facing the situation if Mary had only
stood by her curiosity and insisted on being treated like a reasonable being. But such an attitude would have endangered her
goal, for she must be Latimer's prisoner in order to constellate a
modern Perseus.[43] So she allowed herself to be treated like a child
and consented to stay in Rome until he sent for her.

> She wondered vaguely why he was so reluctant to show her
> La Vignaccia, but, used to his eccentric ways, she did not
> attach much importance to it; although a sense of uneasiness
> worried her when she recollected the note of anxiety that she
> thought she had remarked in his voice when he had spoken
> of the place. Perhaps it was haunted and he wished to lay the
> ghost? What a stranger George Latimer was to her after eight
> years of marriage! How little she knew of the workings of his
> mind—of his soul![44]

Mary has told us the story up to this point as she leans out
of her window at the Hotel in Berne where she is waiting for
Latimer to take her for the first time to the Casa di Ferro. She
continues: "Oh! I wish I had someone to speak to about it all."[45]
And as if in answer to her mental call, a knock comes on her door
and Fraulein Alten enters.

Fraulein Alten is a German spinster who had been "put to
fight" in the hall of the hotel an hour or so before by an English

---

43. [Perseus is best known for having decapitated the snaked-infested head of the goddess
Medusa and rescuing Andromeda by beheading a sea monster. Barbara Hannah apparently
implies here that the divine heroic act will reoccur in the unconscious: Mary's Perseus-like
animus will kill Latimer's Medusa-like anima. *Ed.*]

44. Hay, *The Evil Vineyard*, p. 49.

45. Ibid.

acquaintance of Mary's who claimed that the "old hag is a well-known spy." Mary replied that it was useless to prolong the conversation, and she now welcomes Fraulein Alten eagerly.

Emma Jung first drew my attention to the importance of this shadow figure, who comes up, as it were, just this one time out of the unconscious.[46] The conversation begins with some true shadow advice. She asks Mary if she has been "glooming." "Yes, just about that . . ." is Mary's reply, "looking back into my past life." "Oh! Never do that, my dear!" cries Fraulein Alten, "Life is so sad it doesn't bear thinking about."[47]

It then turns out that Fraulein Alten, who is full of macabre stories, has actually sketched the notorious Casa di Ferro, and it is she who tells Mary the legend of the place that she heard about from the priest while she was at her easel in front of the castle. She particularly emphasizes the end of the legend when Heinrich von Brunnen summoned the local priest to read the funeral service over the two shrouded forms of his victims laid out in the little private chapel right beside the house—the lady of La Vignaccia and her young lover—while the cruel and evil Heinrich shuddered in an agony of tears.

She thus supplies Mary with the key to her whole plot, but by emphasizing the fate of the innocent medieval victim, she encourages Mary to identify with the lady victim and to see the whole thing as a plot of Latimer's to rid himself of Mary.

Yet the very next day, Mary herself, in another compartment of her psychology, pursues this point of view. Mary lies awake most of the night tortured by all the ghost stories she knows. The next morning she makes up her mind that if La Vignaccia is "a sort of Glamis Castle," most people in Switzerland would know.[48]

---

46. [Barbara Hannah writes: The shadow also appears at the beginning of the story in the shape of Mrs. Gunten, Lady Carlton's sister, who plays a rather similar role. Mrs. Gunten is concerned with the salon, while Fraulein Alten with the Casa di Ferro. *Ed.*]

47. Hay, *The Evil Vineyard,* p. 50.

48. [Glamis Castle, with its many turrets and spires and its romantic, even poetic, architecture set among the forested hills of Scotland, is known for its numerous legends and ghost stories. It has been the residence of British royalty since 1372, childhood home of the contemporary Queen Elizabeth, and the legendary setting for Shakespeare's *Macbeth.* It certainly has more stories and legends attached to it than probably any other castle in the

Therefore, she is determined to get Fraulein Alten to take her to see some Swiss friends. As if in answer to her thoughts, Fraulein Alten offers to take her to see Mme de Villeneuve, who has a beautiful old apartment in the Junkerngasse in Berne.[49]

Mary finds a tea party in progress; her fellow guests are the wives of diplomats. She reflects that they are *pauvres deracinees*, "vapid things," only as important as the females of those male animals who "deflect the world-stream into channels that mean peace or war."[50] And "as the female is, so is the male!" Whichever the primary cause of beauty or ugliness of being, the next result is the undeviating law: as the female is, so is the male.

This amounts to a confession that Latimer is what she has made him, but of course this conclusion is never directly drawn. It is the "undeviating law," but somehow or other she does not state it to apply to Latimer and herself. Had Mary brought this conclusion into connection with the legend she had heard the night before—which was constantly in her mind as she sat with Mme de Villeneuve—she would have had to ask herself: "What have I done to my husband that he has bought this place of evil memory?" But such a conclusion would have disturbed the fulfillment of her plot. And as is the case with women's plots, she misses, once again, one of so many possibilities granted by daily happenings to become conscious of what she is up to—and do to something constructive with it, for life and self-realization.

Mme de Villeneuve can tell Mary nothing of La Vignaccia and explains that the Ticino is "as strange to us Bernese as a foreign country." But she sees that Mary is frightened, so she offers impulsively to help her if she is ever in need of a friend.

British Isles. Possibly the most interesting of several ghosts witnessed even in recent times is the Grey Lady, haunter of the family chapel, who is said to be the spirit of Lady Janet Douglas, burned at the stake as a witch on Castle Hill, Edinburgh, in 1537. The charges were probably fabricated for political motives. In recent years as well, the apparition has been seen in the chapel by a number of witnesses. The Grey Lady is also said to appear above the Clock Tower. *Ed.*]

49. [One of the old, quaint, and romantic "alleys" in the center of the city of Berne. *Ed.*]

50. Hay, *The Evil Vineyard*, pp. 50f.

JOURNEY TO THE VINEYARD

When Mary returns to her hotel, she finds that Latimer has arrived from Zurich accompanied by his old servant Race. Race is a most charming person, the most human character in the book, and he is loud in his complaints of having been left "for months in that old Zoorig." And "when Mr. Latimer did come to me in Zoorig, 'e was as glum as an undertaker. Just like an 'ippotized thing 'e's been all this time . . . Lor' bless you, mum, 'e don't even listen when I give 'im notice, no more than if I 'and't spoken."[51]

But Race has no intention of leaving his beloved master—"ipp[n]otized" or not—so the next day they all travel from Berne via Lucerne over the Gotthard Pass and down into the canton of Ticino to take up life in the Casa di Ferro.

Interestingly enough, the Latimers traveled down to Locarno as a quaternity. We read:

> Mary's English maid, a chronically affronted damsel, sat in a corner of the second-class compartment adjoining the Latimer's first-class carriage, sulking and refusing all offers of nourishment; while Race stood in the corridor ruminating gloomily, the Continental Daily Mail and an ancient number of Tit-Bits peeping out of his pocket. Latimer was engrossed in the "Yearly Report of the British School of Archaeology" in Rome.[52]

Mary also tried to read, but says that "there are moments when the written word fails to grip even the ardent votary of books, moments when there is no response in the reader."[53] Though Mary did not yet know it, it was not only a matter of the moment, for we hear that when she got to the Casa di Ferro she again tried to read and to study but could no longer concentrate her attention on books.

---

51. Ibid., p. 92.
52. Ibid., p. 95.
53. Ibid., p. 96.

Unable to read on her journey over the Gotthard Pass, she then dozed and dreamed of walking in the garden at Darnfield with her deceased brother, Jim. And this somehow turned into the golf course near the Aqua Santa outside Rome where she was "topping a ball."[54]

The *acqua santa*—that holy, healing water—brings in the idea of the *acqua permanens*. And the ball, like the circle, sphere, square, and quaternity, ushers in the symbolism of totality. This gives us the confirmation in the actual material of the dual nature of the animus. We have seen that Mary failed to follow her individual feeling in its quest for the totality of her personality, and that the matter then passed into the hands of her animus. As a matter of fact, Mary was already possessed when she went to London. This again is confirmed in the book, for Hay writes that she was not only vanquished in the matter of the gallery seat at the opera but also by a "lameness" thus induced and by a sense of inevitable defeat. Yet no matter how inevitable the defeat, it was still the original sin by which she became involved in her plot. But we see now that such a plot has a double aspect. On the one side, it is indefensible; we risk our lives and those of our environment for purely egotistical ends. And the animus, in his diabolical aspect, helps us to do so. But on the other side, he is fishing us out of our conventional and deadened surroundings and placing us in circumstances where we have an opportunity to realize our totality.

We will return to this dream later, but for the moment it seems to me that it can be taken as a sort of prognosis of both aspects. On the egotistical side, Mary is evidently fed up with the father figures, and we can hardly hope that she will make any serious effort with Latimer, for she clearly intends to repeat her experiment with the brother—in other words, to abandon the senex and try the puer. On the side of the totality, the prognosis seems to me definitely bad. She "tops the ball," that is, she just strikes the top

---

54. [Acqua Santa is a grandiose park and health spa outside of Rome with holy waters that reportedly cure numerous ailments. The holy water—*acqua santa*—emerges from the ground at a temperature of 33°C (91°F). Its high content of bicarbonate, sulphate, and calcium is said to purify and cure the body's organs. *Ed.*]

of it in swinging her golf club. This means that it will likely roll off the green into the rough grass, and she will be in a worse plight than at the beginning, farther away than ever in squarely meeting the realization of the individuation and totality of the Self.

Back in the train, Mary awoke with a start:

> Latimer was looking at her across a railway compartment with such an unusually kindly gaze that it seemed almost pitiful and yearning. She smiled in response and took the opportunity to ask him whether the Vignaccia was haunted. Latimer's faced changed. His expression grew strained. Was it fear? Was it anger, Mary asked herself while wishing with all her heart that she had not put the question to him . . . . Latimer replied: "All houses are visited by the spirits of those who have lived in them; it is useless to deny it, it is so; but they do not affect the living. We do not see them, cannot see them . . . though we know they are there, even be in association with them—yes, be bound up with them, with our consent or against our will!" His eyes were intent on some inward vision, and he no longer heard Mary when she spoke. But at last she arrested his attention again and insisted: "Is it haunted?" she asked.[55]

Latimer responded: "I have never seen anything supernatural in the Vignaccia . . . . Let that be enough, Mary . . . . Remember that the house has been unoccupied for many years, and that spook stories are always invented by peasants and illiterate persons when a house stands empty."[56]

After a prolonged silence he began to tell her of the rare and beautiful things he had collected for the house. These thoroughly aroused her interest and even her delight. But then he spoke with an accent of appeal in his voice. "Mary, I want you to like Vignaccia—to appreciate it."[57] Whimsically she said to herself

---

55. Hay, *The Evil Vineyard*, p. 97.
56. Ibid., p. 100.
57. Ibid., p. 101.

that Signor Enrico might have spoken thus to the woman whom he afterwards murdered.

Torrents of rain had greeted the Latimer's in Lucerne, and when the train lumbered into Goeschenen at the top of the Gotthard Pass, the snow was falling in heavy flakes (as it can any time of the year). But as they reached Bellinzona, the rain had ceased and there was a breath of the warmth of northern Italy in the air. It came as a greeting and a benediction to Mary. Eagerly she told herself that she had left the gloom and the storm and "come back into the light."

The Latimers arrived late at Locarno and spent the first night at a hotel. Mary woke up in the middle of the night and heard a hoarse muttering from the next room where Latimer slept. She sat listening with the blood throbbing at her temples, for this muttering was no ordinary sleep-talking. A tortured, restless dread in the voice was uncanny. When it ceased, she slipped out of bed and cautiously closed and locked the door.

Then she felt stifled. Of course! Her maid had forgotten to open the window. With a sense of relief she laid the blame on the maid's remises and opened the outside shutter. She was met by such a miracle of beauty—characteristic of these lakes in the Ticino—that her irritation and anxiety fell fully away.

> In the deep untroubled blue of the sky the moon rode clear and proud, a perfect crescent, with a single star—a rapt and yearning adorant—gazing down at her, while the waters of the lake were hastening on some mysterious errand of the moon's behest. The thousand sounds of day were banished, all slept and the world was given up to a rhapsody of moon and hurrying waters. A little vagrant breeze came sighing, touched the stiff leaves of a magnolia tree in the garden, making a gentle metallic clamour, as of muted cymbals— passed on to flutter the tremulous leaves of a clump of bamboos and to whisper a message to a group of slender pines— then sped away, sighing farewell to woe some other garden; or perhaps to bring the moon's commands to some forest far

away, leaving the world of the lake and the hill-land to its commune with the Spirit of Night—moving mysteriously in that faint ripple of swift flowing waters beneath the moon's calm sway .[58]

NATURE IN THE PLOT

This is the first mention of nature in the book, but from here on it appears on almost every page, so we must now look at the role that nature has played in Mary's plot. To nature per se Mary was a uterus, and it was nature's job, so to speak, to see that the right seed fertilized that uterine egg. The direct path was blocked by Mary's refusal to marry a commonplace youth and by her incestuous relation to her father which was the true cause of her mother's poisoned dart. From the "tremors of fear" we may assume that nature did not approve of the marriage with Latimer, and indeed it made little sense from nature's point of view, for, biologically, no children were begotten. In such circumstances nature generally behaves like water and flows back, seeking the weak spot where at last a breakthrough can occur. In this case Latimer seems to be that weak spot, and nature seems to be simply eating away at his foundations until at last she can destroy them. We begin to see how our plots support the "blind dynamism of nature." Mary just wanted a brilliant house to attract the right man, and the animus moved Latimer to fulfill her desire. As he was fundamentally unconscious of his feelings and motives, he naturally was malleable to any whim of nature (and to his anima which, of course, is a mighty piece of nature), and he ended up allowing himself to be used as mere building material toward nature's ends. He did not know enough about the instincts to examine the ground on which his marriage was built, and he did not realize that he might become a hindrance to yearnings and desires of nature that have no respect for brilliant brains or learned men. Does water stop to consider the value of the

58. Ibid., p. 107.

building that it destroys? And does an unconscious woman who marries a man whom she does not love stop to consider the role that nature is likely to play and the risks to which she is exposing both the man and herself?

Mary speaks of "the mystery" having appeared in nature. She imagines herself perhaps as "the single star" gazing up as "a rapt and yearning adorant" at the perfect crescent of the moon.[59] We see now why books have lost their charm for her. She no longer worships the sun, the enchanted garden of the mind, but has become a worshipper of the moon, of nature silently and secretly helping her to obtain her heart's desire.

We hear that the limpid air held promise of spring and a breath of the south, and that Mary's heart was light as she set out after breakfast to see La Vignaccia with Latimer. They walked along the shore of what seemed a magical dream lake and suddenly came upon the Casa di Ferro. It sprang up before them as if conjured up by magic. For Mary it was like stepping into another age, as if the hurried modern world had slunk away leaving this castle cut off from time. It seemed to her a place of destiny:

> "Yes, a fateful place . . . ." "Don't say that, Mary, for God's sake, don't say that," Latimer answered. "You are to be happy here . . . . You are mine, and this house is mine—you will live here and be happy. Yes, happy with me." Never had [Latimer] spoken with such uncontrolled passion, such fierce possessive force. And it had its effect. An unexpected tenderness for him stirred in her. "George," she whispered, "be kind to me and I will be happy."[60]

Evidently, Heinrich von Brunnen would have been pleased, and had Latimer really been Heinrich, Mary might have followed Faust's example when he was confronted with Helen of Troy.[61] But, of course, Latimer was not Heinrich, and he was only

---

59. Ibid., p. 107.
60. Ibid., pp. 111f.
61. [Faust and Helen of Troy begot a child. *Ed.*]

intermittently possessed by this figure. When Mary responded to Heinrich, she suddenly found Latimer in his place, a desperately embarrassed Latimer who had evidently no idea how he had become involved in such a scene.

> "Come now, let me show you the place," he said, and without looking at her further, strode on towards the house. She could see that a wave of color had surged over his face, a dark flush as of angry blood.[62]

And they approached the front door, Latimer with key in hand.

> Mary wanted to gain time before entering that gloomy castle, and the chapel on her left seemed to her a refuge. She begged him to let her see it, but he responded roughly: "Never mind the chapel, it has nothing to do with you . . . . Never will have anything to do with you."[63]

Here, Latimer tells her the forthcoming truth. Her "shrouded form" is not to lie in the chapel. That is clear from the beginning. But has he a premonition that she is to place his shrouded form in that chapel? At any rate she notes an appealing look in his eyes as he then turns toward her.

It is understandable that Mary dreads entering that gloomy castle. The castle and fortress are, as we know, symbols of the Self, symbols of that vessel that will turn into a retort from which she cannot escape. The ball that she topped has gone askew. But the retort is unfortunately in possession by the animus, and thus entering the door of the castle means entering a materialization of the animus possession that, though entirely unrealized, has been driving her toward this impending showdown from the beginning in the library of her childhood home. Moreover, it is this castle, this retort, that contained and imprisoned her fantasies in Rome; this is the very thing she has long been asking for. And it has often

---

62. Hay, *The Evil Vineyard*, p. 113.

63. Ibid., pp. 113f.

been said that the best punishment for the plot of many a woman is to give her what she wants! At all events, I must add from my own experience that there is nothing so terrifying as an insufficiently realized plot when it finally appears in concrete reality.

As they enter the castle, Latimer surprisingly held out both hands to her: "Welcome," he said, "Welcome." And here Heinrich von Brunnen appears again, for Mary felt as though she were suddenly confronted with a stranger. It was all like a fevered dream, unreal, yet painfully vivid. But this time the possession is not so effective, for "it seemed as if he were play-acting." But George Latimer play acting? And so it goes on as they walk about the castle: one moment he is Heinrich von Brunnen . . . and the next Latimer the archaeologist. Mary comments on the beautiful carpets and rugs, for instance, and asks: "Oughtn't we to have the floor strewn with rushes?" "Your dates are wrong," smiled Latimer. In her relief at hearing him speak so naturally, she attempted a joke: "When you lived here before, you had carpets?" "Yes," he answered simply, "after she came."[64] He apparently spoke to himself contemplating a memory of his own past.

> "George," she said, "you speak as if you had lived here before, as if you had known the place . . . when it was inhabited by Signor Enrico and the lady of the Casa di Ferro . . . ." "What do you know of Signor Enrico?" Latimer asked . . . , "I insist on your telling me . . . ." "They say he haunts the Vignaccia . . . ." "That's what they say, is it?" he returned angrily…, "Must fools gossip about the dead?" "It's only an old story, after all," she said soothingly. "Yes, yes . . . ," he replied, "only an old story! A mad story of evil. Let us forget it."[65]

At this moment Race's voice, raised in expostulation, came from below (he was speaking to the Ticinese porters who were bringing Mary's luggage from the hotel):

---

64. Ibid., p. 116.
65. Ibid., pp. 120f.

"Hi, you there. Vous! Porter! Donnay me that bag. Sacco do you call it? Well, I'll give you sack-oh! in a minute, I can tell you that, my man, if you don't 'urry up with the luggage. The bagg-gage, d'you comprennay me? 'Ere, take it up them stairs. Yes, yes, up the escal-liay!"[66]

Both Mary and Latimer laughed. Race's prosaic voice came as a relief, and Latimer went down to intervene.

THE SPIDER

We hear that the first week at La Vignaccia passed tranquilly. Mary had promised Latimer to be happy, and she meant honestly to try, sternly putting off all thoughts of Signor Enrico and his hapless lady. Latimer's study was a large central room serving as a passage-way of sorts, a central area adjoining the oratory (the small, internal, private chapel) and other rooms. Mary notes that it is an odd choice since Latimer hates being interrupted when he is working. When Race was asked to see that Latimer was not disturbed, he replied: "Why, Mum, it won't be possible not to disturb 'im. Why can't 'e take another room? There 'e is, sitting like a spider in 'is web, right in the middle of the 'ouse, to catch us like so many flies whenever we move. One of 'is whims again, Mum?"[67]

The entrance to the network of secret passageways was in the oratory, and when Latimer was supposed to be working in his study, he was often really prowling about the passages in the thick walls that he had secretly restored. At many points there were apertures where the wall turned on hinges leaving only a thin perforated layer of plaster. Latimer was thus able to hear and see everything that happened at the Casa di Ferro.

The spider suggestion worked on Mary as a sort of catalyst for her plot. Coming from Race, who was devoted to his master, it was a welcome confirmation of what she had always hoped to be the truth, and it was just too tempting, so she swallowed it whole.

---

66. Ibid., p. 121.
67. Ibid., p. 123.

As we have seen, one can say that she was the actual spider, for Latimer was just blindly compelled to spin the web of her animus. As usual, Mary provided herself with an alibi, for she suggested that Latimer take another room for his study, but he answered curtly that this one suited him. He was so visibly irritated by the suggestion of changing that she felt he must have a reason for his choice. As he was so obliging as to settle down in the center of the web, he formed an almost inevitable hook for the projection of her spider. But actually he was much more like a fly consoling itself with the foolish conviction that it chose to be the boss entangled at the center of a spider's web, the spider itself far more clever and adept than himself.

It would not have been very difficult for Mary to unravel the mystery of the secret passages. Race immediately drew her attention to the fact that one never knew whether Latimer was in his study or not. "'E's all over the place nowadays, Mum. Gives me quite a turn sometimes, 'e does, appearing from nowhere. 'E's 'ere and there and right down in the basement too, as likely as not. Yes, in the orifices, Mum, just as sudden as sudden." But Mary cut him short, for occasionally Race's freedom of speech annoyed her. Yet the spider remark, which was really a good deal more outspoken, did not annoy her at all.[68]

A few days after this conversation Mary was confronted with evidence that was more difficult to ignore. She had seen Latimer go upstairs to the study before her and, after an instant's hesitation, followed him into the room. He was not in the study, nor could she find him in the other places he could have reached from that staircase. She noticed that the curtain over the oratory was drawn back, and for the first time the oratory was unlocked. She entered, but when she put out her hand to feel the texture of the woven carpet that concealed the entrance to the secret passages, she heard Latimer's voice speaking close to her: "Leave that alone." Hastily, like a child caught trespassing on forbidden ground, she stepped out of the oratory. The study was empty.

She called Latimer, but he did not reply:

---

68. Ibid., p. 124.

Then a fearful thought shot through her mind: perhaps it was
not her husband who was so strange, perhaps she herself was
not sane, perhaps she was subject to hallucinations. "Am I
mad?" she whispered. She felt her throat go dry; a wave of ago-
nizing fear surged over her, leaving her weak and trembling.[69]

When at last Latimer entered from the staircase door, she questioned him adding: "Oh, George, I am frightened, it is uncanny."[70]
He assured her that he had turned back on the staircase and
gone down into the Lower Hall. "Are you satisfied?" he eagerly
asked. "Tell me you are satisfied." "Yes," she answered dubiously,
"I suppose I am."[71] But a few minutes later she found old Race
polishing furniture in the Lower Hall, a mania of which he was
rather ashamed.

> "I do wish Mr. Latimer would tell me if 'e wants that 'pree
> Dew' polished or not. I daren't touch it without his permis-
> sion, Mum," Race said in an aggrieved voice. "Why didn't
> you ask him when he was here just now?" [Mary] said care-
> lessly. "'Ere just now?" he grumbled. "Why, I 'aven't seen Mr.
> Latimer since breakfast, Mum . . . . I'm not blind as I know of
> and 'e 'as not been in the Lower Hall this last hour, Mum."[72]

Then Mary realized that Latimer had lied to her, in fact had
lied elaborately. Yet although she well knew the walls were eight
feet thick, she did not draw the obvious conclusion. Presumably
it would have disturbed the fulfillment of her plot if she had discovered the secret passages before the fatal night. Therefore, she
shut up Race, remained oblivious to the facts in front of her face,
and even shuddered in fear of going insane rather than thinking
long enough to solve that rather simple mystery too soon.[73]

---

69. Ibid., p. 126.
70. Ibid., p. 127.
71. Ibid., p. 128.
72. Ibid., pp. 129f.
73. [As occasionally found in mental disorders, "falling" into a psychosis is sometimes preferable to facing the devastating and unconscionable truth of what one has been involved

MARY'S FAMILIAR SPIRIT

This panic regarding her sanity had a very interesting result. She was sitting that afternoon in her bedroom looking out at the smiling beauty of the lake; that one room in the house which she really liked, where she felt safe and had a sense of guarded peace. How still it was. "There is so much comfort in the great silences of the world," she thought. "In silence and beauty the wounded soul can heal its hurts."[74] She knew that her soul was wounded although she had nothing further to expect from it. Suddenly she heard a movement in the room behind her, and then a faint sigh. At first she was afraid, and then fear fell strangely away and a feeling of tranquility and solace stole over her.

> Whatever it was in the room with her—be it spirit or human being—it was good, kind and strong, it meant well by her . . . . The world of external consciousness slipped away . . . . She did not lose the certitude of being in her room, she even saw the furniture distinctly and perceived the fragrance of some lilies-of-the-valley which were on the writing table; and yet she understood that she had passed beyond the world of everyday cognizance, that she had strayed into a plane where Time does not exist. She was aware of sitting motionless in the carven chair; she realized that she herself was unchanged, but she had almost achieved full possession of a knowledge which, although she had never discerned it before, she had always held. There was someone with her whom she instantly recognized, but whose face and aspect she could not see; whose name she could not recollect although had an integrant part of her mind been freed from a kind of haze, she understood it would be a name which was familiar to her. Someone was near her, leaning over the back of her chair, and a hand rested on her brow with a touch so tender and compelling that it drew all the pain and anxiety from her soul. Then a whisper reached her: "Have no fear," it said, "have no

in. *Ed.*]
74. Hay, *The Evil Vineyard*, p. 131.

fear, I watch over you, I guard you until you pass from my keeping to his; until he comes, he for whom you wait." . . .

Slowly, as a cloud floats past a hill-top, the touch on her brow was lifted and, after a pause—a pause like a space of serene blue in an April sky—she knew she was once more alone. . . .

Half dazed, she sat up and turned fearlessly towards the room, fully expecting to see someone—something—standing near her. There was no one, and she felt a keen sense of disappointment, as though a beloved friend with whom she had been speaking had left her without warning.[75]

The book explains this presence as someone who had passed on. But this does not explain Mary's instant recognition or her feeling that a beloved friend had left her. Fraulein Alten had told Mary that it was certain that it was Heinrich von Brunnen who was the ghost of La Vignaccia, but this figure has no resemblance to Heinrich. After Latimer's death, the priest suggested that it might have been either the earlier lady of the Casa di Ferro or the other victim, the younger lover of earlier days. When one examines the material carefully, there is no evidence that this figure is feminine except perhaps the absence of jealousy in regards to Maurice Drummond, a point to which we will later return. Therefore, I think it would be too optimistic to interpret this figure as the Self, for we know that Mary has "topped the ball" and that the castle is in the possession of the animus, though indeed the figure must be related to the Self, for it turns out to be more powerful than Heinrich von Brunnen. We get a hint in the book itself, for when this same figure wakes Mary on the fatal night, she says that it was "as if her soul had woken her body." Therefore, this figure must be a personification of a part of her own psyche, perhaps the more positive side of her animus, the part which is not projected onto Latimer.

There is another possible explanation which I would like to briefly consider. You will remember the definition from Ruland's *Lexicon alchemiae* that Jung gave in *Psychology and Alchemy*:

---

75. Ibid., pp. 132ff.

"Imagination is the star in man, the celestial or super-celestial body."[76] Commenting on Ruland's statement Jung adds:

> This astounding definition throws a quite special light on the fantasy processes connected with the opus. We have to conceive of these processes not as the immaterial phantoms we readily take fantasy-pictures to be, but as something corporeal, a "subtle body," semi-spiritual in nature. In an age when there was as yet no empirical psychology, such a concretization was bound to be made, because everything unconscious, once it was activated, was projected into matter—that is to say, it approached people from outside. It was a hybrid phenomenon, as it were, half spiritual, half physical; a concretization such as we frequently encounter in the psychology of primitives.[77]

Emma Jung suggested in the discussion after the last lecture that, as we first hear of the love story from Fraulein Alten—who certainly represents the shadow—it might not belong to the legend, but rather it might have originated in Mary's imagination. This idea casts an interesting light on the book's suggestion. This figure would then be a figure made by Mary's own fantasy out of the substances of her subtle body, the "celestial or super-celestial body" of Ruland's definition. Naturally, the lover or lovers would be entirely on Mary's side, and thus mean well by her, and they would be bent on their revenge on Heinrich.

The celestial—let alone the super-celestial of Ruland's definition—seems a bit marvelous for what we know of Mary's situation. We must remember that the alchemists used active imagination in conjunction with repeated sublimations of their substances in the retort in order to attain their so-called celestial, sky-blue fluid. Mary's fantasies were mainly unconscious and, in essence, passive imagination. Therefore, it seems reasonable to suppose that the substance that she had produced may be something like the raw

---

76. Jung, *Psychology and Alchemy, CW,* vol. 12, par. 394.
77. Ibid.

material from which the celestial or super-celestial body is extract-
ed by active imagination and sublimation. When one remembers
the effect that Mary's fantasies have had upon Latimer, one is
forced to the conclusion that if she used active imagination at
all, it was more witchlike than alchemistic in character, that is, it
was used for personal ends. This figure would then take on the
character of the familiar of the witch; and I think we should also
consider it from this point of view, for all of Mary's psychic libido
was in the unconscious, she had no activity or relationship worth
mentioning in the outer world, and, moreover, she was living in a
sixteenth-century stronghold with a medieval animus. The familiar of the witch was closely related to the medieval incubus, and I
do not think we can exclude the possibility that Mary actually may
have had some psychological form of an incubus.[78] The woman's
incubus can be said to be a representation of a possessed part of
the psyche and can be seen to consist mainly of a host of masculine demons who in one sense are unconscious yet take possession
of a smaller or greater portion of the psyche. Jung notes that they
assert their "hateful and harmful existence undeterred by all our
insight, reason, and energy, thereby proclaiming the power of
the unconscious over the conscious mind, the sovereign power
of possession."[79] Whether this psychic phenomenon is strictly
subjective or objective, a purely projected visionary experience or
whatever, is for us here not the question.

To delve even further into this theme we will turn to a book
called *The Discoverie of Witchcraft* by an Englishman, Reginald

78. [The incubus (plural *incubi*; from Latin *incubare*, "to lie upon") is a demon in male form
supposed to lie upon sleepers, especially on women, in order to have sexual intercourse
with them, draining their energy in order to sustain itself, and in most cases leaving the
victim dead or in very weak condition. Here we find a parallel to the psychology of vampires,
that is, a type of animus that drains a woman—and all those around her—of her energy.
A female version was called a succubus. During the witch hunts, alleged intercourse with
demons was one of the sins for which women were executed. Sometimes incubi were said to
conceive children with the women they raped, a well-known case being that of Merlin of the
Arthurian legend. In some legends, incubi and succubi were said to be able to change their
sex; the succubus would sleep with a man and collect his semen, transform into an incubus,
and use that seed on a hapless woman to beget human offspring, a "plausible" medieval
argument resolving the question of inexplicable pregnancy. *Ed.*]
79. C. G. Jung, "The Relations Between the Ego and the Unconscious" (1928), in *CW*, vol.
7 (Princeton, N.J.: Princeton University Press, 1953), par. 370.

Scot, that appeared in 1584 to see what we can learn about the incubus. The book was written to prove that there was no such thing as witchcraft in an age when everybody believed in witches—very much including the author's own unconscious. But it is full of quotations from the medieval literature on the subject. The idea that spirits are connected with any kind of substance, or that they consist of a sort of subtle body, is particularly objectionable to Scot, but nevertheless he devotes the fourth book of this large volume to the incubus and succubus. I am sorry to inflict this rather obscene material upon you, but it casts an interesting light on our problem. The book is written in Elizabethan English, so for the most part I only give the sense of what Scot says:

> James Sprenger and Henrie Institor in *Malleus Maleficarum,* agreeing with Bodin, Barth, Epineus, Daneus, Erastus, Hemingius and the rest, doo make a bawdie discourse, labouring to prove by a foolish kind of philosophie that spirits can take on earthly shape, that they can hear and see and even devour meat and expel the same, and that they "specialiie excel in the use and art of venerie." T. Brabant says that until the year 1400 the incubus used to ravish women against their will, but that since that date witches consent willingly to the desire of the incubus.
>
> Sprenger and Institor affirm that witches have often been seen apparently alone in coitus on the fields, and that, after "a convenient time has elapsed for such a piece of work," a black vapour has been observed to ascend from them about the length and bigness of a man. They also say that many a husband has seen the incubus in bed with his wife, and has sometimes struck off his head with a sword, but because the body is nothing but air, "it closeth together again." The wife will then persuade the husband that he is mad or possessed and that he did not know what he was doing, and this because she had more pleasure and delight with the incubus than with any mortal man, "whereby you may perceive that spirits are palpable."[80]

---

80. Reginald Scot, *The Discoverie of Witchcraft* (1584) (New York: Dover, 1989), p. 42ff.

The parallel between the wives who persuade their husbands that they are mad or possessed and Mary's case is striking. Moreover, it was presumably Mary's doubt of her own sanity that led to this manifestation and reassurance, for she thought perhaps it was not her husband but herself who was mad.

The incubus is often seen in the fields and out of doors, according to Scot, and in other books that I have read it is stated that the incubus is a sylvan being, a relation of Pan's, and is to be found in nature. This would fit in with Mary's new fascination with the moon, with nature, and might also explain her feeling that this presence meant well by her. Nature certainly meant well by Mary and was entirely on the side of her plot. One would, however, rather expect such a figure to show jealousy of Maurice Drummond. But Latimer is so madly jealous that one could almost assume that the whole of Mary's animus that was susceptible to jealousy was projected onto him. Moreover, the incubus is so close to nature that he is perhaps hardly differentiated enough to be troubled with this sort of jealousy.

As regards the message given by this tangible presence, the book assumes that it was Maurice Drummond who was meant by "he for whom you wait." On the personal side of the plot, this is presumably correct. We are thus confronted with the fact that this voice knew of Maurice's existence some weeks before he appeared. When Maurice writes to Latimer to ask if he may come to La Vignaccia, Latimer states that Mary has "never heard of him." It becomes clear later, however, that Latimer and Maurice met in London while the former was engaged to Mary. Therefore, it seems a little peculiar that he can remember so definitively after nine years that he never mentioned Maurice to Mary. Being as it may, since this voice—which is admittedly outside space and time—knew of Maurice's existence at the time of Mary's experience in her bedroom, presumably it also knew of him from the beginning. Therefore, the whole plot—on the personal side—may well have been aimed at Maurice from the start. This would fit in with Drummond's statement to Mary after Latimer's death: "We belong together, have belonged together always." Maurice would simply be the puer of Latimer's senex.

But on the side of totality, this "he for whom you wait" takes on a much deeper significance. Rivkah Schärf Kluger has drawn my attention to the fact that the introduction—"Have no fear, have no fear"—is the classical introduction of the voice of God in the Bible. During this experience Mary herself realized that she was "beyond the world of everyday cognizance, in a plane where Time does not exist." Had she been able to hold to this realization, to use her undoubtedly strong power of imagination in meditating upon it, her imagination might have lost its witchlike character and gained an alchemistic aspect. It seems to me that this figure might then have developed into the psychopomp, the Poimen or "good shepherd," and "he" could have led her to the integration of that part of her psyche projected onto Heinrich von Brunnen (the negative aspect of the same figure). He has miraculously brought Mary to a point where—unconscious as she was—she could have taken the inward path that would have led her toward the Self, the totality.

Had Mary actually been living in the Middle Ages, this experience might well have led her to find a vocation as a nun, but in her age and circumstances it really would have been very difficult for her to find a form in which she could have taken her experience wholly to the subjective level. She was only twenty-nine at this time, and thus the part of wholeness would almost certainly include more experience in actual life. Moreover, we know that she was entirely possessed by the goal to fall in love. Therefore, it seems to me that we can assume that the voice, at any rate outwardly, really meant Maurice by "he for whom you wait," or at all events some actual man, and that his advent was rapidly approaching. From this point of view one is struck by the complete absence of shock. We hear that she was "infinitely comforted" knowing now that there was someone who watched over her in that "place of strange memories." But what about the blatant and complex dilemma of another man entering the life of a married woman? She speaks herself of the innate conventionality that was in her blood, thus one is surprised by the lack of conventional reaction when she heard it directly stated that she was waiting for another man; one would expect such a realization to shatter the walls of the compartments.

The innate conventionality does indeed react, but in an unexpected place, and in a meek and unconvincing manner.

> The warm spring days went by quickly, and nothing came to disturb the monotony of life in the Vignaccia. Mary was tranquil; she no longer feared Latimer, though she watched him narrowly, not with anxiety for herself, but with a kind of solicitude for him. She knew instinctively that this quiet was only a pause in a drama wherein she was destined to play her part—what that drama would be she could not even guess, but since that afternoon in her room she was fearless. She saw that Latimer was filled with unrest; often she was conscious of his eyes fixed upon her with such a hungry, miserable look that her heart went out to him in pity. She was no inexperienced girl, and she wondered if there was a physical cause for this devouring gaze. Well, he was her husband, by all the rites of Church and Law, and if he chose to return to her, she was bound to give what he craved. Night after night she waited, praying it might not be, yet *honestly ready to meet his demands* if need be. He never came.[81]

We see here that her conventionality makes an attempt to persuade her that "he for whom you wait" is her husband, but it is anything but convincing. Yet, in terms of plots, her conviction effectively deflects her conscious attention into channels that reestablish and reinforce compartmental thinking. One feels that she was pretty confident that her prayers would be heard. And if Latimer had come, her laboriously dutiful attitude would again be as discouraging as her obedient and disinterested behavior during the first months of her marriage that so effectively extinguished any sexual interest he had. Moreover, Latimer did actu-

---

81. Hay, *The Evil Vineyard,* pp. 137f; Barbara Hannah's emphasis.

ally come on the fatal night, and she refused him. Therefore, we can put a question mark by the phrase "honestly ready to meet his demands." The book continues:

> He was frequently absent for the day, then he would return unexpectedly. Occasionally she recollected that she heard not his footsteps on the terrace—yet suddenly he was standing beside her. It flashed across her that he was watching her. Perhaps he planned to surprise her? She smiled a little bitterly. There was nothing in her life to surprise; she was absolutely alone. Was he jealous of her loneliness?[82]

It is interesting that Latimer watched her and was jealous even before Drummond's arrival. Presumably, he was dimly aware of that presence in her bedroom. We saw that the medieval husband took the incubus exceedingly seriously, and Latimer was possessed by a medieval man and his consciousness was partially in a medieval state of development. As Mary made no attempt to mediate upon that presence from beyond space and time, we may be pretty sure that it would tend to regress toward the incubus rather than progress toward the Poimen.

The next paragraph gives us the key to why there was no shock. We read that she was waiting, for what she did not know, but there was no doubt in her mind that she waited for something. The "he" of "he for whom you wait" has simply disappeared. We could give her the benefit of the doubt, when she married, as to whether she knew that she expected the "brilliant house" to produce the lover in time. But now there is no doubt by which she can benefit. She has told us herself that she has discerned this knowledge that she always held and has recorded it, so to speak, in black and white. Therefore, she must have forgotten what she was waiting for more or less on purpose. Had she remembered, she would have been forced into conflict. She would then have realized that there was an excellent reason for her new solicitude for her husband, and that it was he and not herself who was in

---

82. Ibid., p. 138.

danger at the Casa di Ferro. She was very near this realization, for she tells us again that her fear was for him and not of him. Had she pursued this line of thought, sooner or later it would have collided with "he for whom you wait," and then she would have had to ask herself: "What do I intend to do about my husband when this man who has been promised me appears?" Such a problem might have led her toward her totality and offered a path by which she could escape from "the blind dynamism of nature."

But it belongs to the very nature of the unconscious that it offers us the way of escape, the path to self-consciousness, and if we do not grasp it, it takes it back again. You will remember the treasure, so often mentioned by Jung, that ascends to the surface during nine years, nine months, and nine days.[83] Jung was discussing the difficulty in integrating contents from the unconscious and dream motifs that repeat over and over even when the dreamer may outwardly seem to grasp the meaning. One shows a dream content to a patient, and the patients says: "Yes, I see that perfectly." So there must be some new recognition of that motif. But

> real recognition, a full realization, of these unconscious contents never happens all at once. It always comes in waves, wave after wave, with a pause in between before a new and more intense realization of what that thing is [that emerges]. There are cases where a dream in the beginning of analysis contains the whole analytical procedure. If one realized it, one would possess everything that one needed . . . . At first you get only a very vague glimpse, it is as if you have never seen it. Then it comes again and you think: that is it, as if you have never seen it. Then comes a third wave and you think, is it not marvelous?—a perfect realization. Then that ebbs away, and a fourth and fifth wave come, and many waves must come until we realize that what we call progress is really always one and the same thing, which we are simply unable

---

83. C. G. Jung, *Dream Analysis: Notes of the Seminar Given in 1928–1930* (Princeton, N.J.: Princeton University Press, 1984), p. 651.

to realize and which only dawns upon us very slowly. It is as if the sun, in order to become visible to us, must come up and go down again and again until we realize that it is the sun and it is day.[84]

Jung then proceeds to speak about the repeated attempts on the part of the unconscious to portray a problem in the dreams of a male patient.

He cannot make up his mind to see the thing exactly as it is, and to give it the right value. This seems to be a tremendous difficulty, and I never hastened him, never bullied him, because I know quite well that it cannot be forced . . . . One must not push the thing. It needs to mature slowly. If you push it you might injure vital instincts. I have never made any conditions [on a patient]—if you do not do this, and all that stuff. That won't work at all. One has to be exceedingly patient in such a case. But we shall encounter quite a number of dreams where the wave comes on again and again and where [the dreamer] has a new chance to take it. One often finds that motif, the hidden treasure, or the blossoming of the treasure of the flower in mythology and folklore. It is supposed to blossom after a certain period, say nine years, nine months, nine days. On the ninth night, the treasure comes up to the surface, and whoever happens to be on the spot on the ninth can take it, but the next night it goes down to the depths, and then it takes nine years and nine months and nine days before it blossoms again. That is the demonstration in folklore of the difficulty of psychological realization.[85]

Curiously enough, almost exactly that much time has elapsed since Mary failed to stand by her feeling in the matter of the gallery seat at the opera. Again she missed the opportunity and again it disappears into the unconscious.

---

84. Ibid.
85. Ibid., pp. 652f.

It soon becomes evident that "he for whom you wait" has been taken very seriously by Mary's fantasies, for Maurice Drummond's letter arrived a few weeks after her experience. Latimer exclaimed: "Upon my word, pretty damned cool!" and indeed the letter was cool, for Maurice not only invited himself for a fortnight's visit to a cousin whom he had not seen for nine years but also asked for a telegraphic reply. And then he arrived on the next day, that is, the day before he was expected. This behavior is in flagrant contradiction to everything that Mary tells us about Maurice, for he is always depicted as an exceedingly polite and considerate young man. One can only account for this extraordinary and inconsiderate haste by the hypothesis that Mary must have been broadcasting an SOS in the unconscious and that this young Perseus had unconsciously come hastening on his winged sandals to rescue a fair lady in distress, in other words, that something in the unconscious had taken possession of him. Moreover, Latimer's behavior is an exact parallel of Sir Arthur's before his own first visit to Darnfield. Mary asks him "carelessly" why he does not tell Drummond that it is no time to come, and Latimer replies: "Because—well, I hardly know why myself; I suppose it is difficult to refuse."

Drummond has hardly been in the house for half an hour before Mary is establishing an alibi for him and herself. When they all meet before dinner in the study and Latimer introduces them to each other, Maurice says to Mary: "It's awfully good of you to let me come here," and she replies simply: "I am glad you have come . . . but it was really your cousin who invited you." She was to wonder later why she had instinctively stressed this "fact" from the outset.

I remarked earlier that when Latimer returned to Rome and showed the first signs of his possession by Heinrich von Brunnen, he was half like a hypnotized thing and half more friendly and human than he had ever been before. This development continued at the Casa di Ferro. The cold scientist had almost entirely disappeared, and when Latimer was not possessed, he sometimes showed an astonishing understanding of Mary and a real sympathy for her youth and loneliness. Curiously enough, Maurice's arrival at first strengthened this human side, and for a whole week there was no sign of Heinrich von Brunnen. Latimer actually felt increasingly pleased with his kinsman. He talked more than Mary had ever known him to talk, and it seemed as if the shadow had been lifted from his mind. Moreover, he gave up using the secret passages and ceased appearing suddenly from nowhere.

Mary also had moments of insight. She realized, for instance, that she had married from ambition while her heart had been banished from her council, and she knew that she was wildly and desperately in love with Maurice. She also realized that it was a "situation to be dealt with calmly and reasonably" and was even aware that "she had a task before her which she must accomplish, not for her own sake alone, but for the sake of the man she loved. And for the sake too of that other man, for him she had married in the 'foolish pride of her youth.'"[86] One has the impression that, in a way, she was capable of accomplishing this task, but this would have meant abandoning her lifelong passivity and sacrificing the further development of her plot in its personal aspect. Moreover, it would of course draw her into the most terrible conflict. Yet here was certainly another chance to approach her totality. As we know, the path to the Self is tortuous and always leads through conflict, for the Self is a *coincidentia oppositorum*. But Mary had just fallen from one opposite into the other; she no longer valued the "enchanted garden of her mind" but was now the "rapt and yearning adorant" of the moon and of nature who had now brought her the man with whom she had fallen in love. Here was the man promised her by means of the voice in the bedroom and into his keeping she shall pass.

Therefore, all of her conscious realizations are conveniently swallowed up again in bursts of emotion, yearning, and resentment. Latimer had been a "bird of prey, hungry for flesh" and now he was old and satiated, and she felt that she had missed her youth's fair rights. She was also convinced that the marriage was all his fault, and now he was a jailer in charge of his prisoners or, better said, his single prisoner: a weak and helpless woman

---

86. Hay, *The Evil Vineyard,* p. 189.

irretrievably captive and in his power. She was aware that in a few days Maurice would go away, back to the world of youth and freedom, and she would remain withering away in the Casa di Ferro until Nemesis overtook her.

This is, indeed, not really surprising when we remember that Jung has said that the plots occupy the compartment between consciousness and the animus. Presumably, therefore, it is only possible for a woman to reach a lasting awareness of the animus, and of the other figures of the collective unconscious, after she has succeeded in realizing the existence of the plots. It seems to me that this realization is of paramount important. The book is, indeed, written from the traditional standpoint where woman automatically projects the activity, and thus also the blame, onto man. But it seems to me that she thus gives away her greatest opportunity. Jung writes in *Psychology and Alchemy*:

> Only a fool is interested in the guilt of other people, which he cannot alter. The wise man only learns from his own guilt, and he will ask himself: "Who am I that all this happens to?" To find the answer to this fateful question, he will look into his own depths.[87]

Indeed a profound thought. How much further we would be today if those who preach would look into their own depths and search their own guilt, relieving us of the burden of carrying their guilt as well as our own.

As this lecture is written from the standpoint of woman, I have tried to look into her depths. I have made little attempt to apportion the blame between Latimer and Mary but have concentrated on the latter's unconsciousness, or guilt, wherever I felt that this could help us to see our own.

On the eighth day of Maurice's visit, the three were in the study discussing a splendid meal of risotto à la Milanese that Maurice had promised to treat his cousin to at the Ristorante del Grotto ten minutes' walk from the Vignaccia. Maurice hurried

---

87. Jung, *Psychology and Alchemy*, *CW*, vol. 12, par. 152.

away to order the risotto leaving Latimer and Mary in the study. "What a child it is!" Latimer said, looking after him affectionately. "Yes, yes, youth about the house is good. Perhaps if I had had a son I should be a more genial companion to you, Mary."[88]

It seems to me that this would have been a moment when Mary could have begun that "task," but she replied with a cheap evasion: "Shall we adopt a child; would you care to?" she asked lightly. Heinrich von Brunnen sees his opportunity:

> "Were you proposing to adopt Maurice Drummond? You would be a very young stepmother for him. What would you feel when he called you mother?"
>
> His words sent a hot flush to her cheeks. She bent down, pretending to fasten her shoe; somehow she felt she must hide her face from him at that moment. When she raised her eyes she found him looking at her with so sinister a gaze that her heart stood still. It was the fierce searching look which had haunted her when they first came to the Vignaccia. There was menace, question, pain and mockery in it. Now it seemed to her more threatening than ever before.
>
> "Why do you look at me so?" she asked. She scarcely knew what she was saying.
>
> "I was seeing a very young woman blushing," he answered slowly, and then he rose up and came towards her. For a moment she thought he meant to take her by the throat. Suddenly he paused, swaying backwards slightly, as though a powerful grip had arrested his movement towards her. He looked behind him.
>
> "Who's there? Who touched me?" he cried furiously.
>
> The sunlit room was empty.
>
> Mary sat there silently with a white set face. For an instant they were thus, and she heard the water of the lake lapping upon the shore and the whirr of wings as a bird flew by.
>
> With an effort she rose and, looking Latimer unflinch- ingly in the eyes, said calmly: "There is no one here, George.

88. Hay, *The Evil Vineyard*, p. 162.

Did you think you heard someone?"

"I fancied I-I-I felt . . . It's nothing . . ." he muttered hoarsely, and without another word, he hastened from the room as though fleeing from a great dread.[89]

The book explains this invisible force as the same presence that materialized in Mary's bedroom. Of course this is quite possible, but it could also have been Latimer's own better side that did not want him to hurt Mary. At all events, this invisible force had a totally different effect on her from that of the manifestations of the presence in her room, for instead of being "infinitely comforted" at this intervention on her behalf, she sensed disaster. One cannot make any definite statement about such phenomenon. The fact that Latimer was fleeing as from a great dread does not seem to have moved her at all.

As so often happens in real life, this return to the Heinrich von Brunnen solution of her problem was strengthened by a chance remark that afternoon. Latimer introduced the old priest to her at the Ristorante del Grotto, and he greeted Mary by saying: "It is a pleasure to me to make the acquaintance of the 'Lady of the Casa di Ferro.'" This came to Mary as a shock. She realized that in the thoughts of the neighborhood she was instinctively linked with that other victim of La Vignaccia. She had steadfastly refused to let her mind dwell on that old story, but she now realized that she had always subconsciously admitted her connection with it. It was futile to deny it any longer.

This remark had the same effect as Race's spider. It simply receded into the unconscious; it was swallowed whole. (It was the priest who first told the story to Fraulein Alten and later to Latimer. It is perhaps worth mentioning that, according to Scot, medieval priests were often suspected of having a dubious relation to the figure of the incubus.)

It is also interesting that three days before the fatal act Mary tells us that she has, so to speak, decided to "identify completely with the medieval lady" and thus she gives free rein to her fan-

---

89. Ibid., pp. 163f.

tasy (as well as to her animus in his negative aspect). The priest's remark fell on particularly fertile soil, for it had been directly preceded by an experience with Maurice that she called "destiny fulfilled." Their eyes had met and, as the author explains, they were swept together irresistibly, wrapped in a union that was of the spirit, of the flesh, of the essence of their beings. Directly afterward, Mary became conscious that Latimer had watched the scene, that "hateful watcher," as she calls him.

Mme de Villeneuve arrived the same evening, and Maurice made an attempt to escape the next day, but we are told that Latimer would not hear of his leaving. As they all sat in the study having tea on the third day of Mme de Villeneuve's visit, and as it turns out, on the afternoon of the fatal night, we hear from Mary that Race's simile, considerably developed, has been constantly in her mind. The large sunlit room (the study) had grown to represent the spider's vantage point whence the web depended—it waxed or waned according to the will of the spider, spinner of her destiny. She looked across at Latimer—the spider—smiling at Mme de Villeneuve who was complimenting him on the arrangement of La Vignaccia. Mary thus concedes that she is having a fantasy about herself as the silly fly struggling in Latimer's web on the very day of the tragedy—a parallel to the helpless lady, the prisoner of Heinrich von Brunnen.

There was a duel of wills that night between Mary and Latimer. The latter seemed bent on keeping his guests with him, and Mary on going to bed. Latimer won at first, and fascinated both Mme de Villeneuve and Maurice by pouring out a wealth of knowledge. At last Mary succeeded in breaking up the party, but Latimer followed her into her bedroom. She soon accused him of being her jailer and, in the ensuing scene, repulsed his advances violently. (So much for "honestly ready to meet his demands.") Latimer then accused her of loving Maurice. "And if I do?" she retorted.[90]

> The face near her changed, it grew haggard like one in physical pain . . . . There was fear in his face—fear which made

90. Ibid., p. 208.

him look almost imbecile. "It was here before, here before"
he muttered hoarsely . . . . He looked at her with dazed eyes,
a piteous, hunted gaze it was. . . . "Oh! Why do you torture
me?" he said in a low, moaning voice. "I, torture you?" she
cried. "What have I done?" He laughed harshly: "What have
you done? That you must know best yourself—but I know
too. Don't delude yourself; I know, too."[91]

From notes found in the secret passages after his death, Latimer
was forced by Heinrich von Brunnen to wait and watch while he
thought they might be innocent. When Mary told him that she
loved Maurice, it was apparently the signal that he must start on
"his errand of death" through the secret passages. We see that it
was no impulsive act of jealousy or revenge, but a task that was
forced upon him, an agony and a terror.

As we have heard, Mary herself records this agony and terror,
but it made no impression on her. When Latimer left her, she
remained adamant in her role as the medieval lady, and lay down
on her bed with the reflection that perhaps "Sleep" would bring
her his mighty brother "Death." But she did not care; she was
too weary to care. As we know, the voice fulfilled its promise that
she should pass into Maurice Drummond's keeping, and it was
Latimer and not Mary who died upon that bed.

One can understand why Latimer's anima—even in her
positive aspect—had thrown him into Mary's plot, for had she
not done so, he would have remained entirely one-sided in the
aloof, impersonal realm where he lived, albeit desiccated, lacking
anything other than academic meaning. Latimer also missed—or
avoided—numerous opportunities to confront and discuss the
deeper problems in the marriage. A confrontation with both his
wife and his own feeling life could have redeemed his anima,
although his suffering would have been great and long. Clearly
it was anything but an ideal solution to spend the last months of
his life creeping about in the secret passages, prey to jealousy
concerning his wife, in possession by a "cruel taskmaster." But

---

91. Ibid., pp. 209f.

at least he was experiencing his other, personal feminine side, and it bore some conscious fruit in the new understanding and sympathy that he occasionally showed toward his wife. And even Mary owned once that perhaps if he was so madly jealous, it meant that he cared for her, that in his strange way he loved her. And we must not forget that when they looked at the dead man's face, there was only a great weariness in it, as of one who rests at last having accomplished a task of magnitude almost beyond his strength. (Here, we might compare this with "the task" that Mary said she must accomplish, of reconciling the claims of Maurice and Latimer, a task that she never even began.)

Mme de Villeneuve insisted on concealing the tragedy from the public. At first Mary refused to listen and seemed actually to want the world to know that Latimer had died raving mad, for as she said, it was true. But Mme de Villeneuve carried her point, Latimer was removed to his room, and Mary was made to help her with remaking the bed and concealing the bedclothes that Latimer had hacked to pieces with his dagger. We read: "It had been an almost sordid work, fraught with the hideous suggestion of the efforts of accomplices to conceal a crime."[92]

This is the nearest Mary gets to a realization that she was actually an accomplice in this crime. But the next day, when she is in the secret passages with the priest, she again reverts to Race's simile: "'Oh! Thank God the web was destroyed with the spider.' She shuddered; it was so awesome to think of the man who had been her husband, of the fine scholar, the owner of a great, cultivated brain, as a cruel animal—as a spider."[93] It would have been still more awesome, and a great deal more salutary, if she had thought of herself as Mrs. Spider . . . who is well known to eat her mate.

From the point of view of nature, Mary has had the perseverance to live her plot right through to the fulfillment of its goal. But, from the standpoint of the totality, she has also fulfilled her dream on the Gotthard Pass, for her ball is now entangled out in

---

92. Ibid., p. 237.
93. Ibid., pp. 254f.

the rough of nature. It is no good omen for Maurice Drummond that in the same dream it was just Jim, her dead brother, with whom she was walking. Is Mary on the way to becoming a young daughter of Antinea and to start a salon of dead men? There are other facts that point in this direction. The very first song that Maurice sang to Latimer and Mary was Braham's *Zigeunerlied* which ends with: "Täusch' mich nicht! Verlass' mich nicht" ("Do not deceive me, do not leave me"). And when Mary compared the two men she said that one had authority and strong intellect, and the other had youth.

Apparently the net result of the book is that nature, repressed and exiled at Darnfield, has been freed. But Latimer was the last visible remnant of the "enchanted garden of her mind," and if the peasants are right, and if "his troubled spirit is wandering behind the barred windows of the Casa di Ferro," then the mind that was free (if neglected) at Darnfield has been imprisoned in nature's place. If this is the case, it is almost inevitable that, sooner or later, a new plot will begin with a goal that would lead out of nature back to its repressed opposite: the "enchanted garden of her mind."

But fortunately there is an X in the situation to dampen my prophetic ardor! There is the presence that manifested in Mary's room and that apparently did not remain in the Casa di Ferro. When Maurice assured Mary that they belonged together, she begged him not to speak of it there, for there was a curse on La Vignaccia. But Maurice insisted, saying:

> "We owe it to the unseen being who has shielded us to acknowledge that we have found that most beautiful thing on earth, that the curse has been lifted . . . ." They both heard a movement near them—a long-drawn breath as of one who is infinitely relieved—and it seemed to Mary that once more the touch of gentle fingers came on her brow . . . . A faint breeze signed around the Casa di Ferro for an instant, then passed out over the tranquil waters of the lake.[94]

---

94. Ibid., pp. 242f.

This image of the breeze passing out over the tranquil waters recalls the spirit of God moving upon the face of the waters in Genesis and thus reminds us of "have no fear." Apparently this enigmatic, paradoxical being may well be related to "the spirit of God" or the spirit of life. Yet, what role has it played in the events that have taken place since its first manifestation in Mary's room? We can only say that it was "the one who knew the goal and did what was necessary to achieve it." In the last feverish days that led to Latimer's death, we have seen that Mary apparently forgot the promise of the voice. But, if we examine her behavior more carefully, we can see that somewhere, in one compartment, she was relying upon it implicitly. It was surely because of her inward certainty that she was "to pass into Maurice's keeping" that she risked everything for the fulfillment of her goal and did not even stop short at what worked out as murder. Again and again she told us that her fear was for Latimer and not of Latimer, and she repeatedly recorded his anguish and his fear. But she stopped up the ears of her human side and was willing to die herself rather than fail to fulfill her goal, for she baited her trap with her own body. Then this tangible presence warned her, and perhaps even took her place upon the bed, for although we do not know what, if anything, Latimer was experiencing and envisioning, there is no prior evidence that Latimer was mad enough to simply stab and mutilate an empty bed. You will remember the passage in Scot's book where we were told that many a medieval husband had imagined that he has seen the incubus in his wife's bed and had cut off his head with a sword. (And the incubus presumably remained visible even afterward, for we hear that the head and the body grew together again.) I should perhaps have mentioned that Scot regards the incubus and the devil as practically synonymous, for we are already used to the idea of the close relationship, or even identity, between Satan and God through the lectures of Rivkah Schärf Kluger.[95]

---

95. Rivkah Schärf Kluger, *Satan in the Old Testament* (Evanston, Ill.: Northwestern University Press, 1967).

We cannot say that the book is entirely without result, for this strange presence has been constellated. But Mary did not realize anything of her own connection with the events. Moreover, marrying the puer will not itself free her from her possession by the senex. Therefore, it is only too possible that a part of her will remain with Latimer in the Casa di Ferro until she learns the eternal truth in Christ's logion (so often quoted by Jung): "If thou knowest what thou doest, thou art blest, but if thou knowest not, thou art curst and a breaker of the law."[96]

---

96. C. G. Jung, *Visions: Notes of the Seminar Given in 1930–1934* (London: Routledge, 1998), p. 1226.

Women's Plots: An Analysis of Mary Webb's Precious Bane

Editor's Note: This lecture was presented at the C. G. Jung Institute, Zurich, November 3 and 10, 1970.

PART ONE

It is now almost forty years since I began to work on the subject of animus possession presented in this lecture. But in all this time I have lectured only twice on this theme. The reason for this is the following: Jung encouraged me very much in my initial venture in 1946 and was pleased with the result on his patients' unconscious, which seemed to welcome the opportunity to bring up dreams concerning the plots hidden in the dreamer's depths. Yet he told me later that, with but few exceptions, he had given up trying to make women conscious of their plots, for they just cannot see them. On another occasion he told me that he never shoots at birds he cannot hit. The more a woman is a "plot factory," the less she seems able to see her plots.

Why then have I ventured to speak of this subject that is tricky and dangerous, for people naturally hate things they cannot see? The interest in plots seems to have increased as the years have gone by. And I am more and more impressed by the disastrous effects that the general unconsciousness of plots is having all round us today. These effects are not only in women, but also in men, for though I am speaking primarily here of women's plots—I am a woman and know much more about the subject from our side—I should be sorry to awaken the impression that unconscious plots only exist in women. Weaving the plots of lives, like weaving in general, has indeed been a feminine activity. The goddesses, not the gods, wove the web of fate. So weaving belongs to the feminine principle per se. But, through the anima, men are no less involved in weaving unconscious plots. The gigantic plot woven by Hitler's anima, for example, killed millions while—to quote his own words—he walked with the unconsciousness and certainty of a sleepwalker guided by God himself.[1]

But before we go on, I should try to make clear to you in what sense we are using the word *plot*. Jung used it freely in conversation, but because of the great difficulty of making people, especially women, see what he meant, he seldom or never used the term in his books.[2] We do not use it in the sense of a wholly conscious plot, such as the "Gunpowder Plot," the plot of a detective story, or practical plots of all kinds where the goal is carefully created, kept clearly in mind the whole time, and everything possible is done to consciously achieve it.[3] The word *plot* as we are using it is quite the contrary. It refers to a purpose that is either fundamentally unconscious, or at best compartmentalized, and thus but partially known and at all events left to the unconscious to bring about. An oversimplified example would be when a wife drops a hint about a diamond brooch she recently saw, then more or less deliberately thinks no more about it and is just amazed when it appears for her

---

1. [With the conviction his was a divinely inspired calling, Hitler stated in a speech on March 14, 1936: "I go with the certainty of a sleepwalker along a path laid out for me by Providence" (*"Ich gehe mit traumwandlerischer Sicherheit den Weg, den mich die Vorsehung gehen heisst"*). See Ian Kerschaw, *Hitler 1936–1945* (Munich: Deutsche Verlags-Anstalt, 2000). *Ed.*]

2. [There are no references to the word *plot* in the general index of Jung's *Collected Works. Ed.*]

3. [The Gunpowder Plot of 1605 was a failed attempt by a group of provincial English Catholics to kill King James I of England, his family, and most of the Protestant aristocracy in a single swoop by blowing up the House of Lords during the State Opening of Parliament. The Gunpowder Plot was one of a series of unsuccessful assassination attempts against James I and followed the Main Plot and the Bye Plot of 1603. This event is celebrated in the United Kingdom and the Commonwealth on the 5th of November—called Guy Fawkes Night, Bonfire Night, Fireworks Night, or Plot Night. Here the plots were consciously calculated, organized, and blatantly enacted as opposed to unconscious plots. *Ed.*]

birthday. In another compartment of "good faith" she swears that she never thought of—much less mentioned—such a thing. She may actually have "forgotten" the incident. Who is not susceptible to, or even guilty, of such plotting?

Although the mechanism is very near the surface, the plots I have in mind go down into the strange and but partially fathomable depths of the unconscious and are, therefore, always very difficult to pin down. It is not possible—as is so often the case with other aspects of the psyche—to give a straightforward definite description of them. One can only circumambulate them, as it were, and say "they look like this from here" and then move on and say "they look like that from there." Their development indeed depends on being in the dark, and the deeper they are in the unconscious, the more likely the unconscious can subtly here and there manipulate the environment until they succeed. Therefore, they emulate the "hush-hush" tactics of the witch, which largely explains why it is so difficult for women to see them: from the efficiency point of view, it just does not pay to do so.

Men's plots are different in this respect from women's plots because men's plots are not nearly so directly accessible to them as they are to women. This is because the anima weaves her plots entirely behind their backs, as it were, and until they know their anima, they cannot possibly see what she is doing in this respect. Moreover, the leading principle in man is Logos. It is on this principle that he builds up his main outer life, which is less directly affected by the anima's weaving activities, that is, unless she is quite out of bounds and possessing him. Woman, on the contrary, is directly involved with the feminine principle; it is her principle (unless she is completely animus possessed), and, therefore, she is directly connected with plots and even knows all about them in one compartment of her mind. However, she seldom remains longer than a fleeting second in that compartment while in all the others she is blissfully ignorant of the whole matter, even genuinely and completely blind to it.

Compartment psychology is a very widespread phenomenon. Jung spoke at length on this subject in his seminar in the winter semester of 1929. The most vivid example he gave there is the best I know, so I will tell it again at the risk of repetition. The story goes likes this: A man went to see Jung for his first consultation. As he was talking, Jung noticed that he seemed to have affairs with a good many women, so he made a pencil mark for each on his blotter: five. Presently he said something very mild about the polygamous nature of man. The man at once went up in the air and said: "Polygamy, that is a thing I have no patience with, I am strictly monogamous." Jung asked him about his secretary. "Oh, that is something quite different. The work goes ever so much better if I take her out to dinner sometimes, then naturally I have to take her home and then . . . Oh, well, sometimes something happens." "And Mrs. Green?" asked Jung. "Oh, that again is quite different. A man must have exercise and Mrs. Green plays golf so well, and her house is just by the golf course so naturally I go in to tea and then well . . . ." At about the fourth example the penny dropped, and with horror the man exclaimed: "Well, it is true, I am polygamous." The shock was actually extreme; the man suffered from impotency for nearly a year. That is compartment psychology, and here Jung mentioned the danger of fusing compartments too quickly.

I remember well the surprise this story gave us all in 1929 and how diligently we all tried to find the same phenomenon in ourselves.[4] Although not in such an extreme form, it turned out to be a profitable exercise as I stumbled over a couple of compartments which I had quite unconsciously kept completely separated and was, I'm sorry to admit, shocked about myself.

This compartment psychology explains a phenomenon that I am sure all the analysts among you have met time and again. People often show a remarkable insight into their shadow, and one can spend, for instance, a whole hour talking about how it appears in a dream with their full agreement. Then a situation comes up in real life and, despite their apparent knowledge, they

---

4. [Barbara Hannah was twenty-eight years old when she arrived in Zurich in 1929. She began her studies with Jung and had this self-searching experience at the beginning of her analysis. *Ed.*]

blindly act out their shadow doing what they were quite abhorrent to admit the hour before. So one points it out, and then all hell breaks loose: they vehemently and furiously deny it. At first you think they are trying to deceive you or even themselves, but then one begins to learn about compartment psychology. True, they knew it yesterday, but they genuinely do not know it in the place where they are today, and when that is the case, it is useless to force the point. Say it once and then "retire to your estate" as Jung used to say. A violent fusion of the two compartments might have disastrous results, so one is patient and relies on drop by drop fusion. Although it may take months or even years, gradual infusion is the most helpful way of reaching the goal.

We find this phenomenon in perfectly "normal" people. It is not in itself a sign of pathology. In 1929, Jung pointed out it is largely the result of conventional morality. We have so many opinions about how we ought to be, and they lie, as a rule, so far from what we actually are, that a situation easily arises in which one is induced to form compartments.

Plots are an extreme case of just this compartment psychology in women. The hook on which a plot forms is usually a strong wish for something that is incompatible with conventional morality or with our usual point of view. There is a wonderful example of this in Jung's *Two Essays on Analytical Psychology.*[5] I recommend anyone who does not know the case to read it, as it is the simplest example of a plot that I know of. Just to give you an idea of the incident, Jung tells the story of a woman who has fallen in love with her best friend's husband. As this is incompatible with everything she believes to be right, she only glances at this distressing fact for a moment in one compartment while ignoring it completely in all the others. To convince herself it does not exist, she gets engaged to another man and is quite unenlightened when she actually throws her engagement ring out of the window. This blindness goes so far that one night she runs wildly before a pair of horses and is only just prevented by bystanders from throwing

5. C. G. Jung, "On the Psychology of the Unconscious" (1943), in *CW*, vol. 7 (Princeton, N.J.: Princeton University Press, 1953), pars. 7–11.

herself into the river. All this is an incredibly subtle arrangement in her unconscious which leads to her being taken to the nearest house, naturally that of her best friend, where she just happens to know that her best friend is absent and the husband is alone. The husband was far more conscious of the situation, but his making love to her that night—and not for the first time—was not enough to wake her up to the situation. Such a false position, however, produced a violent hysteria that brought her to Jung who slowly dug out the story. Of course, falling in love with one's best friend's husband is an awfully awkward business. But if fate plays one such a trick, one cannot blindly escape the suffering involved. This girl tried to, but it eventually overtook her in a crippling hysteria. It follows the pattern so ably described in Stevenson's figures of Jekyll and Hyde, where the whole development of the story hinges on escaping suffering. No one has ever realized the opposites of which human nature is composed more vividly than Stevenson. He speaks, for instance, of the incongruous opposite bound together in the agonized womb of consciousness: polar twins that are continuously struggling. The pain of these struggling opposites was the sole reason that Dr. Jekyll learned to dwell with pleasure, as a beloved daydream, in the thought of the separation of these elements. He writes:

> If each, I told myself, could but be housed in separate identities, life would be relieved of all that was unbearable; the unjust might go his way, delivered from the aspirations and remorse of his more upright twin; and the just could walk steadfastly and securely on his upward path, doing the good things in which he found his pleasure, and no longer exposed to disgrace and penitence by the hands of this extraneous evil. It was the curse of mankind that these incongruous fagots were thus bound together—that in the agonized womb of consciousness, these polar twins should be continuously struggling. How, then, were they dissociated?[6]

---

6. Robert Louis Stevenson, *Dr. Jekyll and Mr. Hyde* (Cheswold, Del.: Prestwick House, 2005; first published in 1886), p. 60.

When we keep our plots in a watertight compartment, we also apparently achieve something of this "beloved daydream" and thus, for a time, escape suffering. For it is this same wish to avoid suffering that leads—more than anything else—to the formation of plots. They usually start in women quite consciously with an "I want" or "I must have," then comes the "but . . ." and the whole thing is quickly repressed.

A woman who was in the same position as Jung's patient (that is, in love with a married man) told me years afterward that, as Jung's patient, she never denied that she loved him or even that she wanted to marry him or be his *femme inspiritrice*. "No," she said, "what led to my plots was that I never really believed I would go over corpses to get what I wanted. I was sure that I was much too decent, and I thought that, since I knew the whole thing, there was no danger. The truth is, I see now that I did not stay with the pain of knowing what a bitch the natural woman in me is, so of course she went behind my back and got me time after time into the most humiliating positions. Still worse, she made me blind to the valuable relation I could have had . . . had I seen facts as they were instead of cherishing worthless illusions." This woman was in the end forced to suffer far more than if she had faced the original pain of seeing herself as she was and the facts as they were.

Dr. Jekyll's effort to escape suffering from the realization of his dual nature met, as you will all recall, with an even worse fate. I shall never forget Jung saying, in October 1939, at the beginning of the war, that it was man's constant attempt to escape suffering that brought about such appalling catastrophes. "Man has forgotten that life is sacrificial" were his actual words.[7] Like every other phenomenon, life is made up of equal parts of light and shadow, and if we try to avoid the latter, we only obstruct the course of the former.

The rather dramatic dream of a woman about age forty gives an excellent example of this problem. The woman was:

---

7. For more on the theme of sacrifice, see C. G. Jung, *Nietzsche's Zarathustra: Notes of the Seminar Given in 1934–1939* (Princeton, N.J.: Princeton University Press, 1988), pp. 1516–1527.

standing outside the gate of a most beautiful garden where she saw all the people she loved best. Everything was pervaded by a most divine harmony. As she wondered whether she might enter, a voice said: "Yes, you can go in freely, but only because you have promised to spend just half your time here." The beautiful garden disappeared and an appalling place came in its stead. Everyone she disliked and had difficulties with was there and her worst problems were all lying in wait for her and everything was horrible. The voice continued: "All the while you spend half your time here, you may go to the beautiful garden freely, but if you try to cheat—even by a minute—the door of the garden will close against you forever."

When we directly avoid the pain of something which is incompatible with our own picture of ourselves, we have already begun to cheat and to try to stay longer than our allotted time in the beautiful garden, and then the doors begin to close.

I have spoken a great deal about suffering because it is my considered opinion, based on over thirty years of observing the plots in myself and other women, that every plot starts from the wish to avoid suffering in some form or other, or to get something for nothing: the penny and the cake. Yet the really happy people I have known in the course of my long life have all realized the value of suffering and have done their best to accept it.[8] It is indeed human—all too human—to enjoy happiness and hate suffering, but life is really like the woman's dream: if you try to cheat the half-half rule, the door of happiness closes against you.

In fact, it really is the acceptance of suffering that makes happiness possible. You will all remember Jung's description in *Memories, Dreams, Reflections* of the agony he went through when, on a beautiful summer day, he saw the cathedral in Basel glittering in the sun and thought of God sitting on a golden throne above it. And then he was unable to think the thought through

---

8. [Barbara Hannah was approximately eighty years old at the time of this lecture. *Ed.*]

to the end.[9] He was only about eleven years old at the time, but he could not sleep or rest till, on the third night, he screwed up all his courage and committed the sin he knew that he must and thought what he had seen to the end. To his astonishment he saw God in heaven defecate, which then fell on the cathedral shattering not only the sparkling roof but the entire house of worship. He expected to be damned forever for such an apparently blasphemous thought—don't forget, he was a pastor's son—but instead he experienced "indescribable relief." Grace and a freedom from guilt had come in the place of the expected damnation, and with it also came "unutterable bliss," so much so that he wept "for happiness and gratitude." Jung once told me many years ago that this experience had formed his whole attitude to life. Jung was, I think, one of the happiest people I have ever known. He had a genius for enjoying life, and yet not many have suffered more. And I never knew him try to avoid it. He says in "After the Catastrophe":

> If only people could realize what an enrichment it means to find one's own guilt, what a sense of honor and spiritual dignity! But nowhere does there seem to be a glimmer of this insight. Instead we only hear of attempts to shift the blame on others.[10]

But if this insight could only be reached, the plots would soon be deprived of their richest nourishment.

Another thing that nourishes plots is laziness, a vice that is indeed very nearly related to avoiding suffering. Failure to work, particularly when it is a matter of creative work, has a fatal effect on the plots. I am certain that you all know the very great difference between busying or "employing" oneself and really working. I have known many people who could truthfully say they never passed an idle moment who yet never really worked at all.

---

9. C. G. Jung, *Memories, Dreams, Reflections*, A. Jaffé, ed. (New York: Vintage Books, 1965), p. 37.
10. C. G. Jung, "After the Catastrophe" (1945), in *CW*, vol. 10 (Princeton, N.J.: Princeton University Press, 1964), par. 416.

The saddest case I ever knew of this kind was a woman who was about age forty when she came into analysis. She was highly extraverted, a feeling type, but broke down in her self-denial with a really crippling neurosis in the middle of life. Everything started very propitiously. She painted a long series of inner paintings and seemed all set to know herself. But this first spurt did not last, and it soon became clear that she was no longer really putting herself into her work. She employed herself without cease, it is true, but after the series of paintings gave out she no longer put her creative libido into her work. After a very good start in seeing her plots, I saw she was getting discouraged with her situation in reality, and instead of putting herself back into doing what she could with it, she began secretly to foster illusions. In her case, it was a matter of a man who was very willing to give her everything he could, if she would only respect the limitations his life imposed on their friendship. But it was outwardly very restricted, and she began to prefer secret fantasies of how it would have been if she had met him earlier . . . and so on. From there, it was only a step to the pernicious illusion that she was the one and only woman in his life, his true *femme inspiritrice*, that they were divided by a cruel fate, and all the rest of the plot factory. He soon began to notice that she was no longer real when he saw her, that she was lost in plots to such an extent that he himself was no longer seen, nor was his reality respected, and she thus slowly but surely—and entirely at her own doing—undermined and destroyed the relationship. A miserable old age, cut off from everything searched for, was the inevitable result.

Although a man is the most usual goal of a woman's plot, this is of course by no means always the case. There are also a great many plots where ambition or money plays the leading role. As an example, I remember a young German doctor who used to come every year to work with me for a few weeks during her medical training. When it was finished, she started in on a very interesting practice in an unattractive manufacturing town. She was at first full of enthusiasm about the wonderful experience unfolding before her. But before a year was up, I noticed a difference in her letters, which were now always full of weekends she spent by the sea. Then she came for a few weeks for some more analysis, and the dreams immediately took up an exceedingly critical attitude. Then it all came out. An old friend, also a woman doctor but much older than the dreamer, had a flourishing practice at this seaside resort. It was in no way more than she could manage, and the very first dream pointed out that she was in no need of the dreamer's help; in fact she refused it. But it soon became clear that the dreamer had simply given up doing more than the minimum in her own practice and all her psychic libido had flowed into pirating her friend's practice and establishing herself in her place.

Usually a very intelligent and self-critical woman, this plot made her more stupid and dense than one could believe. It took a month's hard labor to make her see the possibility that she could have a plot at all! And even after she had seen it—and I never saw clearer or more emphatic dreams—she thought just seeing it was enough, then she could go on going there without any danger. The only favorable circumstance was that a friend of hers had just spun a very similar plot which she had carried so far that it had cost her her livelihood. It then became clear too late that had she only kept quiet, the very thing she so passionately cherished would have fallen like a ripe cherry into her mouth. My analysand had followed this whole plot step by step, and, as so often happens, outside herself she had seen it most clearly. The first thing that really began to convince her about her own plot was when a dream deposited her on this very friend's doorstep. This taught me again how much plots are similar to a weed like ground elder, which has such long roots that it is impossible to get them all out.[11]

I was in despair for over twenty years while I was working intensively on my own plots. There was a certain very disagree-

11. [*Aegopodium podagraria* (ground elder, bishop's weed, goutweed) is a common weed in the carrot family that grows in shady places. Purportedly introduced to England by the Romans and into northern Europe by monks, the tender leaves have been used as a spring leaf vegetable much like spinach, and the plant has also been used to treat gout and arthritis. In some areas this plant is considered among the worst of weeds, rapidly spreading over large areas by pernicious underground roots. *Ed.*]

able, out-of-myself feeling that always warned me when a plot was around. I realized that my whole process of individuation depended on getting rid of the ubiquitous weeds. I seemed to weed and weed in vain. Now I had known intellectually for years that the unconscious never repeats and repeats senselessly, there is always something beneath such seemingly tedious repetition, but it took years for this realization to get right down to where it convinced my whole psyche. Indeed Jung had told me this very early on, but I was still too blind to be able to see what it actually was, so the unconscious went on rubbing my nose in what seemed to be senseless surface manifestations. What I mean to say here is, as difficult as it is to see, there is a complex weaving activity in the process of individuation behind one's plots. To put it unjustifiably simply: the Self eternally weaves the pattern of our whole fate, of our unique process of individuation, but when we have egotistical purposes, things we want at any price, the ego takes threads from the Self's pattern and pulls them right out of the original design, spoiling the whole pattern. The plots are so powerful and unbelievably efficient just because they are, so to speak, using material that belongs to the gods. I am aware from my own experience that words cannot describe this phenomenon. I never understood it at all, even when Jung himself explained it to me, for it is a matter of experience. Only through experience will one really know it in oneself. Nevertheless, it is so much easier to see it in other people and to understand it in outside material.

Now another way to look at this problem is to say that the Self entices our egos to drag us through plots in order to force us to integrate our shadow and learn to find an inner center, free from ego desires and closer to the Self. All in all, both ways are the way of individuation.

And I hope at any rate that the way of individuation woven within the plot is visible in the following literary example I am going to lay before you. At least I hope you will keep this aspect in mind as we consider our story. It is the mystery behind our unconscious plots that makes the painful, wearisome, and discouraging work of facing our plots so rewarding. But of course the mystery is

different in every individual case, for after all its universal character belongs to the collective unconscious. Therefore, one can say
very little about it. Just to give the barest hint (which should in
no way be taken literally), I have the impression that in the most
frequent form of women's plots—those concerning a relationship
to a man where there is practically always an immovable obstacle
to a simple biological solution—there is the whole problem of the
coniunctio, of the union of the opposites behind the apparently
purely personal desire. In other words, as well as the fate-weaving
activity of the Self, there is also the most vital and mysterious
goal of the process of individuation behind the plot; for the Self is
highly concerned with the relationship between the sexes and the
union of opposites in general.

As Goethe says: "Where love is missing, power usurps the
empty place," and this, I think, is usually the case when the goal
behind the plot is not about a relationship to a man but about
power and monetary gain. Power and financial plots are more
natural to men than to women, for these plots have more to do
with the Logos principle than with Eros. Such a man as Hitler, for
example, never got around to taking the Eros principle seriously
at all, and all the outer hooks that he offered to his anima were
power hooks. He longed to "come, see and conquer" the whole
world. When a woman offers such hooks—alas a frequent enough
occurrence in these days—she is not living by her principle of
Eros at all but has allowed the goals of her animus to become
her own.

The best example of a woman's plot that I know of is found
in Marie Hay's *The Evil Vineyard* and was first shared with me
by Jung, who mentioned it briefly in the 1925 seminars.[12] But I
took this example first in 1946, and it has since been printed in
the Guild of Pastoral Psychology lecture series. For this reason,
and because the archetypal background or foundation is exceedingly thin in that book, I decided to take a completely different
example in these lectures. Such hooks are difficult to find due to
their "hush-hush" quality and also because the animus is usually

---

12. [See the previous essay. *Ed.*]

very careful not to reveal a portrait of himself in women's books. He is seemingly careful to obliterate any traces of the plots in women's novels. But before we turn to our material, I should like to say a few words about the role of the animus in plots.

Weaving plots is actually a "feminine" activity, and it is the conscious personality or the shadow that is usually responsible for the existence of a plot. But as the latter just remains in the dark in order to be effective, a plot offers the animus an irresistible opportunity to strengthen his own position. Therefore, women's plots have a great deal to do with the animus although he is not their original creator. A woman's plots are useful to him particularly in his role as possessive lover, for the more unreal they are, the less chance they have of succeeding with an earthly lover. And this naturally provides meat and drink to an animus in his original, untransformed, and negative aspect state. When the plot fails, for instance, there is a brilliant opportunity for the animus's possessive and eternal song to be heard: "There, he turned out no good. That is how men are, just as I always told you. Give up men, they're hopeless . . . and rely on me, I am your only hope" and so on. If the animus succeeds in this song, he can often cut off the woman completely from men, possess her entirely, and thus cheat her of her whole life. Therefore, one of the most disagreeable consequences of having unconscious plots that one knows nothing about is that such unconsciousness strengthens the negative aspect of the animus.

The example I propose taking is *Precious Bane* by Mary Webb, a book that I have already spoken of here some years ago but from a different standpoint: the creative animus in women.[13] This

---

13. Mary Webb, *Precious Bane* (Notre Dame, Ind.: University of Notre Dame Press, 1980). [Mary Webb (1881–1927) was an English romantic novelist of the early twentieth century whose novels are set chiefly in the English countryside around Shropshire, a county in the West Midlands region of England bordering Wales. It is renown for its wild and picturesque landscapes, its hill ranges, pine forests, small pastoral valleys in the south, sweeping agricultural plains in the north, and numerous significant historical, geographical, and geological landmarks. The designated Shropshire Hills Area of Outstanding Natural Beauty covers about a quarter of the county. It is one of England's most rural and sparsely populated counties. Mary Webb's cottage was outside of the village of Bayston Hill, a few miles south of Shrewsbury. Webb's poetically vibrant prose, along with the developments and unfolding of her stories, make her one of England's most outstanding authors. *Precious Bane* won the

was taking it mainly from the positive side. Several years later, as I was using Mary Webb as a chapter in my book, I discovered a much more questionable side to the story, namely, that it may well reveal a broken process of individuation. And, as I examined it more closely, I saw that the trouble really came from a determination to avoid suffering. Then only did its main characteristic dawn on me, namely, that it is a woman's plot par excellence. It is difficult to find these deep unconscious plots in women's books. *Precious Bane* was the last of Mary Webb's finished novels, and it is generally regarded as her last. As you know, certain stories give an amazingly accurate portrait of the psyche of the author, and *Precious Bane* strikes me as one of these books. Not that we know very much as yet of Mary Webb. Two short biographies were published within four years of her death, and since then, as far as I know, not a word. Her husband and all of her five much younger brothers and sisters were still in the prime of life, which naturally—though it yielded a lot of outer information—handicapped the biographers as to many intimate details. The book is of very much higher literary value than *The Evil Vineyard*, for Mary Webb's use of language is practically poetic.[14]

Mary Webb's life was short. She was a father's daughter par excellence, had a very happy childhood and a lifelong passion for happiness. When she was twenty, however, she contracted Graves disease, that most depressing of diseases, which, in her case, never really cleared up. Complicated by pernicious anemia, the disease eventually led to her early death.[15] This was a fate that

---

Prix Femina in Paris in 1924–25, an honor to which the book was "preeminently entitled." Gladys M. Cole considers the book to be one of the outstandingly successful novels of the century and further notes that, in *Precious Bane,* Webb creates a half-real, half-fantasy world uniquely her own. Such is the pace, the passion, the sincerity and persuasiveness of her writing that, in spite of the occasional extravagances and melodrama, she compels readers into her world and keeps them there. See www.literaryheritage.org.uk. In her essay "Animus Figures in Literature and in Modern Life," Barbara Hannah provides a more complete synopsis of Webb's story; see volume 1 of this work. *Ed.*]

14. [For an example of Mary Webb's literary style, see the excerpt from the first pages of *Precious Bane* in Barbara Hannah's essay "Animus Figures in Literature and in Modern Life" in volume 1 of this work. *Ed.*]

15. [Graves disease is an incurable thyroid disorder. It engenders the typical protrusion of the eyes and goiter, which caused Mary Webb to become self-conscious and motivated her to

forced the dark side of life upon her. Although she was never able fully to accept it, in *Precious Bane* she made a valiant effort to do so. "Her God was nature," one of her brothers declared after her death, and her native Shropshire represented a paradise she could hardly exist without. We hear that even in nearby Chester (that is, in the next county) she was inclined to pine.

She married when she was thirty-one, three years after her beloved father's death, and the marriage unfortunately took her away from Shropshire. Her relationship with her husband was naturally taboo ground for her biographers at that time, so we know little or nothing about it. Probably her writing was more important to her, at least, that's the impression one gets. Although the two usually lived where her husband's profession took him, nevertheless, the household apparently revolved round her writing. They had no children. She was unpractical and almost criminally so where money was concerned. She gave it away recklessly, pretty much to anyone who even indiscriminately asked, and then complained that an ungrateful public left its authors to starve when in reality she was paid well for her books.

Her interest in nature and her writing, however, kept her alive, and—all things considered—she was even fairly healthy up until the completion of *Precious Bane*. But after that, for reasons we will consider later, things declined rapidly until her death three years later. She died in 1927 at the age of forty-six. Webb was increasingly unable to write, sleep, or even eat, but, very much like Emily Brontë, she declined to take her health seriously until it was far too late. *Precious Bane* is in a way her testament.

Mary Webb lived from 1881 to 1927, but the background of *Precious Bane* was placed a century earlier during the Napoleonic wars. Now, Prudence Sarn, the heroine and narrator of much of the story, was "the best girl in the 'orld . . . very jimp and slender, with a long silky plait to the knees, and dark, meltin' eyes, and such pleasant ways, merry and mocking and pitiful" (so

retreat into her own solitary world, relying ever more on the joy and solace she found in nature. It was during this illness that she seriously began to write poems and essays. Although she recovered somewhat from the illness, she had a recurrence after the death of her father when she was twenty-eight. *Ed.*]

said Prudence's mother) for she was cursed with a harelip which, in those days, was regarded as the hallmark of a witch. Gideon (her ambitious, money-loving brother) used this handicap to get her to swear to obey him in everything he did and said, for he promised to pay for an operation to correct her disfiguration.[16] He proposed unremitting work in order to make a large fortune out of Sarn, their ancestral farm, and then to sell it and leave it forever. Prue knew she was wrong, and when she made the vow, she "felt as if Sarn Mere was flowing right over us" and shivered as if she had an ague.[17] But Gideon could "make you feel as if you wanted what he wanted, though you didna."[18] So, as always, Prue gave in.

For some years, Gideon worked his sister on the farm like a slave, but then something happened which might yet have saved the situation: Gideon fell in love with Jancis, the local wizard's daughter. Prue tells us that:

> Jancis was a little thing, not tall like me, but you always saw her before you saw other people, for it seemed that the light gathered round her. She'd got golden hair, and all the shadows on her face seemed to be stained with the pale colour of it. I was used to think she was like a white water-lily full of yellow pollen or honey. She'd got a very white skin, creamy white, without any colour unless she was excited or shy, and her face was dimpled and soft, and just the right plumpness. She'd got a red, smiling mouth, and when she smiled the dimples ran each into other. Times I could almost have strangled her for that smile.[19]

At Jancis's "love spinning," Prue first saw Kester Woodseaves, the weaver, and fell in love with him at first sight. But she was afraid for him to see her on account of her harelip. It soon

---

16. Webb, *Precious Bane*, p. 159.
17. Ibid., p. 43.
18. Ibid., p. 40.
19. Ibid., p. 23.

became clear that Kester would not allow that to deter him. In
spite of many ups and downs, everything seemed set for a double
wedding and the establishment of an enduring symbol of the
quaternio. And due to the result of a phenomenal harvest and the
Corn Laws, Gideon's goal of the large fortune was even realized.[20]
Gideon and Jancis were to be married in a week, and Kester and
Prue in a year.

But then things went wrong. Jancis's father, the old wizard, discovered his daughter and Gideon in his own bed and, infuriated,
set fire to the corn ricks. Much of Gideon's fortune was burnt in a
single night. Every bit of the humanity that his love for Jancis had
given him was also burnt out; he abandoned Jancis and even killed
his own mother because she could no longer work for her keep.
Nine months later when Jancis brought him their child, he rejected
them both, and Jancis drowned herself and the child in the mere.

From then on Gideon was haunted, partly by the mother he
had murdered, but even more by Jancis and their child, and four
months later, he followed them into the mere. Prue was left alone
with the farm that her ancestors had owned for centuries. But
only for one night. She decided to leave Sarn to its fate and "flee
away as they did from the cities of the plain."[21] But she could not
leave the animals and—as it was the day of the annual fair at Sarn
Mere—she took her flocks and herds there to be sold.

Her harelip had always laid Prue open to the accusation of
being a witch, and now the people—partly puzzled and frightened
and partly out of revenge—slowly "reasoned" it out that all the
terrible happenings at Sarn were Prue's work. Ably worked up by
Prue's enemies, the crowd shouted: "Hare-shotten! A witch! Three

---

20. [The Corn Laws were a set of tariffs enacted in 1815, imposing duties on imported corn.
They were designed to preserve the abnormally high profits of the Napoleonic war years
and to safeguard farmers from the consequences of their wartime euphoria when farms had
changed hands at exorbitant prices, loans and mortgages having been accepted on impossible terms. The Corn Laws, however, resulted in skyrocketing costs for food, depressed
the domestic market for manufactured goods (people spent the bulk of their earnings on
food rather than commodities), and caused great distress among the working classes and
manufacturers in the towns. After more than thirty years of heatedly debated revisions, they
were repealed in 1848. *Ed.*]
21. Webb, *Precious Bane*, p. 275.

times a murderess! . . . Suffer not a witch to live," and Prue found herself tied to a ducking stool and already in the water.[22] At the last moment she was rescued by Kester, the weaver. The two married, and many years later Prue wrote the story as an old, childless woman at the bidding of the parson who knew "of the lies that were told" about her and wanted "the whole truth and nothing else."[23]

This is the bare bones of the story, and we shall have to fill in some details as we proceed. We'll keep the spotlight on the plot this time and analyze the book from that point of view. But I should like to point out from the beginning how clearly this story shows the individuation process behind and below the plot, and how nearly a symbol of wholeness, a quaternio of the dark and light figures, was established. It was, when we examine the material closely, destroyed by the plot which, could it have been made conscious and the humiliation and pain of seeing it accepted, would instead have woven the warp and woof of the totality. One could certainly say here that the Self is weaving the process of individuation, and the ego distorts this into the plot.

As we shall see, the accusations of Prue as a witch were not entirely without foundation. Jung once defined the witch as one who tries to use the powers of the unconscious for personal, egotistical purposes, whereas one who truly strives toward the process of individuation thus turns everything—conscious and unconscious—toward the goal of wholeness for which the purely personal and egotistic factors have to be sacrificed again and again. Although innocent of any actual outer witchlike activity, we will see that she is anything but innocent of cultivating unconscious or subconscious machinations to achieve, at any cost, her egotistical goals.

As I think most of you know, when we attempt to take a novel such as *Precious Bane* as a sort of portrait of the state of the author's own psyche, we roughly divide the cast of characters into the various figures of which the personality consists, much as one generally does in analyzing a dream. But these classifications

---

22. Ibid., p. 283.
23. Ibid., p. 16.

should never be rigid or carried too far. Prue would definitely represent the ego of Mary Webb. This representation was almost conscious for Mary Webb herself, for she gave Prue many of her own characteristics and experiences. Moreover, Prue is the narrator of the story, that is, we see everything through her eyes as we necessarily see through the author's as well.

Jancis, although definitely the anima of Gideon, is also an aspect of Prue's shadow. Prue nearly accepted this aspect and might have well integrated it had it not been for a far worse shadow aspect in the background, and that is the sexton's daughter Tivvy, who we will come to later. Moreover, Jancis is the wizard's daughter and thus a figure, for good or ill, who was closely connected with the magical aspect of the unconscious. Gideon, of course, is the animus par excellence, although he appears, through his ambition and passion for money, in an almost entirely negative aspect, whereas the weaver, Kester Woodseaves, represents his almost wholly positive counterpart.

These are the four main figures in the book, the four who could have developed into the four cornerstones of Mary Webb's individuation process. The minor figures would then have grouped themselves around these four, as it were, and formed the individual pattern of this special process. We must now consider what it was that prevented this eminently desirable solution from settling itself through, as it so nearly did.

The first thing we must consider is Prue's ancestral background and the farm she where was brought up, both dark and difficult as it usually is in places where the individuation process is constellated. Prue says of Sarn, which had been in the family for many generations: "there's a discouragement about the place . . . . there was always a breath of October in our May. . . . It was true, what folks said of Sarn, that there was summat to be felt there."[24] And she says of the family:

> "Sullen as a Sarn," they say about these parts. And they say
> there's been something queer in the family ever since Timothy

---

24. Ibid., pp. 14–15.

> Sarn was struck by forkit lightning in the times of the religious
> wars . . . . And seemingly the lightning got into his blood. . . .
> Sarns have the lightning in their blood since his day.[25]

Already as a child, Gideon showed the dark side of the Sarns
far more clearly than his younger sister Prue. He envied Jancis for
being the wizard's child and thus not forced to go to church, and
when he was seven years old he said in a fury to his father: "I do
will and wish to be Maister Beguildy's son, and the devil shall have
my soul. Amen."[26] Prue, left to herself, was an exceptionally good
and pleasant child, but nevertheless she followed where Gideon
led and got a good many advantages in this way without being
held responsible for having instigated the mischief. It was one of
these escapades that led to their father's death. He was furious
at having caught them out in a lie about having been to church,
and Gideon, who was seventeen but looked twenty-four, knocked
him down as he was advancing with the horsewhip. And whether
as a result of his fall or his rage, he had an apoplectic fit and died
without regaining consciousness. Gideon once again sold his soul
to the devil and took his father's sins upon him at the funeral
(instead of paying the sin eater as was usual at that time), and he
did this in no way out of love for his father but entirely and solely
to get the farm from his mother.[27]

So far in this story the unusually dark Sarn side has been carried entirely by Gideon—in other words, it had been completely
in the unconscious—while Prue was able to be unusually good
and charming in consciousness. And indeed it is very common

25. Ibid., p. 18. [The entire passage, which well illustrates the darkness looming over the family, reads: "Well, Timothy went against his folk and the counsels of a man of God, and took up with the wrong side, whichever that was, but it's no matter now. So he was struck by lightning and lay for dead. Being after awhile recovered, he was counselled by the man of God to espouse the safe side and avoid the lightning. But Sarns were ever obstinate men. He kept his side, and as he was coming home under the oak wood he was struck again. And seemingly the lightning got into his blood. He could tell when tempest brewed, long afore it came and it is said that when a storm broke, the wildfire played about him so none could come near him. Sarns have the lightning in their blood since his day." *Ed.*]

26. Ibid., p. 20.

27. [A sin eater was a man who took upon himself the sins of a deceased person. See "Animus Figures in Literature and in Modern Life," note 44, in volume 1 of this work. *Ed.*]

to find destructive unconscious plots in particularly positive girls and women. Although this seems a point that people find difficult to see, the better the qualities in consciousness, the worse their opposites tend to be in the unconscious. We find this even in the age-old story of Tobit and Sarah, where Sarah was possessed by a devil which had led to the death of seven husbands. Naturally, her reputation in the environment was exceedingly bad; Tobias had heard the worst of her and was most unwilling to be added to her victims. Yet the archangel Raphael said of this girl of ill repute: "The maid is wise, steadfast and exceedingly honorable."

As a matter of fact, such positive qualities are a condition sine qua non for being able to see and eventually integrate the plots. One needs all the good qualities one has to counterbalance one's shadow side. The art of seeing the darkest shadow requires above all never losing sight of the positive qualities. Then it is possible to establish a balance between the two. But it is never safe for any member to identify with the light side as Prue did, and even more so when a family has such a dark ancestral background as the Sarns. If we knew more of Mary Webb, or rather of the Meredith family, for Webb was her married name, I should expect to find that she also had a great deal of darkness in her ancestral background. We already know that her mother was Scottish, from the wild border clans, and exceedingly proud of being related to Sir Walter Scott. Mary Webb's novel *The House in Dormer Forest* points particularly clearly to such a background although her own outer childhood was seemingly happy.[28]

At all events, just after her father's funeral, Prue takes a fatal step that makes her—at all events in one compartment—directly and consciously responsible for the debt. Gideon, having obtained full possession of the farm through being his father's sin eater, reveals his wildly ambitious plans to his sister: to make a fortune from the farm and then sell it and take on a gentleman's place where he can be "chief among ten thousand."[29] These plans alone

---

28. Mary Webb, *The House in Dormer Forest* (New York: George H. Doran, 1921).
29. Webb, *Precious Bane*, p. 40.

would not have bought Prue, although a few words that she drops show her to be far more caught up in the shadow aspirations than she allows. But then Gideon plays a master stroke, in fact, one that is very typical of an ambitious, unscrupulous animus who just wants to possess the woman.

Prue, like most country girls of her age, is counting on getting married and having a babe "grand and solemn" in a "cot of rushes" as she expresses it.[30] Gideon shatters these hopes with a single stroke by suddenly confronting her with the effect of her harelip on her chances of marriage. Up until then Prue had bothered very little about it, she was used to the moans of her mother who often repeated: "Could I help it if the hare crossed my path?" But what it meant to have the mark of the witch in these days never came to Prue's consciousness until Gideon delivered his shattering blow.

At first Prue's instincts react perfectly and she replies: "Not wed, Gideon? Oh, ah! I'll wed for sure."[31] This turns out to be the exact truth, the weaver never thinks of letting her harelip be an obstacle, and if only Prue could have stayed with her sound instinct, there would have been no plot. The instincts are our great protection against plots, and the terrible prevalence of plots today is due in part to how far we have moved away from our instincts. But Prue, like so many of us still today, cannot remain true to her instinctive conviction, and she allows Gideon's rational arguments (typically animus) to win the day. "Not wed, Gideon? Oh, ah! I'll wed for sure." And he answers:

> "I'm afeerd nobody'll ask you, Prue."
> "Not ask me? What for not?"
> "Because—oh, well, you'll soon find out. But you can have a house and furniture and all just the same, if you give a hand in the earning of 'em."
> "But not an 'usband, nor a babe in a cot of rushes?"
> "No."
> "For why?"

---

30. Ibid., p. 41.
31. Ibid.

"Best ask Mother for why. Maybe she can tell you why the hare crossed her path. But I'm main sorry for ye, Prue, and I be going to make you a rich lady, and maybe when we've gotten a deal of gold, we'll send away for some doctor's stuff for a cure. But it'll cost a deal, and you must work well and do all I tell you. You're a tidy, upstanding girl enough, Prue, and but for that one thing the fellows ud come round like they will round Jancis."[32]

This is a point where—if women look back critically—they can often see the starting point of their own plots. To doubt the validity of our feminine instinct is to invite the animus to come in with an opinion, and with the absolute convincing character of such opinions, it becomes "God's truth" to us and thus very hard to see through and dislodge later on.

This is what happened to Prue. Gideon convinced her that she was inferior as a woman, that no man would accept her harelip. And then she was lost, a man and children honestly and truly being the one thing she wanted of life, her purely feminine, biological, and legitimate goal. But once she accepted the opinion of her animus that this could only be reached through Gideon and his ambitious plans, it was no longer legitimate, for she wanted to force it, whether it belonged to her pattern or not. She even gives herself wholly to Gideon's plans although she was conscious that he could "make you feel as if you wanted what he wanted though you didna."[33] But until she learns that Gideon has murdered their mother (and even then she only threatens to leave him), she never once wavers in wholeheartedly working with her entire strength to fulfill Gideon's plot.

And Gideon reinforced his position by making her swear an oath that is strangely reminiscent of the medieval witches' oaths to the devil: "I promise and vow to obey my brother, Gideon Sarn, and to hire myself out to him as a sarvant, for no money, until all that he wills be done. And I'll be as biddable as a prentice, a wife,

---

32. Ibid.
33. Ibid., p. 40.

and a dog. I swear it on the Holy Book. Amen."³⁴ And thus in
return for her servitude and her pact with the devil, she hopes to
buy a cure for her harelip at the end.

PART TWO

The last time I tried to make clear what we mean by the word
plot as Jung used it in conversation with us here. Then we began
speaking of *Precious Bane* by Mary Webb because I hope to show
you by means of a fairly modern novel how a plot works in the
conscious and unconscious of a woman. We are taking the story
as we might take a dream or active imagination, and we are trying to examine the actual state of Mary Webb's psyche, both in
consciousness and the unconscious.

As I see it, Prudence Sarn represents the conscious personality
of Mary Webb, and the rest of the people in the story represent
the various autonomous figures that make up her whole personality. I base the assumption that Prudence could be called the ego of
Mary Webb on the fact that many of Prue's experiences were Mary
Webb's very own and that, as the narrator of the story, she represents the conscious point of view of the author more than any other
figure in the book. I may say that I am not the first to identify Prue
as closely mirroring Mary Webb. Hilda Addison, Mary Webb's first
biographer, writing shortly after her death, says that other characters in her novels, such as Deborah Arden in the *Golden Arrow* and
Amber Danke in *The House in Dormer Forest* have a good deal
of Mary Webb in their composition, but no other single character
mirrors her spirit as perfectly as Prudence Sarn.³⁵ Mary Webb also
directly speaks of parallel experiences that she and Prue had.

In Prudence Sarn we can see exactly how much Mary Webb
knew of the dark side of human nature, how tolerant and intoler-
ant she was of it. Above all, we can see how Prue, presumably
also the author, walks in and out of her compartments. Prue

---

34. Ibid., p. 42.

35. Mary Webb, *The Golden Arrow* (London: Kessinger Publishing, 2004). [This was Webb's
first novel, published in 1916. *Ed.*]

sees through what is happening and at times even almost sees her own contribution to the fatal end of everyone in the book except herself and her weaver. But she remains in that particular compartment only for a moment and then slips back into all the others where she believes implicitly that she had nothing but good intentions. From the point of view of this conviction, all the deadly destruction in the book comes from outside, especially from her brother, Gideon. It is quite true that the evil was mainly concentrated in this animus figure but, as we shall see, Prue had many opportunities, which she failed to take, to influence his fate for the better, just as we may or may not take the risk of dealing with our own animus figures. The same is true of Prue's shadow figures, the beautiful Jancis and Tivvy, the amazingly stupid but sly and cold-blooded daughter of the pious and conventional sexton. Prue makes efforts to accept Jancis and to have a helpful attitude toward her, but she can never carry them through (as so often happens in our own efforts to integrate our shadow). And at first she is even friendly to Tivvy, her worst shadow aspect (of stupidity, power, manipulation, jealousy, viciousness, and greed), but she eventually rejects her entirely (instead of integrating her in some manner) which contributes not a little to the tragic fate that overtakes the old family of Sarn.

We ended last time with Prue's vow to obey her brother Gideon and her feeling, after she had sworn on the Bible, as if "Sarn Mere was flowing right over us, and I shivered as if I'd got an ague."[36] Here Prue describes rather dramatically the result of giving oneself to plots, a feeling that I found to be a most helpful factor in detecting their presence. A plot is always something inhuman; one has given the reins out of one's human and conscious hands, and one is hoping that the unconscious will produce the desired result while we wash those hands in innocence. But one is thus cut off from human relationship and warmth, and it does literally feel as if cold water was flowing all over one, or as if a bitter, icy wind was blowing through. Probably this feeling is individually different in everyone, but I can testify that one can

---

36. Webb, *Precious Bane*, p. 43.

learn to recognize it and thus bring the plot up into consciousness at its very beginning.

There is one point, however, in Gideon's cheese-paring tactics that means a great deal to Prue. To save the expense of employing an accountant and scribe—the whole of the peasantry and farmers and most of the squires' lads of England were illiterate in those days—she is to learn reading, writing, and arithmetic from Beguildy (the old wizard and Jancis's father), paying him by working on his land as well as her own. Even the negative animus is not wholly negative, and Prue says it made her "gladsome to be getting some education, it being like a big window opening."[37]

We can see that in spite of Prue's vow to her negative animus, the Self has by no means given her up or stopped weaving the pattern of the process of individuation. To be able to read, reckon, and write means an enormous gain in consciousness for an illiterate girl, and, as Emma Jung made so clear in her excellent paper on the animus, nothing is so helpful in overcoming animus possession as to work with the conscious mind.[38] Prue was quick to seize this opportunity, for she thinks that the writing will give her a hold over Gideon, since if he was "too harsh with Mother or me, I could be a bit awkward about the writing."[39]

During the following years, however, she worked like a slave for her vow, "grew lanky as a clothes prop," just wearing old sacks and clogs until people called her "the barn-door savage of Sarn."[40] But she would think of the beautiful house and lovely clothes they were to have which helped her fresh heart persevere. Yet the time seemed long, the work endless. One evening Prue had the idea that perhaps she could bathe in Sarn Mere at the "troubling of the waters," reciting the curious ancient prayers which the parson still kept in an old book from the days when everyone believed that the water of Sarn, like Bethesda, could cure all ills. But Gideon

37. Ibid., p. 45.
38. Emma Jung,"Ein Beitrag zum Problem des Animus," in *Wirklichkeit der Seele*, C. G. Jung, ed. (Zurich: Rascher Verlag, 1934).
39. Webb, *Precious Bane*, p. 50.
40. Ibid., pp. 62, 47, respectively.

and even her mother are dead against such a public display and forbade her to do it. She ran away to the attic and cried a long time. But the very idea of weakening her vow to Gideon and finding another way of dealing with her harelip and feelings of inferiority as a woman has an effect. In the attic that evening, Prue has a vision (that is, a visual experience of the Self) which "was a great miracle, and it changed my life; for when I was lost for something to turn to, I'd run to the attic, and it was a core of sweetness in much bitter."[41] This visionary experience is beautifully described, and Mary Webb admitted that it was her own. She also had her "harelip" in the protruding eyes that usually accompany severe cases of Graves disease and which never cleared up in her case. I will not attempt to describe the experience except by quoting a few of Prue's own words:

> there came to me, I cannot tell whence, a most powerful sweetness that had never come to me afore. It was not religious, like the goodness of a text heard at a preaching. It was beyond that. It was as if some creature made all of light had come on a sudden from a great way off, and nestled in my bosom. On all things there came a fair, lovely look, as if a different air stood over them. It is a look that seems ready to come sometimes on those gleamy mornings after rain, when they say, "So fair the day, the cuckoo is going to heaven."[42]

And later she says it was as if the nut-hatch came to its own tree and found it "all to the nut-hatch, and this was all to me."[43]

Above all, she herself likens it to love which she had already detected in the singing of the many birds, as a "weaving of many threads with one maister-thread of clear gold, a very comfortable thing to hear." And now she describes her experience as "a seed from the core of love."[44] The Self is manifesting here on the Eros

---

41. Ibid., p. 59.
42. Ibid., p. 58.
43. Ibid., p. 59.
44. Ibid., pp. 58, 60.

side, her own buried feminine principle is breaking through, and
for a while it looks as if it will succeed in winning back the leading
role in Prue, driving out the animus and the goals of ambition and
money to which she has been sold by her vow to Gideon. And in
a way it did succeed: Prue never lost touch with this experience,
and it gave a meaning to her life. But there were too many compartments in her psychology where she either ignored or really
did not know her plot.

Despite her visionary experience, the plot (well established
and strengthened by her vow to Gideon) will go on functioning in
the unconscious unless she is able to see it and then sacrifice the
egotistical wish, its raison d'être. For instance, if this vision of the
divine had really been "all" to Prue as she says, she would have
sacrificed her ego demands, in her case the insistence on facial
normality at all costs. And then she could have let the pattern
of her process of individuation develop on its own lines, unhampered by egotistical plots of her own. It is very hard to realize
the depth and the destructive consequence of an enticing plot
until old age when one sees far more clearly how one hampered
one's own natural growth by one-sided, shortsighted egotistical
demands that deviate from and spoil the total pattern.

And Prue was far more set on what she wanted from her vow
than she realized; she was prepared to sacrifice even herself for
that promised cure for her harelip. She wanted above all to be
beautiful and to attract men as Jancis did. When Gideon forbids
her to see if the troubling of the waters in Sarn would cure her
"ever in life," she even goes so far as to say:

> "And in death I shanna mind . . . . For if I do well and go to
> heaven I shall be made all new, and I shall be as lovely as a
> lily on the mere. And if I do ill and go to hell, I'll sell my soul
> a thousand times, but I'll buy a beautiful face, and I shall be
> gladsome for that though I be damned."[45]

Here Prue was definitely in the compartment where she con-

---

45. Ibid., p. 57.

sciously knew her plot. She condemned Gideon for selling his soul first as a child just to avoid going to church and then again later to get the farm from his mother, but here she says she is willing to do exactly the same, even a thousand times over, for a beautiful face. For a moment she really sees her whole plot, as women so often do, but alas only for a moment. And later it is as if she never knew it at all. This is what I mean when I say in the introduction that women do know their plots but rarely stay with their own knowledge. Like Prue, they know they would even risk damnation for the object of their plot, but it is too painful a realization and, as usual, they run away from this pain.

It is interesting, however, that this full realization of her plot instead leads not to being damned but is followed by a blissful experience, one could even say by grace, for Prue's experience of the Self in the attic was certainly what Christianity would call grace. This experience of grace parallels Jung, at the age of eleven, thinking his thought about God through to the end. It was the greatest encouragement to recall and re-experience her realization; if she only could have kept to her realization and known that it was the chief cause of her experience in the attic.

But although its cause never dawned on Prue—and one must admit it would have needed unusual penetration for it to do so— her experience nevertheless provided an unforgettable experience for the conscious ego. It also had an effect on the figures of the unconscious, for it was just after this time that Gideon fell in love with Jancis. Such experiences of enlightenment, or such realizations on the part of the conscious personality, always have an effect on the figures of the unconscious whether we know it or not. Here Prue's experience possibly affected Gideon's unconscious: even against his will, love has overcome him. He realized at once that Jancis is lazy and reckless, and that his love for her will endanger the entirety of his ambitious plans. But this love was too strong for him, and for a long time he was wholesomely torn between the two urges.

At Jancis's love spinning yet another factor enters the scene. It is here that Prue falls in love with Kester Woodseaves at first sight. And thus her love for him becomes "the one maister-thread of clear gold." He is the purely positive side of the animus and thus, in every respect, the opposite of Gideon. So an immense step toward wholeness is taken when Prue becomes conscious of his existence and of her own love for him.

The shepherd's wife, Felena, also falls in love with the weaver at first sight. Felena is compared to Mary Magdalene and is claimed to be a woman willing to sleep with any man who attracts her. She is, of course, also a shadow figure of Prue, but she has a faith in her own attractiveness that would have been very helpful to Prue had Prue brought it into her own consciousness. On the whole, Felena is a good-natured woman who is helpful to Prue, but unfortunately a strong rivalry breaks out between them over their love of the weaver. They play against each other in the "game of Costly Colours," and Prue plays like a demon and wins against all expectations.[46] But while they are playing, Prue has a vision that becomes a sort of leitmotif in Prue's plot. It is essentially foreknowledge of the end of the book where the weaver passes by Felena and takes Prue up onto his horse and rides away with her from a crowd of people by Sarn Mere until the sound of the people was "less than the hum of a midge."[47]

This vision left Prue with a very narrow idea of her love for the weaver. Only he and she matter, everyone else is less than the "hum of a midge." Though she really loved him, he became too much of a monomania, and her conscious thought, as well as her unconscious plot, were directed to that one thread in the pattern of her life. And this in turn had a great deal to do with the fact that the larger design of the Self was unable to put itself through whereas the one-sided goal of the plot succeeded. From the moment of her vision and her first sight of the weaver, the goal of her ego was marriage; marriage was the thread, along with the thread of longing for a beautiful face, and these two threads were pulled out of place in the wider design.

---

46. [The "game of costly colors" is apparently a card game, indigenous to Shropshire, with some similarity to cribbage. *Ed.*]

47. Webb, *Precious Bane,* p. 107.

Even though she won the "game of Costly Colours" against Felena and knew that the weaver was her chosen partner, she was yet still possessed by Gideon's fatal barrier which he had fixed to her harelip, so she hides from the weaver and leaves the room whenever he is there. This lethal and dangerous course leads to a surrender in consciousness and leaves the activity in the hands of the unconscious. Here, once again and almost as fatally as in her vow to Gideon, she gives her goal over into the power of other figures in her psyche. And they begin to work on the plot at once. Old Beguildy, the wizard, decides the very same evening to "raise Venus" for the young squire. He intends to raise his daughter, Jancis, naked through a trapdoor with only her face veiled, but Jancis goes crying to Prue, telling her it will ruin her chances with Gideon should he ever hear that the young squire had seen her naked body. Prue agrees to take her place, as she is well able to do, having a beautiful figure. And when she is raised with only her face veiled, she sees that not only the squire but also the weaver is in the room. Half deadly ashamed, half triumphant, she sees the desire kindling in the weaver and asks herself: "Was it all of the flesh . . . or did my soul, that was twin to his, draw him and wile him, succour his heart and summon his love, even then?"[48]

This incident is a marvelous example of what can be achieved by a good plot and how the unconscious in a girl like Prue is far more efficient than consciousness could ever be. It even shows the secret motivation that makes women form unconscious plots on the wily path of attaining their goals. The amazing subtlety of showing her beautiful naked body, with only the face and its harelip veiled, within two or three days of first falling in love would conflict so incompatibly with Prue's traditional morality that only an unconscious plot could achieve such an end.

From the point of view of individuation and establishing a totality, its very unconsciousness gives the story a fatal twist in the next few days. The squire offers Beguildy a large sum of money for a night with "Venus," whom they both believe to be Jancis. The old wizard gives her the choice of accepting the squire's

48. Ibid., p. 116.

offer or of being hired out as a servant for three years at the hiring fair. She comes crying to Prue and Gideon and implores the latter to marry her at once as her only escape. Gideon is very much in love, but he is highly suspicious of the squire's passion for Jancis and also afraid of marrying her out of hand "in the teeth of [the young squire's] longing after her."[49] Jancis's eyes implore Prue to let her explain the whole Venus matter to Gideon. And indeed, although Jancis was bound to secrecy, there was yet a clause in their arrangement that in "utmost need" Gideon might be told. But Prue refuses to allow Jancis to speak, seeing that it was "too much" and "it might get round to Kester Woodseaves" (and thus interfere with her plot), so Gideon (left with his suspicions) decided against love and favored his ambitious plans, condemning poor Jancis to three years' slavery as a servant hired at the hiring fair. Moreover, Gideon decides on a particularly unpleasant situation for Jancis, partly because the wages are higher but mainly because it is far away and she will be beyond the reach of the young squire. Prue definitely broke her word to Jancis here. She knew and said more than once that it was "Gideon's hour of choice," so certainly she could have spoken out under the heading, so to speak, of "utmost need." Yet she refuses, partly, as she says, for fear of the weaver hearing, although she really instinctively recognized that he already knew. She even gives away that she knows that he did in fact know, although only in one compartment. Partly, however, it was also undoubtedly jealousy. Being "debarred from marriage," she somewhere begrudged the matrimony to Jancis, for she often admits how jealous she was of Jancis's beauty. Moreover the very fact that she only sees it as Gideon's hour of choice is a projection. It was really Prue's hour of choice. To have told Gideon would have furthered the Self's pattern of the totality, the double marriage, whereas her silence (for fear of it hurting her egotistical chances with the weaver) pulled the thread further out of its place and used the whole energy of the union of the double opposites for the one marriage that mattered above everything

---

49. Ibid., p. 129.

to the ego. Jealousy generally distorts such a decision deplorably because it robs the woman of any wish to become conscious of the actual human issues regarding its object (that is, Jancis) and makes any means seem fair to further one's own ends.

But there was another reason that is also characteristic of a plot: Jancis is going too far away for Gideon to see her. So he thinks up the plan of Prue writing to her for him and, as the weaver goes regularly to the place he has chosen for Jancis, it is he who shall answer for her. Thus Prue is provided with the chance of writing regularly to the weaver and—as neither Gideon nor Jancis can read or write—the letters rapidly become love letters between the two writers. Now, of course Prue's conscious could not know of this favorable result for her when Jancis is sent away, yet empirically observed, the unconscious (in which time is so relative) does know such things. These letters, as in the matter of Venus, again brought about a great advance in Prue's personal goal with the weaver. When we examine such situations later, we can often see how it was actually ourselves who brought about what otherwise seems to be a gift from the gods.

On the day of the hiring fair, Prue does take a great step forward, this time from the side of consciousness. By the greatest presence of mind and amazing foresight, she saves the weaver's life when he is attacked by fierce dogs. She manages to keep out of sight until he is presumably unconscious, but nevertheless he owes his life entirely to her, and she learns later that he heard all of what she said to him. This has a quite direct result on the part of the unconscious, for when Prue's mother hears what Prue did to save the weaver, the mother realizes that she must be in love with the weaver and, spinning day and night, persuades Gideon to send for him to weave her yarn. Prue sticks to her fixed idea and goes off to faraway meadows for the day, but her mother praises Prue to the weaver until he says: "Well, single I am, and single shall stay, I do believe. But if ever I did think of asking to wed, it ud be just such another as that'n." And her mother implores her that night: "Now dunna you hide from him, Prue.

Be well plucked and risk all, like a good player in the game of Costly Colours."[50]

Prue here gets the full support of the mother instinct, of the good earth so to speak, for Mrs. Sarn, though weak with Gideon, was a good mother to Prue, and the latter had a wonderful chance here to return to her instinct as a woman and to trust herself to its pure guidance. Had Prue been able to take the chance, or rather to remain with the instinct, she might yet have finally given up the plot and let the Self, and not the ego, weave the pattern. And indeed the next two or three years are the time when there seems every hope that the pattern of the totality will set itself through. All four are bound together by the regular letters in which all four are concerned. This hopeful time even survives Jancis's breaking her contract, running away from her servitude, and thus losing all her wages. Gideon forgives her and promises to marry her next harvest at home. For Gideon to forgive the loss of three years' wages is a sure proof that he really loves Jancis.

The harvest is phenomenally good that year. By unremitting hard labor, Gideon and Prue have got practically the entire farm ploughed and under grain. The Corn Laws have raised the price of corn to such an extent that Gideon has actually made the great fortune he coveted. And just before the harvest and the arrival of the love-carriage for Gideon and Jancis's marriage, Prue at last meets the weaver face to face. She tries to run away, it is true, even to jump into the mere to avoid having him see her, but he is near enough to prevent her, thanks her for saving his life, discusses the letters, and makes it quite clear that he loves her. Together they watch the dragonflies coming out of their shrouds, "ether's mon or ether's nid" as they were called at Sarn, for it was supposed that where the serpent, or adder or "ether," lay hid in the grass, there above hovered the dragonfly as a warning.[51] Happy as the day was, yet it contained a fatal mistake, this time due to the influence of the weaver who was as exaggeratedly on the positive side as Gideon was on the negative. The weaver held

---

50. Ibid., pp. 160–161.
51. Ibid., p. 189.

the fatal doctrine that if you think of sin rightly, it just isn't there, and he was so optimistic that he never spoke of winter but of "summer sleeping," nor of caterpillars but of "butterflies-as-is-to-be."[52] So both he and Prue identify with the dragonflies and fly with them to heaven, while they forget all about the adder hidden in the grass.

But the adder is far from sleeping and takes the form of old Beguildy, the wizard. Now Prue always underestimated evil, particularly in Beguildy, though she adds that he has no heart. Yet she always made excuses for him. Indeed while thinking of him she came very near to a philosophy, strangely Eastern in character, that would have saved the whole situation if only she could have lived it in actuality. She realized, namely, that evil as well as good is part of God's design. She says, for example:

> We are His mommets[53] that made us, I do think. He takes us from the box, whiles, and saith, 'Dance now!' or maybe it must bow, or wave a hand or fall down in a swound. Then He puts it back in the box, for the part is played. It may be a Mumming, or a Christmas or Easter play, or a tragedy. That is as He pleases. The play is of His making. So the evil mommets do His will as well as the good, since they act the part set for them. How would it be if the play came to the hour when the villainous man must do evilly, and see! he is on his knee-bones at his prayers. Then the play would be in very poor case. There was a mommet once called Judas, and if he had started away from his set part in fear, we should none of us have been saved. Which is all a very strange mystery, and so we must leave it. But it being so, I think we do wrongly to blame ill-doers too hardly. It is a dreadful fate to be obleeged to act in a curst, ugly way, when surely none would choose it. Needs be that offences come. How should Gabriel show

---

52. Ibid., p. 13.

53. [A "mommet" is a scarecrow. The scarecrow has different names all over the United Kingdom, for instance: "mommet" in Somerset, "murmet" in Devon, "mammet" in Yorkshire and Lancashire. *Ed.*]

his skill with a two-edged sword if Lucifer wouldna fight? But woe be to him by whom they come. Ah! So if the play has a murder in it, or if a good maid is brought to shame, a mommet must be found to do the bad work, though very like, if they could choose, never a one but would say, 'Not me, Maister!' Only they know naught. For I think we be not very different from the beasts, that work deathly harms in the dark of their minds, knowing nothing, weltering in blood, crouching and springing on their prey, with a sound of shrieks in the night, and yet all the while as innocent as a babe. And I think we be not very much other than the storms that raven in the forest, and the hungry fire that licks up lives in a moment, and the lips of the water, sucking in our kin. It is all in the Play. But if we be chosen for a pleasant, merry part, how thankful we ought to be, giving great praise, and helping those less fortunate, and even being grateful to that poor mommet which goeth about night and day to work our destruction. For it might have been the other way.[54]

This contains very deep insight, amazing for Mary Webb writing in the second decade of the twentieth century, but alas she could not carry it through and did land her story in tragedy as she here so clearly foresees. The very name of the book has this problem in it. "Bane," according to the Oxford Dictionary, means a slayer or murderer, anything which causes ruin or destroys life, as in the bane of one's existence. It is also a poisonous herb, widely distributed in the northern temperate zone and found frequently in northern England. Prue often refers to this plant, and blames it for Gideon's mistakes, but I have not been able to find out if "Precious Bane" is a local way of referring to it, or if Mary Webb herself supplied the adjective.[55] At all events, the very title of the book declares the value that lies in the dark, evil, destructive ele-

---

54. Ibid., pp. 157–158.

55. [Barbara Hannah notes that a Major Fenwick, an acquaintance of hers who had spent some time in Shropshire, told her that "precious bane" was the local name for a plant that is regarded as a sort of golden poison. *Ed.*]

ment. If only Mary Webb had been able to hold to this insight, then the Self's pattern could have set itself through in her own life, and the light and dark elements could have been established as an enduring symbol of the quaternity. But she could not hold to her own philosophy concerning the evil moments, an aspect we will return to later.

In the meantime, the whole countryside comes to the love-carriage and about fifty men successfully stack all Gideon's wonderful corn. The weaver comes too and tells Prue that he is going to London for ten months to learn the colored weaving and will then come back with a question for her; Prue knows he definitely means marriage. Gideon and Jancis are to be married in a week, and everything seems set for the double marriage of the four principal figures.

But then one of those mistakes occurs that seem at the time to matter little and yet is so fatal, the type of error into which we are lured when we give ourselves over unconsciously to the powers of unconscious plots. We may be on the alert for many other things, but one inevitably is blinded, and then one falls, either before or after one has achieved what one unconsciously sought. At the feast with which the love-carriage ended, the young squire turns up again with his request for "Venus," and this makes Gideon so suspicious again that he insists on sleeping with Jancis before the wedding, so as to "make sure of what's mine" and to ascertain as well that the young squire has not slept with Jancis. Now Prue overheard this being arranged, and knew well that it was again the Venus incident that caused it, but once again—and far, far more fatally this time—she held her tongue and left Gideon to his fears that Jancis had yielded to the squire.

Now that very day, the weaver has told Prue that he knows she was Venus, so she no longer has the excuse that it may come to his ears, and—although Mrs. Beguildy has lured the old wizard away—she knows well that he always returns when least wanted. Yet she allows Gideon to go down to sleep with Jancis in the old wizard's very bed, dismissing it with the thought "maybe it was no harm, for they would be wed so soon" and withdrew with the moral reflection that she is overhearing a conversation not meant for her and that she could not "abide an eavesdropper."

If only Prue could have come out of her egotistical dreaming here—the weaver had promised that very day to come back for her in a year—and seen Gideon's and Jancis's situation as well, she would never have left Gideon at this fatal hour hanging onto his illusion that Jancis was Venus. But unfortunately, his jealousy of the young squire did not seem important to her. Yet, it is her attitude in this matter that directly brings about that catastrophe which an unseen plot so often releases as if a bolt from the blue. Beguildy returns and finds the pair in his bed. He always hated the wedding—for he hoped to make more money in those nights with Venus—but now he has an excuse to wreak his vengeance on Gideon. He sets fire to all the ricks, and in a single night most everything that Gideon has achieved is destroyed. It is quite clear that Beguildy—though he always hated Gideon—would never have dared to set fire to the ricks without the excuse of avenging his daughter, for at that time arson was still a capital offence, punishable by hanging. But with the excuse of "extreme provocation" concerning his daughter, he actually got off with a very light sentence.

But the unseen adder (unseen on account of the *privatio boni* attitude of the weaver who turned everything upside down so as to ignore the absolute character of evil) coupled with Prue's repeated omission of clearing up the Venus situation with Gideon has disrupted the whole process of individuation and—to use alchemistic language—has broken the retort and scattered its contents.[56] Gideon identifies Jancis with her father, not only

---

56. [*"Privatio boni"* ("absence of good") is a concept found as early as Basil the Great (330–379), who claimed that God cannot be the author of evil nor can evil have any subsistence in itself. The concept was further developed by St. Augustine, who argued that evil is merely a lack of good. Augustine equates "being" with goodness and "non-being" with evil and draws the conclusion that evil is not a thing at all, and complete evil is simply nonexistence, thereby laying the groundwork for the theological conviction that evil does not really exist. Jung notes that the psychologist shrinks from such a metaphysical assertion. See C. G. Jung, *Aion: Researches into the Phenomenology of the Self* (1951), *CW*, vol. 9ii (Princeton, N.J.: Princeton University Press, 1959), pars. 80ff. An excellent discussion can be found in the letters dated April 5, 20, and 30, 1952, in *The Jung-White Letters*, Ann Lammers and Adrian Cunningham, eds. (London: Routledge, 2007). *Ed.*]

refuses to marry her but to see her at all and, as Prue says, "the milk of human kindness in my poor brother had been scorched up in the fire" and his face became like "the face of one without hope, spent and foredone, a lost face." The only thing that aroused him was the thought of vengeance of Beguildy, but Prue prevents the encounter telling him they would take Beguildy to prison and he must not have murder on his soul. "It would have eased me," Gideon answered with a strange look. "It's all dammed up within. Choking, choking me. T'would have eased me to kill un. I'll never mend of it now."[57]

One cannot blame Prue for fearing such an encounter, but Gideon merely murdered someone else, and his words came true, he "never mended" from the blow. The animus regressed into a state far worse than at the beginning, Jancis left her home, from which they'd been evicted, like a "dead maid" and went to the small town of Silverton with her mother to await her father's fate at the higher courts without money or hope. Nothing is left but the actual goal of the plot, for Prue knows that the weaver loves her and that her marriage with him will be the one thing saved from the burning.

If there is anything worse than the pain of plots that fail, it is a plot that succeeds, for I have never yet seen an unconscious plot succeed without the destruction of something fundamental in that individual's process of individuation. Prue got what she wanted, but at the cost of the whole pattern which the Self was weaving. Undoubtedly, the ego can often see through anything it wants, but only at the cost of the whole pattern of the totality.

But worse was to come, and Prue says she can hardly write of that time of "grief and bitter woe." Gideon decided to start all over again with the work, Prue was still bound by her vow and forced to help him. The old mother became more bedridden, and one of the most amazing things in the whole book is Prue's blindness to her brother's intention to rid himself of the burden of his mother's keep. But again she sees it in one compartment, her mother even tells her so at the very beginning and begs her not to let Gideon

57. Webb, *Precious Bane*, p. 231.

come to see her, for he always makes her feel she is a burden. The old woman says that Gideon has no love for her, and he would be better pleased to have her dead and buried. This could hardly be clearer, yet Prue lets Gideon go to see her every evening and listens passively to his efforts to get her to say she would sooner be dead than alive. The old mother holds out bravely for several months, but Gideon wears her down and at last he tells her she would sooner be dead than alive. Thus one evening in March she wearily says that maybe she would. Then Gideon, having attained his object, ceased going to see his mother. Prue records that this was a great relief to the old woman. Moreover, Prue knows her brother would do anything for money. He constantly complains of the expenses for the "doctor's man" and the meals they have to give to Tivvy, the sexton's daughter, who looks after their mother since they are both out working in the fields all day.

Tivvy is Prue's darkest shadow. She is a miserable creature and everything that Prue is not in consciousness. She is lazy, deceitful, untruthful, vicious, manipulative, and above all abysmally stupid. Yet Prue quietly leaves her mother to Tivvy's tender mercies, although she knows well that Tivvy only comes to further her own plot to marry Gideon. She hates and despises Tivvy, but she is nevertheless quite willing to make use of her.

Prue was quite fond of her mother and consistently kind to her. Why then was she so blind to Gideon's intentions to rid himself of her keep? When he poisoned her with foxglove tea, Tivvy knew it.[58] Prue had even heard Gideon talking to the doctor's man about the effect of foxglove tea, but she had no suspicions whatever, even when the doctor made it very clear that he believed

---

58. [Foxglove (*digitalis purpurea*) is a highly attractive biennial plant that has been used from early times in heart conditions. Several important pharmaceutical drugs such as digitalis and digoxin are derived from this plant. It increases the activity of all forms of muscle tissue, but more especially that of the heart and arterioles, the all-important property of the drug being its action on the circulation. Direct ingestion of this plant can cause toxic reactions that lead to severe sickness and death in animals, while in the case of an overdose in humans, it can lead to increased heart rate and heart failure. Other symptoms include stomach upset, mental confusion, and convulsions. Due to the unpalatable nature of the plant, poisoning is infrequent, although when it does occur, it is often severe, dramatic, and fatal. *Ed.*]

her mother to have been poisoned. She just thought he was a peculiar man.

Prue certainly had no plot to kill her mother, but she was so wrapped up in her own plot to marry the weaver that everything that went on around her was less to her than the hum of a midge. She even tells us that she was lost in thinking about the weaver's promise to return when Tivvy came running to tell her that Mrs. Sarn was dying. Her mother is just able to tell her it was the tea, but although she hears it and records it quite naively, Prue again fails to register what she says. Such side effects of plots are only too common since ego consciousness is taken up with the attainment of the ego's goal. Prue even plays no small role in the death of her mother, for in one compartment she knew what Gideon was up to and neither uttered a word against it nor did anything about it. When Tivvy brazenly stated that she was using the murder of his mother to blackmail Gideon into marrying her, Prue was not surprised and knew at once that it was true. From one point of view, both girls were practically accomplices to a murder: both knew, both let it happen, both profited from it. But for Prue it was not just a neighbor, it was her own mother.

In this case, the consciousness of what was happening slipped away into the unconscious and was picked up by the shadow, in this case Tivvy, who used it for her own ends. As Jung once said in a seminar: when we leave things to the shadow, they are done, but usually against us instead of for us. And this painful knowledge was left to the shadow which almost destroyed Prue as a result.

Now, we have mentioned that the goal can be furthered by leaving it up to the unconscious. We saw Prue appearing as Venus before the weaver, which he later tells her lit a fire in him hard to put out. Yet it can just as well lead to the reverse. Killing the mother is killing the instinctive and creative, the bearer of the seed, and Prue, like Mary Webb herself, thus had no children. A single passionate desire, such as Prue had for the weaver, can be obtained by such a plot, but not only does such a success break up the process of individuation, it also kills the creative seeds. Prue's original longing had been for a child, but such a creative solution cannot be brought about by such means. This is shown very clearly in our story. Prue is so abysmally unconscious that she fails to prevent the blatant murder of her own beloved mother, and this condition of unsolvable and repressed guilt may well have sufficed to allow her whole feminine creativity to be destroyed.

A month or two later another tragedy takes place at Sarn. Jancis brings the child she has borne to Gideon and risks everything in an attempt to awaken his paternal feeling and reawaken his love for her. Gideon repulses her cruelly and mocks his son, who is indeed a weak, half-starved creature. Tivvy, terrified that Jancis might yet succeed and herself now pregnant with Gideon's child, tells Prue that in that case she will denounce him for the murder of his mother. Prue, understandably horrified, loses sight of Jancis and the child and Jancis drowns herself and the child in the mere. Thus the last weak creative seed is lost, and another mother is allowed to die through Prue's unconsciousness.

Right to the end, Prue never sees her own contribution to these disasters. They seem to her to be bolts from the blue, and that is another characteristic of deeply buried unconscious plots: they use the forces of the unconscious for personal ends. The ego is blind and unconscious, it would never commit murder itself, yet it allows murder to take place under its very nose when a little more consciousness could have saved the whole thing.

The ghosts of his mother and Jancis begin to haunt Gideon, and before many months have passed Gideon follows Jancis into the mere. Here Prue's failure to register the danger signals is clearer than ever. He spoke more and more of the ghost of Jancis and even told Prue it beckoned to him from the boat on the mere. And one evening, when he was more than usually haunted, he got up and said he was going to see to the stock, telling her not to wait up for him if he was late. Gideon says:

> "If I'm late, put the key over the stable door."
> I thought, no, if he was out so much as a half-hour, I should go after him. Indeed I almost did then. Summat told me to go. But it seemed so queer when he was only going to see to

the stock, to run after him. So I stayed where I was and began
looking in Beguildy's book, that I bought at the sale, and in the
Bible, to see if I could find any cure for such bewitchments.[59]

While she is still reading, two children come running to tell her
they believe Gideon had gone into the mere. Then she runs fast
enough, but it is too late. They never find Gideon's body, for
he had plunged into the deepest dark depths of the mere from
which, we are told, no body was ever recovered.

The whole of the positive potential in the depths of the individuation process of the psyche has returned to the unconscious,
and only the conscious ego remains. Such a condition is indeed a
complete breakup of the process of individuation but might yet
be retrieved if the ego could remain with the ruins and suffer the
whole anguish of what has happened, particularly seeing its own
guilt. Such tragic crises do occur at least once in most deep analyses that involve the whole personality. It is possible to pick up the
broken pieces and begin all over again, as the alchemists did when
their retorts blew up and shattered. One also sees such a development in Emily Brontë's *Wuthering Heights* where everything
is blown sky high by the death of the elder Catherine. But the
broken pieces are gathered together and brought to a satisfactory
conclusion in the younger Cathy.

But Mary Webb was not made of quite the same courageous
substance as Emily Brontë, although there are points of similarity
between their fates. Faced with complete disaster, Mary's Prue
gives up the fight. Sarn now belongs to her, but she decides to
quit. She knows she will find no peace after what has happened
there, thus she decides to leave the old ancestral home to ruin and
its ghosts and the land to return to nature not "for any fault in the
place," she says, "but for what Gideon had made of it."[60] Everything
is blamed on Gideon, so she experiences nothing of the enrichment
or new spiritual dignity that occurs after one finds and encounters
one's own guilt, as Jung put it in "After the Catastrophe":

---

59. Webb, *Precious Bane*, p. 270.
60. Ibid., p. 275.

It is indeed no small matter to know of one's guilt and one's own evil, and there is certainly nothing to be gained by losing sight of one's shadow. When we are conscious of our guilt we are in a more favorable position—we can at least hope to change and improve ourselves. As we know, anything that remains in the unconscious is incorrigible; psychological corrections can be made only in consciousness . . . . Without guilt, unfortunately, there can be no psychic maturation and no widening of the spiritual horizon. Was it not Meister Eckhart who said: "For this reason God is willing to bear the brunt of sins and often winks at them, mostly sending them to people for who he has prepared some high destiny . . . ."

Where sin is great, "grace doth much more abound." Such an experience brings about an inner transformation, and this is infinitely more important than political and social reforms which are all valueless in the hands of people who are not at one with themselves . . . . Every demagogue exploits this human weakness when he points with the greatest possible outcry to all the things that are wrong in the outside world. But the principal and indeed the only thing that is wrong with the world is man.[61]

Prue just walked out on everything, and it is only too easy for us to do the same when the disastrous consequences of our unconscious plots become manifest. But the initial suffering of seeing our own part in such guilt is as nothing compared with its alternative, the slow disintegration of the whole process of individuation along with the goal of the meaning of our life.

But Prue keeps enough humanity to look after the animals and realizes that they cannot be left on the farm she is leaving to its fate. The next day is the fair at Sarn, and at the outset of that day Kester does not appear. Although she tells us this specifically, it now suits her to say he has forgotten her and why should he remember a "hare-shotten woman, in danger of being accused

---

61. Jung, "After the Catastrophe" (1945), in *CW*, vol. 10, pars. 440f.

of witchcraft."[62] No, she says, he will have taken up with another woman by now. She even maligns him by saying it would be a woman he had written most disparagingly of. This also is very characteristic of a plot: one convinces oneself that its goal is completely unobtainable and even loses trust in the man one loves. If Prue had honestly admitted to herself, "It is today he promised to come," it might have struck her that her vow to Gideon, the great obstacle to her marriage, was cancelled by his death. And once she realized her own advantage and how convenient his death was, the way would have been open to seeing her own role in the drama and deaths of four relatives and friends as well as her own guilt. But by choosing to say he had "forgotten her," she can still hold the truth at bay and see herself as the innocent victim of Gideon.

But to doubt the word of the man she loved was perhaps the worst of all Prue's sins because it was undeniably conscious and she knew what she was doing. The results of her unconsciousness are at least not deliberate and are so far from her consciousness that it would, I admit, have needed unusual self-criticism to see them. But if she had said to herself now, "The weaver promised to come today," she would have had to see she must remain quietly at home for him and do nothing irrevocable until he came. And that of course did not recommend itself to her plot, which was still colored by her vision. So she chooses to burn her bridges and decides to take all the animals to sell at the fair.

But her failure to see that her own unconsciousness was largely responsible for all that had happened came back to her brutally at the fair from outside as these things often tend to do if our eyes open to admit the connections. Thus at the fair she is denounced as a witch. The actual outer accusations are all false, or grossly exaggerated; she has done none of the things she is accused of, either actually or consciously. But, as we have seen, her unconsciousness has offered her worst enemies the very hooks on which to hang all their accusations. The worst of these comes from Tivvy, Prue's darkest and completely rejected shadow. Prue had boxed her ears and declared she hated her on the occasion of Jancis's

---

62. Webb, *Precious Bane*, p. 277.

return with the baby. And now Tivvy revenges herself by accusing Prue of having murdered her mother and hindered her marriage to Gideon out of sheer jealousy, declaring that Gideon loved her right well. This turns the scale, and Prue finds herself tied to the seat of the ducking stool to be drowned as a witch. The plot has pinned Prue down into the middle of the shadowy center of her plot. She is within minutes of paying for the whole thing with her life when the weaver, true to his word, appears and saves her.

What has happened here? We see the whole reason why women are so blind to their plots and why Jung had to give up trying to make them conscious of them. If everything is sacrificed for them, even life itself, then (as Jung used to say) plots always succeeded. Prue got what she wanted. For as in her vision so long before, the weaver took her on his horse and rode away with her toward the mountains, leaving everything else behind. But at what a price! And, I must say, this story bears out what more than thirty years of observation has taught me. I have seen many plots consistently or even ruthlessly carried through, and their object attained. But always at the price that was also paid in our story: the loss of all creative seeds and of the individuation process itself and the totality of the psyche.

It is not particularly surprising that Mary Webb was unable to write anything more after she finished *Precious Bane*. She tried indeed in *Armour Wherein He Trusted* but became so discouraged that she rang up Mr. Adcock to tell him she had destroyed all there was of it and sobbed miserably "she would never write any more." Unbeknownst to her, the manuscript was saved from the fire and published after her death. Mary Webb had not carried through her own conviction that the "evil moments do God's will as well as the good" and had thrown out all her evil moments, leaving her story "in very poor case." Interestingly enough, these are the very words the weaver uses when he finds her tied to the witch's stool in the water. "Well, Prue, my dear, you be in poor case," and she replies: "in very poor case."[63] Mary Webb also failed to be true to the title of her book.

---

63. Ibid., p. 285.

But having thrown out the evil and identified with the philosophy of the purely white *privatio boni* of the weaver at the end of the book, Mary Webb could only go back to a time when such an ending was still the right and fitting solution, a time when good still had to be strictly differentiated from evil, when evil was still so consuming and possessing that it had to be adamantly denied, and this entailed a psychological war so vital that the Crusades were fought for it. But we cannot return to a blind and earlier age; we must take up our own, however dark and hopeless it seems. So it is not surprising that Mary Webb fell into despair while she was writing *Armour Wherein He Trusted* and could write no more.

We have already mentioned the misery into which Mary Webb fell after she finished *Precious Bane*. Not only could she no longer write, but she also became increasingly sleepless and her health deteriorated. There seems to have been very little that was positive in her last three years. Reading the account of them, one feels she gave up hope and may have died of sheer discouragement.

A book like *Precious Bane*, written from both consciousness and the unconscious, is nearly related to active imagination and seems to have had the same effect on its author. We do not know—and perhaps never shall know—if there was any outer man at all like the weaver in Mary's actual life. But most certainly, projected or inwardly, she had fallen in love with the positive animus, with the light side, and entirely sacrificed the dark to it. We know this from many things she said as well as from *Precious Bane*. She was always deploring the wickedness of man and asserting her conviction that he could "watch and be clean" and that life could be all positive. Yet we know she did realize that God needed evil moments as much as good ones to aid His will, and such a realization cannot be lightly set aside, for it has set one on the road to wholeness from which one can only turn back into very great misery.

When discussing this point, Jung used to quote the example of Angelus Silesius, who, after the amazing insight shown in his collection of poems *The Cherubinic Wanderer*, listened to the charges of blasphemy against his poems, became a Roman Catholic, and spent a miserable old age writing narrow-minded and even vitriolic pamphlets against his former Protestant faith.[64]

If we look at the plot from Mary Webb's point of view, we can say its goal was to destroy evil utterly and completely and only to save the pair she felt to be guiltless and worthy to live. Mary Webb did not remain a Christian (her father was a clergyman or rather became a kind of pantheist), and her God was nature. As her brother said, she was permeated with its ideals, as indeed most of us are. Life in a way must have been much easier when one could fight crusades for right and for one's ideals and believe that evil could be completely vanquished and repressed. But unfortunately, time has proved again and again that this is a vain illusion. The atrocities particularly of World War II and the Stalinist and Communist regimes have laid this illusion forever to rest. We live in days where the only hope seems to be the individual's struggle to hold out through the warring conflict of the opposites until a union of the opposites is attained and that we, as with Prue and the weaver, can no longer afford to entirely repress one element of the opposites, as Mary Webb did in *Precious Bane*.

I hope I have not given you the impression that I blame Mary Webb or that I in any way depreciate her life or her book. On the contrary, we are just at the beginning of the search for a new attitude to evil, and I regard Mary Webb as an early pioneer in this field. Her life strikes me as a parallel to the early expeditions to reach the North or South Pole. Many people have to lay down

---

64. [Angelus Silesius (1624–1677) was born Johannes Scheffler into a noble Polish Lutheran family. Silesius was fascinated in his youth by the writings of the mystic Jacob Boehme. He received a doctorate in philosophy at the University of Padua and practiced medicine as the court physician to the Prince of Oels in Silesia. He converted to Catholicism at the age of twenty-nine and retired to a monastery in Breslau, donating his family fortune to the education of orphans and other social causes. He was fanatically opposed to Luther—"the devil himself"—and rabidly preached against the Reformation. *The Soul's Spiritual Delight* and *The Cherubic Pilgrim* contain his poetic works, several of which are used today in hymns in both the Catholic and Protestant churches. His poetry touches upon a quiet mysticism which advocates that the soul, serene, can know of God without the intermediary of church or priest. Jung mentions the work of Silesius in several of his volumes and quotes the following verse from *The Cherubic Pilgrim*: "I am as great as god, and he is small like me; he cannot be above, nor I below him be." C. G. Jung, "Paracelsus as a Spiritual Phenomenon" (1942), in *CW*, vol. 13 (Princeton, N.J.: Princeton University Press, 1967), par. 151. *Ed.*]

their lives to gain the knowledge that may eventually enable someone else to reach the goal. And it is just by the mistakes that these earlier explorers make that posterity learns. Therefore, I am aware that I have perhaps sometimes unkindly emphasized Mary Webb's mistakes, but that is because I think that they crucially point out just where we can learn.

I would like to point out, however, that Mary Webb was able to be a pioneer in this field just because she always made the effort—so difficult for women—of doing creative work to the very best of her ability. And at all events I feel very grateful to her for her book *Precious Bane,* for in it she has entered an unexplored territory of the feminine mind and left us most valuable testimony. As I see it, it may have cost her her life, and I am reminded of what Jung said the last time he was in America. He spoke of Christ having seen on the cross that his life had been built on a mistake when he said: "My God, my God, why hath thou forsaken me?" But he had the courage to accept his mistake fully, and so he won through to an immortal soul. Then Jung added: "Go and make your mistakes and have the courage to accept them." Mary Webb made her mistakes, and suffered terribly for them, and who shall say she did not win through to an immortal soul.

The Religious Function of the Animus in the Book of Tobit

Editor's Note: The persons and themes found in Tobit have enjoyed a high level of popularity during the past millennia and can be found in numerous cultures. For instance, material in Tobit has appeared in religious literature and pseudepigrapha in Judaism, including the Talmud and the Midrash Tanhuma. The influence of the book in the New Testament can been seen in 2 Cor. 9:7a (cf. Tob. 4:7, 16); Gal. 6:10 (cf. Tob. 4:10); 1 Thess. 4:35 (cf. Tob. 4:12; 8:7–8); and 1 Tim. 6:19 (cf. Tob. 13:6). Here, the book was used by numerous patriarchs of the Christian Church. Linguistic affinities with the records of the Transfiguration, Resurrection, and Ascension of Christ can also be found.

The Catholic Encyclopedia writes that it is likely that the elder Tobit wrote at least that part of the original work in which he uses the first person singular. As the entire narrative has a historical base, this part is generally considered to be autobiographical. If we accept the story as "fact-narrative," we naturally conclude that it was written originally during the Babylonian exile, in the early portion of the seventh century B.C.E. and that all save the last chapter was the work of the elder Tobit and the younger Tobias. Almost all Protestant scholars consider the book post-Exilic and assign it to the third century B.C.E. or even date it as late as 226 A.D.

Tobit is excluded from Jewish canon probably because the book postdates the closing of the Palestinian Jewish canon. What are considered to be the possible Semitic language originals had been lost by the third century A.D. with only Greek translations known to Jewish scholars or the patristic fathers. Jerome, for example, did not consider the work canonical, yet he translated it from the Aramaic.[1] The Council of Hippo in A.D. 393 recognized the book as canonical. In general, the Western church considered Tobit to be canonical, while in the East, the fathers were divided. The canonicity of the entire Old Testament, including Tobit, was settled for the Roman Catholic Church at the Councils of Florence and Trent. In 1672, the Synod of Jerusalem declared Tobit to be canonical. The Anglican Church, in the Thirty-nine Articles of Religion, separated Tobit and the rest of the Apocrypha from the canonical Old Testament, while permitting its use for reading and instruction. Luther translated Tobit but segregated it, whereas in practice most Lutherans use the Hebrew canon. The rest of Protestant Christianity rejects the canonicity of Tobit.

Tobit and the tale of the grateful dead involve a hero on a journey who comes upon people refusing to bury the corpse of a man lying unburied or otherwise abused. For the dead to lie unburied and set out as carrion to be devoured by vultures and the like was a curse inflicted on criminals, paupers, and those who offended the state. By securing burial for hapless corpses, the hero reveals his altruistic goodwill and respect for the less fortunate. Among the many reasons why the dead return to the living in folktale is the motive of fulfilling an obligation, in this case, an obligation incurred when a hero ransoms or buries a corpse lying without burial. The hero risks his life or gives his last penny, either to pay the man's debts or to bury him properly, and within a short period of time he is joined by a "supernatural" fellow traveler, usually in human form but occasionally in the form of an animal. The companion aids him in securing a fortune,

---

1. [Aramaic is a Semitic language known since the ninth century B.C.E. as the mother tongue of the Aramaeans and later used extensively in southwest Asia as a commercial and governmental language. It was adopted as customary speech by various non-Aramaean peoples, including the Jews after the Babylonian exile. *Ed.*]

or finding some anima figure, or saving his own life. Many of these elements can be found in tales worldwide, but possibly the earliest transcribed version of the story is actually the Book of Tobit itself.

As we shall also see, Ahikar—or Achiacharus—was an Assyrian sage known in the ancient Near East for his outstanding wisdom. Many of his purported sayings have been found in an Aramaic papyrus of 500 B.C.E. Some of the sayings are similar to parts of the biblical book of Proverbs, others to the apocryphal Ecclesiasticus, and others still to Babylonian and Persian proverbs. The collection of sayings is, in essence, a selection from those common in the Middle East at the time. Achiacharus, apparently a nephew of Tobit, was cupbearer, keeper of the signet, steward, and official accounts auditor at the court of Esarhaddon (681–669 B.C.E.) at Nineveh. Ahikar and the Achiacharus of Tobit are apparently one and the same person. Various sources indicate that the legend was undoubtedly oriental in origin.

Despite the rejection of Tobit from the Protestant canon, its place in the Catholic canon is undoubted, and it is esteemed as inspired. In Judaism, the Book of Tobit is deuterocanonical, that is, contained in the canon of Alexandria (but not in that of Palestine). Although today no longer canonical, it can be argued that Jews revered Tobit as a sacred book, as seen from the existence of the Aramaic translation as well as the four extant Hebrew translations. Most of these Semitic versions were found, for example, as Midrashim of the Pentateuch, the first five books of the Bible. That the Jews of the Diaspora accepted the book as canonical scripture is clear from its place in the great fourth- and fifth-century manuscripts of the Septuagint (the Greek version of Jewish scripture). Not only the Jews, but all Christians once viewed Tobit as canonical. The Apocrypha were part of the original King James Version of 1611 but have since been dropped. Against the canonicity of Tobit the Protestants set forth several objections that, to Catholics, would seem trivial and that seem to be aimed at impugning the inspiration of the narrative. Proponents of this line of reasoning tend to dismiss the Book of Tobit as the assimilation of Persian folklore in the minds of Jews until it is fixed in their imagination and serves to minister comfort to many generations. The original language was probably Aramaic, although both Aramaic and Hebrew versions are found in the Dead Sea Scrolls. At least three Greek, three Latin, one Syriac, and four Hebrew recensions of the book are extant.

For her psychological analysis of the Book of Tobit, Barbara Hannah relies on the Apocrypha and pseudepigrapha of the Old Testament, edited by R. H. Charles, in which the special editor, D. C. Simpson, analyzes the story of Tobit. Simpson was a lecturer in theology and Hebrew, St. Edmund Hall, and a reader in Hebrew and Old Testament in Manchester College, Oxford. He writes a twenty-five-page introduction to the work.[2] Barbara Hannah writes elsewhere that:

> Simpson was an Oxford lecturer in theology, Hebrew, and the Old Testament. He takes considerable trouble to iden-tify sources and has been allowed much beyond the usual space in this edition. Charles says that Simpson has used these twenty-five or so pages to very good purpose; but I should not like to put my hand in the fire. I know too little.

The two main archetypal figures of the story are the angel Raphael and the demon Asmodaeus. Raphael is one of the four angels at the head of the angelological system described in rabbin-ic literature along with Michael, Gabriel, and Uriel. Raphael (לאפר— standard Hebrew) translates "has healed," "God heals," and also "God, please heal." Israfil (Arabic) is the name of an archangel of Judaism and Christianity who performs all manner of healing. The Hebrew word for a doctor of medicine is *Rophe*, affiliated through its root to the name Raphael. Of the seven archangels (Rev. 8:2) in the angelology of post-Exilic Judaism, only the archangel Michael (Dan. 12:1) and Gabriel (Dan. 8:16, Luke 1:19) are mentioned by name in the scriptures.

---

2. R. H. Charles, ed., *The Apocrypha and Pseudepigrapha of the Old Testament* (Oxford: Clarendon Press, 1923).

The name Raphael occurs only in the religious traditions that consider the Book of Tobit as canon, that is, Catholic and Greek Orthodox canon, whereby the reference in John 5:4 to an angel who descends to create healing waters is thought by many scholars to refer to Raphael. From the second century on, Jewish traditions referring to Raphael were taken over by both Christian angelology and syncretistic magic, and his name appears repeatedly on amulets and incantations. In kabbalistic literature, he maintains his high rank and takes on new responsibilities. Among Catholics, he is considered the patron saint of medical and paramedical professionals, as well as of matchmakers, newlyweds, and travelers and is petitioned as such.

Among the four elements, he governs the earth; in the colors of the rainbow, he represents green. He oversees one of the four rivers coming out of Paradise. In the Zohar, he is the angel who dominates the morning hours that bring relief to the sick and suffering. His association to healing, to the color green, to the sun, and to the river flowing out of Paradise fit well into the symbolic role he plays in Barbara Hannah's psychological interpretation of the story.

Asmodaeus, or Ashmedai, is an evil demon who appears in later Jewish tradition as the King of Demons. He is sometimes identified with Beelzebub, Abaddon, or Apollyon, the angel of the bottomless pit who rules over all demons (Rev. 9:11). The name is now generally held to be associated with Zoroastrianism, with which the Jews became acquainted during the exile and by which later Jewish views on the spirit world were greatly influenced. In the Talmud he plays a central part in the legends concerning Solomon. In the apocryphal Book of Tobit (iii. 8) there occurs the well-known story of his love for Sarah, the beautiful daughter of Raguel, whose seven husbands were slain in succession by the demon on their respective bridal nights. At last Tobias, by burning the heart and liver of a fish, drove off the demon, who fled to Egypt. From the part played by Asmodaeus in this story, he has been often familiarly called the genius of matrimonial unhappiness or jealousy, and as such may be compared with Lilith. Both the name and the concept seem to have been derived originally from the Persian. The name has been taken to mean "covetous" or related to the Persian "Aeshma-Deva," the spirit of concupiscence. But the meaning is not certain. It is generally agreed that the second part of the name Asmodaeus is the same as the Zend daewa, *dew*, "demon." The first part may be equivalent to Aeshma, the impersonation of anger.

The story evolves a journey to the city of Rages (Rhagae), one of the world's most ancient, strongly fortified cities on a very ancient road that traveled through Babylonia on to Ecbatana (where Sarah, the central figure of the story, lives with her father, Raguel and mother, Edna). The road then passes on to Rages in Median, in Persia. The northern branch of this road was to become known as the Silk Road and traveled into China; its southern branch went into the Indus Valley and India. For millennia traders have journeyed along this road that passed through Rages (Rhagae), where they could then choose one of three roads to the Caspian Sea. The city is thought to be three thousand years old, its magnificent fortress celebrated long before the time of Tobit. Rages is the traditional birthplace of the Persian prophet Zarathustra and the seat of this great religion. It is known for its fire priests, charioteers, and husbandmen. Later it was the religious center of the occult and of magism. Of significance is also that a large colony of captive Israelites settled there. It was destroyed in Alexander's time and rebuilt circa 300 B.C.E. only to be razed in a massacre by Genghis Khan in 1221. Today Shahr-e Ray (or Rayy), an industrial and residential suburb of Tehran, occupies the site. The city is home to the Shiite Muslim shrine of Shah Abdol Azim, where more than one million pilgrims visit yearly.

Ecbatana, the home of Sarah and her family, is also worth mentioning. Herodotus writes that the walls of the fortress city of Ecbatana stood in circles, one within the other, each so contrived that one circle was higher than the next, seven circles in all, an actual architectural work of art. Within the last circle were housed the royal palace and the treasure houses:

The battlements of the first circle are white, the second black, the third scarlet, the fourth blue, the fifth orange. Thus the battlements of these five circles are painted with colors; but of the last two circles, the one had its battlements coated with silver, the other with gold.[3]

The Greek historian Polybius of Megalopolis writes that the city was richer and more beautiful than all other cities in the world.[4] Although it had no town wall, the citadel had impressive fortifications. The builders purportedly used cedar and cypress wood, which was covered with silver and gold. The roof tiles, columns, and ceilings were plated with silver and gold. Despite apparent elements of truth, this description lends itself to the fantastic: the seven walls may in fact be a ziggurat, a kind of multistoried temple tower that was common in the ancient Near East. The psychological significance of Ecbatana for Barbara Hannah's analysis of Tobit are the parallels to be drawn between this city and the New Jerusalem in Revelation. Barbara Hannah notes that:

At the end of Tobit's prayer of joy and thanksgiving we find a beautiful description of the New Jerusalem with its gates of sapphire and emerald, its towers of pure gold, its walls and battlements of gold as well. Such cities are, of course, well-known symbols of the Self. Tobit's vision here can be called a forerunner of the heavenly Jerusalem in Revelation that must have been another two or three hundred years later.

The following essay, "The Religious Function of the Animus in the Book of Tobit," has been gleaned from five manuscripts, written for lectures and publication between 1951 and 1974. From the manuscripts Barbara Hannah used for lectures, it was not always possible to determine where one lecture concluded and the next began. Moreover, her notes were occasionally sketchy, some of her lecture material being given ad hoc. The later lectures are more

---

3. Herodotus, *Histories*, 1.98.
4. Brian McGing, *Polybius' Histories* (New York: Oxford University Press, 2010), 10.27.5–13.

concise, her psychological analysis more accurately developed. Much of the earlier material is, however, more elaborately presented. The lecture material is abridged or elaborated depending on the audience and the lecture series. But, for the most part, a great deal of the material repeats itself. In order to avoid considerable redundancy, the following essay has been synthesized from all of Barbara Hannah's material, complete and incomplete, on the subject of the animus in The Book of Tobit. The goal has been to include everything while repeating as little as possible.

A SHORT SYNOPSIS OF THE BOOK OF TOBIT

Tobit, a devout and wealthy Israelite who has been deported by the Assyrians along with other Jews to the city of Nineveh, introduces the story with an autobiographical observation: "I, Tobit, have walked all the days of my life in the ways of truth and justice, and I did many alms-deeds to my brethren, and my nation." His devotion to God leads him to sever his relations with the members of his Israeli tribe, Naphthali, as he remains faithful to Jerusalem while his tribe falls away to Jeroboam's worship of Baal and the cult of the bull. Tobit alone has gone to Jerusalem to participate in the feasts, tithed ten percent to the priests, and—fulfilling the remonstrance of his grandmother— donated another thirty percent of his income to the poor and destitute. He himself had been orphaned as a child after the early death of his father. To the hungry, he gave his bread; to the naked, his clothes.

In Nineveh, together with his wife Anna and his son Tobias, he gives alms to the needy and buries the outcast bodies of the slain, keeping himself pure, moreover, from the food of the Gentiles. He was in favor with King Enemessar, however, and so prosperous that he was able to deposit ten talents of silver in trust with a friend in Media.

With the accession of Sennacherib (the successor of Enemessar) the situation changed. The Assyrians slew many of the nation of

Jews and left them to decay; Tobit could not bear to look on passively, so against the king's decree, he privately buries the slain. Eventually his deeds are betrayed and he has to flee Nineveh, whereupon all of his possessions are confiscated. Thereafter he and his family live in poverty.

During the Feast of Pentecost,[5] yet another Jew is slain at the marketplace, and when Tobit hears of the deed, he ascends to his room and weeps. After the sun has set he slips out to prepare the man a grave. His neighbors mock him: "This man is not yet afraid to be put to death for this matter, he who once fled away, and yet he burieth the dead again." When he returns from the burial late at night, he has to sleep by the wall of his courtyard as he is, according to Jewish tradition, "unclean": he has touched a corpse and now has to wait until dawn to reenter his house. As he lays near the wall resting, sparrows "mute warm dung" into his opened eyes and a whiteness comes over them. Thereafter the physicians of the city can do nothing; Tobit is blind.

His wife takes up women's household labor so that they can survive. Tobit's destitution is then crowned when he has a terrible spat with his wife (who is equally honorable as Tobit). He adamantly (and falsely) argues that she has stolen a kid (a goat) from the family she is working for, and she counters by mocking his principles of almsgiving to the poor when he himself has nothing but poverty and blindness, being a fool to have thrown away everything near and dear by insisting on burying the dead.

Grieved and weeping, he prays to the Lord not to turn His face from him and to deliver him out of his distress so that he may depart the earth and go into that everlasting peace.

At the same time, in the city of Rages in Media, a young woman, Sarah, is upstairs in her bedroom also praying to be taken

---

5. [In Judaism, Pentecost (from the Greek, "fiftieth") is the Shauvot festival held on the fiftieth day after Pesach (Passover) commemorating the day that God appeared to Moses on Mt. Sinai and passed down the Ten Commandments. The holiday was assimilated by Christianity as Whitsunday, noted as the day on which the spirit appeared to the apostles (as God appeared to Moses) and on which, under Peter's preaching, so many thousands were converted in Jerusalem (Acts 2). *Ed.*]

up to heaven. She is plagued by Asmodaeus, a demon who loves her so much that he has killed each of her seven husbands-to-be on their wedding nights. On that morning one of her father's maids has mocked her for strangling all of her husbands, consummating none of her marriages and thus failing as a woman. "If they be dead, then go after them, let us never see any more of you nor a son or daughter." With no hopes that any man would now ever offer himself in marriage, she prays: "Take me out from the earth that I may hear no more this reproach. Thou knowest Lord that I am pure from all sin with man. My seven husbands are already dead, why should I live?"

Hearing their prayers, the Lord sends the angel Raphael to aid them both.

Later that day, Tobit recalls the large sum of silver that he had deposited in trust with a relative far off in Media. He plans to send his son Tobias there to claim the money so at least his son will have an inheritance if he himself dies. He calls in his son and speaks to him as a father taking his farewell. He reminds him to cause his mother no grief and to bury her next to him, to be mindful of the Lord, to deal justly, give alms of substance even when one has little, lay up money for his own old age, avoid whoredom, marry a woman of one's own kindred, love thy brethren, be respectful even of those one hates, do not fall victim to drunkenness, ask counsel of the wise, and bless the Lord daily. These are the words of a deeply religious man.

Tobias goes out to seek a companion for this journey and comes across a wanderer, the angel Raphael in disguise. Back at Tobias's home, Raphael introduces himself to Tobit as Azarias, son of a respected Jewish family.[6] Tobit offers him wages for accompanying his son on the journey and soon, despite great weeping on the part of his mother (who is convinced she will never see her son again), the two depart on their journey to Media, accompanied by the family dog.

On the first evening they lodge by the Tigris. Tobias goes down to wash himself and is attacked by a fish so large that it could have

6. [*Azaris* is Hebrew for "God helps." *Ed.*]

eaten him. Raphael orders him to seize it and to remove its gall, heart, and liver because they make useful medicines.

Later, Raphael instructs Tobias to take Sarah as his wife, praising the fair and fine qualities of the woman. Tobias, however, has heard of her plight and, filled with fear for his life, states he is not enthusiastic about the prospects of spending the marriage night with her. Raphael instructs him to burn the heart and liver of the fish on coals of the incense burner so that the wedding chamber fills with smoke; this will drive the evil demon away.

When they arrive at the house of Raguel and Edna, Sarah's parents, they are received with kindness. Raguel is touched to hear again from his good kinsman, Tobit, but all weep when they hear of his blindness. At a festive dinner, Tobias asks "Brother Azarias" to speak of their business. Raguel warns Tobias of the fate of Sarah's first seven husbands, but Tobit is no longer worried.

Sarah is given to Tobias as his wife, but not without Edna and Sarah shedding tears in fear. And Raguel secretly prepares a grave for Tobias in the hopes that if he dies, no one will learn that yet another husband has been killed. The marriage night begins, and when Asmodaeus appears, Tobias drives him away with the smoke of the fish's heart and liver, and Asmodaeus flees to the uppermost parts of Egypt. Tobias and Sarah arise from their bed, Tobias leads the two in prayer, asks for the Lord's blessing of their marriage, and prays that he might be upright with his wife and that they become aged together.

When a maid returns to Edna in the morning to report that both are alive and sleeping, there is great rejoicing, and a fourteen-day celebration is prepared. Raphael is sent to pick up Tobit's silver which has been kept by their relative Gabael in Media. When he returns, the festivities begin.

When the fourteen days of festivities draw to a close, Raguel and Edna send Tobias and Sarah off with half of their fortune along with wishes for a prosperous future and many children and with the hopes to see their grandchildren before they die.

In the meantime, Anna is certain her only son is dead and that her husband is responsible. She spends every day waiting on the roadside for his return, refuses to eat during the day, and bewails her son at night. She is overwhelmed with joy when she sees her son returning. As instructed, Tobias places the gall of the fish on his father's eyes, and when his eyes began to smart, he rubs them and the white glaze peels away. Tobit and Anna call for seven days of rejoicing for the wedding of their son. When Tobit wants to pay Raphael, he answers that it is right to keep the secrets of a king but honorable to reveal the works of God. He then reveals that he is an angel who has always been with Tobit and Sarah when they prayed and that he had also been with Tobit when he had buried the dead. All are overwhelmed by this revelation and fall to the ground in fear, but Raphael tells them not to fear and that he has come to fulfill the wishes of God. And with this farewell, he departs.

Tobit concludes the story with a beautiful hymn of praise extolling the greatness and wonders of the Lord, reminding his son to turn to God with all his heart, and that the Lord will not hide His face. Give praise to the Lord for He is good, praise the everlasting King that His tabernacle may be built with joy, the walls of Jerusalem built with jewels and the streets paved with precious stone. He ends with a forewarning of the fall of the wicked city of Nineveh.

After the death and proper burial of his father and mother, Tobias and Sarah depart with their children for Media where they live for many years with Raguel and Edna. Tobias grows old with honor and dies when he is one hundred and twenty-seven years old. But not without learning of the destruction of Nineveh and the fall of the Assyrians.

PART ONE

There seems to be little record of the animus before the Middle Ages, although there are certain writings on witches and in the chronicles of the female saints. A clear figure of the anima is given in Saint Perpetua, about whom von Franz has written.[7] It is only in more recent years that the animus has become a generally recognized figure. Signs of this recognition can be observed even outside Jungian psychology. Emily Brontë speaks of the animus in her poems, where she writes: "And tell why I have chosen thee! . . . Thee, ever-present, phantom thing— / My slave, my comrade, and my king"[8] George Sand, who evidently did not recognize that the animus belongs to the woman, wrote to her friend Gustave Flaubert (that supreme master of literary realism) asking him why he did not let the animus write as she did. These pre-stages should not be ignored.

Probably the best known of these anticipations, and one of the clearest and most enlightening examples of the animus, is to be found in the Book of Tobit, which, although excluded from the Bible, is printed in every Bible that contains Apocrypha between the Old and New Testaments. In my youth, at all events, this appeared in more Bibles than not, and I was brought up on the story of Tobit with the Old Testament stories and was even much astonished in later years to find it was not in the Old Testament itself. Despite my inability to read Aramaic, purportedly the original language of the text, I will risk analyzing it here, as the story is an excellent example for our animus theme as well as the prototype of demon possession, a phenomenon quoted again and again in medieval texts where it is usually found in connection with a possessed girl. It certainly makes sense from this angle, as I hope you will see.

The Book of Tobit combines Jewish piety and morality with Oriental folklore in a story that has enjoyed wide popularity in both Jewish and Christian circles. Prayers, psalms, and words of wisdom provide valuable insights into the faith and the reli-

---

7. [Marie-Louise von Franz's first public lecture was on the visions of Perpetua (*"Einige Bemerkungen zu den Visionen der Heiligen Perpetua"*) at the Psychological Club of Zurich on June 7, 1941, when she was twenty-six years old. The lecture became the theme of her first book, *The Passion of Perpetua: A Psychological Interpretation of Her Visions*, published by Spring Publications in 1949 and republished by Inner City Books in 2004. *Ed.*]

8. [From the poem "Speak, God of Visions," retrieved April 27, 2010, at http://famouspoet-sandpoems.com/poets/emily_bronte/poems/4232. *Ed.*]

gious milieu of its author who employed the literary form of the religious novel—similar to Judith and Jonas—for the purpose of edification of the divine, for instruction regarding righteous behavior and the proper social relations to brethren, for advocating religious piety, and also for the narration of "a good tale." The book contains numerous maxims of theology and wisdom including the function and deeds of angels, honor and piety toward parents, just and pious behavior, the sacredness of marriage, and the value of almsgiving and prayer. Apparently written in Aramaic, the original book was lost for centuries. The Greek translation, existing in three different recensions, was the primary source until 1955 when fragments of the book in Aramaic and in Hebrew were recovered from cave 4 at Qumran. Its popularity occurred almost from the moment it was written right down through to the twentieth century influencing Jewish and Christian literature and medieval art. Carefully revised by Jewish circles by 150 A.D. into its present form, it was immediately translated into various languages following the spread of Christianity to Odessa in the East, to Rome and Africa in the West, and to Ethiopia in the South.

Egypt, Persia, Media, Assyria, and Palestine—over the years virtually every geographic area of possible origin—has had its advocates as well as its equally convinced critics. And even today among students of Tobit there is no consensus. For many scholars, Tobit's geographical and historical errors rule out Mesopotamian origin, and yet the book may well reflect Diaspora conditions and be designed for a Diasporic audience. Although an Egyptian provenance was the dominant theory for the first half of the twentieth century, during the second half of the twentieth century the weight of scholarly opinion shifted in favor of an eastern Diaspora provenance. Within the last 150 years, Tobit has been dated as early as the seventh century B.C. and as late as the second century B.C. Based on historical confusions concerning Assyrian history and the presence of post-Exilic customs, most modern scholars date the book somewhere between 250 and 175 B.C.E. This places the writing of Tobit after the canonization of the prophets as the word of God (Tob. 14:4) but before the

Maccabean period with its turmoil and strongly anti-gentile spirit
(Tob. 13.11; 14.6–7).

The Book of Tobit was most likely written down somewhere
between the third and second century A.D. yet was presumably
based on still older Egyptian or Persian sources. In the field of
analytical psychology, all such books that have passed through
a great many hands can be analyzed in a manner similar to the
method of analysis applied to myths and fairy tales. And they
can usually be considered from both the masculine and the
feminine points of view. After the title of my lecture was already
announced, I realized that the wording might seem odd to some
readers who are acquainted with this text. "Why the animus?"
they may rightfully ask, for this story could very well be taken as
presenting masculine psychology and the anima. In fact, it may
thus be more suiting, in which case Sarah would be the demon-
possessed anima instead of an animus-possessed girl.[9]

Now, as in the case of Jacob and Esau, or of the Egyptian
"World-weary Man," or of Norbert in Hugh de St. Victor, I feel
considerable hesitation in using this story because of my ignorance of its original language. As a matter of fact, in the case
of Tobit, no one is quite sure in what language it was originally
written, and there is also a great deal of controversy as to where
it was written and its exact date. But the earliest copy we have is
in Aramaic (a term applied to the northern branch of the Semitic
family of languages including Syrian and Chaldean).

Most of the versions commonly used in the Apocrypha are
Jewish from about 175 B.C.E. For the purpose of this lecture
I have used the Apocrypha and Pseudepigraph of the Old
Testament edited by R. H. Charles and published by the Oxford
Clarendon Press in 1923. Charles, the general editor, fellow
of Merton College, Oxford, and of the British Academy, was
a renown biblical scholar with an excellent reputation worldwide. D. C. Simpson, the special editor for the Book of Tobit,
is an extremely careful compiler who was highly respected
in England.

9. H. G. Baynes, *The Mythology of the Soul* (London: Routledge and Kegan Paul, 1940).

I have just picked out a few suggestions made by Simpson, an Oxford lecturer in theology, Hebrew and the Old Testament, that bear on our topic. He takes considerable trouble to identify sources and has been allowed much beyond the usual space in this edition. Charles says Simpson has used these twenty-five or so pages to very good purpose; but I should not like to put my hand in the fire. I know too little. One of Simpson's seemingly illuminated suggestions is that the Hebrew author wrote the book in Egypt. He is generally admitted to have been in exile and to have written for others in exile, for he speaks of his hope of going home.

At one time it was believed that Tobit came under Zoroastrian influence, but there is now a good deal of evidence to show that Persian elements would naturally be picked up by Jews at that time without the entire text being directly derived from Zoroastrianism. The author is obviously a staunch adherent to Judaism, but Simpson points out that this is accompanied "by a belief in demons and magic, side by side with a breadth of culture and a liberal outlook on life unequalled by any Palestine author whose work has survived."[10] According to Simpson, the hypothesis that the book was written in Egypt has recently received additional support from the discovery of actual sources upon which the author depended for his plot, outline, literary allusions and the non-Jewish stratum of his religious and speculative materials.

Simpson has additional support for his hypothesis, which is not a new one, grounded in the discovery of the Dead Sea Scrolls. He further tries to prove how much it owes to the Egyptian fable of the grateful dead and to the folktale of Ahikar, the vizier and one of the chief counselors of Sennacherib, King of Assyria (704–681 B.C.E.), a story that has certain prototypical characteristics of the biblical Job. (According to Tobit, Ahikar was actually Job's nephew.) Above all, it is said to be a refutation of the Tractate of Khons (the Egyptian moon god) where one finds the myth with discernable traces of similar subject matter. In this Tractate, Khons, the "beautiful resting one," dispatches himself in another

---

10. Simpson, in the Introduction to Charles, *The Apocrypha and Pseudepigrapha of the Old Testament*, p. 185.

form to successfully cure a demon-possessed princess. Here, we find an association to Nannas, the moon god of the Chaldeans at Ur, as I discussed in the Jacob and Esau lectures. Several scholars have even contended that Tobit was written to refute the Khons Tractate and to testify that only Yahweh, and not any of the Egyptian company of gods, would be capable of dealing with and curing a demon-possessed girl like Sarah, the central female figure of the story. The motif of a girl rescued from possession by a male demon occurred long before Tobit.

Be all this as it may, the interesting point for us is that the motif of a girl possessed by a male demon, along with her recovery, evidently appears long before the Book of Tobit, which was presumably written in the last quarter of the third century B.C.E. It is obviously an archetypal motif and can thus appear quite independently of transmigration or a direct connection—a possibility that authors such as Simpson never realize—and it appears so often and over such a wide geographical area that it apparently belongs to the archetypal background of our theme. Thus I think it is as necessary for us to begin with this aspect, just as it was helpful, in the case of the ego and shadow, to begin with Jacob and Esau. I doubt, however, whether we can hope for as much from the Book of Tobit as we gleaned from Jacob and Esau. For one reason, the problem of ego and shadow is much the same for both sexes, so the fact that the narrators were probably men helped, rather than restricted, the material. But the same probability in the case of Sarah in Tobit is a definite drawback—although I am glad also for the chance to see the problem though the eyes of men. Moreover, not only in the case of Sarah in Tobit, but in most, if not all of the recorded cases of possession, it is of course not just a matter of an opinionating substitute for the real animus that needs throwing into the resin for transformation.[11] It is a case of an extraneous devil that does not belong solely in the woman's psychology and that, for reasons we will later discuss, has been able to invade her psyche and take possession of it. Not that

---

11. [For Barbara Hannah's discussion of putting the animus "in the resin," see "Animus Figures in Literature and in Modern Life" in volume 1 of this work. *Ed.*]

this makes it less important from the practical point of view of our problem. We heard in *Aion* that the personal shadow, which belongs in our individual psychology, is comparatively easy to integrate.[12] The real difficulty with the shadow (apart from hurt pride and so forth) is caused by the contamination of the personal shadow with the collective shadow.

The problem of the ego and the shadow is much the same for both sexes. Jung once said that it did not really matter whether the dreams of Socrates were authentic or not, for they show us the state of the unconscious at that time.

In the story of Sarah in Tobit both narrators are men even though the original story may well have referred to an actual young woman. Nevertheless, we must allow for a good deal of projection of the anima. In most if not all the recorded cases of possession in actual people, the possessing entity is naturally not just a matter of the opinionating substitute of the individual animus, but more a matter of an extraneous devil that, for reasons that we will discuss later, has been able to invade the psyche and take possession of it. In those lectures on Jacob and Esau, it was shown that the personal shadow is comparatively easy to integrate. Psychic possession is caused by the contamination of the personal shadow with the collective shadow. Apart from the wounding of one's dignity at the idea of having such things in oneself, the less one knows of one's personal shadow, the more it is exposed to contamination by the archetypal devil to the extent that there is often complete identification of the two.

In Tobit we have the name of the devil, Asmodaeus, who is said to be the king of demons although he is occasionally identified with Beelzebub or Apollyon, the angel of the bottomless pit.[13]

---

12. C. G. Jung, *Aion: Researches into the Phenomenology of the Self* (1951), *CW*, vol. 9ii (Princeton, N.J.: Princeton University Press, 1959), par. 35.

13. "And they had a king over them, which is the angel of the bottomless pit, whose name in the Hebrew tongue is Abaddon, but in the Greek tongue is his name Apollyon" (Rev. 9:11). *Apollyon* or *Abaddon* literally means "destruction, ruin, or perdition." Apollyon is the chief of the demons. As described in Revelation, Apollyon opens the gates of the abyss and unleashes upon the earth his swarms of demon-locusts who then proceed to torture all those who do not bear the seal of God upon their foreheads. Then he is supposed to seize Satan himself, bind him and toss him into the bottomless pit for a thousand years. The role

One is reminded here of Adolf Portmann's report on the hydrophobia (rabies) virus in the Eranos lectures of 1952, a virus that takes possession of the victim in such a way as to ensure its own future propagation.[14] In a similar vein, the demon takes possession of the human being and makes the person live for its own purposes. Either the virus must be destroyed or the victim will die, much as in psychic possession. The demon must be cast out of the woman's mind; otherwise she will become highly neurotic or mentally ill.

As far as my limited knowledge goes, possession tends to be found more commonly in women than men, in myths, folklore, and fairy tales as well as in recorded history. In "medical records" of possession from antiquity and in modern times, most of the actual individual cases are women. Of course, possession by a demon is a highly exaggerated case of animus possession. But as you know, it is generally easier to learn about the essential characteristics of an illness by examining the exaggerated case. In more normal forms, where we are used to the symptoms, we shall never see it at all unless we are woken up by something more dramatic.

Essentially, there are two parallel stories in the Book of Tobit: one about Tobit, his wife Anna, and their son Tobias, and the other about Sarah, the daughter of Raguel, nearest kin to Tobit, who lives a considerable distance away in the town of Ecbatana in Media. Apparently there is no connection between the two households at the beginning of the story: neither has knowledge of the other. In fact, Tobit apparently does not know whether or not Raguel is still alive.

The book begins with the previous history of Tobit in exile, his sojourns to Jerusalem, and his persistent persecution for unlawfully burying the bodies of exiled Jews who had been persecuted and found executed or murdered, regardless of their crime. No matter what the penalty to him might be, and despite the remon-

---

of Apollyon in biblical references is thus ambiguous, sometimes being described as a good angel who serves God and sometimes also being described as a fallen angel who succumbed to evil. *Ed.*]

14. [Hydrophobia is popularly known as rabies. Adolf Portmann, *Die Bedeutung der Bilder in der lebendigen Energiewandlung* (Zurich: Rhein Verlag, 1952). *Ed.*]

strations from his wife and others, he continued to slip out at night and bury the dead. At one point, Tobit indeed had to flee for his life and all his possessions were confiscated (that in no way pleases one's wife). Later, when he returned to his home, he resumed his notorious nocturnal activities.

The second chapter begins with Tobit's arrival home late at night after burying a murdered countryman. Having handled the dead, he was, according to Jewish law, impure, and thus he had to sleep outside his house. While dozing beside a courtyard wall, sparrows dropped dung into his eyes, which were then soon covered by a film causing blindness. No physician could cure him, and he remained blind.

Being blind, he was unable to provide for his family, and his wife Anna had to support them both by doing menial housework. We are told that an employer paid Anna her wages and gave her a kid (a goat) as a gift. When she brought it home, Tobit, in a pernicious mood, accused her of stealing the kid and demanded that she return the goat to its lawful owners. Anna, rightfully indignant, retaliated . . . and a full-fledged marital spat ensued. "Where are thy alms and thy righteous deeds," she snapped back at her blind and infirm husband. "Behold, all thy works are known," she added, ridiculing him about the illegal deeds he had done. Aggrieved by the intensity of their quarrel, Tobias turns to the Lord in prayer and begs to be delivered from his worldly existence.

On that very same day in the distant city of Ecbatana, one of Raguel's maids inexorably mocks Sarah, his daughter, for killing her seven husbands on their wedding nights. So Sarah, too, prays to the Lord for her release. Thus Tobit and Sarah—unbeknownst to one another—simultaneously petition the Lord to be released by death.

Although it is the story of Sarah that directly concerns us, the two stories belong together, for there is a parallel between Tobit's and Sarah's fate that reveals a close connection between the two even long before Tobias meets her and she becomes Tobit's daughter-in-law. Due to their simultaneous prayers to God, the archangel Raphael was sent to earth to help them both. Both prayers are reported in approximately the same length, both petition the Lord for death. Tobit's wish to die is due to the wretched conditions of his life as well as his wife Anna's vigorous reproaches (for his fully unwarranted and hefty criticism) that led him straight away to turn to the Lord in prayer. His actual fate was indeed far from enviable: blind, in exile and captivity, pursued by the king's soldiers, on no good terms with his wife and neighbors, recently bereft of his and his wife's possessions. He ends his prayer saying:

> and command my spirit to be taken from me, that I may be released from off the earth and become earth: for it is more profitable for me to die than to live, because I have heard false reproaches, and there is much sorrow in me. Lord, command that I be released from this distress, let me go to the everlasting place, and turn not thy face, O Lord, away from me. For it is more profitable for me to die and not to hear reproaches, than to see much distress in my life.

Sarah is also driven to despise her life on account of reproaches (in her case from one of her father's maidservants). She had been given in marriage to seven men, but the evil demon Asmodaeus had slain each one before the marriage could be consummated on the wedding night. The maidservant naturally does not distinguish between Sarah and the demon, thus Sarah ascends to her father's upper room and, planning to hang herself, prays:

> Blessed art thou, O merciful God, and blessed is thy name for ever: and let all thy works bless thee for ever. And now unto thee my face and mine eyes I lift up: command that I be released from the earth, and that I no more hear reproaches.

As Marie-Louise von Franz points out, it is only possible to deal with an old story that has passed through many hands as a myth. One cannot take the characters as parts of an individual's psychology but must take them as basic psychological structural elements of the collective unconscious and anticipations of individual elements. Sarah would be the prototype of the young woman who falls victim to possession, while Tobit would presumably be a representative of traditionalist Hebrew culture. His blindness has not been inflicted by his anima but rather by sparrows. He is also blind in his determination to bury the dead despite persecution for so doing. Thus Tobit's blindness gives us a hint that points symbolically in the direction of the ruling principle of consciousness. In a similar context, Christ broke with the ruling religious tradition and said: "Follow me, and let the dead bury their dead" (Matt. 8:22), thus placing the emphasis on the necessity for the individual to live in this present world. In contradistinction to Christ's injunction, Tobit can thus be regarded as a representative of the traditional consciousness gone blind and now in need of renewal. The prototype of Tobit is still clearly actuated in our time where the whole idea of traditional religion has come into question. On the one hand, for example, Communist or dictatorial regimes pursue mass repression while, on the other, religious traditionalists seek to preserve strict practices and beliefs. (As Jung once noted: religious fundamentalists hold us to a two-thousand-year-old tradition actively given to us by God at that time without, however, allowing God to add anything new since.) Tobit belongs to this latter class of believers. He is as much concerned with traditionalist dictates as were the old Egyptians. Neither way is open for new ideas.

A member of our audience has noted that in the religious melting pot of the Middle East during Tobit's time (probably the second century B.C.E.), new ideas of the Anthropos were popping up. The idea of the Messiah was stirring in the unconscious, and there were sects and monasteries developing these ideas in the area of the Jordan. Claimants to the title of "Son of Man," as Christ would call himself, were manifest in various Gnostic sects. John the Baptist was considered by many of his followers to be such a prophet. But with Tobit, it is at best a case of old wine in new bottles. This brings us directly to the fact that old Tobit is blinded by the droppings of sparrows.

Von Franz has pointed out that the sparrow was, at that time, a worldly aspect of Aphrodite and Venus.[15] Sparrows are birds of these oriental goddesses of love. There are said to be two Aphrodites—or rather two aspects of this goddess: the heavenly aspect symbolized by the dove and the common earthly aspect symbolized by the sparrow. The chthonic aspect of Eros has always been a problem for Orthodox Judaism, a problem that we have inherited and that by no means is solved today. These droppings, then, could be considered as new psychological material—not allowed for in the dogmatic traditions represented by Tobit—and thus devalued as dung. Through the sparrow's connection with Aphrodite, the goddess of love, the droppings can be seen as germinating ideas especially connected with the Eros principle. Birds generally represent ideas that are still in a preconscious, natural, and untamed state. Such ideas either enlighten us . . . or blind us. For instance, the result of Jung's psychology on people who, like Tobit, are in highly traditional positions comes down to the question of whether or not they will be enlightened or whether they will completely misunderstand. In the latter case, they appear considerably more stupid and rigid and even become fanatical and antagonistic.

Angelus Silesius is a classic example of someone who wrote mystical poems about the identity of man and God but could not withstand the revelations that came to him:

> I am as great as God
> And he is small like me;
> He cannot be above
> Nor I below him be.
> In me is God a fire

---

15. [Francis Fawkes (1720–1777) in his "Hymn to Venus" gives a beautiful example of Venus's sparrows: "Venus, bright goddess of the skies, / To whom unnumbered temples rise, / Jove's daughter fair, whose wily arts, / Delude fond lovers of their hearts; . . . The radiant care your sparrows drew; / You gave the word, and swift they flew, / Through liquid air they winged their way, / I saw their quivering pinions play: / To my plain roof they bore their queen, / Of aspect wild, and look serene." Francis Fawkes, *Poetica Erotica* (New York: Crown Publishers, 1921). Ed.]

And I in him its glow;
In common is our life
Apart we cannot grow.

This is a most wonderful description of the relation between the
ego and the Self. But Silesius lived in the seventeenth century,
and he apparently could not make the step of realizing the ego
and the Self. The ego is, so to speak, the stable in which the Self
is born, yet out of the Self the ego arises (although it dare not
identify itself with its master). Silesius wrote these most beautiful
poems but then could not stand up to them. It was difficult to see
that he was as great as God, but in no sense God. He therefore
could not withstand the heresy in his verse. So he concluded his
life writing scurrilous pamphlets against Protestantism in a rather
hopeless and neurotic fashion.

There is a striking parallel in the fact that the old Tobit and
the young Sarah are both in captivity, one to his enemies and
the other to a demon. Moreover, one can also say that they were
both blind, since nothing blinds a woman quite like being possessed by the animus, to say nothing of an extraneous demon. It
is easy to see the connection between Tobit's traditionally based
conscious blindness and Sarah's possession—if we take her as an
anima figure—because when the reigning collective conscious is
blind, the anima is always possessed, that is, she is autonomous
and contained within the unconscious. It is only when consciousness admits new creative material that the anima can be in her
right place as an intermediary function between the conscious
and the unconscious principles. And when she is not in her right
place but repressed within the collective unconscious and cut
off from consciousness, she is open to possession by any demon,
even a collective demon, which is actually quite extraneous to the
psychology of the individual.

But it is also true that, when the Logos principle is in captivity or blind, real women cannot flourish either and fall victim to
possession, which shows us how the two principles are closely
connected. As an example of how a wrong form of Logos, such

as contemporary communism, breeds animus possessions and an animus-possessed type of woman, one need only think of Ana Pauker[16] or the so-called Red Hilda,[17] who actually claims that the law has nothing to do with justice, but must only be used as a political instrument. Von Franz has told me that Red Hilda looks fairly ordinary compared to Pauker, but she is, nevertheless, a marvelous example of how an animus opinion can twist the most elementary feelings of justice into the justification of things totally inhumane.

A further example of this type of animus-possessed woman can be found in Philip Wylie's *Generation of Vipers*, which is about the cult of Mom in America.[18] Of course we can also turn this around and say that American women are in a difficult position since so many American men are living examples of the *puer aeternus*, mother's boys, lacking masculine maturity.

In the chapter on the animus in *Aion*, Jung asks whether the mother or the son is to blame.[19] The answer is both. The mother because she secretly clings to the archetypal idea of the *hieros gamos*, the archetypal form of the union of the opposites of male and female that lies at the very heart of alchemy, and the son because he hesitates to cause himself pain and discomfort in the world, and in the back of his mind, he is convinced that what

---

16. [Ana Pauker (1893–1960), known to her opponents as the "bloody demoness," was a top-ranking government official in Rumania, a hard-line communist politician and a staunch supporter and personal colleague of Joseph Stalin. As a communist boss, she was responsible for the deportation and execution of thousands of her opponents. Toward the end of the 1940s, however, she began to deviate from the party line and to oppose several fundamentally Stalinist issues, and in 1952, she was disposed due to her "softness" and her "Jewish bourgeois origins" and was subsequently imprisoned and interrogated. After Stalin's death in 1953 her court trial was dropped, and she lived thereafter under house arrest. She facilitated the emigration of roughly 100,000 Jews to Israel from the spring of 1950 to the spring of 1952, as all other Soviet satellites had shut their gates to Jewish emigration in line with Stalin's escalating "anti-Zionist" campaign. *Time* magazine portrayed her on its title page in September 1948 as the most powerful woman in the world. *Ed.*]

17. [Rote Hilde (Hilde Benjamin, 1902–1989) was a gifted lawyer and judge who functioned in the services of the Nazi regime, served as the minister of justice, and later as a supreme court judge in the former GDR. She showed no hesitancy in condemning people to death in the name of socialistic ideology, independent of the testimony and the facts. She was well known for her interpretation of justice in Berlin as early as the 1920s. *Ed.*]

18. Philip Wylie, *Generation of Vipers* (New York: Rinehart, 1955).

19. Jung, *Aion*, CW, vol. 9ii, par. 22.

he cannot get by his own efforts, mother will provide. Mom is a devouring demon, but the son likes to be devoured.

If man's Logos is out of order (an extreme example would be a Nazi or Stalinist mentality), then woman's Eros is disturbed or even ruined. If woman's Eros is out of order (animus-possessed, an extreme example being Sarah, whose seven husbands have died next to her), then man's Logos is disturbed or even ruined. A certain quality of anima Eros in man destroys woman's Logos. A certain quality of animus Logos in woman destroys man's Eros. Neither man nor woman can be destroyed (or destroy him- or herself) without ruining the other. This applies not only to their anima and animus, but also to the anima and animus of the partner. It applies to every deeper relationship between the sexes. A time is thus described in the condition of Tobit and Sarah that has a strong resemblance to our own, where we also are faced with the alternative of gaining a completely new consciousness or ushering in destruction.

It is by no coincidence that Tobit and Sarah actually say their prayers on the same day. The motif of mutual redemption, that woman cannot be redeemed without man, and vice versa, is to be found everywhere. The motif of mutual redemption occurs frequently in myths and fairy tales. There is an excellent example in "The Phenomenology of the Spirit in Fairytales" in which a swineherd climbs the "world tree" where he comes across a village, a castle, and an enchanted princess.[20] In the castle there is a forbidden room—into which he naturally goes—and here he finds a raven secured to the wall by three nails. The raven complains of thirst and the swineherd gives him water. With every swallow a nail falls away, and with the third the bird is free and flies out the window. When the princess hears about his escape, she is frightened, for the raven was the devil who had bewitched her, and now the devil will come back and fetch her. Which is just what happens. It is a long and involved story, so I

---

20. C. G. Jung, "The Phenomenology of the Spirit in Fairytales" (1948), in *CW*, vol. 9i (Princeton, N.J.: Princeton University Press, 1968), pars. 421ff. [Barbara Hannah notes that the first English translation was at that time just coming out along with the publication of the Eranos lectures. *Ed.*]

will only say that the hero (the swineherd) and the princess must constantly help each other, and the redemption of one cannot possibly take place without the redemption of the other. There is a male sorcerer and a female who both have to be overcome, and this undertaking needs the utmost efforts of both the hero and the princess.

Another interesting point in our story is the fact that the reproaches of women drive Tobit and Sarah to despair, with Tobit from his wife, and with Sarah from her father's maidservant. The fact that women are less inclined than men to continue under bad conditions is evidenced here. They get restless and expect something to be done about it. This theme is demonstrated in Jung's *Visions* seminar in the story of the Hopi Indians:

> When the world was new, men and creatures lived not and things were not on the top of the earth, but below. All was black darkness above as well as below. There were four worlds: this world, the top of the earth, and three cave worlds, one below the other. The first men and creatures lived in the lowest cave world and increased until they overfilled it.
>
> Then the Master sent "The Two" to see what they could do. (These were two divine brothers who figure in somewhat different forms in the mythology of North and South America.) They pierced the roofs of the caves and descended to the men in the lowest cave. There they planted all the plants, and then finally a cane grew up which was high enough to go through to an opening in the roof, and which was jointed like a ladder. So many men and creatures climbed into the second cave world and took the ladder with them. After a long time the second cave became as overfilled as the first one, and they placed the cane under the roof and escaped into the third cave world. Here, The Two made fire with which torches were set ablaze, and by the light of these the men built huts and kivas or traveled about. But again evil times came and especially the women became crazed.

Jung then points out a general maxim here seen in the women of the Hopi tribe who:

> got neurotic because they were no longer at one with that eternal darkness, they could not stand it. This is a parallel to the Bible where the woman began the experiments with that famous apple, she apparently knew that she would get hysterical in no time if she did not make a move, so she made the first move. Apparently the Hopi women felt the same way about it so they also made the first move, anticipating the spirit of the time and receiving it in full grown hysteria. You see hysteria is not a negligible symptom, it makes sense if you understand it. But men are always convinced that it makes no sense, you never can teach them, they will always say: "Of *course* the world is dark; it is foolish to say it should be light, you must be satisfied with things as they are." The men did not get nervous because their highest ambition is always to be adapted to things as they are, while women cannot stand being adapted to things as they are, they always raise some devil somewhere. Obviously these men realized that the women were getting absolutely intolerable, and that something would have to be done so they tried to make light.[21]

Woman is really less frightened of new ideas. There is an enormous preponderance of women in psychology almost everywhere. Men tend to be more conservative in this respect, generally more afraid of new ideas because they upset their world. A university professor here in Zurich said that he simply could not believe Rhine's idea that the psyche can influence the dice.[22] It if turned out to be true, he was firmly determined to shoot himself. This is

---

21. C. G. Jung, *Visions: Notes of the Seminar Given in 1930–1934* (London: Routledge, 1998), p. 998.

22. [J. B. Rhine and his fellow workers performed experiments—one with dice—with adequate safeguards. The results provided evidence for acausal connections beyond space and time and an acausal transference of energy, indicating that space, time, and physical matter are psychically as well as physically relative. See C. G. Jung, "Synchronicity: An Acausal Principle" (1952), in *CW*, vol. 8 (Princeton, N.J.: Princeton University Press, 1969), par. 833ff. *Ed.*]

reversed when it is a matter of Eros. Women are just as conservative about family forms, or anything based on relationship, as men are about ideas. A woman confronted with a big change in her most important relationship will panic just as badly as a man when his Weltanschauung is threatened.

When he is in his right place, the animus is a *logos spermaticos*, and he can impregnate the anima of man with his seed, so to speak. For in the marriage of animus and anima the roles are reversed. Just as the displaced, opinionating substitute can drive a man nearly mad with irritation, so the animus, in its right place, can give him most valuable germs of new ideas that he could hardly get in any other way. That is the true function of the so-called *femme inspiritrice*.

In *Zarathustra,* Jung continues:

> It is the same with women; it is of course not expressed there in terms of pregnancy, but in masculine terms. It is the *logos spermaticos* that plays the same role in a women, the seed word. Her playful mind is not sentimental—well, you know what an animus is, I don't need to repeat it. It is irritating to a man and he is rightly irritated and is quite right in beating back . . . . A man's brutality is always aroused by the animus of a woman, but she needs and wants it, her unconscious cannot come to itself if she is not manhandled in a way; that is the reason why the animus drives him quite mad. But in that wrong form of the animus there is a kernel of truth, there is something for which a women should find the right form. There is a form, but it is only in her Eros and not in her mind, she cannot make it through her mind, only through her feeling. You see, a woman's Eros is inspiring to a man provided that it is not animus; if it is animus he beats it back and he is quite right to do so. As a woman is quite right in refusing that slimy sticky sentimentality a man produces. But that wrongness is pregnant, as the animus is full of seed.[23]

---

23. C. G. Jung, *Nietzsche's Zarathustra: Notes of the Seminar Given in 1934–1939* (Princeton, N.J.: Princeton University Press, 1988), p. 739.

PART TWO

The maidservant in the story would represent the ordinary woman, born to the common fate. She is closely connected with the sparrows, the chthonic, so-called common aspect of Eros. The maidservant is often less cut off from that aspect of Eros than we are, or at all events, we are inclined to project this aspect onto such figures. Think of the old nurse who is the go-between in Shakespeare's *Romeo and Juliet* and who carries the love letters and messages. Here, Shakespeare carries on the old traditional roles, for maids have been the go-betweens since ancient times. The more cut off and repressed the sexual aspect of Eros is, the more low and vulgar it tends to become. This is both a positive and a negative fact: in going down it re-approaches deeper nature. But on the other hand, its expression tends to go so much below the mark that is almost impossible for someone of the other sex to accept it, which then of course leads to more repression and thus into a vicious circle. In any case, the maid would be much nearer the instinct than Sarah, who was evidently quite cut off. We all have such a woman in us, and she is mortally offended if we go off with the animus and refuse relationship to real men as Sarah was doing. In fact, it was much worse, for according to the maid, she had killed seven husbands. So the ordinary woman—here the maid—utterly rejects her. It is simply hell to be cut off from the biological woman in oneself, that is, from one's instinct, particularly when it reproaches us. And so Sarah goes up into an upper room with the desire to hang herself.

There is an interesting parallel to this theme in the actual medieval case of possession of the nun Jeanne Fery, born circa 1559 in northern France.[24] In her own account Jeanne Fery tells of having been possessed due to her father's curse already when she was quite young. In spite of this curse, she became a nun. She had previously signed a contract with evil spirits and had to sign another after entering the convent. In this way the spirits apparently obtained even more power over her, and they got her to steal pieces of the host and similar things that apparently had

---

24. [See the previous two essays on Jeanne Fery in this volume. *Ed.*]

a very great value for them. Later, when being exorcised, they protested that, if they left her, she would no longer be intelligent, since they had given her the gift of being extremely witty and intelligent. Later, when piercing the host with a dagger (as demanded by the spirits), there was a sudden radiance, and the spirits all shrieked and left the place. Afterward, they came back with a nasty twist, claiming that Christ was their God, and they told her that the only thing left to do was to hang herself. To this she intelligently replied that if they wanted her hung, they would have to do that themselves.

Jeanne Fery's case affords a parallel with the animus-demon in Sarah who tries to convince her that she should hang herself. If we watch him carefully, we can catch him out in this kind of trick all the time. I told you of the woman who let herself be cheated out of an analysis with a good analyst.[25] She suffered hell later on from her animus when it was too late and the analyst had given up his practice. For he, the animus, then reversed his own former opinion and told her she had lost her only chance just "as he had always said," thus dexterously twisting the thing so that it looked as if the woman herself had given up the chance. Or there is the case in which Jung describes that encounter with his anima.

> The anima might then have easily seduced me into believing that I was a misunderstood artist, and that my so-called artistic nature gave me the right to neglect reality. If I had followed her voice, she would in all probability have said to me one day: "Do you imagine the nonsense you're engaged in is really art? Not a bit." Thus the insinuations of the anima, the mouthpiece of the unconscious, can utterly destroy a man. In the final analysis, the decisive factor is always a consciousness that can understand the manifestations of the unconscious and take up a position towards them.[26]

---

25. [See Barbara Hannah's essay "Animus Figures in Literature and in Modern Life" in volume 1 of this work. *Ed.*]

26. C. G. Jung, *Memories, Dreams, Reflections*, A. Jaffé, ed. (New York: Vintage Books, 1965), p. 187.

So one can be ground to pieces in this enantiodromia, and here is thus one of the urgent reasons for putting the anima and animus in the test tube for analysis and transformation; for they can cheat one of the whole of life in this way.

The reproaches also have a positive aspect, in particular with Sarah as, in the end, she gives up the idea of suicide lest her father be reproached. She then turns the tables on God, so to speak, claiming that she has the right to reproach him if he leaves her alive in such an intolerable situation.

The inability to bear reproaches is particularly acute in any civilization where the law is the supreme religious criterion. Then it is a matter of life and death when reproaches are made. This was very much the case with the Jews of that time—the law was most vitally important—and it also provides Simpson with possible internal evidence to support his conviction that Tobit was written in Egypt.[27] For the fear of reproaches was a critically important feature in ancient Egypt. I remind you here, for instance, of the negative confession in the Egyptian Book of the Dead. Helmuth Jacobsohn reports that:

> When the man who has died on earth appears before the judges of the dead, he must first recite the so-called negative confession. He mentions every conceivable sin in a long stream with the protestation that he has not committed them. The dead man thus takes the side of Maat, of Justice, the collective religious and ethical pattern to which every Egyptian must submit as a matter of course. He even feels the obligation to identify with this pattern. A statement which admitted "I have committed this or that sin against religion or morality" would probably have seemed to be blasphemy or sacrilege to an Egyptian of ancient days.[28]

---

27. [See Charles, ed., *The Apocrypha and Pseudepigrapha of the Old Testament. Ed.*]

28. [Jacobsohn speaks of the negative confession that the Egyptians made before their gods wherein they mentioned all of their sins, claiming they themselves had not committed them in their lifetime. The entire responsibility for these sins was then in the hands of the gods who would have regarded it as an insult if man had had the hubris to say that he alone had broken the laws without returning the responsibility to them. H. Jacobsohn, "The Dialogue

To sin is considered here to be a prerogative of the gods; therefore, a reproach is most terrible, for if the gods hear, they will probably take dire revenge, as only they have the right to deviate from the pattern. Both Tobit and Sarah share the same terror. Orthodox and dogmatic religions perpetrate the powerful fear of deviation from the laws of scripture to this day. Neither old Tobit nor young Sarah can stand for the reasonability of deviating from the prescribed, deeply engrained pattern. Both realize that everything is wrong in their environment, but neither can bear reproaches. Here also lies the great difficulty of being humble enough to stand being wrong without collapsing into inferiority, that is, escaping from the real facts. No one, neither old Tobit nor the young Sarah, can stand and take the responsibility. They both realize things are all wrong in their environment, but it is just too much when they feel people blame them, particularly those who are close. (Parsons' children suffer terribly from having a bad conscience. Their fathers are supposed to set a fine example for the whole parish, so their children heap up a most awful terror of reproach or blame.) Jung once noted insightfully that it would be better to take the blame until it is too much, and then one day you will say: "Damn it all, it's not my fault . . . ." And then you can live. But here it is awful for Tobit and Sarah. And it was in fact a bit too much: Tobit's wife cast doubt on his whole integrity in her fury at his skepticism about the kid goat. She said, "And where are thine alms deeds? Where is thy righteous course of life? Behold this thy case is known." She takes the whole ground from under his feet, as women unfortunately can do to men. Jung says in that respect Swiss women have a better instinct than Anglo-Saxon women, as they feel that they must emotionally support their men.

Also in Sarah's case there is a similar severity, this time from the maidservant who says: "It is thou that slayest thy husbands." Now, an unconscious, animus-possessed woman is always unconscious of what her animus is doing, and in this case it was hardly a case of her individual animus, but of the collective Asmodaeus,

of a World-Weary Man with his Ba," in James Hillman, ed., *Timeless Documents of the Soul* (Evanston, Ill.: Northwestern University Press, 1967), p. 7. *Ed.*]

the devil per se. One can be pretty sure, therefore, that Sarah felt very misunderstood and even innocent in the matter when she was accused of killing her husbands.

My attention has been drawn to Stella Benson's *Tobit Transplanted*.[29] Benson draws a parallel between the White Russians living in China and the Jews living in exile in the Book of Tobit. Her work holds closely to the original apocryphal text, but in the matter of the death of the many husbands she undoubtedly lets her unconscious come into play, for here, in one of but few places, she changes a lot of the detail. She draws the Tobit parallel much closer to the way in which things happen in modern life, for in her story the men do not die in the night; they go away, starve, join the army, and get killed or even commit suicide. Here, she shows more clearly how the devil in woman can kill men. It would be too much of a strain on our imagination to think of it happening on the first night. One could not find such a modern parallel, but the animus actually does sometimes kill or drive a husband to suicidal destruction, yet in such indirect ways that the wife sees no connection with herself at all.

Such a case is well depicted in *The Evil Vineyard* by Marie Hay. The whole realm of women's plots has been in the dark for so long that it is a thankless task to try to shed light on them. Jung said that unless women brought their plots to him themselves, he had given up trying to make them see what they were up to. But the very fact that Sarah's demon kills seven husbands—as well as the widespread character of such stories—should give skeptics pause, for it is an idea held by a *consensus gentium*. Jung's description of the standpoint of his psychology toward such things is given particularly clearly in "Psychology and Religion."

> This standpoint is exclusively phenomenological, that is, it
> is concerned with occurrences, events, experiences—in a

---

29. Stella Benson, *Tobit Transplanted (or: The Faraway Bride)* (London: Macmillan & Co., 1931). [Stella Benson (1892–1933) was a feminist, travel writer, and novelist. She left a significant—and often irreverent—record of life during the late teens, twenties, and early thirties in England, the United States, Hong Kong, and China and enjoyed literary recognition throughout her career. This novel won the Prix Femina Vie Heureuse in 1931. *Ed.*]

word, with facts. Its truth is a fact and not a judgment. When psychology speaks, for instance, of the motive of the virgin birth, it is only concerned with the fact that there is such an idea, but it is not concerned with the question whether such an idea is true or false in any other sense. This idea is psychologically true inasmuch as it exists. Psychological existence is subjective insofar as an idea occurs in only one individual. But it is objective in so far as it is established by a society—by a *consensus gentium*.[30]

So it really does not matter at all to us whether Sarah's demon actually could kill those seven husbands in bed or not. The vital point here is that the archetypal motif of women, or the woman's devil who kills men, is widespread in folklore, mythology and fairy tales. It is an idea that has been well established. We also see the demonic murderous side in the animus of contemporary women who are, for instance, in intolerable existential relationship situations, but these are rare exceptions to the rather common everyday rule. Modern women would be well advised to meditate on this fact and not dismiss it as a projection of men. The anima also has murderous tendencies. Pierre Benoît's *L'Atlantide* is an example. The choice is still open to woman as to whether she will remain unconscious of the situation and let her devil destroy men, or whether she will protect him to the utmost of her ability. As Jung noted, a really loving woman can hold the fort against the devil himself. A firm hold on the Eros principle can work miracles.

When Sarah decides against hanging herself so that no one could reproach her father and "bring his old age with sorrow unto the grave," she shows her ability to think of someone else and relate to her father. She shows that she is not entirely in the hands of the demon, for she stops his murderous impulse that is turned toward her and sees reality from the point of view of Eros. But she is still in an infantile situation, for the only place where

---

30. C. G. Jung, "Psychology and Religion" (1940), in *CW*, vol. 11 (Princeton, N.J.: Princeton University Press, 1969), par. 4.

she is related to anyone seems to be her father. This is a paradoxical sort of business: on the one hand due to her infantility and, for instance, her subjection to the father complex, she is indeed possessed, while on the other hand she definitely shows Eros and feeling. She is not wholly egotistical here nor identical with the demon, and this just shows how careful we must be in breaking up infantile or incestuous ties, for if we are not careful, we may destroy the very seeds of Eros. She prays to God at this point, for the love of her father has led her on to the larger archetypal figure, that is, to God.

One cannot just equate God with the Self, particularly not in a woman, but one could perhaps say that there is a certain relationship between God and the masculine aspect of the Self. Jung often points out that one cannot distinguish between the images of God and the Self. Schärf Kluger, in her lectures on Jewish women in the Old Testament, describes the great problem that burdens Jewish women, which is that their God has no feminine aspect.[31] The Protestants have inherited this problem and suffer just as well. This lack of the feminine has had tremendous consequences for women down through the past two millennia. For Catholics, the Virgin Mary partially fills the gap, particularly since the introduction of the dogma of the *Assumptio Mariae*.[32] The animus fits into the masculine deity to a great extent, but the feminine aspect was nowhere represented. It is true that in certain Gnostic tracts one finds the heavenly Sophia—who descends to earth—as a central figure. Or in the Kabbalah where the feminine aspect plays at least as significant a role as the masculine. Between about the fourteenth and eighteenth centuries the mystical branch of Judaism had a genuine form of

31. [See Rivkah Schärf Kluger, *Psyche in Scripture: The Idea of the Chosen People and Other Essays* (Toronto: Inner City Books, 1995). *Ed.*]

32. [In 1950, Pope Pius XII made the Assumption of Mary an official theological doctrine of the Roman Church, announcing that when the earthly course of the "immaculate mother of God" was run, she "was assumed in body and soul to heavenly glory." The 1950 proclamation of the Assumption of Mary as "divinely revealed dogma" was consistent with beliefs that date back at least to the third century, and perhaps even before. Pope Pius's proclamation—still assailed with criticism—was delivered ex cathedra and is one of rare uses of the Pope's supposed "infallibility." *Ed.*]

the feminine—the Shekhinah—but by the nineteenth century this feminine form had fallen into disuse.[33]

To return to Tobit: Sarah turns toward the window to pray. In primitive concepts heaven was beyond the sky, therefore you were closer to God if you prayed toward the window. The Virgin Mary is called a window of escape and a window of illumination. These attributes were given to her in the *Mariali* of Albertus Magnus.[34] A deeper meaning is to be found in the writings of the medieval alchemist Gerhard Dorn, who speaks of the window of eternity as the way into the *unus mundus*, the one world.[35]

Sarah takes great merit for not having given herself nuptially to a man. She has not "polluted her name or the name of her father." She had married all these men with her father's consent, so she was presumably bound to them, but they all died before the marriage was consummated. Therefore, it is rather odd that she boasts in this manner. She was so caught up in the father complex that unconsciously she was at least partially identified with being her "father's wife." This infantility prevented her from giving herself to a man. Also the insistence on her purity is in keeping with Tobit's insistence on his righteousness; a wish to be purely on the light, positive side. Even later, before she could give herself to Tobias, the demon first had to be smoked out. This is again the old enantiodromia of the animus who blames her for doing what he has advocated.

---

33. [Shekhinah is the divine feminine presence or the great radiance considered to be an emanation of God. She is a controversial yet highly popular concept introduced by Kabbalism, reflecting the belief that one could not see God in his fullness, but could see the emanation of God in the glory and light of the Shekhinah. Thus the Shekhinah is also considered to be the consort of God, or bride of God, and mother to all. *Ed.*]

34. [Albertus Magnus (circa 1193–1280) was a Dominican friar who aspired to synthesize and advocate the peaceful coexistence of science and religion. Magnus regards the Virgin Mary as the "clear shining star of the sea . . . divinely born for the enlightenment of nations . . . . Ornament of the world, queen of heaven . . . . Lovely as the moon." Mary appeared to Magnus in a dream and reproached him for his lack of gratitude toward her. See C. G. Jung, *Psychology and Alchemy* (1944), *CW*, vol. 12 (Princeton, N.J.: Princeton University Press, 1953), par. 481. *Ed.*]

35. [Gerhard Dorn (1530–1584) was a Belgian physician, philosopher, and alchemist, advocate and translator of the works of Paracelsus and the theoretical study of the mind. As an alchemist, he is renown for his concept of the *unus mundus*. *Ed.*]

Sarah prays to God, asking that he should either kill her or alle-
viate her lot since she could no longer stand these reproaches. The
question here is whether the woman has reached the limit of her
endurance. We had something of a similar nature in the World-
weary Man. If Sarah has really reached the limit of her endurance,
she will be heard. But if not, then she has complained too soon.
The World-weary Man was to pray if he really could not stand
it any longer. I have seen many times that we have to make the
reality of our conscious lives known to the unconscious and not
assume that it knows. We find the same idea in *The Green Isle of
the Great Deep*, a modern Scottish story by Neil M. Gunn.[36] Jung
said this story was the Scottish version of communism, for if they
were to turn to communism, then they would have a condition
similar to that which is described in this novel. Gunn describes
how God has delegated his authority to a committee that became
too rational while he went to meditate on a western peak. The
meditations of God can last a thousand years. But at least the committee had one rule: if anybody asked so see him, then God had
to be sent for. Old Hector at last asks to see God, who is woken
up and, on looking at his world, sees how terribly his injunctions
have been misunderstood. It is interesting that we have here the
modern idea that God can meditate in retreat for a long time and
be unaware of every thing that happens down here on earth.

After Sarah's prayer, the text proceeds. The prayers of both
Tobit and Sarah are heard. Soon Raphael is sent to heal their
plight. The text, taken from the Apocrypha and Pseudoepigrapha
of the Old Testament goes as follows:

> At the self-same time the prayers of both were heard before
> the glory of God. And Raphael was sent to heal them both;

---

36. Neil M. Gunn, *The Green Isle of the Great Deep* (London: Faber & Faber, 1944).
[Neil Miller Gunn (1891–1973) wrote novels dealing with Scottish Highland life, particularly
the destruction and disintegration of cultural tradition and the Highland Clearances, during which more than a quarter million indigenous people were burned out of their homes,
murdered, sold into slavery, or forcibly assimilated into a foreign culture in order to clear the
land for sheepherding by English landowners. Gunn's final novels deal with the problem of
violence in society after he became interested in Zen Buddhism. *Ed.*]

> in the case of Tobit to remove the white film from his eyes,
> that he might see the light of God with his eyes, and in the
> case of Sarah . . . to give her for a wife to Tobias, the son
> of Tobit, and to unbind Asmodaeus, the evil demon, from
> her; because it belonged to Tobias that he should inherit
> her rather than all those who wished to take her. At that
> time did Tobit return from the courtyard into his house and
> Sarah . . . herself also come down from the upper chamber.
> (Tobit 3:16–17)

Apparently the two had reached the limit of their endurance.
It seems that both the man's and the woman's prayers were
required. In fairy tales the efforts of both hero and princess are
often needed. Kirsch remarked that the idea of prayer coming
before the appearance of the glory of God can be found in Persian
Zoroastrianism, where the glory of the light is considered to be
one of the five emanations of Ohrmazd, the supreme deity of
light, life, and truth. This idea apparently emanated from India
across Persia to Iran. (There was obviously a great deal of communication and exchange between these areas of the Middle East
and the Asian continent, more than might even be expected.)
Toward the end of the story, the angel Raphael states: "I am
Raphael, one of the seven holy angels, which present the prayers
of the saints, and which go in and out before the glory of the Holy
One." Raphael is the direct link between man and God, and just
as he is one of the archangels, so Asmodaeus, according to all
accounts, is a special demon. In the Zoroastrianism of Persia the
light and dark are clearly defined. There are six archangels and six
arch demons. The most clearly defined of these six arch demons is
Aesma and his name is thought to be reflected in the Asmodaeus
of Tobit.[37] At all events, he is an exceedingly effective counterpart,
which is probably why God sent down such an exalted angel as

---

37. [Older etymologists derived the name Asmodaeus from the Hebrew verb *shamadh*, "destroy," but it is now generally held to be associated with Zoroastrianism, with which the Jews
became acquainted during the exile. Jewish views on the spirit world were greatly influenced
from Persian mythology. It is now held to be the equivalent of the Persian Aeshma-Deva, the
spirit of concupiscence and a demon of wrath. *Ed.*]

Raphael. We are inclined to think of angels in the Christian way, but here they are definitely taken in the Jewish sense.

Angels are such a well-known theme that one is inclined to feel rather confused about them. (Or at least I am.) You can find a great deal of valuable information in Rivkah Schärf Kluger's *Satan in the Old Testament*.[38] The *Encyclopedia Britannica* defines the word as a general term "denoting a subordinate superhuman being in monotheistic religions, i.e., Islam, Judaism, Christianity and allied religions such as Zoroastrianism. The Mal'akh Yahweh in the Old Testament sometimes means 'messenger of Yahweh' and sometimes 'angel of Yahweh.'" These are superhuman beings, distinct from Yahweh, and therefore inferior and subordinate to him. However, it is sometimes said by those who have seen the Mal'akh Yahweh (angel of the Lord) that they have seen God.[39] The *Encyclopedia Britannica* says:

> The identification of the Mal'akh Yahweh with the logos, or second person of the Trinity, is not indicated by the references in the Old Testament, but the idea of a Being partly identified with God, and yet in some sense distinct from Him, illustrates the tendency of religious thought to distinguish persons within the unity of the Godhead and foreshadows the doctrine of the Trinity.

The appearance of Raphael—not forgetting his dark counterpart Asmodaeus—also foreshadows the appearance of the Anthropos. Speaking psychologically, I think we should be justified in taking Raphael as representing a symbol of the light side of the Self and Asmodaeus as the shadow side, the dark side, so to speak. Schärf Kluger has shown, for reasons too long to give here and which you can read in her *Satan in the Old Testament*,

---

38. Rivkah Schärf Kluger, *Satan in the Old Testament*, Hildegard Nagel, trans. (Evanston, Ill.: Northwestern University Press, 1967).

39. [Genesis 31:11–13 reads, "The Angel of the Lord spoke to me in a dream saying . . . I am the god of Bethel where you anointed the pillar and where you made a vow to Me." In Judges 13:21–22, Manoah and his barren wife meet and converse twice with "the Angel of God," yet Manoah subsequently says: "We shall surely die, because we have seen God!" *Ed.*]

that Satan is really the dark functional aspect of Yahweh which is turned toward man, just as one could say that Raphael in Tobit represents a light functional aspect of Yahweh.

In a dream that I had just prior to the beginning of this course I saw an animus figure the size of a normal man, yet behind him was another figure a bit larger, and behind him another and another, larger and larger, seemingly ad infinitum until they were so high that they were completely out of my sight. In the archangel Raphael and archfiend Asmodaeus we see something of those figures which were completely out of my sight. Those are the great and ineffable figures to which the animus leads.

A woman only really enters the spiritual aspect of the religious field through the animus. If she were only female and had no male side, she would probably be contented with satisfying only the Eros side, and her religion would then tend toward timeless earth cults concerning fertility. Greek women used to meet and tell each other sexually risqué stories to ensure the fertility of the fields. It is the animus that introduces women to the spirit and connects them with the spiritual problems of our time. The personal problem of that opinionating substitute—who often seems only set on making mischief in our relationships and life—may seem irritating and banal. But if we follow it up, he leads to such figures as Raphael and Asmodaeus and right to the problem of the dark and light sides that forms the subject of Jung's "Answer to Job."[40]

It is noteworthy that it is the dark side, that is, Asmodaeus, who is on earth at the beginning of the story, and that it is the dark and not the light side that is in possession of Sarah. This agrees with our own experience of the animus: we almost always meet him first in his negative aspect, as the opinionating substitute that has to be caught and put in a test tube for transformation. In extreme cases of animus possession he can almost be as destructive a demon as Asmodaeus. It also strikes me as interesting that it is only when both Tobit and Sarah have reached the

---

40. C. G. Jung, "Answer to Job" (1952), in *CW*, vol. 11 (Princeton, N.J.: Princeton University Press, 1969).

limit of their endurance—have suffered the maximum—that the positive side is constellated; and this again agrees at any rate with my experience.

Now what about this light of God? In the case of Tobit, the healing process entails that removal of the white film caused by the sparrows so that "he might see the light of God with his eyes." Darkness comes before the dawn. Presumably Tobit could never have had this new illumination without the darkness beforehand. Tradition dims the light—which is necessary, as we could not stand the light all the time. Evidently something new is on the way.

Jung brings some interesting quotations from St. Augustine that throw a light on this theme. Augustine discriminates between two forms of cognition, a cognition of the morning, *cognitio matutina*, and one of the evening, *cognitio vespertina*. Jung says that if we equate *cognitio* with consciousness rather than strictly with cognition, this would mean that, toward evening, consciousness is gradually darkened. But as the evening turns toward morning, so a new light dawns from the darkness, the *stella matutina*, and this is the evening and morning star in one, as in Lucifer, the light-bringer.

Jung notes that the *cognitio matutina* (morning knowledge) corresponds to the *scientia Creatoris*. The other kind of knowledge or consciousness is the *cognitio vespertina* (evening knowledge) and corresponds to the *scientia creaturae*.[41] Jung quotes St. Augustine who writes:

> For the knowledge of the creature, in comparison with the knowledge of the Creator, is but a twilight; and so it dawns and breaks into morning when the creature is drawn to the love and praise of the Creator. Nor is it ever darkened, save when the Creator is abandoned by the love of the creature.[42]

---

41. C. G. Jung, "The Spirit Mercurius" (1948), in *CW*, vol. 13 (Princeton, N.J.: Princeton University Press, 1967), par. 299ff.

42. From St. Augustine, *The City of God* (11:7); ibid., par. 299n.

Jung writes:

> If we equate *cognitio* with consciousness, then Augustine's
> thought would suggest that the merely human and natural
> consciousness gradually darkens, as at nightfall. But just as
> evening gives birth to morning, so from the darkness arises a
> new light, the *stella matutina*, that is at once the evening and
> the morning star—Lucifer, the light-bringer.[43]

Jung suggests that the *cognitio matutina* means the experience of
knowledge and understanding in the blessed moment it happens;
whereas the *cognitio vespertina* is the result of imitation, repetition, dogmatization, conceptualization, polishing, and so forth,
until it has become a mere formula that is used by man as if he
were its creator. Jung goes on to say:

> It seems to me that Augustine apprehended a great truth,
> namely that every spiritual truth gradually turns into some-
> thing material, becoming no more than a tool in the hand of
> man. In consequence, man can hardly avoid seeing himself
> as a knower, yes, even as a creator, with boundless possibili-
> ties at his command. The alchemist was basically this sort of
> person, but much less so than modern man. An alchemist
> could still pray: "Purge the horrible darkness of our mind,"
> but modern man is already so darkened that nothing beyond
> the light of his own intellect illuminates his world. "*Occasus
> Christi, passio Christi.*" That surely is why such strange
> things are happening to our much lauded civilization, more
> like a *Götterdämmerung* [twilight of the gods] than any nor-
> mal twilight.[44]

Augustine identifies the evening cognition with the knowledge
of the creature, of man (*scientia creaturae*), a cognition turned
toward the outer object, while he identifies morning cognition

---

43. Ibid., par. 299f.
44. Ibid., par. 302.

(*scientia Creatoris*) with the knowledge of the creator (psychologically considered, this would be knowledge of the Self). And
the latter is a revealed morning light after the darkness of the
night. What is originally revealed by this morning light becomes
human science or traditional religion, that is, the science of the
man who asks, "Who knows and recognizes all of this? That is I."
And here we have the ego. This is the beginning of the darkness
that, in its turn, gives birth to the seventh day of rest. The Sabbath
is thus the day when man returns to God and once again receives
the light of the morning. In Tobit this is called "the Light of God."

Jung goes on to say that St. Augustine would certainly have
known the heathen names for the days of the week. It is darkest
on the fifth and sixth days, *Veneris* being the darkest. We speak
of Friday, but in French and Italian it is *venerdi*.[45] Then comes
Saturday, the day of Saturn, which turns into Lucifer and the full
light of Sun-day. We could say that the old Tobit represents the evening cognition of St. Augustine, and Tobias the morning cognition.

In Sarah's case we also get a new light on the matter. She is the
predestined wife of Tobias because she belonged to him rather
than to all those who tried to take her. This is a typical game
of the animus. He behaves abominably, but only when there is
something wrong in the conscious attitude. Sarah, we are told
here, should not have been given to those seven men. Presumably
this was her father's mistake. But she also could have said no. One
death should have been enough. To go on to seven really seems
unnecessary. (But then the number seven is most significant for
the Persians.) Here again is a favorite game of the animus in his
old possessive form. He seems to push women directly to the
wrong man and then has the easy task of destroying the marriage
so that he may turn around and say "I told you so." Jung says, in
his "Two Essays," that the animus behaves like the jealous lover. It
is also interesting that Asmodaeus was bound to her. Raphael has
to go and free Asmodaeus, to "unbind" him. In the case of Jeanne
Fery it took forever to exorcise all the demons. In Sarah's case,
Asmodaeus was presumably bound by God, perhaps because of

---

45. [French: *vendredi*; Italian: *venerdi. Ed.*]

God's tendency at that time to incarnate. The play *The Green Pastures* goes right through the Old Testament, and toward the end God says: "It does not seem to work out this way, the only thing I can do is to become man and see it from that side."[46]

The fact that Asmodaeus had to be bound also points to a fact that is slowly becoming clearer as we learn more of the animus, namely, that he is not happy himself in the state of possession. It looks as if he wants to possess a woman body and soul, but the evidence is mounting that what he is really doing is a kind of challenge. He wants to incarnate, so to speak, and if the woman does not realize him, if she does not take up his challenge and have an *Auseinandersetzung* with him, he possesses her. She makes a vacuum by her neglect of the problem, so to speak, and automatically he moves into it. It is absolutely useless to try to escape the animus. The only possible thing to do is to try to realize him. To the extent that you can realize him—or to the extent that he becomes incarnate—he is more or less assimilated. You see this clearly with women who have a spiritual fate, so to speak, and animus possession is the first step where one is given a chance to realize the spiritual dimensions entailed.

The binding of Asmodaeus is another hint in the direction of an Egyptian source. In the World-weary Man we learn that he thought his Ba soul should be bound in body with "bond and rope."[47] This binding is more or less a magic procedure, dependence through projection, that is, being bound by fascination. It also reminds us of what we discussed in the introduction where the animus is found in the amber, apparently stuck fast in the

---

46. [*The Green Pastures*, a Pulitzer Prize–winning play by Marc Connelly, is a reenactment of stories of the Old Testament in which all the characters (including God) are African American and speak in a black southern dialect. The theme of the Lord walking on the earth evolves with utter simplicity, producing a play of emotional depth and spiritual exaltation, a divine comedy of the modern theater. It was first performed at the Mansfield Theatre in New York City in 1930. *Ed.*]

47. [See Jacobsohn, "The Dialogue of a World-weary Man with His Ba," lines 3–30. The "Ba soul" is comparable to the Western concept of the soul and includes that which is individual and unique and thus extends into the idea of personality. Objects were thus possible of having a Ba soul as well. The Ba also departs from the body at death and is sometimes depicted as a human-headed bird that flies out of the tomb and joins in the afterlife with the Ka soul, that is, the life force and the "self" of the individual. *Ed.*]

sticky resin.[48] We compared this with Maria Prophetissa who used glue to attach the fugitive Mercurius to the bottom of the retort. And here again we get a demon, a first cousin of the animus—even if in a rather collective form—bound in Sarah and her environment. Moreover, although it is claimed to be necessary to "unbind Asmodaeus," he is actually not free for long. Once he is smoked out of Sarah, we read that the demon was baffled and fled only to be pursued and bound again by Raphael. Now, this binding or imprisoning of demons or the devil himself is a pretty common occurrence, but it fits well into our theme of the necessity of putting the opinionating animus into a test tube so that he may transform.

PART THREE

Just as Tobit and Sarah prayed on the same day, so the two go where they belong at the same time: Tobit in from the courtyard, Sarah down from her father's room. It is necessary to be where one belongs when one has to face the divine. Here, there is a difference: Tobit goes in and Sarah comes down. He has to go inside himself to face the problems of his life and to open to new ideas and experiences. Sarah has to come down from being caught up in her father complex, that is, in the head. I once knew a woman who complained that there were no men who liked her, but later when I happened to speak to a few men, it turned out that men who tried to get near her came up against her anger and outrage. Jung explained that she would be the princess in a castle tower, her father the king. Although she imagined that she wanted relationships with men, what she apparently really wanted was the wonderful, magical relationship to father to remain untouched. In a similar way Sarah had to come down from her attitude to face the imperative changes awaiting her.

The first result of Tobit's going inside is that he realized that he has prayed for death and is thus under an obligation to set his

---

48. [The "introduction" Barbara Hannah mentions here can be found in her essay "The Animus Problem in Modern Women" in volume 1. *Ed.*]

house in order. He remembers money that he has left in trust with Gabael in Rages and decides to ask Tobias to fetch it for him. As already noted, Tobit only had a cognition of the evening, the *cognitio vespertina,* that knowledge resulting from conceptualization, imitation, repetition, and dogmatization, the knowledge dictated by tradition. One could say that Tobias is destined to bring the new light of morning, the *cognitio matutina,* and he represents the nucleus of the renewal of consciousness. We often see such themes in fairy tales, for instance, those discussed by von Franz in her lectures. Tobit goes on to give his son long injunctions about his favorite burial themes: he must bury his father and honor his mother (that is rather touching considering his conviction that Anna has been so disagreeable to him). True, the only recommendation Tobit brings is that Anna faced dangers when Tobias was in her womb. Tobit also wishes that she should be buried in his grave. He goes on to recommend that Tobias should continue fulfilling the law, giving alms and being kind to the destitute and needy, but rather on the principle of giving in order to receive. I would like to share an anecdote about Page Roberts, the dean of Salisbury, who was noted for his forthrightness. One day, just as he was going to preach, the congregation was singing a hymn about doing good without "seeking a reward." This was altogether too much for him, and he leaned over to the congregation and exclaimed: "What liars you all are, you are just laying up for a deferred annuity in Heaven."

Rebecca enjoined her son Jacob not to take a stranger for a wife but choose a bride from one of his father's tribe (adding many edifying precepts all more or less an exposition of the law). In a similar vein Tobit exhorts Tobias to remember "these commencements" and then tells him of the money. Tobias agrees to help his father but points out that Gabael will not know him and that he does not know the way. His father says that they tore the note of hand in half and that his half will suffice as an introduction to Gabael. Von Franz points out that the Greek word for "symbol" originally meant an object torn in half for purposes of later identification. So Tobias is given the one half and must find the other. One might also suggest that traditional religion gives us half of ourselves before we have any idea of what religion really is. This aspect seems interesting because it shows that a symbol is something that comes purely from the unconscious yet is a phenomenon on the fringe of consciousness; part of it we know and part we do not.

Tobias must also find a "trusty man" to show him the way. He goes out of his house and finds the angel Raphael who he takes for an ordinary man. To cut a long story short, Raphael is examined by the elderly Tobit and passes as satisfactory in every way. Raphael tries to avoid the direct lie as to which family and tribe he belongs to, but when Tobit insists, he claims kinship with him, giving the name of a noble and good lineage. Perhaps the only thing that directly concerns our theme is that, in response, Tobit remarks that he himself lies in darkness like the dead and lives among them, a statement just quickly mentioned as further evidence of our conclusion that Tobit belongs to a tradition in urgent need of renewal.

Anna makes a fuss about this journey, certain that she will never see her son again. But Tobit assures her that Tobias will return in peace and that a good angel will go with him (although he has no idea who Raphael is). One charming turn in the story is that, when starting off with Raphael, Tobias takes his dog along with him. According to Cruden's Concordance this is something more or less unique in the Apocrypha of the Old Testament. In biblical times the dog usually had a negative connotation, but here it is spoken of as a companion. The dog as guide is a widespread motif, but in the context of Persian tradition the dog leads one in death, while the Egyptian Anubis, the jackal or dog-headed god, guides us to the underworld. Dogs however also show us a new paths into life, the motif here being "instinct as friend."[49] Tobias, in contradistinction to Tobit who lived by the law, seems

---

49. In *The Archetypal Symbolism of Animals* Barbara Hannah writes that the dog "lends itself to development and even to a large degree to assimilation . . . . It could, therefore, be called an instinct which we can, to a certain extent, integrate much more easily." In this text she notes that the mythological symbolism associated to dogs includes, among other things, the dog as loyal friend, guide, watchdog, and healer (roles he can be said to play in Tobit),

friendly with this carrier of instinct that presumably had some favorable influence on the success of his mission. A man with a negative father complex is cut off from his instinct and would be badly handicapped in battling with an animus possession. In *Aion* Jung speaks of the dead man giving a piece of bread to the dog so that he may lead him rightly into the land of the dead. Here, however, the dog is not a symbol of death. On the contrary, it accompanies Tobias on his path to a new light via the beyond or the unconscious. The instinct is absolutely indispensable in every dangerous crossing whether it is from "life to death" or an "old worn-out attitude into a new outlook on life." Jung often speaks of the piety of animals and of how much nearer they live than we to God's will—to their true nature. Referring to the logion in the Oxyrhynchus papyrus, Jung writes: "That means the instincts, one could almost say the blind instincts; the way of nature will bring you quite naturally where you have to go."[50]

Tobit was written only two or three centuries before the Oxyrhynchus papyri containing the sayings of Jesus that were found by B. P. Grenfell and A. S. Hunt in their excavations southwest of Cairo around 1903. Here, we find one version of a significant quote from Jesus:

Who are they that draw us to the Kingdom of Heaven? The fowls of the heaven, and of the beasts whatever is beneath the earth or upon the earth, and the fishes of the sea, these are they that will draw you: and the kingdom of heaven is within you: and whosoever knoweth himself shall find it: and having found it ye shall know yourselves that ye . . . are in God and God in you.[51]

---

as well as betrayer, trickster, thief, and corpse eater. See Barbara Hannah, *The Archetypal Symbolism of Animals* (Wilmette, Ill.: Chiron Publications), pp. 3, 54. *Ed.*]

50. [Jung, *Visions*, p. 402. Jung writes: "That is like the figure of the helpful animal in fairy tales. When the hero is in a tight place and doesn't know his way out, one or two animals appear that prove to be very helpful; they show him the way—something very near and very self-evident which he has not seen. This is the function of instinct, and it helps in situations where nothing else helps, when your mind leaves you completely" (ibid. p. 133). *Ed.*]

51. Montague Rhodes James, *The Apocryphal New Testament*. (Oxford: Clarendon Press, 1924), p. 26. [Oxyrhynchus is a city and archaeological site in Upper Egypt located about

In the editions that have been restored, an obliterated passage includes the beasts, as indeed is to be expected. Only a man with instinct can deal with an animus-possessed woman; the animus can argue any man straight into the anima, but if the man has enough instinct he will not fall for it. It is really a test of whether a man is in contact with his instinct or not. A man with a mother complex is awfully handicapped in this way as it cuts him off hopelessly from instinct. As Kirsch pointed out, the Anthropos idea of the complete man was already in the air at that time, and the complete man very much includes his animal side.[52]

On the first night of the journey, Raphael and Tobias lodged by the Tigris. Tobias, usually referred to as "the young man," went down to wash his feet in the river. We read that:

> a great fish leaped up out of the water, and would have swallowed the foot of the young man. And he cried out. And the angel said unto the young man, "Grasp and take hold of the fish." And the young man caught hold of the fish, and hauled it up on to the land. And the angel said unto him: Open the fish, and take out its gall and the heart and liver and put them by thee, and cast away the innards; for its gall and heart and liver are for a useful medicament. And the young man opened the fish and collected the gall and the heart and the liver, and he roasted part of the fish and did eat, and left part thereof salted. And they journeyed both of them together until they drew nigh to Media. And then the young man asked the angel and said unto him: "Brother Azarias, what is the medicament in the

---

100 miles south-southwest of Cairo. The site is considered to be one of the most important ever discovered and has yielded an enormous collection of papyrus texts dating from the time of the Ptolemaic and Roman periods of Egyptian history. The cite essentially consists of the vast, centuries-old garbage dumps of the town of Oxyrhynchus, which were gradually covered with sand and forgotten for about a thousand years. *Ed.*]

52. [James Kirsch was instrumental in introducing the Kabbalah to Jung who drew parallels between the alchemical Anthropos and the Ten Sefiroth. The latter can be conceptualized as an ethereal, formless monad and yet a representation of the very "body" of God, the "Adam Kadmon," a Kabbalistic depiction of the primordial man: an Anthropos figure with a complete body. *Ed.*]

heart and the liver of the fish and in the gall?" And he said
unto him:

"As regards the heart and the liver of the fish, make thou
a smoke before a man or a woman who hath an attack of a
demon or an evil spirit, and every attacker will flee from him,
and they shall nevermore find an abode with him. And as for
the gall—anoint a man's eyes, upon which white films come
up, [or] blow into them on the white films, and they become
well." (Tobit 6:2–9)

This fish is possibly the most important item in the Book of Tobit.
It seems very large as it nearly swallowed Tobias's foot. (In some
versions, the foot is omitted and the fish would have devoured the
whole of the young man.) Evidently, it cost Tobias a Herculean
effort, and maybe it required the help—or the presence—of
Raphael to overcome it. Thus, it is not simply the fishing up of a
content out of the unconscious, as the motif of the hero overcoming the monster is also suggested. The fish is drawn to Tobias and
tries to swallow him. This is necessary, for whatever is going to
redeem the unconscious must first be accepted by the matrix of
the unconscious. Tobias must be able to attract contents himself
from the unconscious in order to become more numinous and
powerful, that is, he must have a constellating effect.

Both sides come into action here, and it is a question whether
the fish will first swallow Tobias, that is, swallow Tobias's consciousness, or whether consciousness will directly overcome the
fish. (The former we see in hero myths such as Jonah where being
swallowed precedes any form of redemption.) Raphael decides
here for consciousness, that is, he backs Tobias in the fight.

It is interesting that although Raphael is sent by God to help
Tobit and Sarah, it is the young man, and not the angel, who takes
the hero's role here. This is not always the case in these mythological journeys among human and divine companions. Chidr
took all the action on his journey with Moses in the Qur'an, for
instance, and as far as I remember, in the case of two companions,
it is often the one with magical or divine qualities who performs

most of the heroic deeds.[53] That it is Tobias and not Raphael who takes action would indicate that the divine is nearer to, or approaching the human, or rather, that the human being is taking over more responsibility and is not remaining passive as we see in Moses in the Qur'an or in numerous fairy tales. The myth is evidently driving toward the human being taking an increasingly responsible attitude.

Von Franz relates a phenomenon that is closely connected with our theme. We find an old myth in northern European folklore of the companion, in this case a ghost, who accompanies the hero. In this myth all the deeds are performed by the human being. But when Hans Christian Andersen took over the story, he turned it around and put all the action into the hands of the supernatural figure. This shows the typical childishness on Andersen's part; he expects everything worthwhile to be given as a gift by the unconscious. This attitude parallels the mother's son described in *Aion* who cannot get out into the knocks of the world because of his secret conviction that there is another way: his mother can give it to him. But Tobias—the human figure of this pair—takes the action alone, after being advised and helped by Raphael.

If we take the story from the feminine side (and, to a great extent, you can generally take such old myths from both sides), Tobias would again represent the hero. But in this case it would not be the archetypal foundation of all egos, but the archetypal basis of the transformed and integrated feminine mind. Looked at from the point of view of Sarah, there are several animus figures in this myth. The first is her father, the second is Raguel, the third is Raphael/Asmodaeus (as the opposite aspects of the

---

53. [Chidr, in Sufi mysticism, is the first angel of Allah, "The Face of Allah." Because Allah is unnamable, ineffable, and formless, he appears in tangible, visible form as Chidr, "the Angel of the Face." A similar reference in the Old Testament occurs when Jacob wrestles with the angel and says that he has seen God face to face (Gen. 32:20). Or where Christ is considered the visible face of God. Barbara Hannah refers here to the story of the angel Chidr accompanying Moses on a journey. They come upon a series of human tragedies—in part created by Chidr himself—which strike Moses as being terribly unjust. Moses repeatedly asks Chidr how God can allow such tragedies, and Chidr repeatedly tells him that he must wait without knowing the answer. Eventually Chidr reveals the greater, humane and invisible plan of God behind such sufferings. Jung mentions Chidr in *Nietzsche's Zarathustra*, pp. 320, 369, 1531. *Ed.*]

divine animus figure), and finally, as the fourth, Tobias. Jung once said that one should choose or support the animus figure that is in connection with the instinct because he is the one who is in direct connection with life. The others also have their function, but they often work *contra naturam*. Here, it is obviously Tobias who is in connection with instinct, for he not only takes his dog with him, but also catches the fish, and thus he is the one who can free Sarah.

In my early analysis with Jung, I had many dreams where I was waiting for the hero to rescue me as we see in theme of Andromeda and Perseus.[54] It took lots of "kicks" from Jung to make me realize that I could wait forever unless I could get my mind to take over the human side of the role. Women are terribly inclined to project this figure, especially onto the analyst. And predisposed to avoid the terrific creative exertion that they must make with their minds in order to take over the role in their own liberation from the old opinionating demon, a possession that usually has quite as firm a hold on them as Asmodaeus has here on Sarah. The old alchemists say that although all the work must be done by man, it can only be completed if God is willing. This divine help is represented here by Raphael. But the point I want to make is that divine help is no substitute for the hard human work of pulling that fish out of the river. It is extraordinarily difficult to make women work creatively; any excuse will do. The exceptions here naturally are women who are driven by a special creative gift.

Tobias here plays the constructive part of the woman's animus. The divine help is represented here by Raphael, but he is no substitute for the hard work implied by wrestling with and pulling up the fish out of the river. To pull a fish out of the river and prevent it from drawing one down into the unconscious is a wonderful example for creative work since all such work consists of drawing

---

54. [Andromeda, the beautiful daughter of the Ethiopian king Cepheus, was chained to a rock jutting out of the sea to appease the rage of Poseidon who had been aggravated by the conceits of Andromeda's mother, the queen Cassiopeia. Doomed to be devoured by a female sea dragon, she was rescued by Perseus who beheaded the monster as it was approaching and took her back to Greece as his wife. *Ed.*]

contents out of the unconscious and doing the best we can with them consciously. On the primitive level, it is enough to escape the monster. But Tobias goes further and draws the essence out of the fish, an apt symbol for the creative side, Tobias being the archetypal image foreshadowing the work of the male ego or the spirit of the woman. Unless a woman has a special creative gift through which she can aspire to worldly "success," it is often difficult to get her to develop her creative side in a disciplined and enduring manner outside her task of raising and caring for a family.[55]

In *Aion*, Jung quotes the Syrian Apocalypse of Baruch who claims that the time preceding the coming of the Messiah will fall into twelve parts, and the Messiah will appear in the twelfth. As a time division, Jung notes, the number twelve points to the zodiac, of which the twelfth is the sign of the fishes.[56] It is then at the end of time—and the coming of the Messiah—that Leviathan will rise out of the sea. "The two great sea monsters which I created on the fifth day of creation and which I have presaged until that time shall then be food for all who are left."[57] According to the Talmud, the "female Leviathan has already been killed by Yahweh, salted, and preserved for the end of time. And the male He castrated, for otherwise they would have multiplied and swamped the earth."[58] We see a parallel here in our text, for apart from obtaining the essence of the fish (the liver, heart, and gall bladder), Raphael and Tobias eat some of the fish and salt more. Now we do not know if Tobias's fish was male or female, but the fish is often connected with the female, particularly in the neighboring cults of Asia Minor. And that may have been known to the author of Tobit. I mentioned, for instance, the Syrian goddess Atargatis, often known as Derketo, who is generally described as the fish goddess. (In one story she was hatched from an egg in the Euphrates; in another, escaping

55. [In the past half century, women have obviously progressed radically on this and many other issues. *Ed.*]

56. Jung, *Aion*, *CW*, vol. 9ii, par. 176.

57. Ibid., par. 181.

58. Ibid., par. 181n.

pursuit, she leaped into the Euphrates and became a fish. Half fish herself, her son was called Ichthys.)[59] There is a legend of Aphrodite whose origin is connected to this Babylonian love goddess, and Venus herself who arose directly out of the sea.

Throughout the history of symbolism, the fish often represents an all-devouring *concupiscentia*. In *Aion* Jung says that the fish owes these bad qualities to its relationship with the mother and love goddesses, Ishtar, Astarte, Atargatis, and Aphrodite.[60] Venus reaches her zenith in the zodiacal sign of the fishes where Atargatis and her son are also found. We still eat fish on Friday, the "Day of Venus."[61]

Fish symbolism is inexhaustible. A great deal is to be found in Eisler's *Orpheus the Fisher* and in *Aion*.[62] There is a certain connection between the projected cure and the malady in Tobit's case since both sparrows and fish are closely related to the love goddess Venus. However, in the case of Sarah and Asmodaeus, I would like to turn again to *Aion*. Where Jung goes into great detail about the symbolism of the fish, we also find a reference from the Zohar. Here, the fish that swallowed Jonah is said to have died to be resurrected after three days when he then spat the poor man out. The Zohar claims that: "through the fish we shall find a medicament for the whole world," an obvious parallel to the events involving Tobias on the Euphrates where the "fish pulled ashore" also contains a powerful remedy. But why does a part of the fish's entrails have such a redeeming effect on Sarah and Asmodaeus?

The opposites are completely separated in our story. Raphael represents the Mal'akh Yahweh (angel of God) on the light

---

59. Ibid., par. 173.

60. Ibid., par. 174.

61. [The tradition of eating fish on Friday comes from many different pagan cultures. Aphrodite Salacia, a fish goddess, was worshipped by her followers on her sacred day, Friday. They ate fish and engaged in orgies. The Christian church assimilated this tradition by requiring the faithful to eat fish on Friday. Throughout the Mediterranean, fish, wine, and bread were used for sacramental meals, and ancient Rome called Friday *dies veneris* or Day of Venus. Ed.]

62. Robert Eisler, *Orpheus the Fisher: Comparative Studies in Orphic and Early Christian Cult Symbolism* (Whitefish, Mont.: Kessinger Publishing, 1992).

side, a wholly positive functional aspect of Yahweh, whereas Asmodaeus represents the dark and evil, a wholly negative functional aspect. If Raphael had taken up the fight with Asmodaeus directly, it would have been a case of two opposites, and the result would have been uncertain. Raphael had to resort to something which had some kinship with Asmodaeus, just as Tobit's blindness was caused—and healed—by something related to Venus: like cures like.

This aspect of the fish is dealt with in *Aion*, but it is highly complicated and subtle. Naturally, the fish, as a content of the unconscious, originally contained both opposites. But as fish symbolism developed, it slowly began to split off. Jung notes that we can see "from the example of Leviathan how the great 'fish' gradually split into its opposite, after having itself been the opposite of the highest God and hence his shadow, the embodiment of his evil side."[63]

Tobit was written much later than the theology that places the Leviathan opposite of God, yet we can see that the great fish was related to the demon Asmodaeus quite early and so it possessed that similarity that seems to be indispensable for a remedy to be effective. In *Aion* we find an exceedingly interesting discussion about the split in the Leviathan corresponding to the rather common theme found in dreams of a double shadow that appears when the conscious ego personality does not contain all the contents or components. A piece of the personality then remains split off, mixes with the normally unconscious shadow, and forms with it a double personality that is oftentimes antagonistic.

Jung continues with the mythological case of the Leviathan and the Behemoth as components of God.

> That this doubling represents an act of conscious realization is clear from Job where we are told that Yahweh smote Rahab "by his understanding" (tebūnā; Job 26:12). Rahab, the sea monster, is cousin . . . to Tiamat, whom Marduk

---

63. Jung, *Aion*, *CW*, vol. 9ii, par. 183.

split asunder by filling her up with Imhullu, the north wind. The word *tebūnā* comes from *bīn*, to "separate, split, part asunder"—in other words, to discriminate, which is the essence of conscious realization. In this sense Leviathan and Behemoth represent stages in the development of consciousness whereby they become assimilated and humanized. The fish changes, via the warm-blooded quadruped, into a human being, and in so far as the Messiah became, in Christianity, the second Person of the Trinity, the human figure split off from the fish hints at God's incarnation. What was previously missing in the God-image, therefore, was the human element.[64]

Our story is, of course, two or three centuries prior to the Christian era, but, nevertheless, we can say that the fish in Tobit contains potentially the same idea. The fish can be said here to be that tendency that is building up the physical vessel in which God can incarnate.

Therefore, a part of the fish is the most apt symbol we can imagine to cure Sarah who, while she was possessed by the demon, was entirely cut off from her own humanity. But note: not the whole fish, but the most vital organs—liver and heart. The fish was originally regarded as both opposites, then as the shadow of God, and finally as the tendency toward incarnation in God. It forms an essence that understandably would be highly effective in releasing Sarah from her inhuman incubus.

I have said that Raphael, as the opposite of Asmodaeus, would not be effective in overcoming the demon alone. The same opinion, based on quite different reasons, can be found in a book by a seventeenth-century monk, Ludovico Maria Sinistrari, an Italian friar of the strict observance of St. Francis who lived between the years 1622 and 1701. He was famous for his brilliant lectures and books and wrote *De Daemonialitate et Incubis et Succubis* toward the end of his life in which he maintained that the incubus and succubus could not be reached by ordinary or even extraor-

---

64. Ibid., par. 185.

dinary exorcism, but only by some kind of corporal means.[65] He quotes two cases. In one he knew the confessor. It concerned a girl of good family who was a boarder in a convent school and who was very much troubled by an incubus who tried to possess her and who was constantly pestering her. The exorcist failed to accomplish anything with ordinary means, and thus he resorted to magic. He noticed that the girl was of an intensely phlegmatic disposition, so he tried fumigation. He got beautiful herbs to make a smoke and made her carry with her fragrant perfumes, and thus freed her. Sinistrari himself was then called in by a deacon in a Carthusian monastery who was possessed by a demon. He also tried fumigation, but the demon flourished on, and the situation got worse and worse. He then recalled the phlegmatic disposition of the other sufferer and realized that the man before him was of a choleric and sanguine disposition. Therefore, the fumigation was of his own nature, but with herbs, water lilies, and water plants. And thus the demon was overcome.

Sinistrari discusses the possession of Sarah in Tobit at length and expresses the opinion, as against that of the learned doctors, that it was impossible to expel such demons as possessed her without physical means.

Physical means are required to expel incubi because they are, in part, of a physical nature. Almost all black and white magic is built upon some such assumption. There is always a physical agency. The medicine man must first ascertain the kind of demon that is in possession. The Navajo sand paintings are an example, for they depend on the kind of demon that is in possession of the patient.

It is of interest that this seventeenth-century monk was already of the opinion that Raphael alone could not have driven out Asmodaeus, a fact that agrees with our own experience of the opposites. A modern dream illustrates this point. A young man dreamed of a terrific struggle between two supernatural beings

---

65. Ludovico Maria Sinistrari, *Demoniality* (London: Fortune Press, 1927). [See Barbara Hannah's essay "The Problem of Women's Plots in Marie Hay's *The Evil Vineyard*" in this volume. *Ed.*]

associated with Ohrmazd and Ahriman in Zoroastrianism. He was afraid that the light side was going to be overcome when a little bit of the dark changed sides. This is comparable to Raphael's need of the fish to overcome Asmodaeus.

However, it is not the parts of the fish themselves, but the smoke arising from burning them, that sets Asmodaeus to flight. Burning and smoke reflect the process of spiritualization. Although the substance of the fish was required, it does not heal Sarah directly. This was achieved by means of the spiritualization of the instinctive factor. The idea of turning material things into smoke and steam always pertains to the process of spiritualization, but here it has a more specific nuance. Once again we can shortly turn to Jung's simile of archetype and instinct in his article on "Patterns of Behavior and Archetypes." Here, he uses the image of the ultraviolet and infrared ends of the spectrum to illustrate psyche juxtaposed to instinct, in other words, the more spiritual archetypal end of the psyche (ultraviolet) as opposed to the infra-red instinctual end. He points out that sinking into the instinctive (infrared) sphere only leads to unconsciousness and panic and not to a conscious realization and assimilation of the instinct.

> This means—to employ once more the simile of the spectrum—that the [image associated with the instinct] is to be located not at the red end but at the violet end of the color band. The dynamism of instinct is lodged as it were in the infra-red part of the spectrum, whereas the instinctual image lies in the ultra-violet part . . . . The realization and assimilation of instinct never takes place at the red end, i.e., by absorption into the instinctual sphere, but only through integration of the image that signifies and, at the same time, evokes the instinct, although in a form quite different from the one we meet on the biological level.[66]

Thus conscious assimilation can only take place at the more spiri-

---

66. C. G. Jung, "On the Nature of the Psyche" (1954), in *CW*, vol. 8 (Princeton, N.J.: Princeton University Press, 1969), par. 414.

tual (ultraviolet) end where the archetype, as the leading image of the instinct, offers an opportunity of rescuing consciousness from the seething abyss of the passions and instincts themselves.

This gives us some idea of why the heart and liver of the fish have to be burnt, that is, spiritualized, for it is only at this end of the scale that consciousness can be renewed and strengthened. Sarah is confined by the old opinionating form of the animus, contaminated and even personified by the collective arch-devil Asmodaeus, and it will require a tremendous conscious realization before he can be made to give way in her and leave her free to receive the renewed and transformed animus symbolized by Tobias.

Here, we find the eternal theme of the hero myth and the motif of innumerable taboos. The nearer one comes to the instinctive world, the more insistent becomes the urge to escape it in order to rescue the light of consciousness from the darkness of the boiling abyss. But the archetype, as the image of the instinct, is psychologically a spiritual aim for which the nature of man longs, the sea to which every river is pressing along its winding way, the prize that the hero wins from his battle with the dragon.

Tobias wins the prize through his battle with the fish, or put it in terms of feminine psychology, Sarah's mind has made the great effort to understand. This in turn clears the path for exchanging Asmodaeus (the old opinionating animus reinforced in her case by contamination with the collective devil) for the renewed and transformed animus represented by Tobias. The old negative animus often encourages women to believe that they can escape from—or even change their animus—by means of an entirely satisfactory sexual experience. But despite whatever this may bring, the assumption is erroneous. Consciousness is far too endangered at the instinctive end of the scale. It is only at the other end that the meaning can be found and realizations made that bring about the change from possession by an Asmodaeus to a free and true relationship to Tobias. This is in no way a depreciation of the sexual or instinctive end. At the right time, when life demanded it of them, Tobias and Sarah also lived out their sexuality, but if they had not gone through the stage of spiritualization of the smoke by

means of the fish, they would have lost their hard-won consciousness in the realm of blind instinct. Tobias—like his seven predecessors—may have inevitably been killed by Asmodaeus.

In the vital task of transforming the animus, it is the archetypal
end that counts. According to age and the demands of life, the
instinctive end must also be faced down, for at the right time it
too belongs to the reality that is needed to pin down the animus.
But we must also be able to face the smoke, that is, the spiritualization of the reality that was previously and necessarily concrete,
just as the fish was substantial when Tobias caught it and was
afterward burnt to make the necessary smoke.

PART FOUR

We have not yet discussed why only the heart and the liver of the
fish were needed to exorcise Asmodaeus, or why the gall was the
right cure for Tobit's blindness. Hovorak-Kroneld's *Vergleichende
Volksmedizin [Comparative Folk Medicine]* provides no information on this point, although the gall of the fish is still used in some
eye remedies. From the psychological standpoint, however, these
organs are very important.

In his seminar on Zarathustra, Jung notes that, in many myths,
the hero cuts out and eats parts of the fish, usually the liver,
which, according to primitive ideas, represents the life and soul of
the fish.[67] He also points out in the *Visions* seminar that the punishment of Prometheus for stealing the divine fire was not only
being chained to the rocks but also to endure an eagle constantly
eating his liver.[68] Jung speaks here thus of the liver being the thing
that lives in us, the symbolic seat of life. In another place, Jung
says that the liver is connected with the emotions, the center of
passion. (As you know, a liver upset is often the result of an outburst of fury or, even more often, due to swallowing emotion.)

---

67. Jung, *Nietzsche's Zarathustra*, p. 1449.

68. [Jung notes here that the liver was regarded as the seat of life, the thing that lives in
one, therefore, the English "liver" and German "*Leber*" are close to "life" or "*Leben*." He
also notes that Prometheus is an eternal image of the creative spirit. See Jung, *Visions*, p.
1013. *Ed.*]

The meaning of the heart is in some ways similar, but it is perhaps more the mainspring of life than life itself. In *Zarathustra*, Jung notes that:

> the idea is that his head is contained in the heart, behind the head and superior to the head. It is a well-known idea that people can argue in an apparently logical and rational way while really speaking the wishes of their hearts . . . . So the will of the heart [in Nietzsche's Superman] . . . forces the head, and no matter what the head may think, it will be forced by the heart which knows [the] goal.[69]

The heart and liver of the fish, that is, the essence of life, emotion, and affection, the essence of relationship, had the power in the form of the smoke to put the possession and the demon to flight. This agrees with our own experience of the animus. The way par excellence to transform the animus from the opinionating demon into a creative mind is a devotion to life, a complete acceptance of its reality, and the sacrifice of all illusion about it. And the heart, representing feeling and Eros, is the greatest help that we know, for it is really only when someone of the other sex matters vitally to us that we have the impetus and the strength to resist the opinions of the animus.

As Raphael and Tobias are approaching Ecbatana where Raguel lives with his wife Edna and daughter Sarah, Raphael tells Tobias the purpose of their visit, namely, that he is Sarah's next of kin and thus Raguel must give Sarah to him in marriage. The most important point of this speech for us is that Raphael tells him that the maiden is wise, steadfast, and honorable, and that her father is an honorable man. (The Vatican version of Tobit, the one usually used, states only that she was wise and beautiful.)

Superficially regarded from the modern point of view, this strikes us as strange, for to be possessed by the devil usually has negative implications. Actually, the possession of such superlatively good qualities is the sine qua non for the ability to meet

69. Jung, *Nietzsche's Zarathustra*, pp. 92f.

the dark side of oneself. Jung recently pointed out that we have never been more in need of the Christian virtues and the symbol of Christ than now. It is a historical fact that the real, personified configuration of the devil only came into existence with Christ.[70] In Luke Christ says: "I beheld Satan as lightning fall from Heaven [sic]" (Luke 10:18). Jung commented that the devil fell from Heaven, that it was removed from God, at the time when Christ was separated from Him by becoming man. Christ thus severed himself from the shadow and called it the devil.

This is necessarily the first step in any process of becoming conscious. The differentiation between ego and shadow is foreshadowed in our study at the point where the death of the seven husbands is not attributed to Sarah directly (except by the maids) but to her devil Asmodaeus. Raphael recognizes her virtues, and these are then the raison d'être for her recovery.

Jung points out that the beginning of our *Auseinandersetzung* with the shadow and with evil is the very time we require every virtue we have. "To keep the light alive in the darkness, that is the point, and only there does your candle make sense."[71]

After he has told Tobias that the maid "is fair and wise," Raphael goes on to say: "I know that Raguel cannot marry her to

---

70. [Barbara Hanna refers here to the historical moment when Satan was detached from his spiritual, dialectical affiliation with Jesus Christ. Schärf Kluger, in her commendable study on Satan, remarks that Satan, in contrast to the real cacodemons, belongs to the divine realm. And in contrast to the mythological figures of the seraphim, the cherubim, Leviathan, and Behemoth, he does not represent the nature side of God (witness their animal shapes). But he is a *spiritual* demon who stands in a dialectical confrontation with God. The animal attributes (horns, goat's feet, tail) "grew" on him later in his development. The Old Testament Satan is a personified function of God, which, as we shall see, develops step by step and detaches itself from the divine personality. Schärf Kluger, *Satan in the Old Testament*, pp. 51. *Ed.*]

71. [Jung writes in a letter to Father Victor White that when a patient in our day begins to emerge from an unconscious condition, the first thing that confronts him is his shadow, that is, dealing with one's own darkness. Here, one must decide for the good, the *imitatio Christi*, or one will go down the drain. The good is here the goal of individuation. Jung emphasizes that if you do not cling to the good, the devils will devour you. "To keep alive the light in the darkness as Evil overwhelms you, that is the point where your candle makes sense." See Jung's letter to Father Victor White, 24 November 1953, in C. G. Jung, *Letters*, vol. 2, 1951–1961, Gerhard Adler, ed., in collaboration with Aniela Jaffé (Princeton, N.J.: Princeton University Press, 1992), p. 135; also C. G. Jung, *The Jung-White Letters*, Ann Lammers and Adrian Cunningham, eds. (London: Routledge, 2007), p. 218. *Ed.*]

another according to the law of Moses, but he shall be guilty of death, because the right of inheritance doth rather appertain to thee than to any other." We hear then that Raguel has apparently incurred "liability to death" when he married Sarah to those other seven men. Yet in chapter 8:11 (in one version of Tobit) Raguel says that he has given his daughter in marriage to seven men "of our brethren." Thus we have another controversial point. Here, Simpson is worried by the fault being apparently with Raguel who, he points out, suffered no penalty. He further notes that Raphael foresaw no danger for Raguel, but only for Tobias, and that the seven men suffered the penalty of death. This is really a puzzle. Why should outsiders bear the brunt?

In the case of Jeanne Fery, the virtues were experienced not directly in her, but projected onto the figure she called Mary Magdalene (who, as you remember, played an essential role in her recovery). The turning point is where Jeanne sees Mary Magdalene after she throws herself obeisantly at the feet of the Archbishop of Cambrai. Jeanne had sided entirely with her devils, and one of the most interesting events in the whole case is the point where she wants both Christ and her other gods, and then receives the sign in radiance. She came to think that if a sign was vouchsafed her as the sacraments were being made by the devout, she then might worship Christ as well as her other gods. This made her spirits angry. They made her take a piece of the host and obliged her to pierce it with a knife. She writes that when she thus pierced the host, blood flowed forth and the whole room was filled with a bright radiance. Then she was frightened, for all her spirits fled with terrible shrieks, and she was left alone exhausted on the floor. Thereafter she was but slowly persuaded to take the side of Mary Magdalene whose appearance coincided with the encounter with the archbishop. Here, we see the necessity of relationship, the positive feeling for someone of the other sex, that gave her the necessary impetus to challenge and free herself from the demonic animus. Sarah, who had the good qualities in herself, was immediately able to side with Tobias.

Taken as a subjective problem of Sarah's, we could say that inwardly the seven men could represent creative opportunities that were not strong enough to break up the possession by Asmodaeus. Such things can be seen in most women's lives. Or looking back on one's own life, one sees how one creative possibility after the other passes by without being seized and put into reality. (This is true of opportunities for relationship to the other sex and also of opportunities to do something creative in art, writing, and so forth.) Looking back, one can only say: It was a pity I missed that, but it was not strong enough to break through my animus opinions. In a great many cases women have to experience the waves of life breaking against her and rolling away again before she is ready inwardly to make the great effort that leads to major changes in her animus and her mind. One creative possibility after another passes by and is lost, in relationship, art, or writing, and so forth, until at last the woman is ready to make the great effort to change her animus, her mind. One may assume that, subjectively or objectively, the possibilities had not yet reached the crucial point that must be lived if one is ever to escape the likes of an Asmodaeus.

In Tobit it can be said that the seven men were without sufficient instinct to enable them to stand up to an animus-possessed girl such as Sarah. Or even to realize the danger they were in. Tobias, on the contrary, is afraid. He says: "Now, for my part, I fear," and then pleads with Raphael to let him off on account of being the only son of his parents. But Tobias has his dog, an accompanying form of sound instinct we might suspect, and is warned by a wholly reasonable fear. Human beings lose their instinct to a great extent, but animals generally lose little if any at all. Tobias would probably never have risked the marriage night with Sarah if Raphael had not persuaded him to do so.

Symbolically seen, the number seven no doubt plays a considerable role. It is the number of the planets as known to the our ancient forefathers and represents the seven gods of fate.[72] Therefore, killing the seven might also have the symbolical meaning of killing a

---

72. [The planets known to the ancients were Mercury, Venus, Mars, the moon, the sun, Jupiter, and Saturn. *Ed.*]

state of dependence on fate. It would thus belong to those themes of liberation and the assuming of responsibility as we have already seen in the motives of "overcoming the great fish" and "smoking out the possessing demon." Jung sometimes speaks of the planets as collective constituents in people. This consideration fits into the idea that the seven may have been symbolic possibilities not so individual that they necessarily had to be lived. Here, it is only when the crucially important eighth comes into action that it is vital that Sarah no longer dallies but grabs the chance. We all have a kind of instinct that says, "The thing must be done, now! or I shall miss my life." These are the turning points in life that one cannot afford to miss and that belong to the process of individuation. If not grasped, the whole process is endangered. Eight, like four, is a crucial number in individuation, and it is vital for Sarah to grab this chance.

Raphael reminds Tobias of his father's command to take a wife of his family and repeats his assurance that the demon need not be reckoned with because he will surely fly from the smoke. Finally he says: "And fear not, for she was set apart for you before the world was; and thou shalt save her and she shall go with you." Again there is clear evidence that this is a fatal moment in the individuation process, for as Raphael says, it was settled before the world began. Tobias and Sarah belong together in the *unus mundus* rather like the Platonic idea of humans being round in the beginning and then cut in half. In the Chinese novel *Dream of the Red Chamber* there is a complex and extremely vital love story in which a wise old man tells a couple that in a previous existence the man was a piece of green jade and she was a red flower growing beside him, and they had then loved each other daily, now to meet again today.[73]

It is rather startling to encounter here such a clear reference to the doctrine of predestination that Calvin later pushed to the extremes. But taken psychologically, this doctrine has its place even in Jungian psychology, for there seems to be a kind of predestined pattern in every individual. It is just as impossible to deviate from the pattern of what we are as it would be for an

73. Tsoa Hsueh-Chin, *Dream of the Red Chamber* (New York: Anchor Doubleday, 1958).

apple to become a tomato or a tiger to cease being a beast of prey and take up vegetarianism. It is as necessary for us to realize our pattern as it is for any animal or tree. From this point of view, the liberated Sarah would be the anima in Tobias's pattern and Tobias the transformed animus in Sarah's pattern. This would also explain the peculiar words at the end of chapter 6: "And then Tobias heard the words of Raphael, and that she was his sister of the seed of his father's house, he loved her exceedingly and his heart clave unto her."

Now Tobias has not yet seen Sarah, so except on the assumption that she is really his anima, and thus belongs to him as part of himself, it would be difficult to understand how he could already love her. As it is, it reminds one of Goethe's words: "Were you not in a former existence my sister, or my bride?" which Jung often quotes as an example of how a man feels when he meets his anima projected into a real woman. When man finds his anima or a woman her animus, there is that complete click, that feeling of coming home, of belonging. This feeling is expressed when Raphael says that Sarah was set apart for him before the world was, to which Tobias responds by loving her exceedingly, his heart cleaving to an unknown woman.

When they arrive at the house, Raguel immediately recognizes Tobias's likeness to Tobit and Tobias admits to being his son, and thus he is warmly welcomed. Raguel, his wife, and his daughter weep. A ram of the flock is then killed, and they all sit down to eat. The ram is an animal of fertility. It is possible that it may have been meant to strengthen Tobias in his dealing with Sarah's demon. But before Tobias will eat, he insists on the wedding arrangements being made. Raguel expresses not only complete willingness but also his inability to oppose the marriage, saying, "I have not power to give her to another man than thee, because thou art my nearest kin." He also admits that he has already given her to seven men and that all died on the wedding night. He then begs Tobias to eat, drink, and be merry, for "the Lord will deal mercifully with you." But he evidently has no doubt that Tobias will follow the fate of his predecessors, for he secretly digs a grave in his backyard late in the night, planning this time to hide the corpse of the victim on his own property so no one will know that yet another bridegroom has met his doom.

Raguel's pessimism fits the animus idea that everything will always go on in the same old way. It is the voice in women that assures them that nothing can possibly change, and it is one of the hardest nuts to crack in the transformation of the animus. Evidently Raguel does not believe that anything can break the power of Asmodaeus. In actual experience it often seems as if there were a secret bond between the fallen animus and the devil, often due to the secret and unconscious incest wish. Although Raguel inevitably rejoices in Tobias's victory over the evil spirit, one wonders whether he had not had an unconscious alliance with Asmodaeus who had enabled him to keep Sarah, his only child, to himself. Moreover, Rafael says that the demon never harms Sarah but kills every man who tries to take her away. Jung remarks that the animus is a kind of jealous lover or husband who can so maneuver the situation as to put an opinion in the place of the real man, thus ruining the relationship.

Animus opinions are invariably collective, and they override individuals and individual judgments in exactly the same way as the anima thrusts her emotional anticipations and projections between man and wife. If the woman happens to be pretty, these animus opinions have for the man something rather touching and childlike about them, and he then adopts a benevolent, fatherly, professional manner. But if the woman does not stir his sentimental side, and competence is expected of her rather than appealing helplessness and stupidity, then her animus opinions irritate the man to death, chiefly because they are based on nothing but opinion for opinion's sake, and "everybody has a right to his own opinion." Men can [also] be pretty venomous here, for it is an inescapable fact that the animus always plays up the animus— and vice versa. "Unfortunately, I am always right," a woman once confessed to Jung.[74]

---

74. [C. G. Jung, "The Relations Between the Ego and the Unconscious" (1928), in *CW*, vol. 7 (Princeton, N.J.: Princeton University Press, 1953), pars. 334–335. *Ed.*]

In the Middle Ages, this aspect was emphasized in literature on the incubus, Asmodaeus here being an appropriate prototype. The incubus was represented as a half-material, half-spiritual being who completely possessed the woman, giving actual physical pleasure, and was a ghostly lover intensely jealous of any real man. Although unpleasant, even obscene, this literature gives a good many hints expressed in a primitive way about the animus as husband and lover. Unless she resists him, he never directly harms the woman herself. But the literature tells of more than one case where he becomes a sort of poltergeist with all its annoying tricks when the woman resists him.

We enter a realm here, the realm between mind and matter, where we know little or nothing, so I only just mention it in passing in connection with the murders of the seven men that Asmodaeus committed.

There is an obvious connection between repressed incest fantasies in the father and such demon lovers. Or, one might say, a secret unconscious bond between father and daughter forms a hook where even a devil from the collective unconscious such as Asmodaeus can attach himself and gain an uncanny power over the girl's father.

There is, nevertheless, some truth in the animus idea that "who we are never changes" since animus opinions usually have a grain of eternal truth in their structure, even though it is twisted. Therefore, they have to be unraveled, and it is unsafe just to throw them away and risk the loss of the gold with the dross. This again emphasizes the importance of understanding the nature of the animus, who says himself that we are attached like Siamese twins, albeit in totally different realities.

According to the law of Moses, Tobias has refused to eat and drink before Sarah is given to him. The young positive animus cannot function in the air, he must have a foot in actual reality, even in traditional reality. His position must be legitimized "according to the law of Moses," indicating a beginning stage in the humanizing of the animus.

Such collective laws represent something human. It is a primitive stage to be legitimized by law, but it is a beginning stage in the humanizing of the animus. It also means that Tobias thus takes a large slice of power away from Raguel in that he insists on being Sarah's legitimate husband according to the law of Moses.

Still, today, it does no good at all just to talk to the animus. If we think we have settled him that way, we need not worry; he will be back in half an hour with the same old opinion. We must legitimize and humanize our position if we are to give our positive animus a chance. This means that we must not move too far from tradition, but try as much as possible to see tradition with new eyes—not throwing it away—and continually striving to make our peace with it without sacrificing our new insight. If we do not find a middle way to work with tradition, we throw away too much of value, get too far from our roots, and end up in an indefensible position. Moreover, the young hero animus is the stronger here and can overcome the apathy and hopelessness of the traditional animus. Historical inertia, says Jung, always comes up and opposes the new and creative love in woman.[75]

Here, the prognosis for Sarah is good. We see that Sarah's animus was personified by several figures: her father, Raguel, Raphael, Asmodaeus, and, as the decisive fourth, Tobias. As Sarah's eighth lover, he is even further connected to her in this numinous number. By analogy to mythical parallels we could expect Tobias to be strong enough to overcome the historical inertia and pessimistic forebodings of the old Raguel animus. Tobias represents a transformed mind in Sarah that has hitherto been unconscious, a mind that only developed and came into action by the suffering she accepted in bearing her lot with Asmodaeus.

It is rather interesting that Edna, Sarah's mother, seems more or less identical with her husband Raguel, whereas Anna, Tobit's wife, is in some ways a more decisive character than her husband. She has no scruples, reproaching her husband so energetically that he prays to God to release him from his agony. Anna is a prevailing personality in the story and (as a matriarchal figure) would presumably have played an equally important role in Tobias's

---

75. C. G. Jung, "Woman in Europe" (1927), in *CW*, vol. 10 (Princeton, N.J.: Princeton University Press, 1964), par. 267.

life, so we can suspect that he has some form of a strong mother complex. Taken from the female standpoint, we see here a parallel with Sarah, for she has an outstanding father complex, Raguel being the singular prevailing influence in her home. Such types tend to marry each other: a man with a powerful mother complex often finds a woman with a powerful father complex and vice versa. Edna, however, weeps bitterly as she prepares the bridal chamber, for Edna, like Raguel, has little doubt that the demon will kill Tobias as he has the other seven predecessors. She tries to cheer her daughter, however, and one is not quite certain whether she is really hopeful that the curse is about to be lifted, or whether she is merely confident that the demon will do Sarah no harm, as he never has done so before. She probably prays for the best and fears the worst, for she makes no attempt to stop Raguel from digging a grave for Tobias during the night.

When he was taken to Sarah, Tobias "remembered the word of Raphael and took the ashes of the perfumes and put the heart and the liver of the fish thereupon, and made a smoke therewith."

We have already discussed the incident of the smoking out of the demon, and I gave you two medieval parallels from Sinistrari, the seventeenth-century monk. I would just like to remind you once again that the parts of the fish had to be burned to put Asmodaeus to flight. Burning and turning to smoke signifies a process of spiritualization of the instinct. This is done by means of a spiritualized instinctive factor that also fits in with the idea of Tobias as the transformed mind and the completing fourth. Sarah has made the great effort to distance herself both from Asmodaeus—that old murderous and opinionating demon—as well as from her father, a man who pessimistically holds to the belief that nothing can change. The parents do nothing about it (following their nature), they just leave the matter to God. So all the action falls to the lot of Tobias, who is later also helped by Sarah. The new things we have here are, first, that Tobias precisely obeys the injunction of Raphael and, second, that this action actually baffles the demon who flees to the upper parts of Egypt only to be pursued straightaway by Raphael and bound on the site.

Theme of binding the demon in an evidently far away place is also noteworthy. The upper parts of Egypt presumably symbolize a place somewhere near the source of the Nile, a place in the unconscious near the secret source of the waters of life. In other words, he is bound deep in the unconscious. The binding is a magic procedure that, in our language, amounts to repression and absolute control. We find this theme fairly often, particularly in primitive stories. It was obviously absolutely necessary at that time and is needed still today. In Revelation, Satan is bound for a thousand years. This is not a "putting into the resin for transformation"—that is a stage that comes much later—but it is still often necessary even if a temporary stage. I recall a case of a difficult animus that I brought to Jung in supervision who then told me that, with a certain aspect of the animus (which was making a lot of trouble), there was nothing to be done other than to just lock it up. If left loose, it would simply wreck the patient's life. "Locking up" would mean encouraging the patient to refuse certain opinions, thoughts, or courses of action, that is, to reject them completely. As an example, I mentioned the case of a young woman who had a relationship that she valued and that had collapsed. The man was a hopeless sort of person, cruel, merciless, and without pity. But her animus always suggested that she must telephone or write to him or, still worse, that I as the analyst must do so. She would suddenly telephone me—often from abroad—with some new, hopelessly idiotic idea that would only have alienated him forever and provoked more cruelty than the girl could possibly stand. Jung also said here that there was nothing else to do but just lock up the animus. Eventually I had to tell her that, if she persisted with her suggestions, there would be no point in seeing me anymore. Such persuasion is obviously a technique of repression and leads nowhere in regards to a transformation of the animus. But it prevented the animus at that time from destroying her altogether. There is a considerable pathological streak in this case, and I am uncertain if it will ever be possible to let him out.

In a normal case, when the emotion over the breakdown of the relationship has partially subsided and the situation is more or less accepted, one can begin to loosen those bonds that tightly restrict the animus. One needs then to bring the woman's thoughts back to what the animus had tried to do and raise the question about the objectivity of his existence. And then one would need to consider what could be done about him. But where there is a latent psychosis, as was the case above, this is seldom advisable.

PART FIVE

With Sarah, this was more a question of time. Apart from her possession by Asmodaeus, she had an apparently more or less untouched personality. She was "wise, steadfast, exceedingly honorable," and we know that she was sane enough to reject the idea of suicide. Also her prayer to God is completely reasonable and sane, so that the greater part of her personality was evidently sound. (The vital questions are always: how big is the swamp and is there enough firm ground from which to drain it?) Of course there must have been a pathological hook for such a murderous devil possession, but with naïve, natural, and simple women such things can be locked up and their lives can then be led quite normally. Apparently this was the case with Sarah, and when the devil was smoked out, she could lead a normal life.

The suggestion was made that the ram might be regarded as the sacrifice in the place of the human (as we see, for example, in the case of Abraham and Isaac). However, I do not want to push this symbolism too far. The Old Testament is replete with the details of animal sacrifice, yet these cannot just be directly compared to that of Isaac, which was a drastic challenge demanded of Abraham. In Tobit, the killing of the ram was probably the type of gesture done for cherished guests in preparation of an ordinary festive meal typical of those times. One can hardly assume that it was intended symbolically. On the other hand, the choice of the ram—instead of ox, goat, ewe or fowl—has a certain symbolical significance for us, of which Raguel himself was presumably unconscious.

Apocrypha, the ram is occasionally used as a sacrifice of atone-Apocrypha, the ram is occasionally used as a sacrifice of atone-Apocrypha, the ram is occasionally used as a sacrifice of atone-Apocrypha, the ram is occasionally used as a sacrifice of atone-in the Bible are in Leviticus and Ezra:in the Bible are in Leviticus and Ezra:in the Bible are in Leviticus and Ezra:in the Bible are in Leviticus and Ezra:in the Bible are in Leviticus and Ezra:in the Bible are in Leviticus and Ezra:tt> And whosoever lieth carnally with a woman that is a bond-
> maid, betrothed to an husband, and not at all redeemed, nor
> freedom given her; she shall be scourged; they shall not be
> put to death, because she was not free. And he shall bring his
> trespass offering unto the Lord, unto the door of the taber-
> nacle of the congregation, even a ram for a trespass offering.
> And the priest shall make an atonement for him with the ram
> of the trespass offering before the Lord for his sin which he
> hath done; and the sin which he hath done shall be forgiven
> him. (Lev. 19:20–22)

Whereas in Ezra we find:

> And among the sons of the priests there were found [those]
> that had taken strange [foreign] wives; namely of the sons
> of Jeshua, the son of Jozadak, and his brethren; Maaseiah,
> and Eliezer, and Jarib and Gedaliah. And they gave their
> hands that they would put away their wives; and, being
> guilty, they offered a ram of their flock for their trespass.
> (Ezra 10:2–19)

Here, the priests who took strange wives (that is, foreign or non-Jewish wives) also had to offer a ram of the flocks for their trespasses.

Now, the seven men before Tobias may have committed some sin, but not the Tobias in our story, nor had he yet lain with Sarah. Symbolically, the ram, an animal of the greatest virility and potency of springtime exuberance, is a truly fitting symbol for the sin of an overabundance of masculine sexual ardor. Presumably the men in Ezra who had taken the bond maidens and the strange women were called upon to sacrifice the ram as a symbol of their own animal instinct that had led them to sin against the law. For Tobias we could assume that the ram represents a piece of Tobias's animal instinct which has to be sacrificed, eaten and assimilated before Tobias could face his struggle with Asmodaeus. And in a similar vein, Tobias and Sarah had to offer up their prayer before consummating their marriage, and the parts of the fish had to be burnt. Symbols and relevant passages on theme of sacrifice, including that of Abraham and Isaac, can be found in Jung's paper on the Mass.[76]

Raphael needed the help of the heart and the liver of the fish in order to prevail over Asmodaeus. But now that Tobias has fully obeyed him, Raphael is strong enough to bind the demon alone. As long as Asmodaeus had a footing in the human being, Raphael was presumably powerless to overcome him. The devil was, so to speak, incarnate, whereas Raphael was pure spirit. We find the same idea in medieval church doctrine. The devil required a witch, a foothold within the human being, in order to be effective. The *Malleus Maleficarum*, written by two well-known inquisitors, is based entirely on this idea.[77] It began with the Bull of Innocent VIII and became the official document used to authorize the execution of "witches" (and hundreds of thousands of other people) for nearly three centuries. Its premise is that the devil cannot be dealt with until his foothold in man is destroyed.

Asmodaeus was baffled by the smell of the fish, that is, he was attacked by an attribute of the fish goddesses, the Eros side, that gives power to the positive aspect of the divine in order to overcome the negative demon aspect. When an animus really interferes in a relationship that is important to you, that is the moment when something can be done about it, for then Eros has a possibility. One can often see this practically. The woman I mentioned, for instance, who made crazy scenes and whose husband said he would leave her unless she stopped, would never have been able

---

76. C. G. Jung, "Transformation Symbolism in the Mass" (1954), in *CW*, vol. 11 (Princeton, N.J.: Princeton University Press, 1969), pars. 296–448.

77. [See Barbara Hannah's lecture "Jeanne Fery: A Case Study on the Animus, Possession, and Exorcism" in this volume. *Ed.*]

to control her demonic animus based solely on the fact that she theoretically and intellectually knew she should. It was through her fondness of her husband, and through his fondness for her, that she gained a bit of Eros, a bit of the fish goddess so to speak, and this gave her positive animus a chance of binding the demon.

There is no direct evidence in the text that Sarah loved Tobias, although this would seem to be indicated. In her prayer she had said that her father had no kinsman or relation for whom she could keep herself alive. When she learned of the existence of Tobias and saw him, it is at any rate possible that her reaction was similar to that of Tobias on learning that she was his predestined bride. The fact that her mother comforts her while the bridal bed is made indicates that Sarah may have cared enough to fear for his fate.

The story works perhaps even better from the masculine side where Tobias can be seen as the ego working for the redemption of the anima. It is clear that it is the work of the man or woman that gives the angel the power to bind the demon. This is the great difference between alchemy and the church, for while the latter puts the whole emphasis on the fact that only Christ can help, the alchemists always contend that it depends on the effort of individual women and men. Actually the middle way lies between the two.[78] Once the demon is out of the room, Tobias and Sarah can shut the door of their chamber. Here, they act concertedly, Sarah now taking an active part in preventing the return of the demon. The rapid exorcism of the demon is to a great extent due to her active participation. Then Tobias rises up from the bed and says: "Sister, arise, and let us pray that God will have pity on us."

Raphael had impressed Tobias beforehand with the necessity for prayer. Without it, they might have fallen victim to the dangerous idea that they themselves had effected the cure, an inflation that would have enabled Asmodaeus to return promptly. In talking to the analysts at the Jung Institute, Jung once said that the most important work of the analyst was in doing active

---

78. [See "Melchior Cibinensis and the Alchemical Paraphrase of the Mass" in Jung, *Psychology and Alchemy*, CW, vol. 12, par. 480ff. *Ed.*]

imagination on himself so that he could keep himself disinfected and in order. So doing, there would then be a good chance of a synchronistic effect in the patient. But if, on the other hand, the analyst takes the credit for having done a good piece of work, then the devil pats him on the back. To keep yourself in Tao is more important than what you say to the patient, and it is also far less likely to get you into trouble.

It is true that Tobias and Sarah had already prayed to God, but continued prayer seems to be necessary in order to assure continued divine intervention. The prayer before their consummation of the marriage emphasizes the archetypal, spiritual end of the scale and reduces the risk of Tobias and Sarah being swallowed by the primitive unconsciousness of the instinctive sphere that they are about to enter. The spiritual, religious side of sexuality is much more clearly emphasized in the East than with us, for there we find sexuality integrated into religious ceremony. Jung once noted that crime and sex are oftentimes synonymous not only in Western thought but at times even the way sex is practiced. In the East, however, sexuality is put in a far better light. In yielding to the unconscious instinctive sphere, it is easy to become possessed by some content of the unconscious, such as a power devil or a possessive animus. Prayer forms a defense against such dissolution in the unconscious and protects one, so to speak, while one is in the instinctive sphere. It can also provide an orientation to which one can afterward return. Prayer forms a bridge between the two ends of the scale of consciousness that is presumably the reason for the particularly solemn rites in the marriage service. One of the main reasons that God sent Raphael was so Tobias would "see the light of God." The ram had to be eaten, the heart and liver of the fish burned, and now prayer proceeded, all to prevent Sarah and Tobias from becoming the blind victims of instinct and to strengthen their consciousness.

Tobias notably says: "I take not this, my sister, for lust but in truth." It is at the ultra-violet spiritual end of the spectrum—"in truth"—where the realization and the new consciousness are born. Only a considerable effort to reach this end (symbolized here by their joint devotion in prayer to God) will suffice to underpin this newborn truth. Thus truth alone can prevent this renewal of consciousness from being swallowed again by the dark, emotional, instinctive unconscious.

It is striking that just as Raphael emphasizes that Sarah was set apart for Tobias before the world existed, so Tobit connects the story back to the archetypal background found in Adam and Eve. It is not just a personal love affair. It is also a divine drama, a sacrament with mystical meaning important to their whole race. Only when the spiritual meaning is brought to consciousness can their bodies be united, although this physical union is also a vitally important part of the psychological climax. Their union is absolutely necessary for the dawning of the new light of the morning and the renewal of consciousness.

When Raguel and Edna discover that Sarah and Tobias have survived the wedding night, they are amazed and overjoyed. And after a prayer of thanksgiving to God, they prepare a fortnight's feasting. Raphael insists that Tobias should stay and partake of the food and drink. Raphael, therefore, performs Tobias's original mission. He not only collects the money, he also brings Gabael (who had held Tobit's money) to the wedding feast, for he is also a kinsman.

Hitherto Raphael has merely accompanied Tobias, but now he has taken over the action and in a surprising and most mundane way. One could say that the money had been left about in the collective unconscious and was now wanted, so the angel collected it from rather far away. Tobias and Sarah have fulfilled all of Raphael's injunctions, and in such cases the unconscious sometimes helps us in an astonishing and unexpected way. Frequently, when we seriously work on our own unconscious (and do not make excuses about time), things turn out well on the outside as if of themselves. The Lapis also says that if you will help me, I will help you. But to funk with outer life and make an alibi of work on the unconscious is every bit as bad. It is a case of Scylla and Charybdis, and one must find out which belongs to the time. But really one always knows somewhere within what one ought to do.

Before leaving theme of the collection of the debt by Raphael, it should be pointed out that such sums of money, from the psychological point of view, represent libido, that is, psychic energy that has disappeared into the collective unconscious. This energy is now required for the new content represented by Tobias and his marriage to Sarah, a *coniunctio* that is apparently important enough for Raphael's personal attention.

In the meantime, old Tobit, and especially Anna, both knowing nothing of Sarah, are distressed by Tobias's long absence, for he should have returned a long time before. Tobias is aware that they will be anxious and insists on returning directly after the fortnight stipulated for the celebration. Raguel's entreaties to send a servant are firmly refused. So Raphael, Sarah, and Tobias set out richly laden, for they not only have the money that they were sent to fetch from Gabael, but also half the possessions of Raguel and Edna that have been given them as Sarah's dowry. At the angel's suggestion, Raphael and Tobias set out ahead of the others and, again accompanied by the dog, they herald the arrival of the entourage at Tobias's home. Anna rushes out to meet them, and blind old Tobit stumbles after her. Tobias then rubs the gall into his father's eyes and restores his sight, parts of that fish curing both Tobit and Sarah. But why was it necessary for Sarah to be cured first?

In myths and fairy tales we often find that the old traditional consciousness is either killed or transformed. This also happens with the primitives in actual practice when the old king is symbolically killed before the new king can be invested. This change can happen psychologically after great suffering such as Tobit endured with his blindness. As von Franz explains, one of the most common causes of the destruction of the old king is when he tries to take the young anima for himself. Practically speaking, one can see a similar thing with every new realization of the truth. Although the Catholic Church fought against the Reformation, it took over much from the upsurging reform movement sacrificing such abuses as the sale of indulgences and the rights to heaven. But when the older tradition tries to take the whole of the new consciousness unto itself, it usually fails to work, and then the old king, the old consciousness has to die just as it does when the king entirely rejects the new consciousness.

For Protestants, taking the bride for oneself would be, in this case, trying to swallow analytical psychology instead of letting it shed new light on the old eternal truths that have become darkened by tradition. Such attempts have already been made in that certain Protestant parsons have taken over the idea of analyzing the people who come to them for help, usually without the indispensable preliminary step of being analyzed themselves and learning what analytical psychology actually is. Of course, for the most part, this is more of a temptation for the Protestant than the Catholic Church, for the former lacks the framework of the confessional where psychological knowledge casts a new light without swallowing it whole and turning it into analysis.

Turning back to the story of Tobit and Tobias, we note that they try to give Raphael not only his wages but also half of what they have brought back from Media. He then reveals that he is an archangel. Raphael himself seems surprised when they tell him that they had not noticed that he had not partaken of food or drink. He then instructs them that not only is he an angel, but his appearance to them was nothing other than their own visions. He presumably reveals his angelic origins only at this point because they would have been too fearful, on the one hand, and on the other, they would have relaxed their efforts, feeling comfortable in the hands of an angel who would take care of everything for them. Also characteristic of suffering and pain is that only afterward does one see the so-called "divine plan" behind the affliction. But even now, when they all know Raphael well, they are afraid, and they fall on their hands and knees with their faces to the ground. The text then continues with Raphael who says:

> "God hath sent me to heal thee and Sarah thy daughter-in-law. I am Raphael, one of the seven holy angels, which present the prayers of the saints, and which go in and out before the glory of the Holy One."

> Then they were both troubled and fell upon their faces: for they feared. But he said unto them: "Fear not, for it shall go well with you; praise God therefore. For not of any favor of mine, but by the will of God I came; wherefore praise him forever. All these days I did appear unto you; but I did neither eat nor drink, but ye did see a vision. Now therefore give God thanks: for I go up to Him that sent me: but write all things which are done in a book."
>
> And when they arose, they saw him no more. Then they confessed the great and wonderful works of God, and how the angel of the Lord had appeared unto them.

Now, at last, they are able to confront the fact that they have been with a messenger of God. The most difficult realization of all is the divine quality in oneself. In his ETH lectures Jung said that seeing the shadow was child's play compared with seeing those supernatural powers within, with which we must never identify. We must know that we are of it, but we are not these powers themselves. This is well illustrated by the figure of the archangel who accompanies them throughout the entire episode, but whom they mistake to be just an ordinary man. As pointed out by James Kirsch in an earlier lecture, the drama is a preparation for the incarnation of the God in man, that is, for the Anthropos.

We must now consider whether our story has revealed anything of practical use to us in understanding the religious function of the animus in woman today. But we should first establish what we mean by the term *religious function*. I use the term in contradistinction to the old opinionating animus that is the original condition in practically every woman. As you know, just as men suffer from anima moods, so women suffer from a whole network of animus opinions that consist largely of what the father, or other male authorities of their youth, taught them, or what was impinged upon them unconsciously from the collective Weltanschauung, that is, the collective worldview in which they were raised. Such opinions have an absolute and exceedingly emotional character.

We do not question them, they are too ingrained; the woman simply asserts—and believes—that they are indisputable facts.

The religious function of the animus really begins when the woman has the courage to doubt the absolute truth of these opinions. This is far more difficult than it sounds, for the animus certainly is a tremendous support on which many women lean unconsciously, exactly as the traditional wife leans on her husband. Moreover, the animus can impart a deceptive but very seductive feeling of being "always right." Certainty is always one-sided, and when we allow the opposite to live, then we become prey to doubt. But this doubt is in place of the certainty that the animus lent us before, and in this doubt we begin to have a dim feeling that actually, in this doubt, suffering, and uncertainty, there is somewhere a purpose, perhaps even a suprahuman or divine purpose, that it is not all in vain.

Jung once said in a seminar that man overcomes by killing the dragon, by masculine activity, whereas woman overcomes in a more passive way, by accepting suffering.[79] If she can accept the suffering of changing her old certainty for doubt, the animus himself begins to change. He no longer supplies her with false remarks that are beside the mark but begins himself to search in the doubt and darkness for hints, for small indications, that show the way to the divine pattern of the process of individuation. Instead of possessing and tyrannizing the ego, he begins himself to serve the Self, to become a religious function that can help the ego in its lifelong task of discovering the Self, the divine part of man.

At the end of Tobit's prayer of joy and thanksgiving we find a beautiful description of the New Jerusalem with its gates of sap-

---

79. [Neither Barbara Hannah nor Jung literally mean that men, per se, should solely challenge adversity in an active and assertive manner, women solely in a passive and receptive manner. Barbara Hannah is addressing here two different ways of coping with adversity—masculine and feminine / active and passive—neither of which is gender specific and both of which are open to men and women alike in accordance to the specific situations in which they are embroiled. She succinctly clarifies any possible misunderstanding on this point in her discussion on the symbolism of the lion in her compilation of lectures on animal symbolism given at the C. G. Jung Institute, Zurich, between 1954 and 1958. See Hannah, *The Archetypal Symbolism of Animals*, pp. 198n and 264ff. *Ed.*]

phire and emerald, its towers of pure gold, its walls and battlements of gold as well. Such cities are, of course, well-known symbols of the Self. Tobit's vision here can be called a forerunner of
the heavenly Jerusalem in Revelation that must have been another two or three hundred years later. The city is definitely a feminine symbol, one could say of the mother anima. In Revelation,
the New Jerusalem is the bride of Christ. We must not forget that
Tobit's tradition was overwhelmingly male. Therefore, it was the
birds of the chthonic aspect of Aphrodite that blinded Tobit, for
he failed to realize the Eros principle. One could say that it "just
formed a white film over his eyes" and, therefore, it is most interesting that his prayer ends with anticipation of an almost purely
feminine symbol, the New Jerusalem.

You can see a somewhat similar phenomenon in modern
dreams when something new and surprising is being prepared
in the unconscious. If one looks back over one's dreams, one can
see that the advent of new events or new forms of awareness and
reflection seem to have been carefully prepared, sometimes over
a period of many years. We all know those dreams that we fail
to remember, yet feel they were clear, numinous, and striking a
moment before we woke up. I always have the feeling—though I
certainly could not prove it—that such dreams are often attempts
of this new and surprising phenomenon to break though directly
into consciousness. And if one fails to "get it"—if it is a vital
and numinous thing—it slowly builds a bridge so that, in time,
it can reveal itself directly, as Raphael does here. Many marvelous things have happened in our story that yet seemed entirely
within the framework of the normal. Tobit was impoverished but
now has received money from Gabael as well as a fortune with
his daughter-in-law. Sarah is cured of her demon, and Tobit's
blindness is healed. (Maybe they could both be explained by the
effects of burning the fish's liver and heart, a medical therapy so
to speak.) But these wonderful surprises have piled up, and now
they are all ready for the real revelation: namely, the numinous
fact that they have seen a messenger of God, and all of this has
been brought about by a supernatural being.

The state described at the beginning is somewhat extreme and dramatic, very much the state of the animus in almost any woman before she begins the task of working on her animus. The two father figures, Tobit and Raguel, are both caught in tradition and the past. Tobit is entirely preoccupied with the dead, and Raguel is firmly convinced that change is hopeless and the fate of his family must go on in the same old negative and destructive way. With such a paternal foundation for animus opinions, Sarah is laid wide open to possession. Asmodaeus, admittedly an archdemon, was a most potent and destructive figure who, fortunately, is usually less preoccupied with ordinary women. (Here, his potency is comparable to the demons of Jeanne Fery.) But the difference is only in degree, an animus/demon possession of a more modest kind in women today is practically always the result of such a paternal background.

The turning point occurs when, following the reproaches of Raguel's maidservant (indicating how the ordinary, instinctive woman regards herself), Sarah decides "against suicide" and "for the acceptance" of almost intolerable suffering. She makes the first turn toward the religious attitude herself in her prayer to God. If he will not let her die, then he must hear her reproaches. Such a desperate appeal, accompanied with the real sacrifice of going on with her life, seldom goes unheard, and the divine side of the psyche can then come into action. In psychological language, the ego sacrifices itself and defers to the Self, giving the Self a chance to take over. In our story, the Self does so very efficiently and dispatches Raphael to help. This divine element is indeed unrecognized until the end of the story, as is still usually the case with us. But it is only the archetypal background that reacts. Old Tobit simultaneously chose to give over the action to his son, Tobias, who, as a human being, can be regarded as Sarah's individual animus.

Tobias did indeed take over the religious function of the animus. As soon as his father had entrusted him with the task of collecting the money from Gabael, a sum of energy lying untouched and unused in the unconscious, he began to look for hints to lead him on the way to fulfill the pattern. It was he who found Raphael and brought him to his father, and throughout their entire journey he allowed himself to be accompanied by his dog and guided by the suggestions of the archangel even when he had to brace himself and overcome justifiable fear.

A great deal of this happened in the unconscious for Sarah, as indeed it often does for the woman of today. If she can once make up her mind to pursue a completely new attitude toward life and her animus, the latter often changes without her knowledge. I have seen more than one case where the woman was as agreeably surprised as Sarah when her Tobias broke through into consciousness.

Sarah accepted Tobias immediately, and thenceforth, seen from the point of view of her psychology, the action was conscious. Together they carried out Raphael's suggestion and thus reached a *coniunctio* "in truth" that symbolized the "light of God"; in psychological language, a new consciousness.

In conclusion, we should perhaps consider the images of the Self in this story from the standpoint of Sarah's psychology. As you know, the images of the Self in dreams tend to be of the same sex as the dreamer, although this is by no means an invariable rule. There are certain indications of a feminine divine figure working behind the scenes in the sparrows of Aphrodite and the fish goddess of Asia Minor. But these are mere hints, details hidden behind the one great overwhelming figure, Raphael. Angels have a certain sexless quality, and at bottom, the Self, as a union of opposites, is hermaphroditic. Therefore, I suggest that Raphael (not forgetting his shadow Asmodaeus) is the image of the Self in our story, whether you take it from the masculine side or the feminine side.

We must not, however, forget that Tobit's and Sarah's prayers were "heard before the glory of God" and that he then sent his archangel to earth to help them both. Then we hear no more of him; everything is done by Raphael. Looked at psychologically, this corresponds to the archetype per se that, as Jung has said in many places, is entirely beyond our apprehension. It is only in its images that we can apprehend and experience it, just as in our story it was Raphael who was experienced intimately by all the characters. Tobias seems to me, therefore, to fit equally well as the archetypal basis of man's ego consciousness which actively has to overcome the dragon (Asmodaeus); that is, as the religious function of the animus in women which will help her actively if she is in a position to accept her suffering and learn the value of her own feminine principle. Tobias, above all, represents the spirit of genuine and ultimate integrity.

Summing up, one could say that the story of Tobit and Sarah begins under the dominance of one opposite: the masculine. Sarah is possessed by a male demon, a sort of super-animus, and Tobit is totally unaware of Eros: he quarrels with his wife "unto death" and only believes in a male world. Then, very slowly, Eros sets itself through: the sparrows blind and thus depotentiate Tobit, and Sarah's Asmodaeus is driven out by means of the symbol of the fish goddess. Sarah is left an ordinary natural girl apparently now under her own principle of Eros, as she accepts with no further trouble the fate of being a wife and potentially a mother. Eros is thus reestablished as a principle along with Logos, and these two principles are united in the marriage of Tobias and Sarah.

The New Jerusalem, which does not come from above as in Revelation, is thought of as Jerusalem itself on earth. One can also say that this final vision represents a new opportunity of social community as found in cities: a more enlightened and altogether freer life than the condition of things at the beginning of our story. From the standpoint of the animus, the city is an especially apt symbol, for the animus and anima are particularly disturbing in our dealings with our fellow men and women. And, therefore, this vision of the feminine symbol, the New Jerusalem, represents anticipation of a new life, quite as different as the contrast given in our story between a captive people living in exile and a people living freely in their own city with golden walls and sapphire gates thrown in. We are so used to being under the power of our animus opinions that we do not even realize the normal state of slavery in which we live.

Bibliography

Adamson, Joy. *Born Free*. New York: Pantheon Books, 1961, 1991.

———. *Living Free*. New York: Fontana, 1962, 1975.

Adler, Gerhard. "A Contribution of Clinical Material." *British Journal of Medical Psychology*, vol. 22, parts 1 and 2 (1949).

Austen, Jane. *Emma*. New York: Barnes and Noble Classics, 2004.

———. *Mansfield Park*. New York: Oxford University Press, 1990.

———. *Northanger Abbey*. New York: Barnes and Noble Classics, 2007.

———. *Persuasion*. London: Penguin Classics, 1998.

———. *Pride and Prejudice*. London: Wordsworth Editions Limited, 1993.

———. *Sense and Sensibility*. Harmondsworth, England: Penguin Books, 1969.

Baynes, H. G. *The Mythology of the Soul*. London: Routledge and Kegan Paul, 1940.

Bennet, E. A. *What Jung Really Said*. London: Macdonald, 1966.

Benoît, Pierre. *L'Atlantide* (1919). Paris: LGF, 1996.

Benson, Stella. *Tobit Transplanted (or: The Faraway Bride)*. London: Macmillan & Co., 1931.

Bolzte, J., and G. Polívka. *Anmerkungen zu den Kinder und Hausmärchen der Brüder Grimm*, vol. 2. Dieterich, Leipzig, 1913.

Brontë, Anne. *Agnes Grey*. New York: Oxford University Press, 1988.

———. *The Tenant of Wildfell Hall*. New York: Oxford University Press, 1992.

Brontë, Charlotte. *Jane Eyre*. New York: Bantam Books, 1981.

———. *Shirley*. New York: Oxford University Press, 1979.

———. *Tales of Angria*. London: Penguin Classics, 2006.

———. *Villette*. New York: Oxford University Press, 1984.

Brontë, Emily. *The Complete Poems*. Janet Gezari, ed. London: Penguin Books, 1992.

———. *The Professor*. London: Penguin Books, 1948.

———. *Wuthering Heights*. New York: Penguin Books, 1959.

Bryant, Arthur. *English Saga: 1840–1940*. London: Collins, 1940.

Charles, R. H., ed. *The Apocrypha and Pseudepigrapha of the Old Testament*. Introduction by D. C. Simpson. Oxford: Clarendon Press, 1923.

Cohen, J. M., trans. *The Life of Saint Teresa of Avila by Herself*. New York: Penguin Classics, 1957.

Coles, Gladys Mary. "Mary Webb" (2003). Retrieved on January 24, 2010, at www.literaryheritage.org.uk.

Deren, Maya. *Divine Horsemen: The Living Gods of Haiti*. Kingston, N.Y.: McPherson, 1983.

de Sade, Donatien-Alphonse-François. *The Complete Marquis de Sade*. Paul J. Gillette, trans. Los Angeles: Holloway House Pub. Co., 2007.

Eisler, Robert. *Orpheus the Fisher: Comparative Studies in Orphic and Early Christian Cult Symbolism*. Whitefish, Mont.: Kessinger Publishing, 1992.

Fawkes, Francis. *Poetica Erotica*. T. R. Smith, ed. New York: Crown Publishers, 1921.

Gaskell, Elizabeth. *The Life of Charlotte Brontë*. London: Smith, Elder and Co., 1857; New York: Oxford University Press, 1996.

Goethe, J. W. *The Sorrows of Werther*. New York: P. F. Collier and Son, 1917.

Görres, Joseph. *Die Christliche Mystik*, vol. 5. Regensburg: Verlagsanstalt GJ Manz, 1836–1842.

Goudge, Elizabeth. *Green Dolphin Country*. London: Hodder and Stoughton, 1961.

Gunn, Neil M. *The Green Isle of the Great Deep*. London: Faber & Faber, 1944.

Hannah, Barbara. *Active Imagination*. Boston: Sigo Press, 1981.

———. *The Archetypal Symbolism of Animals*. Wilmette, Ill.: Chiron Publications, 2006.

———. "The Problem of Contact with the Animus." The Guild of Pastoral Psychology, lecture no. 70. East Dulwich: H. H. Greaves Ltd., 1951.

———. "The Problem of Women's Plots in *The Evil Vineyard*." The Guild of Pastoral Psychology, lecture no. 51. East Dulwich: H. H. Greaves Ltd., 1948.

———. *Striving Towards Wholeness*. New York: C. G. Jung Foundation for Analytical Psychology, Inc., 1971; republished Wilmette, Ill.: Chiron Publications, 2001.

———. "Victims of the Creative Spirit." The Guild of Pastoral Psychology, lecture no. 68. East Dulwich: H. H. Greaves Ltd., 1950.

Harding, Esther. *The Way of All Women*. New York: G. P. Putnam Sons for the C. G. Jung Foundation for Analytical Psychology, 1970.

Hay, Marie. *The Evil Vineyard*. Leipzig: Bernhard Tauchnitz, 1924.

Headlam, Maurice. *Bishop and Friend*. London: Macdonald and Co., 1945.

Herodotus. *The History*. David Grene, trans. Chicago: University of Chicago Press, 1987.

Hogg, James. *Confessions of a Justified Sinner*. London: David Campbell Publishers, 1992.

Hsueh-Chin, Tsoa. *Dream of the Red Chamber.* New York: Anchor Doubleday, 1958.

Huxley, Aldous. *Ape and Essence: A Novel* (1948). Chicago: Ivan R. Dee, 1992.

———. *The Devils of Loudun.* New York: Harper Perennial, 2009.

Jacobsohn, H. "The Dialogue of a World-weary Man with His Ba." In James Hillman, ed., *Timeless Documents of the Soul.* Evanston, Ill.: Northwestern University Press, 1968.

James, Montague Rhodes. *The Apocryphal New Testament.* Oxford: Clarendon Press, 1924.

Jung, C. G. "After the Catastrophe" (1945), in *CW,* vol. 10. Princeton, N.J.: Princeton University Press, 1964.

———. *Aion: Researches into the Phenomenology of the Self* (1951), *CW,* vol. 9ii. Princeton, N.J.: Princeton University Press, 1959.

———. *Analytical Psychology: Notes of the Seminar Given in 1925.* William McGuire, ed. Princeton, N.J.: Princeton University Press, 1991.

———. "Analytical Psychology and Weltanschauung" (1931), in *CW,* vol. 8. Princeton, N.J.: Princeton University Press, 1969.

———. "Answer to Job" (1952), in *CW,* vol. 11. Princeton, N.J.: Princeton University Press, 1969.

———. "Brother Klaus" (1933), in *CW,* vol. 11. Princeton, N.J.: Princeton University Press, 1969.

———. "Commentary on 'The Secret of the Golden Flower'" (1957), in *CW,* vol. 13. Princeton, N.J.: Princeton University Press, 1967.

———. "Concerning Rebirth" (1950), in *CW,* vol. 9i. Princeton, N.J.: Princeton University Press, 1968.

———. *Die Psychologie des Kundalini-Yoga. Nach Aufzeichnungen des Seminars 1932.* Zurich: Walter Verlag, 1998.

———. *Dream Analysis: Notes of the Seminar Given in 1928–1930.* Princeton, N.J.: Princeton University Press, 1984.

————. "Instincts and the Unconscious" (1948), in *CW*, vol. 8. Princeton, N.J.: Princeton University Press, 1969.

————. *The Jung-White Letters*. Ann Lammers and Adrian Cunningham, eds. London: Routledge, 2007.

————. *Kindertraum Seminar*. Zurich: Schippert and Co., 1940–1941.

————. *Letters*, 2 vols. Gerhard Adler, ed., in collaboration with Aniela Jaffé. R. F. C. Hull, trans. London: Routledge and Kegan Paul, 1976.

————. "The Meaning of Psychology for Modern Man" (1934), in *CW*, vol. 10. Princeton, N.J.: Princeton University Press, 1964.

————. *Memories, Dreams, Reflections*. A. Jaffé, ed. New York: Vintage Books, 1965.

————. "Mind and Earth" (1931), in *CW*, vol. 10. Princeton, N.J.: Princeton University Press, 1964.

————. "The Miraculous Fast of Brother Klaus" (1951), in *CW*, vol. 18. Princeton, N.J.: Princeton University Press, 1976.

————. "Modern Psychology." Notes on lectures given at the Eidgenössische Technische Hochschule, Zurich, 1934–1935.

————. *Mysterium Coniunctionis* (1955–1956), *CW*, vol. 14. Princeton, N.J.: Princeton University Press, 1963.

————. *Nietzsche's Zarathustra: Notes of the Seminar Given in 1934–1939*, 2 vols. Princeton, N.J.: Princeton University Press, 1988.

————. "On the Nature of the Psyche" (1954), in *CW*, vol. 8. Princeton, N.J.: Princeton University Press, 1969.

————. "On the Psychology of the Unconscious" (1943), in *CW*, vol. 7. Princeton, N.J.: Princeton University Press, 1953.

————. "Paracelsus as a Spiritual Phenomenon" (1942), in *CW*, vol. 13. Princeton, N.J.: Princeton University Press, 1967.

————. "The Phenomenology of the Spirit in Fairytales" (1948), in *CW*, vol. 9i. Princeton, N.J.: Princeton University Press, 1968.

————. "The Process of Individuation." Notes on lectures given at the Eidgenössische Technische Hochschule, Zurich, June 1939– March 1940.

————. "Psychological Aspects of the Kore" (1951), in *CW*, vol. 9i. Princeton, N.J.: Princeton University Press, 1968.

————. "Psychological Aspects of the Mother Archetype" (1954), in *CW*, vol. 9i. Princeton, N.J.: Princeton University Press, 1968.

————. *Psychological Types* (1921), *CW*, vol. 6. Princeton, N.J.: Princeton University Press, 1971.

————. *Psychology and Alchemy* (1944), *CW*, vol. 12. Princeton, N.J.: Princeton University Press, 1953.

————. "Psychology and Literature" (1950), in *CW*, vol. 15. Princeton, N.J.: Princeton University Press, 1966.

————. "Psychology and Religion" (1940), in *CW*, vol. 11. Princeton, N.J.: Princeton University Press, 1969.

————. "The Psychology of the Transference" (1946), in *CW*, vol. 16. Princeton, N.J.: Princeton University Press, 1966.

————. "The Relations Between the Ego and the Unconscious" (1928), in *CW*, vol. 7. Princeton, N.J.: Princeton University Press, 1953.

————. "The Spirit Mercurius" (1948), in *CW*, vol. 13. Princeton, N.J.: Princeton University Press, 1967.

————. "The State of Psychotherapy Today" (1934), in *CW*, vol. 10. Princeton, N.J.: Princeton University Press, 1964.

————. "The Structure of the Psyche" (1931), in *CW*, vol. 8. Princeton, N.J.: Princeton University Press, 1969.

————. "A Study in the Process of Individuation" (1950), in *CW*, vol. 9i. Princeton, N.J.: Princeton University Press, 1968.

————. "Synchronicity: An Acausal Principle" (1952), in *CW*, vol. 8. Princeton, N.J.: Princeton University Press, 1969.

————. "Transformation Symbolism in the Mass" (1954), in *CW*, vol. 11. Princeton, N.J.: Princeton University Press, 1969.

————. "The Undiscovered Self (Present and Future)" (1957), in *CW*, vol. 10. Princeton, N.J.: Princeton University Press, 1964.

————. *Visions: Notes of the Seminar Given in 1930–1934*, 2 vols. Clair Douglas, ed. London: Routledge, 1998.

————. "The Visions of Zosimos" (1954), in *CW*, vol. 13. Princeton, N.J.: Princeton University Press, 1967.

————. *Wirklichkeit der Seele*. Zurich: Rascher Verlag, 1934.

————. "Woman in Europe" (1927), in *CW*, vol. 10. Princeton, N.J.: Princeton University Press, 1964.

————. "Wotan" (1936), in *CW*, vol. 10. Princeton, N.J.: Princeton University Press, 1964.

Jung, Emma. *Animus and Anima: On the Nature of the Animus*. Cary F. Baynes, trans. New York: The Analytical Psychology Club of New York, 1957.

Jung, Emma. "Ein Beitrag zum Problem des Animus," in *Wirklichkeit der Seele*, C. G. Jung, ed. Zurich: Rascher Verlag, 1934.

Kaigh, Frederick. *Witchcraft and Magic of Africa*. London: Richard Lesley and Co., 1947.

Kerschaw, Ian. *Hitler 1936–1945*. Munich: Deutsche Verlags-Anstalt, 2000.

Koch-Hillebrecht, Manfred. *Homo Hitler: Psychogramm eines deutschen Diktators*. Munich: Wilhelm Goldmann Verlag, 1999.

Kramer, Heinrich, and James Sprenger. *Malleus Maleficarum (Or, The Hammer of Witches)* (1486). Charleston, S.C.: Forgotten Books, 2008.

Le Faye, D., ed. *Jane Austen's Letters*. New York: Oxford University Press, 1997.

Lorenz, K. *On Aggression*. London: Routledge Classics, 1966.

Mead, G. R. S. *Fragments of a Faith Forgotten*. Kila, Mont.: Kessinger Publishing, 1992.

McGing, Brian. *Polybius'* Histories. New York: Oxford University Press, 2010.

Neufeldt, Victor A., ed. *The Works of Patrick Branwell Brontë*, vol. 1. New York: Garland Publishing, 1997.

O'Gorman, Francis. "Editorial Introduction: 'Gaskell and the Brontës,' Literary Manuscripts of Elizabeth Gaskell (1810–1865) and the Brontës from the Brotherton Library, University of Leeds" (n.d.). Wiltshire: Adam Matthew Publications, www.adam-matthew-publications.co.uk.

Peers, E. A., trans. *The Life of Teresa of Jesus: The Autobiography of Teresa of Avila*. New York: Image, 1991.

Portmann, Adolf. *Die Bedeutung der Bilder in der lebendigen Energie Wandlung*. Zurich: Rhein Verlag, 1952.

Ratchford, Fannie E. *The Brontës' Web of Childhood: The Miscellaneous and Unpublished Writings of Charlotte and Patrick Branwell Brontë*. New York: Columbia University Press, 1941.

Read, Herbert. *Zum 85. Geburtstag von Prof. Dr. Carl Gustav Jung*. Zurich: Rascher Verlag, 1960.

Rider Haggard, Henry. *She: A History of Adventure* (serial publication 1886–1887) New York: Oxford University Press, 2008.

Sade, Donatien-Alphonse-François de. "One Hundred and Twenty Days of Sodom, or The Romance of the School of Libertinage," in *The Complete Marquis de Sade*. Paul J. Gillette, trans. Los Angeles: Holloway House, 2007.

Schärf Kluger, Rivkah. *Psyche in Scripture: The Idea of the Chosen People and Other Essays*. Toronto: Inner City Books, 1995.

————. *Satan in the Old Testament*. Hildegard Nagel, trans. Evanston, Ill.: Northwestern University Press, 1967.

Scot, Reginald. *The Discoverie of Witchcraft* (1584). New York: Dover, 1989.

Shorter, Clement. *The Brontës: Life and Letters*, vol. 2. London: Hodder and Stoughton, 1908.

Simms, Norman. "Medieval Guilds, Passions and Abuse" (1998), *Journal of Psychohistory* 26(1): 478–513.

Sinclair, May. *The Three Brontës*. London: Hutschinson, 1914.

Sinistrari, Ludovico Maria. *Demoniality*. London: Fortune Press, 1927.

Stevenson, Robert Louis. *Dr. Jekyll and Mr. Hyde* (1886). Cheswold, Del.: Prestwick House, 2005.

Tillinghast, Richard. "Rebecca West and the Tragedy of Yugoslavia." *The New Criterion* 10 (June 1992).

Trinick, John. *The Fire-Tried Stone*. London: Stuart and Watkins, 1967.

van der Hart, O., E. Nijenhuis, and K. Steele. *The Haunted Self: Structural Dissociation and the Treatment of Chronic Traumatization*. New York: W. W. Norton and Company, 2006.

van der Hart, Onno, Liernes, Ruth, and Goodwin, Jean. "Jeanne Fery: A Sixteenth-century Case of Dissociative Identity Disorder" (1996), *Journal of Psychohistory* 24(1):18–35.

Vine, Steven. "Emily Brontë." *The Literary Encyclopedia* (2001). Retrieved January 24, 2010, at www.litencyc.com.

von Franz, M.-L. *Archetypal Patterns in Fairy Tales*. Toronto: Inner City Books, 1997.

―――. *The Feminine in Fairy Tales*. Boston: Shambhala, 1993.

―――. *The Interpretation of Fairy Tales*. Boston: Shambhala, 1996.

―――. *The Passion of Perpetua: A Psychological Interpretation of Her Visions*. Toronto: Inner City Books, 2004.

―――. *Die Visionen des Niklaus von Flüe*. Zürich: Daimon Verlag, 1980.

Walten, Edith H. "Four Stories by Rebecca West." *The New York Times* (February 3, 1935).

Webb, Mary. *Armour Wherein He Trusted: A Novel and Some Stories*. New York: E. P. Dutton, 1929.

―――. *The Golden Arrow* (1916). London: Kessinger Publishing, 2004.

―――. *The House in Dormer Forest*. New York: George H. Doran, 1921.

————. *Precious Bane*. Boston: Little, Brown, 1987.

Wells, H. G. *Christina Alberta's Father*. London: Jonathon Cape Ltd., 1926.

West, Rebecca. *The Harsh Voice*. Garden City, N.Y.: Doubleday, 1937.

Wilhelm, Richard. *Das wahre Buch vom südlichen Blütenland,* vol. 1 Jena: Eugen Diedrichs Verlag, 1911.

Wires, Richard. *The Cicero Spy Affair: German Access to British Secrets in World War II*. Westport, Conn.: Praeger, 1999.

Woodham-Smith, Cecil. *Florence Nightingale*. New York: Grosset and Dunlap, 1951.

Wylie, Philip. *Generation of Vipers,* rev. ed. New York: Rinehart, 1955; 2nd edition, Champaign, Ill.: Dalkey Archive Press, 2007.

Index

Aborigine, Australian, **vol. 1:** 68n10
absolutism, political, **vol. 2:** 13–14
abuse, **vol. 1:** 28n41, 28n42
active imagination, **vol. 1:** 20–23, 64–65,
    73, 79, 82, 95, 117, 132, 147, 150,
    154, 171, 190; **vol. 2:** 23, 85, 120,
    129, 284, 362–63; used by alche-
    mists, **vol. 2:** 217–18
Adam and Eve, **vol. 1:** 71; **vol. 2:** 155,
    364
Adamson, Joy and George, **vol. 1:** 293
adders, **vol. 1:** 228, 230
Addison, Hilda, **vol. 2:** 261
Adler, Alfred, **vol. 1:** 165; **vol. 2:** 33n4
Adler, Gerhard, **vol. 1:** 262; **vol. 2:** 7n8
adolescence, **vol. 2:** 81–83
Ahikar (Achiacharus), **vol. 2:** 289, 302
Albert I, archduke of Austria, **vol. 2:** 73
alchemy, **vol. 1:** 5, 67–69, 72, 134–35,
    154, 200, 284; **vol. 2:** 47, 49, 62,
    216–17, 311; as a metaphor for psy-
    chological processes, **vol. 1:** 288–89,
    295
amber, **vol. 1:** 131, 134, 135n39, 140,
    153–54, 157; **vol. 2:** 169, 331
amnesia, **vol. 1:** 61n3
analysis (modern), **vol. 2:** 95, 99, 128,
    132, 159; misused, **vol. 2:** 86
analytical psychology, **vol. 2:** 366; femi-
    nine versus masculine, **vol. 2:** 301
Anderson, Hans Christian, **vol. 2:** 338
Andrews, Henry Maxwell, **vol. 1:** 162
angelology, **vol. 2:** 290–91, 300, 326
Angria (imaginary kingdom of the
    Brontë children), **vol. 1:** 264, 267,
    302
anima, **vol. 2:** 6, 24–26, 172, 191–92,
    199, 232, 239, 353, 362; as the coun-

terpart of the animus, **vol. 1:** 98–99;
    defined, **vol. 1:** 2, 263; **vol. 2:** 3;
    levels of development, **vol. 1:** 101–3,
    147; personified, **vol. 1:** 16
anima possession, **vol. 1:** 111; **vol. 2:** 22,
    167, 171
anima and animus, **vol. 2:** 1, 17, 312,
    318; as archetypes, **vol. 1:** 112, 172;
    characters, **vol. 2:** 34–35; control
    over, **vol. 1:** 143–44, 159–60; **vol. 2:**
    22; as deities, **vol. 1:** 116; marriage
    of, **vol. 2:** 315; personal aspect, **vol.
    2:** 20
animus: anesthetic, **vol. 2:** 40; as bridge
    between worlds, **vol. 1:** 40n55, 129–
    30, 151; childhood contact with, **vol.
    2:** 42; coming to terms with it, **vol.
    1:** 297; connected to the shadow,
    vol. 1: 9–10; between consciousness
    and the unconscious, **vol. 2:** 14, 22,
    41; conversing with, **vol. 1:** 21–22,
    25, 53; defined, **vol. 1:** 2, 110, 263;
    vol. 2: 3; dual aspects, **vol. 1:** 15,
    35; **vol. 2:** 22; Father Christmas,
    vol. 1: 165; and instinct, **vol. 1:** 50,
    52; as a jealous lover, **vol. 2:** 5; levels
    of development, **vol. 1:** 101, 103–5,
    147; in literature, **vol. 2:** 299; before
    the Middle Ages, **vol. 2:** 298; nega-
    tive, **vol. 1:** 35, 60, 62, 75, 77, 81,
    83, 132, 140, 151, 153, 165, 213–14,
    224, 226, 229–32, 235; obedience
    toward, **vol. 1:** 214; opinionated,
    vol. 1: 24, 36, 53, 55, 67, 70, 95,
    107, 110–11, 113, 121, 131–34, 136,
    138, 141, 146, 151–55, 164–66, 168,
    273–74; **vol. 2:** 4–6, 9–10, 13, 30,
    117, 167, 260, 303–4, 315, 327, 332,

346, 354–55, 370, 372; personifications, **vol. 1:** 16–17, 106; positive,
vol. 1: 223–24, 226, 233, 235; put
in the resin, **vol. 2:** 168–69, 303;
and reality, **vol. 2:** 117; religious
function, **vol. 2:** 2, 367–68, 370–71;
role in women's plots, **vol. 2:** 250;
as *spiritus rector,* **vol. 1:** 109; use of
symbolic language, **vol. 2:** 117
animus cocoon, **vol. 1:** 97–98
animus possession, **vol. 1:** 216, 218–19,
221, 226, 233; **vol. 2:** 3, 22, 37–38,
48–49, 108, 156, 159–60, 167, 169,
237, 305, 311, 327, 331, 335–36; in
the Middle Ages, **vol. 2:** 2
ant, leaf-cutting, **vol. 1:** 292
Anthropos, **vol. 1:** 72–73; **vol. 2:** 308,
326, 336, 367
Antinea, **vol. 2:** 162, 191, 234
Anubis, **vol. 2:** 334
Aphrodite, **vol. 2:** 309, 341, 371
Apollo, and the nymph Coronis, **vol.
1:** 217
archetype of the Self, **vol. 1:** 300. *See
also* Self, archetypal
archetypes, **vol. 1:** 62, 112, 294–95
arsenic, **vol. 1:** 78
Asmodaeus (Ashmedai), **vol. 1:** 10, 148,
213; **vol. 2:** 18, 291–92, 304, 319,
325–27, 330–32, 370
Astarte, **vol. 2:** 341
astrology, **vol. 2:** 97
Atargatis (Derketo), **vol. 2:** 340–41
Atman (Atman-Purusha), **vol. 1:** 71–72
Augustine, **vol. 2:** 328–30
Auseinandersetzung, **vol. 1:** 19; **vol. 2:**
16–17, 30, 37, 49, 82, 331, 349
Austen, Caroline, **vol. 1:** 183
Austen, Cassandra Elizabeth, **vol. 1:**
177–78, 180–81, 183
Austen, Jane, **vol. 1:** 107, 147, 279; **vol.
2:** 159; biographical sketch, **vol.
1:** 174–83; extreme realism, **vol.
1:** 200; her father complex, **vol.
1:** 179–80, 182, 191, 194; in the
Regency period, **vol. 1:** 313–14
Austen, Jane, *works:*
Emma, **vol. 1:** 178, 181
Mansfield Park, **vol. 1:** 181, 194
Northanger Abbey, **vol. 1:** 180–81
Persuasion, **vol. 1:** 178, 181, 184,

198–99, 201; synopsis, **vol. 1:**
196–97
Pride and Prejudice, **vol. 1:** 180–84,
190–96, 199; Mr. Bennet, as an
animus figure, **vol. 1:** 192, 199;
synopsis, **vol. 1:** 185–90
Sense and Sensibility, **vol. 1:**
180–82, 184

Balzac, **vol. 1:** 272
bane, defined, **vol. 2:** 273
Barrymore, Ethel, **vol. 2:** 165n12
Beaverbrook, Max, **vol. 1:** 162
Beguines, **vol. 2:** 94n34
behavior, patterns of, **vol. 1:** 291–94
Benoît, Pierre, *L'Atlantide,* **vol. 2:** 6, 34,
174, 191, 321
Benson, Stella, *Tobit Transplanted,* **vol.
2:** 320
Berlaymont, Louis de (Duke of
Cambria), **vol. 1:** 30, 60; **vol. 2:** 65,
70, 106, 135–36
Bible:
Ezekiel, **vol. 1:** 305
Ezra, **vol. 2:** 360
John, **vol. 1:** 124
Judith, **vol. 1:** 148
Leviticus, **vol. 1:** 226; **vol. 2:** 360
Naboth's vineyard (Kings), **vol. 2:**
171
Tobit, **vol. 1:** 10, 148, 201, 210; **vol.
2:** 2, 18, 32, 122, 258; canonicity,
vol. 2: 288–89; date written, **vol.
2:** 300; example of the animus,
vol. 2: 299; fish motif, **vol. 2:**
337, 339–43, 345–48, 352, 357,
361, 363; geographic origins,
vol. 2: 300, 302, 318, 331; historical basis, **vol. 2:** 287; motif of
mutual redemption, **vol. 2:** 312;
original language, **vol. 2:** 301;
as Persian folklore, **vol. 2:** 290;
synopsis, **vol. 2:** 294–98, 305–7;
tale of the grateful dead, **vol. 2:**
288–89, 302; Tobit's blindness,
vol. 2: 308, 310
Bigg-Wither, Harris, **vol. 1:** 179
Blavatsky, Helena, **vol. 1:** 218
blood sacrifice, **vol. 1:** 23–25, 28–30,
131, 133, 141, 143
blood spirit, **vol. 1:** 29, 50

Bodin, Jeanne, *Démonomanie,* **vol. 2:** 41
Boehme, Jakob, **vol. 1:** 208–9
borderline cases, **vol. 2:** 86, 91, 105
Bozzano, Ernesto, **vol. 2:** 72
Braun, Eva, **vol. 2:** 164
Brontës, **vol. 1:** 21, 34, 178, 296; **vol. 2:**
    76–77; background, **vol. 1:** 237–40,
    264–66; the father, **vol. 1:** 266; their
    modernity, **vol. 1:** 240, 242, 251;
    their relation to the collective uncon-
    scious, **vol. 1:** 262; writing career,
    vol. 1: 267–71
Brontë, Anne, **vol. 1:** 243–44, 273–74;
    The Tenant of Wildfell Hall, **vol. 1:**
    243, 290
Brontë, Branwell, **vol. 1:** 241, 271–73;
    death, **vol. 1:** 282
Brontë, Charlotte, **vol. 1:** 180, 200,
    244–46, 274–80; **vol. 2:** 76, 116;
    biographical notice of Emily, **vol.
    1:** 258–259; dream, **vol. 1:** 268–70,
    282; in the role of mother, **vol. 1:**
    269; writing as a man, **vol. 1:** 298
Brontë, Charlotte, *works:*
    Jane Eyre, **vol. 1:** 244–46, 270,
        277–78, 289, 298
    Shirley, **vol. 1:** 240, 289
    Strange Events, **vol. 1:** 297–309
    The Professor, **vol. 1:** 278
    Villette, **vol. 1:** 278, 289, 304
Brontë, Emily, **vol. 1:** 108, 280–84; **vol.
    2:** 299; as a mystic, **vol. 1:** 242, 246,
    282
Brontë, Emily, *works:*
    poems, **vol. 1:** 246–47, 258, 261,
        275–77, 281, 285, 290
    Wuthering Heights, **vol. 1:** 164–65,
        190, 247, 258, 270, 278, 284–89,
        296, 280; synopsis, **vol. 1:**
        248–58
Brontë, Maria, "The Advantage of
    Poverty in Religious Concerns"
    (essay), **vol. 1:** 266
Bruno, Giordano, **vol. 1:** 68n10
Bruschveiler, v2; 46
Bryant, Arthur, **vol. 1:** 194; **vol. 2:**
    178–80
Buddhism, **vol. 2:** 13n15
bullbaiting, **vol. 1:** 225, 235
Burney, Fanny, **vol. 1:** 166, 198–99

Calvin, John, **vol. 2:** 352
Carlyle, Thomas, **vol. 1:** 271
Carpocrates, **vol. 2:** 103
castle and fortress, as symbols of the
    Self, **vol. 2:** 210
Catholic Church, **vol. 2:** 103, 122, 288,
    365–66
Chaplin, Charlie, **vol. 1:** 162
Chapman, R. W., **vol. 1:** 179, 195
Charles, R. H., **vol. 2:** 290, 301–2
Chawwa, **vol. 1:** 101–2, 104, 147
Chidr, **vol. 2:** 337
Christ, **vol. 1:** 71–73, 86; **vol. 2:** 18, 35,
    46, 69, 87, 100–1, 107, 109–10, 119,
    121, 124–25, 308, 350, 362; logion,
    vol. 2: 160, 236; identified with
    Logos, **vol. 1:** 124; as a symbol, **vol.
    2:** 349
Christianity, **vol. 1:** 124, 173; **vol. 2:**
    35–36, 46–47, 68
Christie, Agatha, **vol. 1:** 147
Chuang-tzu, **vol. 1:** 68
Churchill, Winston, and Hitler, **vol. 2:**
    163–65
Clement of Alexandria, **vol. 1:** 174
cognition, **vol. 2:** 328–29, 333
collective unconscious, **vol. 1:** 5, 9,
    12–14, 23, 38, 49, 62, 65, 71, 100,
    119, 129–30, 170–71, 262, 266–69,
    272, 274, 280, 283–84, 290; **vol.
    2:** 10, 20–21, 40–41, 71, 120, 132,
    198, 228, 249, 308, 310, 355, 365;
    Charlotte Brontë's *Strange Events* as
    a description, **vol. 1:** 302
Colonna, Francesco, **vol. 2:** 33n3
communism, **vol. 2:** 48–49, 311, 324
compulsion, **vol. 1:** 72–73, 116
concupiscentia, **vol. 1:** 73, 128, 137–38,
    140, 152–53, 230
confession, misused, **vol. 2:** 86
coniunctio, **vol. 1:** 70, 89, 96, 156, 167;
    vol. 2: 249
Connelly, Marc, *The Green Pastures,*
    vol. 2: 331
Corn Laws, **vol. 1:** 222
countertransference, **vol. 2:** 59, 142
country estates, **vol. 2:** 178–80
creative spirit, **vol. 1:** 270–71, 275, 278,
    283
crucifixion, **vol. 2:** 17
Cusanus (Nicholas of Cusa), **vol. 1:** 47

Dante, **vol. 1:** 10, 148n2; **vol. 2:** 18, 33–34

Darcy, as an animus figure, **vol. 1:** 190

Davidson, Emily, **vol. 1:** 161

de Sade, Donatien-Alphonse-François, **vol. 2:** 54

de Stael, Germaine, **vol. 1:** 182

Dead Sea Scrolls, **vol. 2:** 302

Democritus, **vol. 1:** 68

demons (devils), **vol. 1:** 10, 38, 60–62, 66, 73, 146, 263; **vol. 2:** 53, 304–5, 358

Deren, Maya, **vol. 2:** 79

devil, **vol. 1:** 13–15, 27–29, 66, 72–73, 89, 100, 143–44, 160, 214, 230–31, 234; **vol. 2:** 10, 39, 42, 67–69, 349; collective, **vol. 2:** 2, 346; projection of, **vol. 2:** 20–21

devil's mark, and stigmata, **vol. 2:** 46

Diagnostic and Statistical Manual of Mental Disorders (DSM), **vol. 2:** 51–52

diamond body, Eastern symbol of the Self, **vol. 1:** 140

Diana, **vol. 1:** 74, 77, 86, 88, 90, 92, 96

diaspora, **vol. 2:** 300

discrimination, in women, **vol. 1:** 121, 123

Disraeli, Benjamin, **vol. 2:** 180

dissociative identity disorders, **vol. 1:** 26n37, 28n41, 29n43, 29n44, 32n45, 61n3; **vol. 2:** 51–52, 55–56, 126n46

dog, as a guide, **vol. 2:** 334–35, 339

Dorn, Gerhard, **vol. 2:** 323

doves, symbol of Diana, **vol. 1:** 86–88

dragon, in masculine psyche, **vol. 2:** 368, 372

dragonflies, **vol. 1:** 228, 230

dreams, **vol. 1:** 15, 17, 23, 57–58, 67, 78, 82, 132, 171, 305; **vol. 2:** 24, 98, 128–29, 185, 224–25, 243–44, 344, 369

dream analysis, **vol. 1:** 148; **vol. 2:** 255

Dyke, Andrea, **vol. 1:** 81

earth cults, **vol. 2:** 327

Ecbatana (the city), **vol. 2:** 292–93

Edgeworth, Maria, **vol. 1:** 166, 178, 199

ego, **vol. 1:** 5, 8–10, 58, 75, 85; **vol. 2:** 61, 96; and animus, **vol. 1:** 24, 170–71, 301; and plots, **vol. 2:** 152;

and Self, **vol. 2:** 47–48, 310, 370; and shadow, **vol. 2:** 303–4

Egyptian Book of the Dead, **vol. 2:** 318

Eisler, Robert, *Orpheus the Fisher,* **vol. 2:** 341

elephant, at the Circus Knie, **vol. 2:** 111–12, 143

Eliot, George (Mary Ann Evans), **vol. 1:** 147, 178, 180

Eliot, T. S., **vol. 1:** 162

Elsa, the lioness, **vol. 1:** 293

enantiodromia, **vol. 1:** 35n60, 118, 269, 308; **vol. 2:** 63, 95, 318, 323

English gentleman ideal, **vol. 1:** 195

Eros, **vol. 1:** 18, 50, 53, 61–62, 66, 68, 70, 74–77, 88–89, 92–96, 106, 110–11, 113, 121–27, 130, 136, 148–55, 168–70, 193, 213, 215–16, 221, 224, 227, 230; **vol. 2:** 3, 5, 82, 119, 249, 264, 309, 312, 315–16, 321–22, 327, 348, 361–62, 369, 372

Eucharist (the host), **vol. 2:** 78, 350

Eve, **vol. 1:** 71, 101–2, 104, 147; **vol. 2:** 78

evil, **vol. 2:** 84–85, 101, 104, 284–85; omnipresent, **vol. 2:** 11; personified, **vol. 1:** 14; **vol. 2:** 21; the problem of, **vol. 1:** 84–85, 88–89, 96, 210–11, 213, 219, 226, 228, 230, 226, 241 (*see also* good and evil); projected, **vol. 2:** 59

exorcism, **vol. 1:** 26, 29, 38–39, 59–61; **vol. 2:** 55, 57, 59, 63–69, 78, 84–85, 88, 97, 105, 107, 110, 112, 114–15, 118, 124–26, 128, 130–32, 137–38, 143

exorcists, **vol. 1:** 31–32, 61; **vol. 2:** 2, 42, 58

Fairfield, Cicely Isabel. *See* West, Rebecca

fairy tales, **vol. 1:** 3, 41, 49–50, 53, 56, 146–47, 214, 224n53; **vol. 2:** 333; Balkan, **vol. 2:** 162; "The Goose Girl," **vol. 1:** 41–49; in which an old man steals a cow, **vol. 2:** 160; King Thrushbeard, **vol. 1:** 223–24; Siberian, **vol. 2:** 93, 162

fantasy, **vol. 1:** 21, 64–65, 68

father complex, **vol. 1:** 19, 28, 35, 179–80, 182, 191, 194; **vol. 2:** 39, 115,

322, 332, 335, 357; **vol. 2:** 30, 85
father-daughter relationships, **vol. 1:** 202
Faust, **vol. 2:** 189, 198, 209. *See also*
Goethe, *Faust*
feminine (female) principle, **vol. 1:** 53,
75, 89, 92–93, 96, 147, 223; **vol. 2:**
152
femme inspiritrice, **vol. 2:** 315
Fery, Jeanne, **vol. 1:** 1, 26–41, 50,
54–55, 59–62, 65–66, 69, 73, 148,
214; **vol. 2:** 6, 39–50, 61–62, 65–87,
90–145, 316–17, 330, 350, 370;
becoming a nun, **vol. 2:** 124; modern diagnosis, **vol. 2:** 52–53, 55–57;
regression to a child of four, **vol. 2:**
128, 131, 133, 137, 143; transference to the archbishop, **vol. 2:** 112,
119–20, 136, 140; vision of blood
from the host, **vol. 2:** 81, 98, 100,
104–5, 120, 124, 127–28
Flaubert, Gustave, **vol. 2:** 299
food, fantasy, **vol. 2:** 78–80
fountain of wisdom, **vol. 1:** 74, 82
French Revolution, **vol. 1:** 175
Freud, Sigmund, **vol. 1:** 3, 73n21, 146,
165; **vol. 2:** 33n4
fumigation (smoke), and the process of
spiritualization, **vol. 2:** 344–45, 357
fundamentalists, religious, **vol. 2:** 308

Gaskell, Elizabeth, **vol. 1:** 178, 238,
264–65, 269, 274, 277–78, 281, 287,
304
geese, connected with Nemesis, **vol.
1:** 53
George III, **vol. 1:** 174, 194, 313–14
George IV, **vol. 1:** 175, 313–14
Glamis Castle, **vol. 2:** 202
glass breaking, as a symbol, **vol. 2:**
130–31
Gnosticism, **vol. 1:** 5, 71, 101–3, 134,
146, 295; **vol. 2:** 35
God (Christian), **vol. 1:** 10, 174; **vol. 2:**
182–83; and ego, **vol. 2:** 37; as masculine (lacking the feminine), **vol.
2:** 18–19, 37, 322; and Satan, **vol. 2:**
235; as Self, **vol. 2:** 322
goddesses, **vol. 2:** 341; fish, **vol. 2:**
361–62, 371–72
Goethe, **vol. 1:** 77, 108–10; **vol. 2:** 174,
249, 353; *Faust,* **vol. 2:** 171, 189n33

Gondal (imaginary kingdom of Emily
and Anne Brontë), **vol. 1:** 267, 271,
302
good and evil, **vol. 1:** 87, 222, 296;
vol. 2: 61, 93, 272; in plots, **vol. 2:**
154–55
Goodwin, Jean, **vol. 2:** 55
Görres, Joseph, **vol. 1:** 27, 37, 39; **vol.
2:** 39, 49, 66–67, 107, 118–19
Goudge, Elizabeth, **vol. 1:** 147; *Green
Dolphin Country,* **vol. 1:** 17, 192
grace, **vol. 2:** 266
Greek Pantheon, **vol. 1:** 117
Grenfell, B. P., **vol. 2:** 335
ground elder, **vol. 2:** 247
Guild of Pastoral Psychology, **vol. 1:** 1,
261–62; **vol. 2:** 66
gum arabic, **vol. 1:** 135, 154–57
Gunn, Neil M., *The Green Isle of the
Great Deep,* **vol. 2:** 324

Haiti, **vol. 2:** 79
Hannah, Barbara: analysis with Jung,
vol. 2: 108–9, 339; case of a patient
hearing a voice, **vol. 2:** 101–3; example from her own experience, **vol.
2:** 44–45; her dreams, **vol. 1:** 77–78,
99–101, 131, 235; **vol. 2:** 327, 339;
her own plots, **vol. 2:** 247–48;
Striving Towards Wholeness, **vol. 1:**
237, 273n25, 280n35, 296
Harding, Esther, **vol. 1:** 213
hare lip, as the devil's mark or the sign
of a witch, **vol. 1:** 212–13, 218–19,
227–28, 232–33
Hareton, as a Parsifal figure, **vol. 1:** 258
Hay, Marie, **vol. 2:** 175
Hay, Marie, *The Evil Vineyard,* **vol. 1:**
98, 107; **vol. 2:** 34, 42–43, 170, 173–
74, 249, 320; heroine's background,
vol. 2: 178–84; Mary's familiar, **vol.
2:** 215–36; Mary's goal to fall in love,
vol. 2: 184–93, 197, 221; nature in
the plot, **vol. 2:** 208–12; projection,
vol. 2: 193–95, 199; salon motif,
vol. 2: 184–85, 187, 189, 194, 197;
shadow, **vol. 2:** 202; spider motif,
vol. 2: 212–14, 230–33; symbolism
of totality, **vol. 2:** 205–6; synopsis,
vol. 2: 175–78
Headlam, Maurice, **vol. 2:** 64n11

Heathcliff: as an animus figure, **vol. 1:** 190, 202, 216, 275, 278, 286–89; **vol. 2:** 34; as *deus absconditus,* **vol. 1:** 257
Hecuba, **vol. 2:** 151–52
Helen of Troy, **vol. 1:** 101–2, 104, 106, 147–48
herd instinct, in mankind, **vol. 1:** 14, 76, 216; **vol. 2:** 22, 156
hermaphrodite, **vol. 1:** 63, 122
Hermes, **vol. 1:** 101, 103, 105–6, 136, 147; **vol. 2:** 162
hero myths, **vol. 2:** 337, 346–47
hero stage of animus development, **vol. 1:** 101
Herodotus, **vol. 2:** 292
Hicks, Nugent (Bishop), **vol. 1:** 38; **vol. 2:** 64
hieros gamos, **vol. 1:** 75, 86, 90–91, 96; **vol. 2:** 11, 13, 162, 311
Hippodamia, **vol. 2:** 17
Hitler, Adolf, **vol. 1:** 34; **vol. 2:** 110, 118, 238, 249; and Winston Churchill, **vol. 2:** 163–66
Hogg, James, **vol. 1:** 122; **vol. 2:** 124n45
homosexuality, **vol. 1:** 69, 215
Hoover, J. Edgar, **vol. 1:** 162
Hovorak-Kroneld's Vergleichende Volksmedizin [Comparative Folk Medicine], **vol. 2:** 347
Hunt, A. S., **vol. 2:** 335
Hunt, Violet, **vol. 1:** 162
husband stage of animus development, **vol. 1:** 101, 103, 105–6
Huxley, Aldous, **vol. 2:** 48, 65, 114n43
hydrophobia (rabies), **vol. 2:** 73–74, 305
hysteria, **vol. 2:** 114, 125

I Ching, **vol. 2:** 131
Icarus, **vol. 1:** 143
incarnation, **vol. 2:** 343, 367
incest, **vol. 2:** 354–55
incubus, **vol. 2:** 218–20, 223, 230, 235, 343–44, 355
individuation, process of, **vol. 1:** 39, 69, 81–82, 146–47, 164–65, 208–9, 217, 222, 229, 232, 235, 253, 258, 284, 290, 294–96; **vol. 2:** 10, 46, 48, 113, 119, 139, 140n48, 162, 206, 248, 251, 349n71, 352, 368
Innocent VIII, **vol. 2:** 58, 122, 361

Inquisition, **vol. 2:** 41, 57, 121–22
instinct, **vol. 1:** 124, 221–22, 291–94; **vol. 2:** 62, 186, 188–89, 208, 316, 335–36, 339, 346–47, 351, 357; animal, **vol. 2:** 361; feminine, **vol. 1:** 214–15; **vol. 2:** 260; mother, **vol. 2:** 4, 271; religious, **vol. 1:** 219
introjection, **vol. 1:** 28n42
intuition, **vol. 1:** 67, 148, 292
Iroquois, **vol. 1:** 68n10
Ishtar, **vol. 2:** 341

Jacobsohn, Helmuth, **vol. 2:** 318
Jaffé, Aniela, **vol. 1:** 218
James, Henry, **vol. 1:** 162
jealousy, **vol. 1:** 64; **vol. 2:** 5, 47–48, 220
Judeo-Christian religions, **vol. 2:** 153. *See also* Christianity
Jung, C. G.: on alchemy, **vol. 2:** 62; on anima and animus, **vol. 1:** 20, 35, 109–18, 120, 131–33, 144; **vol. 2:** 65, 174; regarding his own anima, **vol. 1:** 117–18, 308; **vol. 2:** 317; on animus development, **vol. 1:** 101–6; allergic to the negative animus, **vol. 2:** 1–2; regarding atomic war, **vol. 1:** 81; **vol. 2:** 8; on Augustine, **vol. 2:** 328–30; on children and their dreams, **vol. 1:** 266, 269; on Christ, **vol. 2:** 286; on the collective unconscious, **vol. 1:** 262; on crime and sex, **vol. 2:** 363; definition of a witch, **vol. 2:** 255; division of novels into two classes, **vol. 1:** 303–4; on doubt, **vol. 1:** 25, 88; his dreams, **vol. 1:** 298–301, 306–7; on historical inertia, **vol. 2:** 356; on instincts, **vol. 1:** 291–94; on integrating unconscious contents and dream motifs, **vol. 2:** 224–25; on jealousy, **vol. 2:** 5; letters to Father Victor White, **vol. 2:** 7, 349n71; on Logos and Eros, **vol. 1:** 122–26; on marriage, **vol. 2:** 192; on masculinity, **vol. 1:** 211; on myths and fairy tales, **vol. 1:** 41; on Nietzsche's problem, **vol. 1:** 127–28; his 1944 vision, **vol. 1:** 305; on the piety of animals, **vol. 2:** 335; on plots, **vol. 2:** 91–92, 110, 228, 241–42; process of individuation, **vol. 1:** 232, 284, 294–96; quoting

Goethe, **vol. 1:** 77; on reincarnation, **vol. 2:** 92; on relationships, **vol. 2:** 93; regarding schizophrenic conditions, **vol. 1:** 212; on sentimentality of men, **vol. 1:** 118–19; speaking of the dead, **vol. 1:** 307; story of the Hopi Indians, **vol. 2:** 313–14; regarding the supernatural, **vol. 1:** 33–34; theoretical standpoint of his psychological studies, **vol. 2:** 63–64; on the transcendent function, **vol. 2:** 71; trekking in the Sudan, **vol. 2:** 15–16; on the unconscious, **vol. 1:** 3, 7, 12–14, 146, 173, 277; on the union of the opposite sexes, **vol. 1:** 90; on women, **vol. 2:** 319–20

Jung, C. G., *works:*
   1938 Eranos lecture, **vol. 1:** 286
   Aion, **vol. 1:** 18, 173, 295; **vol. 2:** 311, 335, 338, 340–42
   Answer to Job, **vol. 2:** 327
   Memories, Dreams, Reflections, **vol. 2:** 13–16, 244–45
   Mysterium Coniunctionis, **vol. 1:** 62–64, 67, 69–72, 74–76, 78–81, 83–87, 93–95; **vol. 2:** 11, 141, 144–45
   Nietzsche's Zarathustra, **vol. 1:** 8; **vol. 2:** 315, 347–48
   "Phenomenology of the Spirit in Fairy Tales," **vol. 2:** 312
   Psychology and Alchemy, **vol. 1:** 19, 52, 82; **vol. 2:** 35, 97, 142, 216–17, 228
   "Psychology and Religion," **vol. 2:** 320–21
   "Psychology of the Transference," **vol. 2:** 128
   Visions seminars, **vol. 1:** 101, 124, 128–29, 131, 137–43, 151, 157–59
   "Women in Europe," **vol. 2:** 166, 172–73
Jung, Emma, **vol. 1:** 2, 18, 23, 131, 178, 216, 226; **vol. 2:** 3–4, 28–29, 35, 64, 202, 217, 263
Jungian psychology, **vol. 1:** 1–2, 4, 6, 8, 27, 261–63, 268, 284; **vol. 2:** 100, 174, 352; applied, **vol. 2:** 168; misunderstood as a philosophy or religion, **vol. 1:** 6

Kabbalah, **vol. 2:** 322
Kaigh, Fredrick, **vol. 2:** 41, 47
Kali, **vol. 1:** 269
Keats, John, **vol. 2:** 79
Kingsford, Anna, **vol. 1:** 218
Kirsch, James, **vol. 2:** 325, 336, 367
knowledge, absolute, **vol. 1:** 67

Lamb, William (Lord Melbourne), **vol. 2:** 179
Lammers, Ann, v2; 7n8
Lawrence, D. H., **vol. 1:** 108–9
Leade, Jane, **vol. 1:** 167
Leibnitz, **vol. 1:** 68n10
Leviathan, **vol. 2:** 340, 342–43, 349n70
Lévy-Brühl, Lucien, **vol. 2:** 71
Lewis, Wyndham, **vol. 1:** 162
libido, **vol. 1:** 23–24, 131, 179, 182; **vol. 2:** 100–1, 104, 186, 218, 365
Liernes, Ruth, **vol. 2:** 55
life beyond death, **vol. 2:** 13–14
lightning, and individuation, **vol. 1:** 208–9, 228
lingam, **vol. 1:** 103
Logos, **vol. 1:** 18, 25, 50, 62–63, 70, 77, 89, 92–94, 96, 106, 110, 120–26, 130, 136, 148–50, 155, 169–70, 215–16, 222, 226; **vol. 2:** 4, 100, 249, 310, 312, 372
logos spermaticos, **vol. 1:** 120; **vol. 2:** 315
Lorenz, Konrad, **vol. 1:** 86; **vol. 2:** 93
Loudun, **vol. 2:** 114
love, **vol. 1:** 105–6; **vol. 2:** 82, 121, 185–87, 189–90, 266–67; at first sight, **vol. 1:** 223; and marriage, **vol. 2:** 183–84; and sex, **vol. 1:** 104, 106; as a stage of animus development, **vol. 1:** 101, 103, 105
Lucifer, **vol. 1:** 87, 167; **vol. 2:** 144, 273, 328–30
Luciferian principle, **vol. 1:** 286; **vol. 2:** 119, 124
lycanthropy, **vol. 2:** 72

Macaulay, Thomas, **vol. 1:** 198
magic, **vol. 1:** 5, 219; **vol. 2:** 57, 344; black, **vol. 2:** 77–78, 344
Magnus, Albertus, **vol. 2:** 323
Maier, Michael, **vol. 2:** 49
Malleus Maleficarum, **vol. 1:** 234;

vol. 2: 57, 361
mandala, **vol. 1:** 284, 295
Maria Prophetissa, **vol. 1:** 135–36, 154,
    156–57; **vol. 2:** 169, 332
Marlowe, Christopher, **vol. 2:** 189n33
marriage, **vol. 1:** 182, 189, 241, 301; **vol.
    2:** 192, 267, 269, 300; double, **vol.
    1:** 290
Mars, **vol. 1:** 166–68
Mary Magdalene, **vol. 1:** 30–32, 37–39,
    50, 61–62, 69; **vol. 2:** 55, 66, 70,
    108–11, 119–21, 126–45, 350; as a
    symbol of the Self, **vol. 2:** 110, 141
Mary, Mother of God, **vol. 1:** 101–2,
    104–6, 147. *See also* Virgin Mary
masculinity, **vol. 1:** 212, 216; **vol. 2:** 166
mass mindedness, **vol. 1:** 79, 86
Mead, G. R. S., **vol. 1:** 103
medicine man, **vol. 2:** 71, 97, 344. *See
    also* witch doctor
meditation, **vol. 1:** 20–21, 299–300, 306
medium, **vol. 2:** 77
Meister Eckhart, **vol. 1:** 8, 73; **vol. 2:**
    48, 59
memory, **vol. 1:** 36
men's plots, **vol. 2:** 163, 239
Mephistopheles, **vol. 2:** 189, 198
Mercurius, **vol. 1:** 135–36, 155
Messiah, **vol. 2:** 308, 340
mind and body, as two separate entities,
    vol. 1: 300
money, **vol. 2:** 364–65
moon, symbol of Eros, **vol. 1:** 89, 93–94
morality, conventional, **vol. 2:** 241
Morienus, **vol. 2:** 173
Moses, in the Qur'an, **vol. 2:** 337–38
mother complex, **vol. 2:** 36, 336, 357;
    negative, **vol. 2:** 85
mother figures, in Jane Austen, **vol. 1:**
    193–94
Moyzisch, Ludwig, **vol. 1:** 132
multiple personality disorder. *See* disso-
    ciative identity disorders
mystics, feminine, **vol. 2:** 18
myths, **vol. 1:** 3, 41, 49, 124, 146–47,
    161, 191, 223, 257, 270

nature, **vol. 2:** 220, 234; blind dynamism
    of, **vol. 2:** 173, 208, 224
Navajo sand paintings, **vol. 2:** 344
Nazis (Nazism), **vol. 1:** 133, 162n16;

vol. 2: 48–49, 85, 157
Neumann, Therese, **vol. 2:** 80
New Jerusalem (in Revelation), **vol. 2:**
    293, 368–69, 372
Nicholas of Flüe, **vol. 2:** 80
Nicholls, Arthur Bell, **vol. 1:** 279
Nietzsche, **vol. 1:** 127; **vol. 2:** 20n28
Nightingale, Florence, **vol. 2:** 96
Nijenhuis, E., **vol. 2:** 61n8
Nous and Physis, **vol. 1:** 134, 136
Nussey, Ellen, **vol. 1:** 283
nuthatch, **vol. 1:** 221–22; **vol. 2:** 264

occult, **vol. 1:** 218–19
Odin, **vol. 1:** 223, 230
Opincinus de Canistris, **vol. 2:** 77
opposites, **vol. 2:** 7–8, 12–13, 17, 60–61,
    63; clash of, **vol. 1:** 66, 79–81; ten-
    sion, **vol. 2:** 11, 38; union of, **vol. 1:**
    83, 95; **vol. 2:** 249, 285
Ouroboros, **vol. 1:** 23, 69, 71; **vol. 2:**
    152–53
Oxyrhynchus papyri, **vol. 2:** 335

paganism, in England, **vol. 2:** 179
Palazzo Barberini, **vol. 2:** 194
Paracelsus, **vol. 2:** 98
paradox, civilization's loss of, **vol. 1:** 296
passion, in Victorian times, **vol. 1:**
    194–95, 275
Pauker, Ana, **vol. 2:** 311
Perseus, **vol. 2:** 201
Petrarch, **vol. 1:** 10, 148n2; **vol. 2:** 18,
    33
phallus, **vol. 1:** 101, 103–4
Philaletha, Eirenaeus, **vol. 1:** 62, 69–70,
    73–74, 77–81, 87, 93, 96
Pistis Sophia. See Sophia
plots: and avoidance of suffering, **vol. 2:**
    243–44, 251; belonging to nature,
    vol. 2: 149–50; defined, **vol. 2:** 146–
    48, 238; differences between men
    and women, **vol. 2:** 149–50, 163; as
    a driving force, **vol. 2:** 150–51, 155;
    and laziness, **vol. 2:** 245–46; reality
    of, **vol. 2:** 147–48. *See also* women's
    plots, men's plots
Poimen, **vol. 2:** 221, 223
Poliphilo, **vol. 2:** 33
Polybius of Megalopolis, **vol. 2:** 293
polygamy, **vol. 2:** 106

pomegranate, as a symbol, **vol. 2:** 49, 68, 116–17, 125
Pordage, John, **vol. 1:** 167
Portmann, Adolf, **vol. 2:** 73, 305
possession, **vol. 2:** 23, 38, 51–53, 57, 59, 61, 63–65, 71–72, 74, 87, 90, 100, 304–5; case at the Abbey of Vallombrosa, **vol. 2:** 88–91; of children, **vol. 2:** 72, 74; as a deliberate sin, **vol. 2:** 121–23; demonic, **vol. 1:** 10, 26, 34, 59–60; **vol. 2:** 94–95, 299, 303; medieval cases, **vol. 2:** 3; by wild animals, **vol. 2:** 73
prayer, **vol. 2:** 58n5, 68, 86, 299, 362–64
predestination, doctrine of, **vol. 2:** 352
primitives, **vol. 1:** 5; **vol. 2:** 74–75; like figures of the unconscious, **vol. 2:** 16
projection, **vol. 1:** 8, 18, 128, 169, 171; **vol. 2:** 3–4, 19, 85
propriety, British notions, **vol. 2:** 179–80
prostitution, **vol. 1:** 105
Protestants, **vol. 2:** 289, 322, 366
psuedo Logos, **vol. 1:** 124
psychological disorders, projected into the body, **vol. 2:** 97–98
psychological types, **vol. 1:** 38
psychology: compartmental, **vol. 2:** 170–72, 239–41; family, **vol. 2:** 44; feminine, **vol. 1:** 262; **vol. 2:** 346; masculine, **vol. 1:** 263; **vol. 2:** 172; nun's, **vol. 2:** 49; of women, **vol. 1:** 262–63. *See also* Jungian psychology
psychopomp, **vol. 1:** 101, 103, 129, 147
psychosis, **vol. 1:** 32n45; **vol. 2:** 109
Pythagoras, **vol. 1:** 295

quaternities, **vol. 1:** 174, 253, 287, 289–90, 295; **vol. 2:** 47n19, 204–5, 254–55, 274

Radcliffe, Ann, **vol. 1:** 199
Radochio, Hieronymus, **vol. 2:** 88
Rages (Rhagae, the city), **vol. 2:** 292
ram, as a symbol of fertility, **vol. 2:** 353, 359–61, 363
Raphael, **vol. 2:** 290–91, 325–27, 330, 332, 334, 336, 371; opposite Asmodaeus, **vol. 2:** 341–45
Ratchford, Fannie, **vol. 1:** 264, 279; **vol. 2:** 75, 115
Red Hilda. *See* Pauker, Ana

Reformation, **vol. 2:** 365
Regency period, **vol. 1:** 194, 313–14
regression, **vol. 1:** 61n3, 129
relationship, **vol. 1:** 18, 25, 38, 62, 65, 109–11, 127–28, 154, 168–69; **vol. 2:** 5, 27–30, 107–9, 120, 249
relationships, with men, as animus projections, **vol. 2:** 28
religions, **vol. 1:** 5, 11, 138; history of, **vol. 1:** 116
repression, and plots, **vol. 2:** 151–52
Rhine, J. B., **vol. 2:** 314
Richard de St. Victor, **vol. 2:** 160
Rider Haggard, Henry, **vol. 1:** 10, 112, 148n2; **vol. 2:** 18, 34, 174
Roberts, Page, **vol. 2:** 333
Rochester, as the animus, **vol. 1:** 289
Roget's Thesaurus, **vol. 1:** 194
rooks, birds of divination, **vol. 1:** 219, 222
Rosinus (Zosimos), **vol. 1:** 68, 70
Ruland's Lexicon alchemiae, **vol. 2:** 216–17
Russell, Ken, **vol. 2:** 114n43

sacrifice, **vol. 2:** 243n7, 359–60
saints: betrothed to Christ, **vol. 2:** 49; female, **vol. 1:** 263; **vol. 2:** 298; lives, **vol. 2:** 63, 134; male, **vol. 1:** 39
St. Francis of Assisi, **vol. 1:** 203
St. Ignatius of Loyola, **vol. 1:** 20
St. Norbert, **vol. 2:** 58–59, 123–24
St. Paul, **vol. 2:** 103
St. Perpetua, **vol. 2:** 18, 32, 35n8, 299
St. Theresa of Avila, **vol. 1:** 263–64
St. Victor, Hugh de, **vol. 2:** 62–63, 123
Sand, George, **vol. 1:** 147; **vol. 2:** 299
Satan, **vol. 2:** 43, 47, 349n70, 358
satipatthana, **vol. 1:** 155n8
Schärf Kluger, Rivkah, **vol. 2:** 43, 221, 235, 322, 326, 349n70
schizophrenia, **vol. 2:** 56, 97, 101, 114
Schopenhauer, **vol. 1:** 199
science, **vol. 1:** 200
Scot, Reginald, **vol. 2:** 218–20, 230, 235
Scott, Sir Walter, **vol. 1:** 198
Self, **vol. 1:** 13, 18, 37–39, 55, 58, 61–62, 71, 73–77, 96, 140, 174; **vol. 2:** 11–14, 17, 19, 94; archetypal, **vol. 1:** 306 (*see also* archetype of the Self);

as a *coincidentia oppositorum*, **vol.
2:** 227; images in Tobit, **vol. 2:** 371;
weaving the pattern of one's fate,
vol. 2: 248–49; in women, **vol. 2:**
121
self-knowledge, **vol. 2:** 160–61
seven, the number, **vol. 2:** 351–52
sexual abuse, of children, **vol. 2:** 53–56
sexuality, **vol. 1:** 90, 147, 195, 199; **vol.
2:** 5, 346, 363
shadow, **vol. 1:** 2–5, 8–10, 12, 24, 50–58,
71–73, 80–85, 99–101, 146, 149, 173;
vol. 2: 10, 17, 20, 240–41, 248, 258;
animal, **vol. 1:** 36; collective, **vol.
1:** 100; personal, **vol. 2:** 6; personal
versus collective, **vol. 2:** 304
Shakespeare, William, **vol. 1:** 164;
Romeo and Juliet, **vol. 2:** 316
shaman. *See* medicine man, witch doctor
Shaw, George Bernard, **vol. 1:** 162, 272
Shekhinah, **vol. 2:** 323
Shropshire, **vol. 1:** 202–3
Silesius, Angelus, **vol. 2:** 284, 309–10
Silk Road, **vol. 2:** 292
Simms, Norman, **vol. 2:** 55, 61n8
Simpson, D. C., **vol. 2:** 290, 301–3, 318
sin eater, **vol. 1:** 209–10
Sinclair, May, **vol. 1:** 243–44
Sinistrari, Ludovico Maria, **vol. 2:**
343–44, 357
Smith, Cecil Woodham, **vol. 2:** 96
Socrates, dreams, **vol. 2:** 304
Sophia, **vol. 1:** 101–3, 147; **vol. 2:** 322
sorcery, **vol. 2:** 41
soul, **vol. 1:** 68, 76, 79–80, 84, 94, 103,
128, 146–47, 172, 210–11, 213; **vol.
2:** 3, 18; feminine, of man, **vol. 1:**
2, 263, 272; **vol. 2:** 18, 37, 153–54;
projected onto the other sex, **vol. 2:**
153–53; of woman, **vol. 2:** 33–34
sparrow, as an aspect of Aphrodite and
Venus, **vol. 2:** 309, 316, 328, 341,
371–72
spinning, related to fantasy and wishful
thinking, **vol. 1:** 223, 230; **vol. 2:** 75
spirit: of blood, **vol. 2:** 69; masculine, in
women, **vol. 1:** 2, 263; **vol. 2:** 153–
54; primitive belief in, **vol. 2:** 42
spiritualization, **vol. 2:** 345–47, 357
spiritus rector, **vol. 1:** 107–9, 147, 150,
168, 201; **vol. 2:** 170–71

Steele, K., **vol. 2:** 61n8
Stevenson, Robert Louis, **vol. 2:** 242;
Dr. Jekyll and Mr. Hyde, **vol. 1:**
198, 296
subconscious, **vol. 1:** 112; **vol. 2:** 255.
See also unconscious
substance abuse, **vol. 2:** 52
subtle body, **vol. 2:** 217, 219
succubus, **vol. 2:** 219, 343
suffering, and happiness, **vol. 2:** 244
suicide, **vol. 1:** 109; **vol. 2:** 70, 103–4,
113, 125–26, 359
sulphur, **vol. 1:** 66–73, 76–78
supernatural, **vol. 1:** 32–33, 288
Surin, Jean-Joseph, **vol. 2:** 114n43
symbol, **vol. 2:** 333–34
synchronicity, **vol. 1:** 67

taboos, **vol. 2:** 346
Tao, **vol. 1:** 68, 91; **vol. 2:** 12, 14, 17,
24, 363
Tardieu, Auguste Ambroise, **vol. 2:** 54
Tertullian, **vol. 2:** 162
Thackeray, William Makepeace, **vol. 1:**
166n19, 244
Thomas, Ulma G., **vol. 1:** 145
Three Marys, legend, **vol. 2:** 121
Tibetan Book of the Dead, **vol. 1:** 157
Tillinghast, Richard, **vol. 1:** 162n16
Tobit. *See* Bible: Tobit
totality, **vol. 1:** 69, 71, 73, 172, 249, 284,
287, 294–96, 300; **vol. 2:** 221, 233,
269, 271, 276, 283
Tractate of Khons, **vol. 2:** 302–3
tradition, **vol. 2:** 356
trance, **vol. 1:** 219n50; **vol. 2:** 51–52
transcendent function, **vol. 1:** 129–30
transference, **vol. 2:** 85, 87, 141
Trinick, John, **vol. 2:** 11
Tsoa Hsueh-Chin, *Dream of the Red
Chamber*, **vol. 2:** 352

unconscious, **vol. 1:** 2–3, 6–8, 10–11, 22,
95, 112, 117–21, 123, 142, 148–49;
vol. 2: 8, 10, 14, 58, 62, 141, 337,
364; androgynous, **vol. 2:** 37; healing
powers, **vol. 2:** 85; personal, **vol. 1:**
5, 8, 173; **vol. 2:** 30–31; personified,
vol. 1: 16; and plots, **vol. 2:** 152,
238–39; the reality of the animus,
vol. 1: 297; and religion, **vol. 2:** 19

unconscious men, **vol. 2:** 166–67
unconscious women, **vol. 2:** 166–67, 171
unio mystica, **vol. 1:** 221
union of opposites, **vol. 1:** 255
unus mundus, **vol. 1:** 90; **vol. 2:** 323, 352

van der Hart, Onno, **vol. 2:** 55, 61n8
Venus, **vol. 1:** 68–70, 166–68, 224; **vol. 2:** 309, 341
Virgin Mary, **vol. 2:** 35, 322–23. *See also* Mary, Mother of God
virtues, Christian, **vol. 2:** 7, 349–50
visions, **vol. 1:** 67, 95, 131, 151, 271, 305–6
von Franz, Marie-Louise, **vol. 1:** 41, 49, 59, 91, 98, 135, 191, 212, 217, 221, 223, 230, 236; **vol. 2:** 32, 59, 116, 299, 307, 309, 311, 333, 338, 365

Walton, Edith H., **vol. 1:** 163n17, 311
weaving, a feminine activity, **vol. 2:** 238
Webb, Mary, **vol. 1:** 107, 147, 178, 184, 201; **vol. 2:** 283–86; biographical sketch, **vol. 1:** 202–5; **vol. 2:** 251–52
Webb, Mary, *works:*
    Armour Wherein He Trusted, **vol. 1:** 205; **vol. 2:** 283–84
    Gone to Earth, **vol. 1:** 204
    The House in Dormer Forest, **vol. 2:** 258
    Precious Bane, **vol. 1:** 202, 205–36, 296; **vol. 2:** 250–52, 283–86; cast of characters as figures of a personality, **vol. 2:** 255–56; process of individuation, **vol. 2:** 255–56, 263, 265, 268, 275–76, 278, 280, 283; Prue as a witch, **vol. 2:** 255; Prue's harelip, **vol. 2:** 259–61, 264–65, 268; Prue's instincts, **vol. 2:** 259; Prue's shadow, **vol. 2:** 262, 267, 277–78; synopsis, **vol. 1:** 207ff; **vol. 2:** 252–61
Wells, H. G., **vol. 1:** 17, 162; **vol. 2:** 24–25, 86
West, Rebecca, **vol. 1:** 107, 147, 161–74, 205; *The Harsh Voice,* **vol. 1:** 163, 172, 311–12
White, Victor, **vol. 2:** 7

Wilhelm, Richard, story of the rainmaker of Kiautschou, **vol. 1:** 81, 90–91; **vol. 2:** 12
wind, as spirit, **vol. 1:** 54
wisdom, **vol. 2:** 60–61
witch doctor, **vol. 1:** 157; **vol. 2:** 47
witches, **vol. 1:** 10, 81, 148, 212–13, 219, 233; **vol. 2:** 50, 78, 239, 298, 361; ducking stool, **vol. 1:** 220, 234–35; familiar, **vol. 2:** 218; history of, **vol. 1:** 264; pact with the devil, **vol. 2:** 38, 46–49, 68, 116, 260
witchcraft, **vol. 1:** 5; **vol. 2:** 38–39, 47, 57–58, 63, 114n43, 116, 121–22, 218–19
wizards, **vol. 1:** 230–31, 233
Wochpe (Lakota Sioux goddess), **vol. 1:** 191
Wolff, Toni, **vol. 1:** 142, 158, 295
women: archetypal motif of devil who kills men, **vol. 2:** 321; authors, **vol. 1:** 99; and creativity, **vol. 2:** 4, 339; drawn to psychology more than men, **vol. 2:** 36, 38, 314; Jewish, **vol. 2:** 322; in masculine professions, **vol. 2:** 36; surplus, **vol. 1:** 98; tendency to be unreasonable, **vol. 2:** 96
women's plots, **vol. 1:** 255; **vol. 2:** 75–76, 170, 173, 237–38; goals, **vol. 2:** 246; rooted in animus possession, **vol. 2:** 160. *See also* plots
Woolf, Virginia, **vol. 1:** 198
Wordsworth, **vol. 1:** 266–67, 281
World-weary Man, **vol. 2:** 301, 324, 331
Wylie, Philip, *Generation of Vipers,* **vol. 2:** 311

Yeats, W. B., **vol. 1:** 247
ying and yang, **vol. 2:** 36
yoni, **vol. 1:** 102–3, 147
Yorkshire, **vol. 1:** 241
yucca moth, **vol. 1:** 291–92

Zarathustra, **vol. 2:** 292
ziggurat, **vol. 2:** 293
zodiac, **vol. 1:** 269, **vol. 2:** 340
Zoroastrianism, **vol. 2:** 98, 291, 302, 325, 345